W9-DEU-487

HISTORY AND EVOLUTION OF SAILING YACHTS

CHARTWELL
BOOKS, INC.

T6

Australia IV

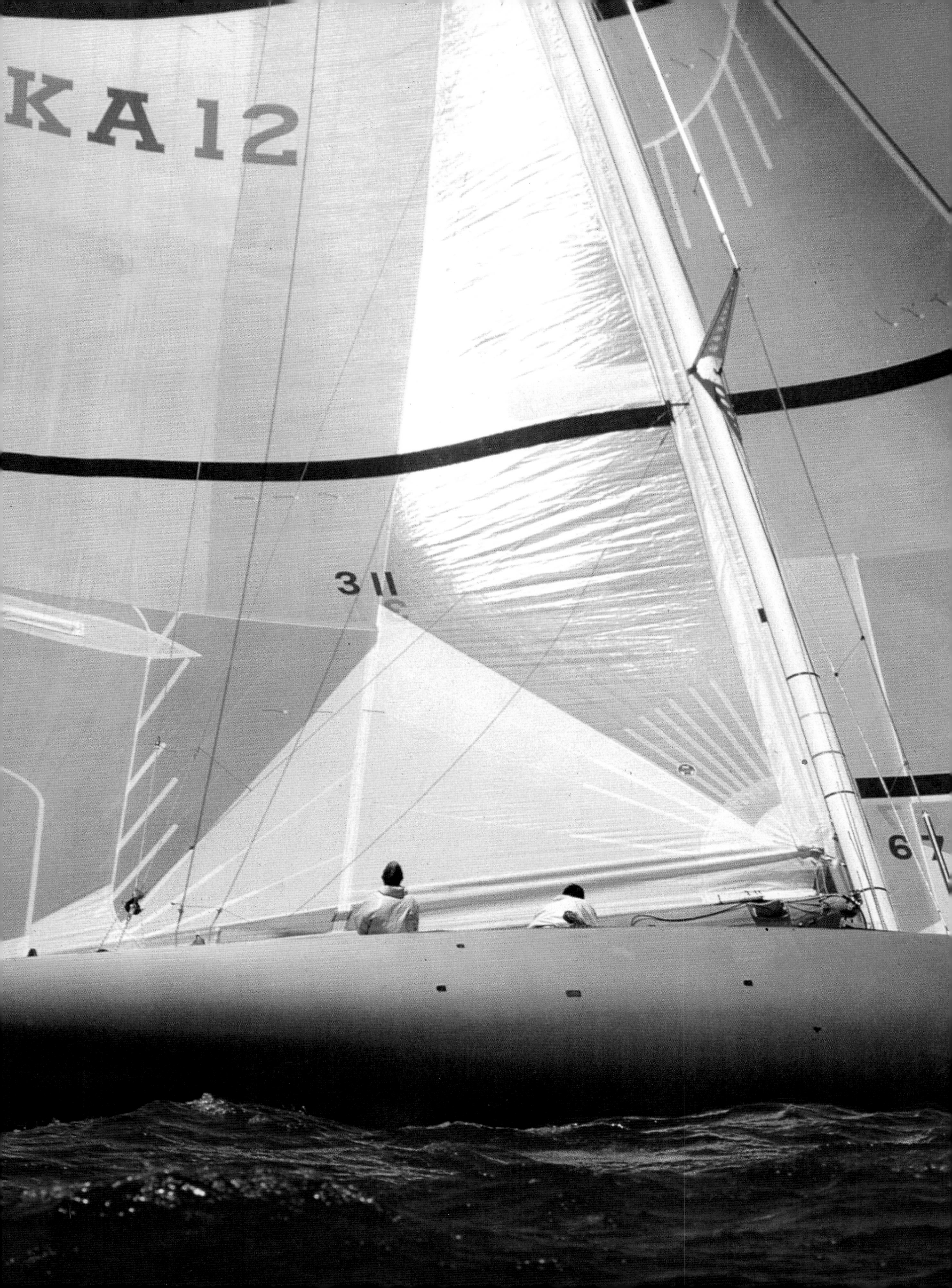
KA 12
311

HISTORY AND EVOLUTION OF SAILING YACHTS

TEXT
FRANCO GIORGETTI

EDITORIAL PRODUCTION
VALERIA MANFERTO DE FABIANIS
LAURA ACCOMAZZO

GRAPHIC DESIGN
PATRIZIA BALOCCO LOVISETTI

CONTENTS

4-5 Ever since the victory of the schooner America on the Solent in 1851, the America's Cup races have continued to represent the ultimate challenge for designers and skippers. It is the best known regatta among the general public and the most significant event in terms of the development of yacht technology. The last edition to be raced with the International Rule 12-meter yachts, perhaps the class most closely associated with the event, was held in 1987.

6-7 In the year 2000 two new names appeared in the eternal battle for the Hundred Guinea Cup, those of Luna Rossa and her sponsor Prada. The Italian boat won the right to challenge Black Magic the New Zealand defender that had snatched the trophy from the Americans' grasp four years earlier.

7 top Three late-nineteenth century American cutters, all small for the era at under 60 feet in length, racing to round the marker represented by the Brenton Reef lightship at the entrance to Narraganset Bay, Rhode Island, in the United States.

Published by
Chartwell Books, Inc.
A Division of Book Sales, Inc.
114 Northfield Avenue
Edison, New Jersey 08837

First published by
Edizioni White Star, Vercelli Italy.
Title of the original edition: Storia ed evoluzione degli yacht da regata
World copyright
© 2000 White Star s.r.l.
English Translation by Neil Frazer Davenport
Printed in Italy by Officine Grafiche De Agostini, Novara.

ISBN: 0-7858-1251-2

1 left More pennants than sails aloft on the first yachts to race in British waters: the highly decorated transom stern, the high topsides, billowing sails and a voluminous prow raising waves and spray. The impression is one of speed but scarce efficiency in the regattas at the dawn of yachting.

1 right Competitive sailing is nowadays established throughout the world with yachts racing on the longest of all possible routes: the circumnavigation of the globe, a race promoted and sponsored by the Whitbread Brewing Company.

2-3 The 1930s saw the domination of the schooner rig which the Americans had adopted as something of a national tradition, although its origins lay in a French naval pursuit vessel. John Alden was one of the great specialists in the field and the Lelantina was one of his most famous schooners.

PREFACE

The origin of the yacht, of a boat destined to be sailed solely for pleasure, is much older than its very particular current form, technology and usages might lead one to presume. The term "yacht" itself has a long history. It undoubtedly originated in Northern Europe, although some authors have identified its first appearance in a French text, *Histoire de la Marine Française*, (1551), in which it is used to describe a boat used for recreational purposes. The word clearly derives from the Northern European terms *yagd* in Danish and German, *yagt* in Swedish and Dutch and *yat* in Lapp, which mean to hunt, rapid and fast. "Yacht" also appears in Danish texts from the

8-9 Two American 12-meter yachts from the late Thirties: the America's Cup was still far off for a class of boat that was very popular in that era. In Britain, as in the United States and Northern Europe, races for this category were keenly contested and also featured in the Olympic Games of 1908, 1912 and 1920.

9 Early in the twentieth century, the Solent was the stretch of water on which the sailing ambitions of sovereigns, aristocrats and businessmen were put to the test: Germania belonged to a group of German industrialists, Britannia was the British royal yacht while Satanita belonged to a British gentleman.

seventeenth century where it is used to indicate a slim, agile boat used for those roles generally performed by escort vessels or frigates in the Mediterranean where to hunt and hunting were military functions.

The *yagt* or *jacht* mentioned in Dutch texts from the late sixteenth century were military vessels, subsequently used for "affairs of state, the transportation of goods or simply for the pleasure of those who sailed them." It was, however, the British who adopted the term "yacht" and who finally and exclusively applied it to a type of vessel in relation to its function, the "pleasance boat", a craft thus devoted to the pleasure of its users.

Today, after three centuries of recreational sailing, regattas and ocean cruising throughout the world, the term "yacht" has become

universally accepted. The yacht, born in the seas of Northern Europe and consecrated in Britain, is the symbol of a pleasure as old as the world itself, that of navigation.

While the history of the term "yacht" takes us back to the sixteenth century, we have to go much further to find the origins of recreational sailing, the practice that was responsible for the creation of the yacht as we know it today. In certain examples from the past centuries, or even millennia given that we have reports of this form of navigation that date back to the pre-Christian era, it is perhaps difficult to find anything in common with the modern sport of sailing.

It is certain, however, that in antiquity men sailed not solely out of necessity but were also prompted to undertake perilous voyages by desire and pure pleasure, to say nothing of their

10-11 The Whitbread race today represents yachting's most demanding ocean racing event: a circumnavigation of the globe in four stages for crewed yachts. The world's leading skippers such as the New Zealander Peter Blake and the American Paul Cayard with EF Education participate in the race.

11 The 1993 edition of the Admiral's Cup: participation in this event, ocean racing's world championship, requires the commitment of substantial economic resources and yachts increasingly rely on sponsorship from companies which see sailing as an ideal promotional vehicle.

yearning for new horizons and the display of power and importance.

The *Thalamegus* was a vessel of state "... and pleasure that we would call a yacht of the type used on the water by kings and great lords.

This type of vessel had a fine stateroom with a magnificent bed. Philopater, the King of Egypt, had a superb ship of this species constructed, aboard which he publicly cruised on the Nile with his wife and children." This note is taken from the eighteenth century text by Stanislao Bechi, *Istoria sulle Origini e Progressi della Nautica*, which also mentions Cleopatra's famous Galea and the ships of Caligula. According to the author, and confirmed by other sources, these examples all testify to a familiarity with a form of sailing difficult to assimilate to the modern sport, but nonetheless recreational. In the past the sea has also frequently represented a source of pleasure and even a master poet of inland origins was given to dream of a "cruise" with friends and their respective companions.

"Guido, I wish that you and Lapo and I, could be as if enchanted and placed in a vessel that with every breeze would take to sea as you and I wished..."

The author was, of course, Dante, and the vessel is that boat *"de joie de vivre et de deport"* of the Wizard Merlin which is mentioned in the stories of King Arthur. We are now talking about the second millennium in which Dante's dream was to become reality in the seventeenth century.

This delving into the past in search of the roots of sailing as a sport effectively reveals only the external aspects of the phenomenon.

In effect, as soon as yachting appeared in the seventeenth century with its independent manners and mores and was accepted as part of the social structure of the day, it revealed a side to its character that the terms "yacht" and "recreational sailing" had never before expressed.

From the seventeenth century onwards sailing for pure pleasure, with boats specifically produced to this end, increasingly signified competition against an adversary, speed, the search for ultimate performance; in a word regattas.

As soon as Charles II of England encountered the yacht of his cousin, a challenge was issued, a race between two boats on a windward-leeward course no different to the present day America's Cup. And this was only the beginning. Subsequently, all forms of recreational sailing, in any part of the world in which the activity gained a foothold, were to take on a competitive connotation.

Perhaps because sailing teaches and demands the virtue of patience and absolute subordination to natural phenomena, it stimulates a continuous quest for perfection: making the most of whatever the wind has to offer, trying to better the efforts of the next man. Which is, when all is said and done, the essence of racing.

Ever since the race between the royal yachts on the Thames in 1661, racing has in fact been a constant feature of yachting and has constantly influenced the development of the yacht.

This is true to the point that writing a history of the yacht without discussing racing would be impossible, and writing the history of competitive sailing effectively means recounting the history of the yacht.

12-13 The conclusion of the 2000 edition of the America's Cup once again favored the defender: the New Zealanders aboard Black Magic *defeated the Italian boat* Luna Rossa *by 5-0. Even after the historic defeat of the Americans in 1983, experience has continued to play a major role in an event that is now well over a hundred years old.*

14 top The Dutch yacht is still today principally if not solely identified by its large leeboards, a characteristic technical feature shared by no other type of yacht and one which responded to precise technical demands. When the yacht was exported firstly to England and then throughout the world, the feature was abandoned as it was closely tied to the particular conditions of the seas in which the boats originally sailed. Holland has extensive shallow and sheltered internal waters and the typical Dutch yacht derived from commercial vessels employed to carry large loads. Hulls were hence very full and flat-sided and unsuited to sailing close to the wind. The large leeboards in fact served to improve the vessel's beating capabilities.

THE ORIGINS OF SAILING

HOLLAND BIRTHPLACE OF THE YACHT

While it is probably correct to identify the 17th century as the historic period that witnessed the official birth of yachting, it is undoubtedly correct to locate the place of this birth in Zeeland region of present day Holland. Between the end of the sixteenth and the early years of the seventeenth centuries, Holland established itself as the world's premier seafaring nation, not so much in terms of its military might but for the merchant fleet that flew its flag throughout the seven seas.

In that period Dutch ports were home to a

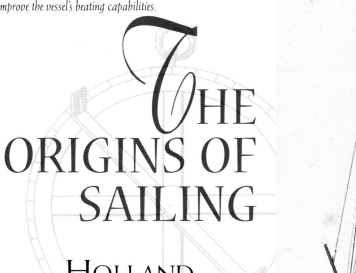

14 bottom In the mid-seventeenth century one of the principal features of the Dutch yacht was the richness of its decoration: the transom stern came in for particular attention, to the detriment of the purely nautical characteristics of the vessels, but emblematic of the opulence enjoyed by the country's bourgeoisie. The wealthy Dutch merchants in fact used their yachts as symbols of their economic success rather than as sporting boats or for cruising along the low, flat coasts in a climate not ideally suited to recreational sailing. The illustration is by Willem van de Velde the Elder. Much of what we know about the origins of yachting we owe to this artist and his son.

14-15 For purely pictorial motives this illustration somewhat exaggerates a situation typical of seventeenth century Holland. The country's internal waters would actually have been congested by the mercantile traffic offering the only easy and economical means of bulk transport, along with the numerous recreational craft that could already be found sailing. Amsterdam in fact boasted no less than three ports reserved exclusively for yachts.

fleet of no less than 3,500 ships of a total burden in the order of 600,000 tons. While it is true that the majority of these vessels were destined to ply shallow coastal waters, many were equipped for ocean crossings and navigation. Committed to extending its territory by reclaiming land from the sea rather than by way of military conquest, Holland took advantage of the state of perennial and turbulent belligerence afflicting other European nations to develop its commercial traffic. It rapidly became a state managed and organized by a wealthy merchant class which soon manifested a desire to express its power through the only means open to the inhabitants of a "land of water," ships. Their *jachten* were so sumptuous, highly decorated and gilded as to become known as *speeljachten* or pleasure boats.

The spread of these boats was rapid and unstoppable, to the point that the first port devoted to recreational craft had to be built at Amsterdam as early as 1622. Three years later, with this first port complete, a second had to be

constructed, followed by a third within the next twenty years. This fleet of small boats (the average length was not more than 33 feet, with many only around 20) was destined exclusively for pleasure. The phenomenon is recorded in numerous pictures of the era depicting the country's barely ruffled internal waters crowded with countless small boats in a chaotic toing-and-froing that nowadays can be seen on the sheltered waters of the Solent, Long Island and the bay at Cannes, to name but a few of the international yachting Meccas—unmistakable evidence of sailing for pure pleasure.

Along with the pre-eminent peculiarity of representing the prototype for an activity that, having achieved world-wide popularity, shows no sign of declining as we enter the third millennium, those Dutch *jachten* had technical features unique in the field of naval architecture that nonetheless had other traditions of no lesser importance. While French, English, Spanish and Portuguese craft

in practice drew on a single model, that of the high-sided cargo galleon, a vessel with a long history but suitable above all for carrying as many cannons as possible rather than a payload, the Dutch hull was distinguished by a number of technical details. These distingusihing features were evidently valid as, while not being adopted by other countries at the time, they have been retained unaltered to the present day. Above all the Dutch hull boasted an unusual fullness of shape. While it is true that ships in that period had wetted areas that were rather blunt at either end (with the exception of the Mediterranean *galere*, vessels constructed for high-speed raiding rather than cargo carrying or broadsides of cannon), the Dutch hull was fuller, especially at the stem. In all probability this was due to the need to maintain a high loading capacity in spite of the shallow draught imposed by the coastal and internal waters of the Netherlands. The full shapes of the stem were particularly suitable for the short, sharp seas typical of

shallow waters and can be seen (although the relationship is somewhat tenuous) in the Grand Banks fishing boats constructed 200 years later. The bottom of the hull was flat, another means of improving loading capacity while retaining a shallow draught. Resistance to lateral drift was provided by two leeboards that could be lowered into the water, a system that was both simple and unique to Dutch vessels.

The rig of these boats, that is to say the system of sails, was also original for an era in which all sailing vessels had square or, in the case of the Mediterranean *galere*, lateen sails. The Dutch boats were rigged with a spanker gaff that was also very efficient when sailing close to the wind. Much has been said about the sailing and seagoing qualities of this type of boat. As far as I am concerned it is sufficient that this rig characterized the world's first true yachts, its worth demonstrated by the fact that it continues to be used.

THE FIRST YACHT

Marine historians are in agreement in identifying the first yacht in history as the Dutch-built *Mary*, donated by the citizens of Amsterdam, or more precisely by the notables of the East Indies Company, to King Charles II of England on the occasion of a state visit to Holland in 1660.

"We sailed for four or five miles with extraordinary pleasure, on a fine day with a following wind, and they brought us on board freshly gathered oysters that were excellent and which we ate with great appetite."

Such was the description of a day's sailing aboard the *Mary* written by the diarist Samuel Pepys, a Royal Navy administrator and attentive observer of public and contemporary events from the coronation of Charles through to the plague and the Great Fire of London.

The *Mary* was a typical Dutch yacht, built for the Dutch East Indies Company with an overall length of 85 feet, a beam of around 20 feet and weighing a hundred tons. Rigged fore-and-aft with a spanker and jib, she had the

typical pivoted leeboards and, like all the boats owned by the wealthy Dutch bourgeoisie, rich decoration at stem and stern and round portholes for cannons (which as we shall see were carried on yachts for another hundred years, up to the end of the eighteenth century), surrounded by gilded garlands sculpted in the timbers. According to contemporary reports (no pictorial evidence of the *Mary* survives) the interior was extremely luxurious, the cabins being decorated with gilding and embellished with paintings and sculptures executed by the leading artists of the times.

Charles II remained enthusiastic about the Mary even when the yacht, having left Dutch waters, proved to suffer from the larger waves encountered in the Channel. This characteristic strong pitching over the crests of the waves had caused considerable distress to Charles' sister Mary, in whose honor, and perhaps to make amends for a bout of seasickness, the yacht was named. In spite of

this royal enthusiasm, the seaworthiness of the vessel was hardly sufficient to satisfy the technical demands of the sovereign. Peter Pett, a master carpenter and son of Phineas Pett, a former boatbuilder to the royal family, was entrusted with the task of designing a new boat similar to the *Mary* but with better handling characteristics. Pett closely examined the Dutch boat, finding much to praise in its design and construction. He nonetheless managed to create a considerably better yacht, the *Catherine*, named after the future wife of Charles II.

The *Mary* was decommissioned and rotted slowly in Irish waters, where she eventually sank off Holyhead in 1675. A group of divers located the hulk in 1973, but quite rightly she still rests in her watery grave.

16 The Mary, a yacht richly adorned with flags and decorations, proceeds up the Thames with its heavy hemp sails filled and distorted by an improbable head wind. Mary was the symbol of an era in which ostentation counted for as much if not more than real substance, but for all those interested in the history of recreational sailing she represents the original yacht. She was the first boat conceived solely for recreational sailing that actually performed all the functions typical of the activity: she represented her owner, she carried him on cruises with no aim other than pure pleasure, she raced and she was the prototype from which, with successive improvements, naval architects and yacht designers eventually derived hull shapes and rigging designed to provide improved performance.

16-17 Into the eighteenth century yachts were still armed. The cannons served for signalling in an era in which rather than sailing freely, yachts took to sea in parades, and for salutes when two boats crossed each others' paths. The presence of these arms is further testimony to the origins of the yacht as a vessel of state. Later, when recreational sailing left the safety of coastal waters, the cannons were to regain their original defensive function. Well into the second half of the nineteenth century, Commandant D'Albertis' Corsaro was armed in view of the adventurous voyages the yacht was designed to undertake.

During Charles II's reign no less that twenty-eight yachts were built and launched for the king and his brother, the future James II, an equally enthusiastic yachtsman.

While the *Mary* is correctly held to be the first true yacht, thus giving to Holland the prestige of being the nation that gave birth to recreational sailing, it is nonetheless true that in England, other boats had been built earlier for the sovereigns' exclusive pleasure. Henry V had the *Trinity Royal* (an oared vessel) but in the late sixteenth century, progress in rigging technology had allowed a sailing yacht to be built for Queen Elizabeth, the *Rat of Wight*, launched at Cowes in 1588, while her successor James I gave a sailing boat just 28 feet in length to his son. The *Disdain* was launched at Chatham in 1604 and was designed by the aforementioned Phineas Pett, a descendent of an already famous family of shipwrights who, along with his son Christopher Peter, was to build all of the royal family's subsequent yachts.

17 bottom From a historical point of view, Charles II, King of England from 1660 to 1685, can be considered to be the first sailing enthusiast, the first true yachtsman. In order to satisfy what was a real passion for sailing, he commissioned no less than twenty-eight yachts that he helmed personall. Following his lead, yachting spread throughout the world.

State yachts

The 18th century was a period of chaotic belligerence on the one hand and scientific and social progress on the other; wars entailed exchanges of experience between nations, albeit on the battlefield, and required immense technical and economic resources. The century of the Enlightenment provided the fuel for these efforts. This was just as true of yachting, a field still very much in its infancy as the previous century had witnessed only the definition of the type of craft involved and the attribution of a name. The activity developed on two fronts with new hull shapes and a scientific approach to design and construction.

This was the century in which the British admiralty developed, on the basis of the Dutch vessels imported in the second half of the previous century, its own craft with deeper stem sections that while perhaps not yet describable as slim were however already canted rather than swollen.

This was also the century in which the *Encylopédie* was published in France, complete with a section devoted to "Architecture Navale-Marine," and the century of Frederik Henrik af Chapman's monumental work published in Sweden under the title *Architectura Navalis*

Mercatoria. This contained lines plans of close to 200 ships of all kinds, accompanied by a text explaining the various methods of calculating hull dimensions, some of which are still used today.

At the same time, the sea-borne conflicts between the various fleets of France, Spain, England and Holland had led to an interesting exchange of experience and know-how. From the seas of the north (England and Holland) came hulls with greater loading capacities while out of the Mediterranean came French and Spanish vessels with more agile hulls and more efficient fore-and-aft lateen rigs.

Out of this wealth of comparative data and notions was to develop the late eighteenth century English cutter that was eventually to lend form to what we understand as yachts today. Throughout the seventeenth century, however, recreational sailing was to remain largely the preserve of the sovereign courts, even though the definition of the term "yacht" in W. Falconer's *Dictionaire universal de la Marine,* published in 1769, reveals early signs of a more widespread popularity: "Yacht: state vessel generally used for the transportation from one nation to another of princes, ambassadors and great figures. The principal function of a yacht

being to receive such passengers, numerous pleasantly furnished apartments are provided and equipped with fittings appropriate to the rank and number of the passengers. Royal yachts are generally rigged as ketches with the exception of the principal vessel reserved for the sovereign which is equipped with three masts like a ship. They are usually elegantly appointed, richly decorated with sculpture and always commanded by naval captains. Alongside these state vessels there are a host of smaller yachts used by customs and excise officials, the navy or as pleasure boats by high ranking individuals."

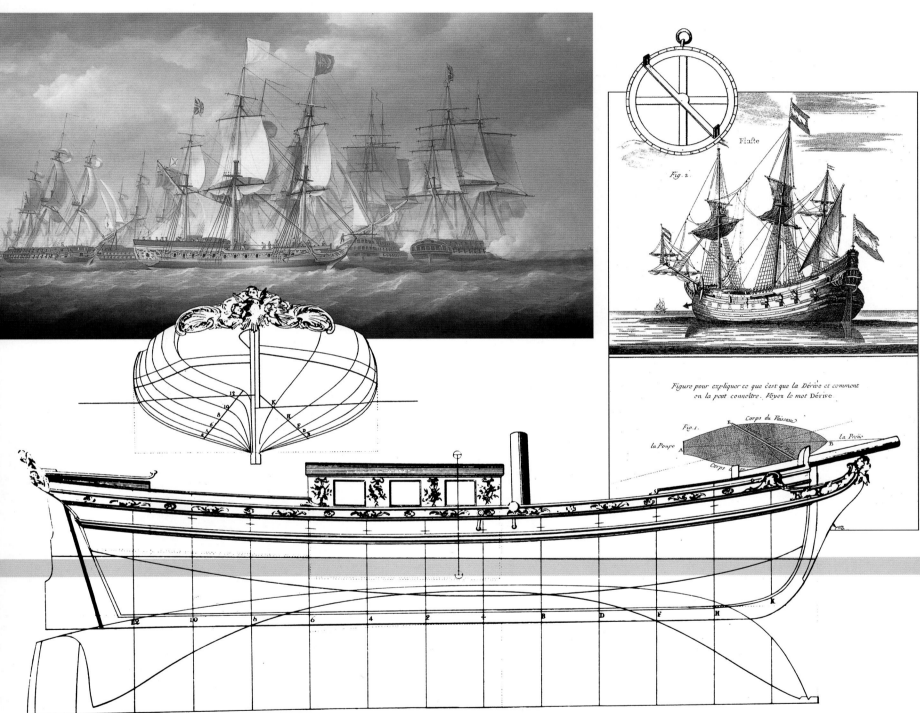

18 In the late seventeenth century Prussia, a nation that comprised present-day Poland and part of the Baltic regions of the former Soviet Union, could hardly avoid drawing on the naval patrimony of neighboring Holland and the yacht of Fredrick Wilhelm I of Prussia, the Liburnica, had all the features typical of the Dutch jaght: leeboards and a heavily decorated transom stern. The sails are carefully furled here but the numerous large flags and pennants aloft would have made any docking maneuver arduous.

19 top left Louis XVIII's return to his homeland could hardly have been made by any other means than a royal yacht. As it had been the British who had supported the restoration of the monarchy in France, the yacht was naturally British, the three-masted HMY Royal Sovereign.

19 top right The first systematic study of techniques, technologies and models was Diderot and D'Alambert's Encyclopédie, which devoted an entire section to the science of naval construction and navigation.

19 bottom The first book dedicated to naval architecture was published in Sweden with texts and drawings by an English engineer working in the service of the sovereign of that country. Frederik Henrik af Chapman's monumental work Architectura navalis mercatoria described both the theories which then lay behind the form and construction of ships, and the typical types of craft to be found in that period. Among the many drawings published by Chapman were a number of yachts which, in the eighteenth century, already represented a well established breed.

20-21 The Sun King, Louis XIV, while a contemporary of Charles II of England did not share his passion for the sea and sailing. He nonetheless wanted to imitate him in form at least. The pool in front of the opulent Palace of Versailles thus became the setting for scale replicas of the English sovereign's royal ships and yachts. In France at that time, form was far more important than substance and, in any case, the country lacked the necessary social conditions for the development of activities such as sailing. The eighteenth century was to bring yacht clubs to England and revolution to France.

AT THE COURT OF VERSAILLES

Although Versailles clearly lacked none of the pomp and magnificence of the English court, a similar interest in the sea and sailing failed to develop in France. In spite of two extensive coastlines, one on the Mediterranean and one facing the Atlantic and the Channel, and even though it could boast well established commercial (fishing above all) and military traditions, the country was notably slow to take up yachting. French recreational sailing only developed in the 19th century; in fact, even from as early as the beginning of the eighteenth century Aubin's *Naval Dictionary* correctly defined recreational craft and a few years later, in 1718, Rachelet's *Dictionary* contained the term "yacht" and even gave instructions as to its correct pronunciation.

The kings of France, evidently more concerned with other forms of "grandeur," never had yachts constructed for either personal or state use until the ascension to the throne of Louis-Philippe. Louis XIV did actually order two scaled-down replicas of the yachts of Charles II, but only to have them float as backdrops in the great pool in the gardens of Versailles. These models, for this is all they were, aroused considerable admiration and interest but still failed to ignite the spark of sailing among a French people perhaps already distracted by the somewhat more significant matters of war and economic crisis that were to lead to revolution. As early as 1613, the end of mourning for Henry IV had been marked by events centered on a regatta on the Seine at Paris with boats raced by professional seamen, fishermen, pilots and smugglers. In spite of the regatta's success it remained a one-off event.

This lack of interest is surprising in a nation that had experience of two different seas, the Atlantic and the Mediterranean, and had gained from the latter shipbuilding notions for the creation of vessels with shapely lines deriving from Maltese, Genoese, Venetian or Algerian galleys (a "galley" being a light, fast military vessel with oars and/or sails used from the Medieval period up to the 18th century. From the classic Greek Galee = weasel) that a hundred years later were to surprise the English when they appeared in the prow of the schooner *America*.

21 *As soon as the period of mourning for the Huguenot massacres was over, Henry IV, the King of France and Navarre, organized a sailing regatta on the Seine. This was late in the seventeenth century and the event could have represented a milestone in the history of yachting. However, the race was actually staged between professional sailors and fishermen, therefore not for pleasure. The tragic reign of Henry IV, that ended with his assassination, was not evidence of nascent interest in recreational sailing.*

KING CHARLES II OF ENGLAND

22-23 and 23 bottom The Charlotte, one of the many yachts in the British royal fleet, clearly derives from the Dutch jaght. Her bow and stern were still rounded, typical of a hull originally designed to carry loads rather than passengers and, above all, in shallow, sheltered waters. The stern was of course richly decorated and was better suited to testifying to the wealth and taste of the owner than to improving the performance of the yacht. Cannons continued to peer from the portholes along the sides, emphasized by gilded garlands. The late eighteenth century oil painting by Robert Dodd is interesting as it illustrates how yachts rode at anchor in that era, sails aloft, albeit furled, with the exception of the square sail which was aback. This is a curious practice, undoubtedly intended to allow for a certain rapidity of movement, but which must have placed notable strain on the anchor.

Without doubt the title of the inventor of yachting should go to Charles II of England, the owner of the first yacht, the *Mary*, and responsible for introducing the very term "yacht" to the country responsible for its diffusion throughout the world.

During his 25-year reign, the sovereign commissioned the building of no less than 26 yachts, the majority of which were the fruit of the creative genius of the master carpenter, Pett, who, in his turn, merits the title of the world's first yacht designer. Among Charles II's many yachts, one of the most remarkable was without doubt the *Fubbs*, built towards the end of the seventeenth century at Greenwich with an overall length of 80 feet, a beam of 21 feet and a weight of 150 tons. This very fast vessel was distinguished by a ketch rig that Charles II claimed to have invented and which he in any case held to be the most suitable for a

recreational craft. *Fubbs* was perhaps not the first ketch in history but certainly the first built in England.

Like all the king's yachts, *Fubbs* boasted particularly luxurious interiors. The royal suite at the stern featured carved oak panelling, an inlaid floor and a huge four-poster bed draped with brocades and silk.

It was the relative costs of this luxury that obliged Charles II to curb his nautical activities: while at that time a naval warship cost £15 a ton and a merchant vessel just £8, the sovereign's yachts cost as much as £33 per ton.

Charles II's successor, James II, maintained a fleet of just 9 yachts (including the glorious *Fubbs* which was to continue sailing until 1781). However, recreational sailing began to spread beyond the royal circles and soon a number of admiralty officials followed their king's example. In the meantime, the royal fleet had severed its ties with the navy which until then had been responsible for its maintenance, had had passed directly into the hands of the royal

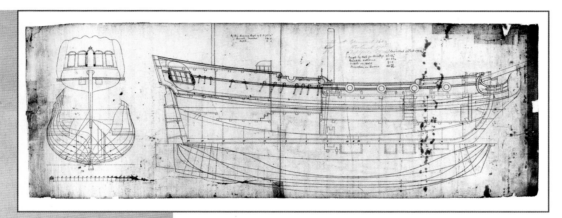

23 top In the second half of the eighteenth century the etymological definition of a yacht was also established. Alongside the technical treaties appeared the first dictionaries of nautical terms: the "yacht" was defined as a boat with official functions and as such generally reserved for heads of state and high ranking courtiers. There was also a precise hierarchy: the yacht reserved for the sovereign would have a rig that together with its size would distinguish it from other boats; it would thus be equipped with three masts like the Royal Charlotte, the former Royal Caroline, the yacht belonging firstly to William II and George I, then to Charles II.

23 center Fubbs was one of Charles II's first yachts, and certainly one of the first to be designed and built in England. She was constructed at Greenwich in 1682 by Phineas Pett. Baptised with the nickname of the Duchess of Portsmouth, one of the King's favourites; she was a particularly fast vessel, beloved of Charles II, a supporter of the ketch rig which was something of an innovation at that time to the extent that the sovereign was actually credited with its paternity. We have been left with a lively account of a cruise aboard the Fubbs in which it is described how Charles II and his brother the Duke of York were not above lending a hand with sheets and sails like ordinary seamen when required. The lines of the Fubb's hull exemplified what was then, as it was to be for the next two centuries, a pillar of naval architecture: the hull should be rounded at the prow and slim in the stern, "cod's head and mackerel's tail."

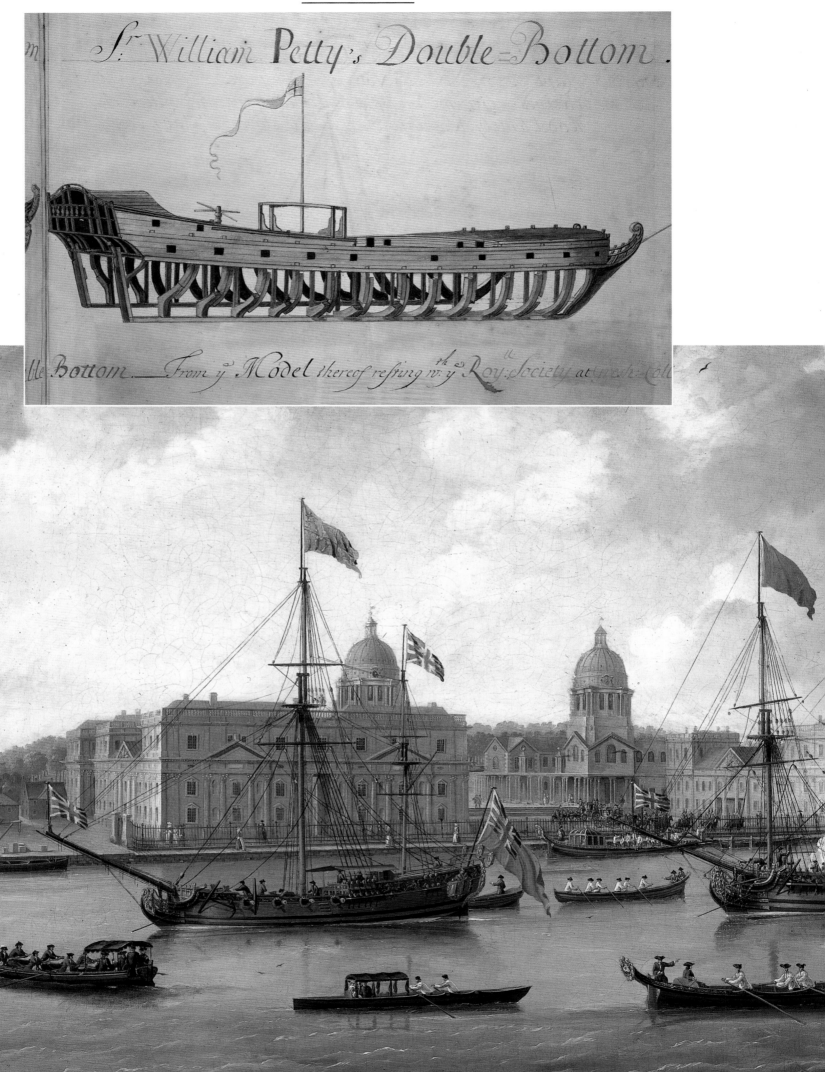

Sr. William Petty's Double=Bottom.

...lle Bottom.— From ye Model thereof resting wth ye Royll Society at Grech=Coll...

family. The port of Greenwich, then the main London port, was adopted as its home.

William II's enthusiasm for the sea and sailing matched that of his father and although he never attained a similar stature in the field he continued to sail for personal pleasure, especially aboard the *William and Mary.* The king entertained his great friend Peter I of Russia aboard this vessel, the czar discovering a shared interest in and passion for sailing.

The succeeding members of the Stuart line were also distinguished by their sailing activities. George I's reign saw the foundation in 1720 of the world's first yacht club, the Water Club of the Harbour of Cork, in the small town in the south of Ireland. As George III found when he came to

the throne, the royal fleet included the Royal *Caroline*, a three-master (according to Falconer and as we have seen, the typical rig for a royal yacht, in contrast with the perhaps more informed opinion of Charles II) which the king renamed as the *Royal Charlotte* in honor of his bride. Despite what had gone before, the *Royal Charlotte* was fitted out in such a luxurious style that when it was sent to the continent to bring the princess back to England she is reputed to have asked, "Shall I be worthy to go aboard?"

While the English yachting movement that was developing under the aegis of the ruling house experimented with new forms (*The Experiment*, the first catamaran or twin-hulled yacht, dates from the late seventeenth century,

and was built by Sir William Petty), the royal yachts and those of the court aristocracy still featured the full lines of their Dutch predecessors and the Baroque style of detailing, such as the cannons protruding from round portholes decorated with gilded garlands seen half a century earlier.

During the reign of George II the first true race with a trophy was held in 1749. A silver cup was offered by the king to the first boat home on a course from Greenwich to Nore and back. As is the case with the major modern regattas, the cup was won by a yacht designed expressly for the event, the *Princess Augusta*.

24 top Over a hundred years before Stevens, in the England of the dawn of yachting, a twin-hulled catamaran (the word derives from the Tamil term, kattumaram, "bound wood", and was used to describe a form of raft typical of Southeast India) had already been built by a certain William Petty in 1662. In reality he had simply divided the hull of a ship into two parts, linking them with a widened deck. The model illustrates the concept well.

24-25 For the whole of the century the River Thames was the home of the royal yachts, seen here at anchor line abreast at Westminster, handy for Buckingham Palace and the Houses of Parliament. In this painting can be recognized the three-masted Royal Caroline and the ketch-rigged Katherine, two typical rigs, the first as the personal yacht of the sovereign and the second for its handling qualities, at least according to Charles II. Banners aloft and cannon salvoes show that we are in the mid-eighteenth century.

CZAR
PETER

Early in the eighteenth century, Russia, the world's most geographically extensive nation, but also the most backward in social and economic terms, had yet to build up a naval fleet, in part because it had no access to the sea other than the port of Archangel which was ice-bound for over six months every year.

This situation prevented the czar of the time, Peter the Great, from becoming one of the first yachtsmen in history alongside Charles II of England. However, his enthusiasm for the sea and sailing was by no means inferior to that of the English sovereign.

Peter the Great's yachts never enjoyed the fame of the *Mary* and the later royal yachts built by Phileas Pett and his son, nor were they as numerous or as technically significant.

The czar's passion for sailing was ignited when he discovered abandoned in the Kremlin stores the hull of a small sailing boat, no more than 20 feet in length, that had been presented to Ivan the Terrible by Elizabeth I a century earlier.

From that moment onwards, Peter the Great's life took what was a remarkable turn for a sovereign. Becasue his country lacked a shipbuilding tradition, the czar decided that he himself should learn the secrets of the trade, travelling to Holland to work as a simple carpenter in the Dutch shipyards. That experience only increased his fervor, laying the basis not only for the satisfaction of his own demands, but also for the creation of the first Russian fleet.

Peter the Great struck up a friendship with William II of England, another sovereign gripped by the same passion for things nautical, who presented him, during a trip to the British Isles, with a yacht worthy of its name, *Royal Transport*. Nothing is known of this vessel other than that it was reputed to be very fast.

Peter the Great was only able to sail his yacht from England to Holland from where he was obliged to proceed overland to Moscow. The *Royal Transport* instead headed for Archangel where it remained trapped for fifteen years by the ice and its draught which prevented it from navigating the rivers. The czar successfully constructed a Russian fleet but never managed to instil a passion for sailing in his fellow countrymen, as yachting without water is of course a contradiction in terms.

26-27 *Peter the Great's passion for yachts was only to be satisfied by a gift from his great friend William II of Great Britain who presented him with the* Royal Transport. *Up until then he had had to content himself with admiring the displays of Dutch yachts organized for his benefit. These events were veritable reviews with the yachts parading in formation and maneuvering according to the patterns codified by the navies of the day. The Czar took part in the events with great pleasure; in the picture here he will be aboard the yacht in the foreground on the right that is flying the imperial Russian flag.*

THE NORTH SEA

Denmark is a small country, like Holland for that matter, with great naval traditions and has been ruled uninterruptedly by a monarchy from 850 AD. In the seventeenth century, when the monarchies of other European courts were launching ostentatious royal yachts, the incumbent king, Christian V, commissioned the *Elephanten*, a yacht based on the vessels of his Dutch neighbors, or rather those of the English who had by that time under Charles II already developed a new more

efficient version of the *Mary*.

The *Elephanten* was built in Denmark in 1687 by the Englishman Francis Scheldon. She had an overall length of 92 feet, a beam of 23 feet and was rigged as a ketch. The stern was richly decorated with friezes, curlicues and garlands to which was added a large elephant sculpted in wood.

Three years later the Danes launched a new royal yacht, the *Cronen*, similar to but larger than its predecessor.

27 *The first attempt to categorize yachts, and indeed ships and shipping in general, was made by Chapman. His was, however, more of an encyclopedia than a technical treatise. The English architect compiled and cataloged almost all the types of craft then in use, making drawings from models or the actual vessels. When he himself turned his hand to designing he simply referred to the models that he had recorded in his monumental work. While the form of the Amphion, the Swedish royal yacht, was clearly derived from the lines of military vessels of the era, she nonetheless had a degree of elegance and formal balance.*

26 bottom *The Czar of all the Russias never had a fleet of yachts like his counterparts in other European countries; however his passion for the sea and sailing was authentic and led him to mix with the carpenters in the Dutch boatyards in order to learn boatbuilding techniques. The painting dates from the nineteenth century and the composition probably reflects what the artist may have seen when wandering around a contemporary boatyard. The layout of the yard as it appears in the background of the painting is nonetheless interesting with two sheds covering two slipways in a very modern and undoubtedly efficient structure. Well into the nineteenth century, boats were in fact still being built in the open on beaches.*

INLAND WATERS

The Netherlands gave birth to the yacht with the gift of the *Mary* to Charles II and their inland waters were (and still are, of course) roamed by fleets of private boats from the seventeenth century onwards. Strangely it was only the sovereigns who failed to equip themselves with a royal yacht at that time.

The *jaght* became a symbol of the wealthy bourgeoisie merchant class and were exported as a model to the old and new worlds. William of Orange and Queen Mary did use this type of boat as private and state yachts but only in England.

Private *jaght* were also launched by Prince Henry of Orange, Charles XI of Sweden and later by Czar Alexander I.

In the present day, Beatrice of Holland enjoys sailing aboard *De Groene Draeck*.

IN THE BALTIC

Only after the mid-eighteenth century, with the accession to the throne of King Gustav III did Sweden emerge from its isolation to enjoy a cultural and economic renaissance. On the crest of this wave, a number of royal yachts were constructed, *Amphion*, launched in 1778, being one of the most interesting.

The boat was designed by F. H. af Chapman, one of the many Englishmen working, especially in the naval sector, in eighteenth-century Sweden. Without doubt he was the most well known of them thanks to the vast and fundamental work mentioned earlier. The 160-foot *Amphion* was rigged as a schooner which was not unusual at that time in those waters and the decoration of the sides was also the work of Chapman.

King Gustav III frequently sailed aboard *Amphion*, using it both as a state yacht and, in preference, for long cruises through the Finnish archipelago.

THE DUTCH INHERITANCE

Early in the eighteenth century, the territory that was eventually to become the United States of America was still a vast unexplored expanse waiting to be colonized. Only the coastal strips had a veneer of Old World civilization in the form of isolated settlements with little contact between one another. These colonies were populated by various ethnic groups, those that in that period were at war with one another in the Old World: the Spanish in California, the French in Louisiana and Quebec (in the far north and today part of Canada), the British, and before them a few Dutch, on the Atlantic coast.

The Dutch, in fact, landed early in the seventeenth century, on an island at the mouth of the Hudson river which the natives called Manhattan. There they founded a city they naturally baptized New Amsterdam. It was only to become New York after having been conquered by the British in 1664. The colonists from the Netherlands thus had no time to build a city or a port, never mind think about yachting which was, after all, an activity associated with situations of economic prosperity, just as it is now and always will be.

A people, a nation, firstly establishes its economy, concentrates on accumulating wealth

and only then, when the economy is booming, does it begin to think about things such as yachts.

At the end of the seventeenth century and through to the beginning of the eighteenth, the economic situation in America was still at the pioneer level: groups of colonists, in conflict with the natives and occasionally amongst themselves, were attempting to secure the conditions for their very survival. Not even the Dutch, who back in their homeland had left a flourishing tradition of recreational sailing, and who had been responsible for introducing the activity to the British, had the physical and economic resources necessary for the building of yachts. While it is true that there are reports of a "yacht" built by a colonist at Manhattan as early as 1614, it is reasonable to presume that it was a jacht rather than a speel jacht, and thus a working boat.

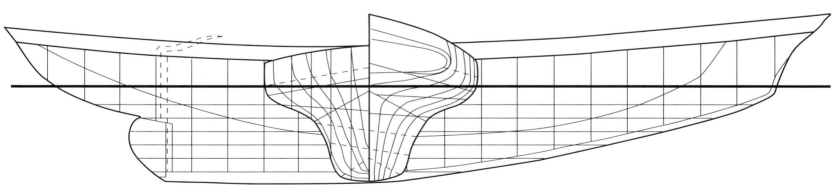

28 top The yacht owned by Colonel Morris enters the port of New York under full sail: the Dutch influence is still evident, especially in the rig and the masses of flags and banners. It was, however, the first American yacht if only because it was actually built on the other side of the Atlantic. In the background of the picture can be seen interesting details of contemporary boatbuilding: no fixed structures, slipways directly on the shore, a beached hull laid on its side for the caulking of the seams which in that era was done with oakum and pitch.

28 bottom Only structural problems, associated with the materials and the techniques available at the time, prevented Robert Livingston Stevens from designing

the first yacht with a ballast fin: Onkaye, so different in her transverse sections with respects to Maria, had a bulge in her lines so as to carry ballast as low as possible and free it from the keel. This was a significant example of the pull towards the new in the search for continued improvements in performance.

29 top From the earliest days the schooner has been a rig typical of American waters. It was frequently employed on the boats used by the pilots who sailed out to meet ships and conduct them to safe anchorages in ports. The American pilot boats were not generally required to tackle particularly rough seas in contrast with the British counterparts, the Channel cutters; they simply had to

be fast. It was thus only natural that they should give birth to high performance yachts. The Dream was in fact a Boston pilot boat before becoming a private yacht.

29 bottom Maria represents an unusual attempt to make the shape of a hull competitive: the great width of fishing and working boats resulting from the shallow waters of the American coasts was exaggerated, as on a modern planing yacht. The Americans, in contrast with the British, immediately tried to find new and independent forms and rigs for yachts, without however forgetting two fundamental elements of their naval tradition: stability of form and mobile keel appendages.

THE FIRST AMERICAN YACHTS

The European colonists who landed on the American coasts in the seventeenth century wasted little time in building solid economic fortunes. The territory was rich in easily extracted prime materials and trade in cultivated, mined or hunted products was particularly profitable; partly because so much of it was carried out in the form of smuggling in order to avoid the Navigation Acts imposed by the British. As we have already mentioned, prosperity was a prerequisite for the birth of yachting.

The first recorded American yacht was the *Francy* belonging to Colonel Lewis Morris, depicted in an engraving from 1717 as she sails across New York Bay.

This vessel was still based on the Dutch model, the hull featuring a very full prow, the richly decorated quarter-deck and the rig with a spanker with a very short jib and free base unequivocally drawing on the vessels seen on

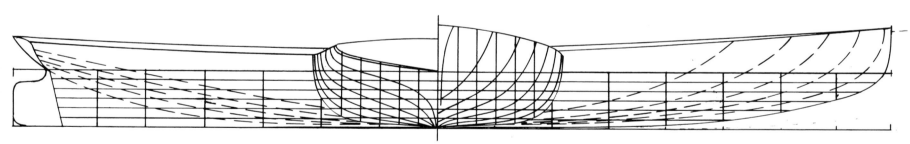

the Zuider Zee a hundred years earlier. Such are the similarities that some doubt remains as to whether this was in fact a recreational yacht or in fact a working vessel.

What is certain is that it was not until the early nineteenth century that recreational sailing really became established on the other side of the Atlantic. Once it had gained a foothold, however, it developed rapidly. In the early years of that century a number of great families had already amassed immense fortunes and among them the seeds of ostentation and passion found fertile terrain.

The Crowinshields, of Dutch origins, began in 1801 with a small yacht, the *Jefferson*, a sloop that while of no great sophistication was particularly fast. She was followed five years later by the famous *Cleopatra's Barge*.

In the meantime, at New York, the Stevens family launched, respectively, the *Diver*, of just 20 feet in length, the *Trouble*, far larger at an overall length of 52 feet 6 inches and built along the lines of the Caribbean pirogues, *Double Trouble*, so named because of its twin-hull construction (it was in fact a catamaran) and lastly the *Wave* of almost 65 feet.

The family was to add further chapters to the history of American yachting with the design of the great *Maria* and *Onkaye*.

The first American yacht club was founded at Boston in the early 1830s (other clubs had actually been founded earlier but had only a brief existence). In contrast with the exclusive and aristocratic English clubs, the Boston Boat Club was constituted by a group of friends with a shared passion for sailing and, above all, a

hedonistic approach to life. In 1835, the club nonetheless managed to acquire the *Dream*, a 46-foot schooner, for the modest sum of 2,000 dollars, and the following year the 52-foot *Breeze*.

The majority of the American yachts were derived from working boats and in particular the schooner. The American schooner appeared around the end of the eighteenth century as a fast cargo or military vessel and was itself based on contemporary French escort vessels. The *Berbice* was launched in 1780 and was the progenitor of the Baltimore schooner and thus the "bankers' schooners."

A typical example of the breed was the *Hornet*, constructed in 1819 in Maryland as a schooner-rigged pilot boat, converted to use as a yacht at New York in 1852 and fitted with a sloop rig.

CLEOPATRA'S BARGE

30 top and 30-31 The Stars and Stripes are hoisted on a yacht: for over a century the Union Jack of the British boats had enjoyed a monopoly on recreational sailing throughout much of the world. In the rest of the globe the sport simply did not exist. Cleopatra's Barge had the form, decorations, rig and so on peculiar to a boat devoted to sailing for pleasure, and she owed nothing and indeed was deliberately distinguished from working and naval boats, and as was frequently the case with American yachts, she paid little heed to tradition.

In the context of an embryonic world, in which a nascent population's inclination towards great undertakings had yet to manifest itself, the yacht *Cleopatra's Barge* was of great import.

This yacht was particularly significant because it was designed and built exclusively as a recreational vessel intended to be used for a remarkably ambitious cruise in an age when cruising was generally a coastal exercise. It was also a deliberate manifestation of status in that it was furnished and decorated to a standard perhaps never before seen in a yacht.

Cleopatra's Barge was above all a symbolic yacht, not only because it was the first true American yacht, but also because it accurately reflects the history and nature of the nation.

Her owner, George Crowinshield, was neither an aristocrat nor a statesman, nor was he a member of one of the great capitalist families. He was a merchant and shipowner and descended from just two generations of modest traders. His great-grandfather who emigrated from Holland was a physician and died in poverty.

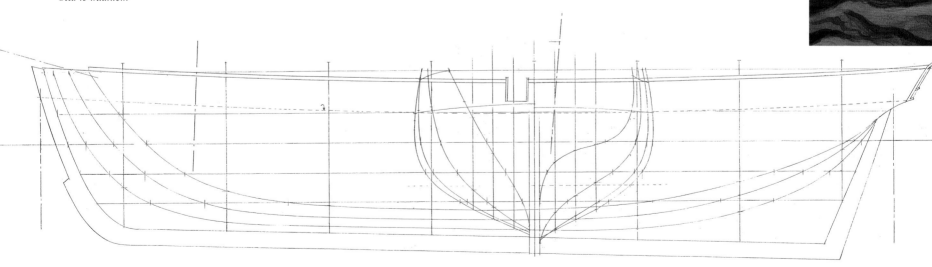

30 bottom The lines of Cleopatra's Barge, *seen here in a drawing made at a later date from original models and illustrations, clearly show the derivation of the design from those of working boats. The hull had very full sections at the prow that tapered towards the stern in the* classic "cod's head mackerel's tail" layout, a keystone of naval architecture up to the nineteenth century. The keel was straight and ran almost the full length between stem and stern, being only slightly inclined from the front to rear. There was a practical question behind this aspect as *when launched the hulls slid directly along the slipways exploiting the natural slope of the beaches. Only the modern yard run by Herreshoff in the late nineteenth century had appropriate equipment and slipways conceived specifically for hulls with appendages.* Cleopatra's Barge *was in fact a yacht only in terms of her decorations, while the British cutters already had a degree of autonomy with respects to ships. The U. S. would have to wait for the Steers schooner* America *to see lines designed specifically for performance.*

31 A formal portrait of the owner of Cleopatra's Barge that confirms the success he achieved in business and testifies to his passion for the sea: his yacht can be seen sailing in the background, while he is gripping a telescope in a pose typically used to portray the great admirals. Crowinshield is both an emblem of the American way of life and a prototype of the modern yachtsman, no longer an aristocrat sailing to respect a social convention, but a wealthy enthusiast. His Dutch origins had imbued him with the restlessness of the inhabitants of barren lands eager to embrace the open sea.

George Crowinshield is representative of the American social model and his *Cleopatra's Barge* was an emblem of that model. The yacht was launched at Salem on the 31st of October, 1816. The hull was over 101 feet long, 23 feet wide, had a draught of 11 feet 6 inches and a displacement of 192 tons. She was rigged as a brigantine-schooner with square-rigged sails on the foremast and a fore-and-aft spanker on the main. The yacht's sides were decorated asymmetrically with painted horizontal bands to starboard and lozenges to port. The constructor Retive Becket presented George Crowinshield with a bill for 50,000 dollars, over twice the price for a merchant vessel of a similar size.

The interiors were as sumptuous and as un-nautical as one could possibly imagine: panelling on the walls in exotic woods, beamed ceilings decorated with gold borders, chairs with backs painted with country scenes, fireplaces, sofas with harp-shaped backs and gold strings and sideboards full of silverware and porcelain.

On the 30th of March, 1817, George Crowinshield set sail in this yacht for a cruise that was all but unthinkable in that day and age. He crossed the Atlantic (probably the first crossing made by a recreational yacht) to the Azores and then proceed to Gibraltar, Tangiers and Majorca. With Mediterranean cruising in mind, George Crowinshield had

ordered a set of light sails to be prepared, a degree of attention to technical detail that was surprising for a man apparently interested only in impressing with his great wealth and eccentricity.

George Crowinshield returned to Salem, leaving his yacht in the Mediterranean in view of a future cruise that was to have taken him to the northern seas. He instead died in 1818 in the city of his birth.

Cleopatra's Barge had a final moment of notoriety when in 1820 she was sold to the king of the Hawaiian Islands, Kamehameha II. The natives had little experience with that kind of craft and soon provoked a dramatic shipwreck.

A NEW NAVAL ARCHITECTURE

While *Cleopatra's Barge* was the first purpose-built American yacht, in reality, apart from her extraordinary exterior appearance and the interiors of a quite stunning opulence, she was still a traditional vessel. American society, finding itself in a situation of sudden and enormous prosperity, could hardly fail to begin to express in the field of naval architecture those qualities of innovation and progress that the Enlightenment on the one hand and the multiple influences of a multi-ethnic society on the other had to offer. The nation was also helped in this respect by the fact that it was starting from scratch with new shipyards, new labor forces and new materials, all established in a setting free of restrictive traditions. The idea of progress is born when a society is struggling to establish itself and, as soon as the nascent economy permits, it flourishes.

The modern yacht developed during the first half of the nineteenth century in an America which had only recently severed its political ties with England. The form it took was determined by an eagerness to experiment with new lines and new technology, used exclusively to advance the concept of the yacht and not subjected to the demands of merchant, naval or other forms of working craft.

Every new idea needs a father-figure, and in the case of yachting this role was played by Robert Livingston Stevens, engineer, inventor, member of a great railroad dynasty and above all fanatically devoted to the cause of progress.

Looking at his two earliest designs for the *Onkaye* and the *Maria*, a basic concept is immediately apparent: the abolition of all that had gone before in order to develop new theories, inventing new techniques where necessary and experimenting with new materials.

Even when R. L. Stevens adopted more traditional technology, he was determined to improve and transform it. This was the case with the centerboards that he used on both the *Onkaye* and, in a more extreme form, the *Maria*.

Leeboards had been invented by the Dutch in the early seventeenth century: two pivoted blades, one either side, were lowered alternatively according to the direction the wind was blowing from. The system worked but was by no means sufficiently rapid and efficient for those looking for speed and performance from a yacht. The vertically sliding daggerboard was invented one hundred and fifty years later. Both of these systems were penalized by a requirement that had nothing to do with performance—the need to devote interior space to cargo. It was not until the eighteenth century and the establishment of recreational yachting as an independent activity that the modern centerboard appeared on both sides of the Atlantic, virtually at the same time.

In England between 1810 and 1824, Captain Molyneux Schudlam developed a system with a centerboard located along the longitudinal axis of the hull that was rotated about a central pivot in order to be raised or lowered. It was not widely taken up in Britain only because English naval architects and boatbuilders had in the meantime, as we shall see later, developed hulls so deep as to render the concept superfluous. Almost at the same time, on the 10th of April, 1811, a patent was deposited in the new-born United States for a similar centerboard system invented by the brothers Joshua, Henry and Jacocks Swain. There are no grounds to suspect any form of plagiary.

Whereas the first system involved the use of a deep keel, the Swains' sole concern was to develop a means of improving a boat's ability to

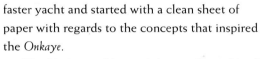

32-33 When Stevens decided to build the schooner America in order to challenge the world of British yachting, the Maria was chosen as the test yacht against which to verify the new boat's performance. At that time Maria was the fastest boat afloat in American waters, although only inshore due to the lack of stability caused by her vast sail area applied to a very lightly ballasted hull. Moreover, she was difficult to trim due to her two centerboards. America was just as up-to-date in terms of her lines, but was more logical and benefited from the professionalism of her designer. Stevens was, after all, an amateur and the Maria in fact never succeeded in beating America.

32 The Maria was in sharp contrast with Cleopatra's Barge. Apart from her size, to all intents and purposes she resembled a working New York Bay sloop but in reality she was a vessel conceived in terms of speed alone, with a shallow hull, a long waterline, two centerboards, one for stability and the other to counterbalance the shifting of the center of effort with respects to the hull center at different points of sailing.
The simplicity of the sail plan tends to take attention away from the aspect for which the Maria is still remembered: with her waterline of 110 feet, she was the largest sloop ever constructed.

sail into the wind. R. L. Stevens used both systems in original designs.

Stevens designed and built the *Onkaye*, which in an American Indian tongue means "dancing feather", in 1840, a 98-foot schooner with a beam of 22 feet, centyerboards and absolutely innovative lines.

With this vessel the designer concentrated on the shape of the hull. He wanted a form that made as little wave as possible when moving through the water, had the ballast set as low as possible and at the same time provided great stability while avoiding excessive width at the waterline.

What emerged was a hull with extraordinary, chalice-like lines that, had it not been penalized by the available materials and constructional techniques far behind those used today, would have been comparable with a contemporary yacht.

The hull had a finely tapering waterline both where it entered, at the prow, and where it exited the water at the stern and therefore raised a very small bow-wave, especially in light winds. As winds rose, the boat would heel and dip the wider upper part of the hull into the water with an

immediate increase in lateral stability. The iron ore ballast (previously stone had always been used as ballast and had been located within the hull) was placed inside the hull at the lowest part of the U-shaped section that ran practically from stem to stern along the full length of the waterline. Such a long keel was imposed by the slipway at the boatyard down which a yacht of the size of *Onkaye* would have to be slipped in order to be launched. The only traditional feature of the *Onkaye* was her schooner rig, and even here the designer had added a boom-less spanker to the foremast, a spanker that in part overlapped that of the mainmast. The yacht proved to be extremely fast and perhaps her only defect was her great stability, due to the shape of the hull and the low-setballast which provoked such a short, sharp roll that on one occasion the masts were snapped cleanly at the base, due to the intense stress placed on rigging that was not yet composed of steel cables.

Stevens' next design produced six years later demonstrated that his ideas were not compromised by technical prejudices. *Maria*, a sloop launched in 1846 had radically different sections as the designer simply wanted a better,

faster yacht and started with a clean sheet of paper with regards to the concepts that inspired the *Onkaye*.

The *Maria* owed her stability to the width of her sections and was designed above all to be particularly light in all areas including the rig. Hollow masts, boom and bowsprit were used for the first time and special tooling had to be invented and constructed to make them. The sections of this light-weight hull were very flat and to allow the yacht to sail close to the wind two centerboards were provided, an enormous central daggerboard that when it was lowered extended the draught to 13 feet 7 inches and was made of steel ballasted with lead. In order to lift it, Stevens invented a twofold differential tackle with chains. The second device located at the stern rotated on a pivot and made of light wood was designed to balance the yacht under different sail loads.

The structure of the yacht reflected her designer's ideas on lightness, although the materials of the day were not always adequate for the tasks to which they were put. During one of her first voyages, *Maria* lost the forward part of the main daggerboard with its seven tons of ballast. Stevens thus invented something new, replacing the daggerboard with another in wood and locating the ballast externally for the first time in history. Around twenty tons of cast lead were cast from the inside to the outside of the hull through holes in the keel, being secured by the fact that the solidified metal remained in the holes.

The *Maria* with her length of 113 feet at the waterline still remains the largest sloop ever constructed. She boasted a sail area of over 8,000 square feet very simply distributed, with consequent weight savings, between a 4,850 square-foot spanker and an enormous boomed jib. Contemporary reports indicate that in light winds and calm waters, the *Maria* was easily capable of seventeen knots.

Man's first challenge when he felt the need to move across water—and this is something he has felt from his very origins—was that of finding a floating means of transport. Having solved this problem with wood that floated naturally, without the need for any intellectual input, there arose the question of the creation of a form that created the least possible resistance as it moved through the liquid medium. The process was similar to that which led to the development of the wheel that permitted movement over land.

It is intuitive that objects intended to move should be pointed or at least have their shortest side in the direction of travel, but it is surprising that with the passing of the brief era of tree trunks and simple rafts, man should have immediately adopted a rounded hull form. Such were the difficulties inherent in creating these shapes that highly complicated technology that has remained unaltered from its inception to the present day had to be developed. This technology involved the use of planking laid over a combined longitudinal and transverse structure, as well as secondary systems of caulking (the means by which the joints between the various planks were made watertight), nailing and joining. The techniques are in fact so complex that they still today require a workforce composed of highly specialized master carpenters and caulkers.

Perhaps it was the very invention of the wheel that rightly convinced Man that the correct hull shape should be rounded both longitudinally and crosswise. At this point, however, he rested on his laurels to some extent. From the first planked vessels, constructed in Ancient Greece, to those of the period of the Enlightenment, no efforts were made to optimize hull shape which only varied according to the role for which the ship in question was constructed. If the vessel was designed to carry cargo, be it rocks or arms, then the carpenter would produce a tubby, swollen shape, restricted only by the need to have a point at either end and the limitations on his ability to curve the planking—as far as he was concerned he would have happily produced a sphere (quite rightly, given that a sphere is the geometric form enclosing the greatest volume and therefore the most cargo in the smallest package). If instead the vessel was required to be fast then the hull would be elongated, although this was due more to the space required by the "engine," that is to say

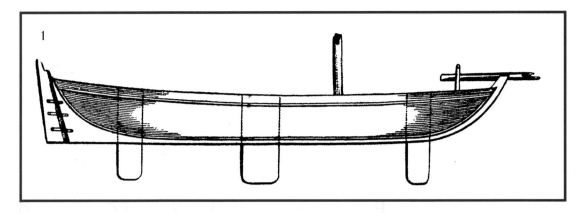

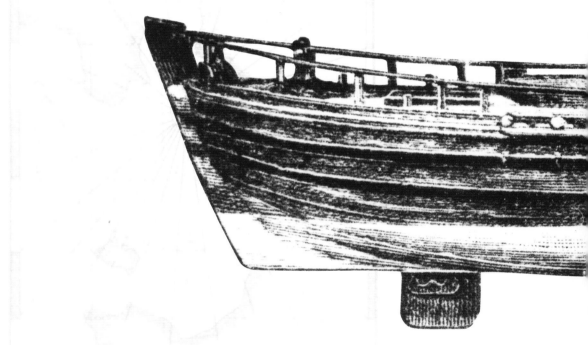

34 and 35 The first centerboard was developed in 1771 by Captain Shank of Boston who built a sloop equipped with three mobile keel appendages. The system was subsequently offered to the British Admiralty which had it applied to diverse vessels. The Commodore of the Cumberland Fleet, Taylor, had no less than five centerboards fitted to his fourth yacht, Cumberland IV. However, the system did not become widespread until patents were issued, one in America and one in Britain in 1811. Historically, the mobile keel has been used above all in American waters, favored or rather imposed, as it had been in Holland since the seventeenth century, by the shallowness of the seas around those coasts. The system is generally complicated to apply: the drawings on the opposite page clearly show the modifications to the structure of a boat required by the installation of a centerboard. The principal elements of the

frame such as the keelson, essentially the backbone of the yacht, are involved. In principal, as mentioned earlier, the Dutch preferred to use leeboards that did not interfere with the frame and left all the interior space for the cargo. The centerboard is, however, more efficient and, despite the complications of the system which demands the creation of a watertight case at the center of the yacht, proved to be the better solution. The five centerboards fitted to Cumberland IV were an attempt to control the balance between the center of thrust and the center of buoyancy: interesting but complicated.

Drawing 1 – An eighteenth century hull with three centerboards: a British design which never got beyond the drawing board but illustrative of the attempts to resolve the problems of leeway and balance under sail.

Drawing 2 – This transverse section shows the mechanism used to lift the cenereboard inserted within a watertight case. The system cuts through the main structural elements such as the beams and keelson.

Drawing 3 – The centerboard is left by means of two chains wound on rollers manually actuated via cranks. It is difficult to see how the buoyant wooden centerboard would instead be lowered.

Drawing 4 – The keelson, weakened by the opening cut for the centerboard, is reinforced with two floor timbers at either end of the slot and a series of intermediate ribs set into the keelson itself.

Drawing 5 – A detail showing the opening in the keelson for the passage of the centerboard, highlighting the joining system for the ribs and the notch for the first external plank.

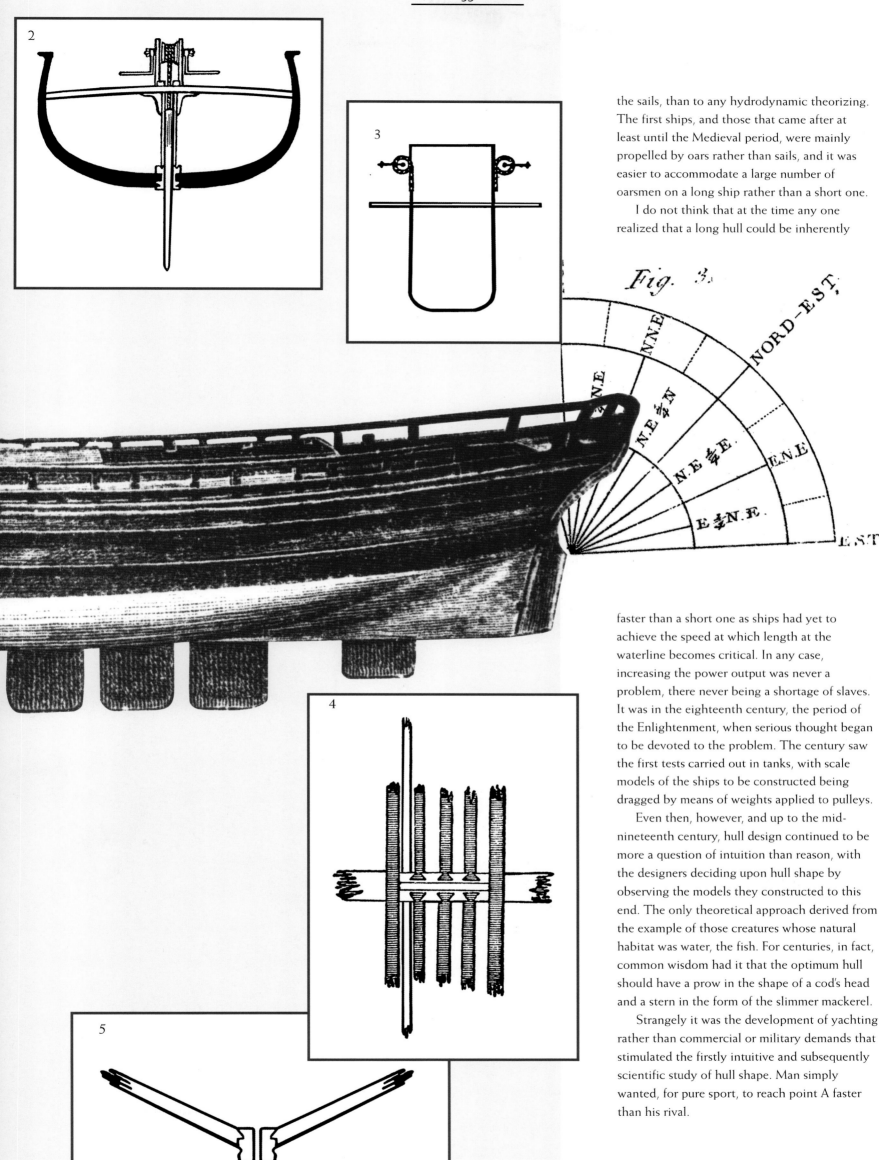

the sails, than to any hydrodynamic theorizing. The first ships, and those that came after at least until the Medieval period, were mainly propelled by oars rather than sails, and it was easier to accommodate a large number of oarsmen on a long ship rather than a short one.

I do not think that at the time any one realized that a long hull could be inherently

faster than a short one as ships had yet to achieve the speed at which length at the waterline becomes critical. In any case, increasing the power output was never a problem, there never being a shortage of slaves. It was in the eighteenth century, the period of the Enlightenment, when serious thought began to be devoted to the problem. The century saw the first tests carried out in tanks, with scale models of the ships to be constructed being dragged by means of weights applied to pulleys.

Even then, however, and up to the mid-nineteenth century, hull design continued to be more a question of intuition than reason, with the designers deciding upon hull shape by observing the models they constructed to this end. The only theoretical approach derived from the example of those creatures whose natural habitat was water, the fish. For centuries, in fact, common wisdom had it that the optimum hull should have a prow in the shape of a cod's head and a stern in the form of the slimmer mackerel.

Strangely it was the development of yachting rather than commercial or military demands that stimulated the firstly intuitive and subsequently scientific study of hull shape. Man simply wanted, for pure sport, to reach point A faster than his rival.

THE BRITISH CUTTER

Today we define a "cutter" as a boat rigged with a single mast and two or more foresails. In reality, cutters were originally defined more by their function than their rig: a cutter was a boat carried by the naval vessels used to counter the activities of smugglers and the term was later adopted to describe any kind of craft whose strong suit was speed rather than cargo capacity, especially pilot boats. Since many English yachts were in fact based on pilot boats, "cutter" came to be used to describe a kind of yacht very common in British waters: fairly narrow, with a deep draught and rigged with a single mast and a long bowsprit to carry more than one jib.

The hull shapes and rigging of "working" cutters were studied to render the vessels fast and maneuverable, these being fundamental qualities of a yacht, and by the end of the eighteenth century, a cutter was an English yacht by definition. By the nineteenth century the category had developed still further and become excessively characterized, much in the same way as in architecture, rococo developed out of baroque and eventually marked its demise.

The motives for the development of this type of yacht lay above all in the ratings then in vogue that considered neither the wetted surface nor the sail area and thus penalized the length of the

boats, and then there was the need to increase the size of the "engine" in order to out-run adversaries. What resulted were yachts ever narrower in relation to their length. Whereas the earliest cutters had a fairly high beam/length ratio (the Pearl, from 1820, that may be considered the first true yacht-cutter, had a ratio close to 3.7 against the 2.7 of the first yacht in history, the Mary), it continued to increase from the 4.0 of the Mosquito of 1848 to the 7.2 of the Spankadillo of 1882.

Prior to reaching the excesses of the late nineteenth-century cutter, however, this category was to produce a series of boats that

were not only extremely fast and blessed with notable ability to sail close to the wind, with respects to other contemporary boats, but were also exceptionally beautiful. Still today the nineteenth-century English cutter has immense appeal and represents a form, both in terms of hull shape and rigging, that had finally freed itself of the trappings of the working boat; the English cutter could only be used for recreational sailing.

It is interesting to note just how many innovations in the world of yachting were introduced on this kind of boat. These included roller booms, actually introduced on pilot cutters that notoriously sailed with skeleton crews, useful for taking in the mainsail as winds increased. As cutters had vertical stemposts and when sailing into heavy

seas had no buoyancy reserves to counter pitching, the prow and especially the bowsprit would be submerged, placing severe stresses on the rigging. Retractable bowsprits were an answer to this problem. The *Mosquito* instead had the first steel hull. Above all, however, the cutters featured the first waterlines that tapered at both stem and stern, the designers beginning to progress beyond the "cod's head-mackerel's tail" formula.

The era of the deep and narrow cutter, which was also defined at its height as the "Plank on Edge" style, inevitably came to a tragic conclusion. The *Oona*, built at Southampton in 1886 by Fay, lost her keel at sea due to the enormous stress to which it was subjected.

A number of people, including the designer, lost their lives in the accident.

36 top The rig of the English cutter derived from models that had been tested throughout the eighteenth century by the Royal Navy and had therefore reached a degree of consolidated efficiency: a large spanker with a gaff that was far more sophisticated than the original Dutch version, two foresails, one attached to the tip of the foredeck, the other to the head of the long bowsprit, and a square sail on the topmast, a relic of traditional large ship rigs used in following winds.

36-37 The British coasts offer little by way of shelter and the ports are frequently situated on river estuaries. Ships thus had to wait at sea for the pilot before venturing into waters that were frequently unknown to the commanders of foreign vessels. For this reason the pilot cutters that sailed in British waters needed to be exceptionally seaworthy as well as fast and easy to handle. The hull shapes and rigs of this type of boat were to provide an unmistakable model for many yachts from the second half of the eighteenth through to the twentieth century.

37 top A vertical bow, a very narrow hull, a running bowsprit, low over the water, black-painted sides: that's the English cutter. These characteristics were to evolve, being taken to extremes rather than actually changed, throughout the nineteenth century to the point where they came to symbolize the concept of the yacht itself, shared this position with the American sloop or schooner and gave rise to a school of thought that still has its supporters today. Without doubt, this philosophy, technical considerations aside, produced the world's most beautiful boats.

37 bottom When plying the cutter would strike the square sail, replacing it with a gaff topsail should the strength of the wind so require. The spankers used on cutters had a free base, that is to say they were not reeved to the boom: it was thought that a sail tending towards a spherical form was more efficient than a flat sail. Aerodynamic studies were to demonstrate the contrary but were far in the future and it was only America's success against the British cutters that sowed the seed of this idea in the mid-nineteenth century.

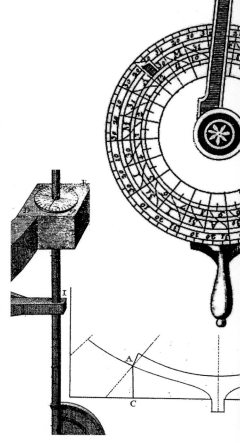

THE AMERICAN SLOOP

Another dramatic incident curtailed the rapid development of yachts in a different direction on the other side of the Atlantic. In 1876, the *Mohawk*, a gigantic centerboard yacht (121 feet at the waterline against a beam of 30 feet 4 inches, representing a ratio of 4, much lower than the ratios of the English cutters, but more importantly she had a draught of just under 10 feet against an overall length of 131 feet!) suddenly capsized when struck by a gust of wind as, with the sails already set, she was raising her anchor and thus had no headway. The owner and his wife, together with three guests, all members of New York's highest society, all perished in the accident.

From that moment the Americans began to revise their "broad and shallow" model that for almost a century they had put forward as a local alternative to the "deep and narrow" English yachts.

Between the late eighteenth and the early nineteenth centuries, a type of yacht had been developed in America that was derived from the fishing sloops as typical of many Caribbean islands (they can still be seen today in those waters, raced in local regattas as picturesque as

they are highly competitive) as the bays of the Atlantic coast and the estuaries such as that of the Hudson in New York.

The terms "sloop" and "cutter" have similarly ambiguous etymologies: both were used to describe a boat carried by larger ships and both were probably of Dutch origin (in Holland there were small boats with a single mast known as *kotter* and others called *sloep*). At the same time, "sloop" is phonetically comparable to the Italian word *scialuppa* and the French *challop* both used to describe ship's boats. Sloop eventually came to be used to describe a type recreational boat that enjoyed great popularity in the Atlantic waters of the United States.

The principal characteristics of the type were a very broad hull with a very shallow draught (in comparison with the seas around Britain, the local waters are not deep; the continental shelf extends for 125 miles whereas there is no such feature off the English coasts), centerboards ensuring an ability to beat against the wind and a large sail area very simply distributed on a single mast in the form of a large spanker with no gaff topsail and a boomed jib. The heeling effect due to the sails was stabilized more by the breadth of

38 bottom *The sheltered, windy waters of the Atlantic coast of the USA favored the spread of racing amongst the various types of boat that had been developed for commercial activities, above all fishing. Feverish gambling accompanied these events; but then even in the more aristocratic world of British regattas, cash prizes had been offered to the victorious owners as early as the eighteenth century. The two boats in the foreground plying at close quarters, represent the prototype of the American sloop: broad, shallow hulls, stability entrusted to mobile ballast, the crew in particular, a large sail area with a simple plan featuring a large spanker (reeved to the boom) and a large boomed foresail.*

38-39 *The American yacht was born free of debts to predecessors or the experience of third parties. The American designer was thus able to experiment with new forms and while his British cousins were stubbornly perfecting a single type he, for example, might accept a clipper bow as seen on the second sloop, or a straight, rather English bow like the one on the boat in the foreground. Between the two yachts is a catamaran which if it does owe a debt it is to its exotic Polynesian forebears rather than William Petty.*

39 bottom *The Mohawk incident was in reality down to the imprudence or lack of expertise of her commander who was caught out by a gust of wind with his gaff topsail aloft (the illustration does not show it but all the reports confirm its presence) when the yacht was still riding at anchor. This was of greater significance than the fact that the stability of the yacht was entrusted to form rather than ballast, but the episode was nonetheless a violent blow to the supporters of the broad-and-shallow approach to yacht design and dramatically slowed the development of the philosophy.*

the hull than by the ballast at the keel (stability of form rather than stability of weight due to a heavily ballasted keel) and by the weight of the crew and the mobile ballast, which on some vessels, the famous "sand baggers" took the form of sandbags that had to be shifted from one side to the other with every change of direction.

As the American sloops increased in size, the pinnacle of development perhaps being the *Maria*, while the hull retained the "broad and shallow" format, the rig evolved in the direction of a two-masted system that in the second half of the nineteenth century was to become the American yachting rig par excellence, the schooner.

THE FIRST RACE

The term "regatta" derives from the Venetian *rigada*, meaning the alignment of the boast prior to the start of a race (specifically the rowing events that were the earliest form of nautical competition). The competitive spirit is so deeply rooted in man that not even boats such as the British prototypes of the modern yacht, those vessels such as the *Mary* deriving from Dutch models and apparently designed for ostentation rather than sailing prowess, were immune to the challenge of racing. The modest stretch of water represented by the River Thames was no obstacle and in fact in October, 1661, just a year after the

belonged to the king's brother, James, Duke of York, was slightly longer at 52 feet, 6 tons heavier and was designed by Peter Pett.

The two yachts were rigged according to the customs of the day, that is to say, along the lines of the Dutch model with a single mast carrying a fore-and-aft spanker, foresails (with only the jib differing from the shorter sail typical of Dutch yachts) and square sails for sailing before the wind.

The first part of the course ran downstream (we are not actually told anything about the state of the tide, but we may presume that it was not

40 left The birth of yacht clubs was a social phenomenon rather than consecration of a sporting activity associated with the practice of sailing. Originally the club was an institution that guaranteed one's position within a certain privileged class and hence paid great attention to ceremonial matters and exclusivity. It is, however, beyond doubt that the yacht clubs contributed to the spread of recreational sailing. While England was the home of the first yacht, one of the Crown territories, Ireland, had the honor of hosting the first sailing club, founded at Cork, in 1720.

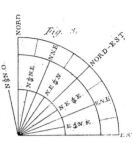

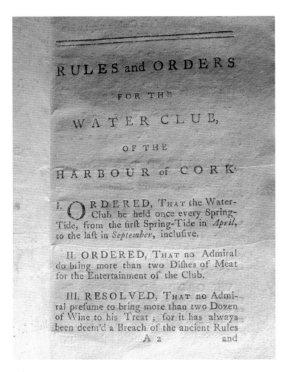

arrival of the *Mary*, the people of London were able to watch the first recorded sailing race from Greenwich, then a suburb of the capital, to Gravesend, downstream towards the Thames estuary and back. This course provided a total length of 40 miles on a river no wider than a mile.

There had undoubtedly been earlier races between the yachts of rich Dutch merchants, just as the earlier vessels owned by the British sovereigns had been raced against each other, but the event held on the 1st of October, 1661, was without doubt the first race held on a well-established course and the earliest of which we have reliable reports that also mention the prize at stake: £100 sterling (at a time when a yacht such as that of Charles II cost around £3,000).

The race was disputed by two very similar boats, both in fact derived from the *Mary* but with a fundamental modification: the designers replaced the laborious and rather inefficient leeboards used in shallow Dutch waters with the deeper central keel of traditional British vessels. The first was the Charles II's *Catherine* built that year by Christopher Pett with a length of 49 feet, a beam of 19 feet, a draught of 7 feet and a weight of 94 tons. The second boat, the *Anne*,

flowing against the boats as they would have had difficulty overcoming it given the direction of the wind) with a strong head wind. The first leg must have involved much laborious tacking given that at some points the river was no more than half a mile wide and that at that time no vessel was truly comfortable sailing close to the wind.

The *Anne* had established a narrow lead over the king's boat at the Gravesend mark. The return leg was completed with a following wind and the two yachts sped towards Greenwich with all sails set, the spanker and foresails goosewinging. It was Charles II's *Catherine* that crossed the finishing line at Greenwich first, with the king in person at the

helm.

From that moment on sailing began its irresistible rise. Other races were held in England, above all as we shall see following the foundation of the first yacht clubs. Throughout the eighteenth century, however, these regattas were closer to exhibition events than true competition, with much demonstration of military-style maneuveres.

One English chronicler has left us with this description of one the events staged in 1784 by the Water Club of the Harbour of Cork:

"I am going to describe a ceremony that they hold at Cork. It resembles the Venetian Doge's

40-41 and 41 bottom The first yacht clubs' sea-going activities were restricted, although this is perhaps not the most appropriate term given the difficulty of handling the boats of that era, to formation reviews and exercises similar to codified naval maneuveres. The yachts were always led by the commodore, the "admiral" of the fleet, a term of clearly military derivation. The yachts sailing out of Cork at that time were identical to their English counterparts with very full bows (it was thought that a large bow wave was indicative of a fast boat) and a sail plan that revealed its Dutch origins.

seaborne wedding. A group of worthy gentlemen who have assembled as "The Water Club" sail out to sea a few miles in a great number of small boats that, with regards decoration and gilding, exceed the king's yachts at Greenwich.

Their admiral, elected each year, raises the colours on his small vessel, leads the avant-guard and receives the salute; the others install themselves in their position and remain in line in the same manner as the king's ships.

The fleet is accompanied by a great number of boats, their colours flying in the wins, drums beating and trumpets playing..."

The challenges accepted and won in 1662 and again the following year by the catamarans of Sir William Petty against launches (probably a sloop) and ships of the king cannot really be described as races either, but historical records do exist of true competitive sailing races. In 1749, for example; the first race was held between yachts owned by *commoners*, that is to say

gentlemen not belonging to the royal family. Won by the Princess Augusta owned by a certain George Bellas, the race was held between Greenwich and Nore, a sandbank about 40 miles from the mouth of the Thames, and back. This was perhaps the first race to leave the sheltered waters of the river and can certainly be described as an early deep-sea race, lasting almost two days.

The Cumberland Fleet, later to be renamed as the Royal Thames Yacht Club, organized various regattas from the 1780s onwards, still on the Thames and reserved for yachts of between 2 and 5 tons. These were no longer "royal" yachts along Dutch lines, laden with decoration and gilding, but were rather single-masted boats of between 20 and 23 feet in length with narrow or deep keels. They were derived from the cutters used to chase smugglers and designed for maximum speed.

True racing yachts had at last seen the light of day.

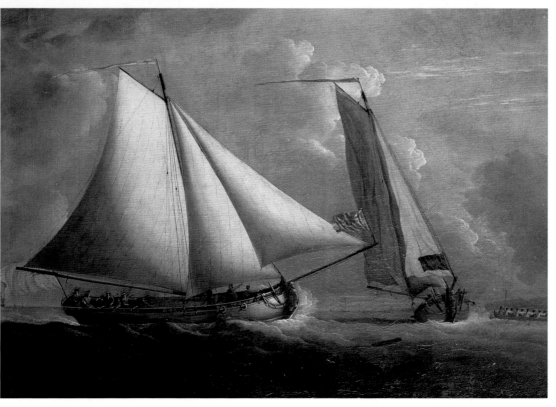

41 top In England, the tradition established with the duel between the Catherine and the Anne was to develop through a club founded in 1770 on the waters of the Thames. The sporting activities of the Cumberland Fleet were distinguished by the fact that they were the prerogative of members of the aristocracy with no direct ties to the royal family, in contrast with the first race in history. In that period, when it was free of the intense commercial traffic of later years, the Thames was the setting for frequent races, while the royal yachts transferred to the more exclusive waters of the Solent.

Racing in america

While Europe, or rather Britain, began sailing for pleasure, albeit with rather baroque yachts of Dutch origins, throughout the eighteenth century the future United States of America was embroiled in rather different affairs and had little time to devote to nautical recreation.

All we generally hear about that period concerns pioneering expeditions in search of fertile new land to colonize and cultivate, skirmishes with Indians that according to one's point of view were more or less ferocious, and most importantly, the War of Independence. Sailing had to wait for the century that followed.

Having achieved nation status, the United States rapidly reached a position of economic strength that permitted yachting to flourish.

As was usually the case, the first to race amongst themselves were the professional seamen. The schooners first to ask for a pilot earned the right to unload first, a significant economic advantage, of course, while the first pilot to reach the incoming ship earned the right to guide it into port. This situation encouraged designers and shipbuilders to create ever faster hulls and ever more efficient rigs, with none of the restrictions imposed by the traditionalist attitudes to yachting of aristocrats and royalty

who left progress to the American up-starts.

The search for improved performance had its most significant results in small fishing boats, the New York Bay sloops, the sand-baggers, the oyster and crab boats of Chesapeake Bay. Yacht builders, designers and owners soon recognized the technical qualities of boats deriving from similar experience and the Atlantic waters saw a constant increase in the numbers of recreational sailors and races for those types of vessels. Classes were created (at New York, for example, 20- and 28-foot sloops were raced), and rules and regulations were defined (the size of the crew of a sand-bagger was restricted to 17 seamen who,

the fastest afloat, not only at work but also in races organized at Boston and New York, as ever attracting cash prizes and enthusiastic gambling. *Mary Taylor*, named after a dancer famous for performances decidedly risqué for the day, was one of Steers' most famous pilot boats. Until the appearance of *America*, naturally.

In the meantime, the first race for yachts, that is to say, boats purpose-built for the sport, had been held at New York, along with another for small recreational boats and fishing sloops in Boston. This city was also, as mentioned earlier, the home of a small club, initially an association of friends devoted to competitive sailing. The club's two boats, the *Dream* and the *Breeze*, raced each other repeatedly for the sole pleasure of the club members.

John Cox Stevens, the son of the genial designer of the *Onkaye* and the *Maria*, Robert Livingston Stevens, also built a yacht, the *Wave*, a 60-foot sloop, successfully challenging and defeating all the New York boats before moving on to Boston in search of worthy adversaries. Stevens was to be a dominant figure in American yachting and even further afield and we shall encounter him in connection with the N.Y.Y.C. and the schooner *America*, but that is another story.

42-43 The waters of the United States were to have to wait until the nineteenth century to witness racing between yachts. Social conditions in a country which had after all only come into being in the second half of the previous century were not yet ripe for the development of the sport. When that time came, however, development was rapid and racing spread along the Atlantic seaboard in the bays of Boston, New York and Baltimore. The lightships anchored to signal the dangerous sandbanks characteristic of those shore, represented ideal route markers and are still often used today.

having no duties other than to rapidly shift the sand-bag ballast each time the boat came about and acting as ballast themselves, were actually recruited from among the stevedores at the port.) The regattas always had cash prizes and attracted feverish betting.

One of the best known designers was George Steers, who was to go on to pen the lines of America. In the 1830's, however, he was involved in the creation of small sloops with overall lengths of around 16 feet 6 inches. He won every races in which he personally participated at the helm these boats and subsequently concentrated on pilot boats, which also proved to be among

RATINGS

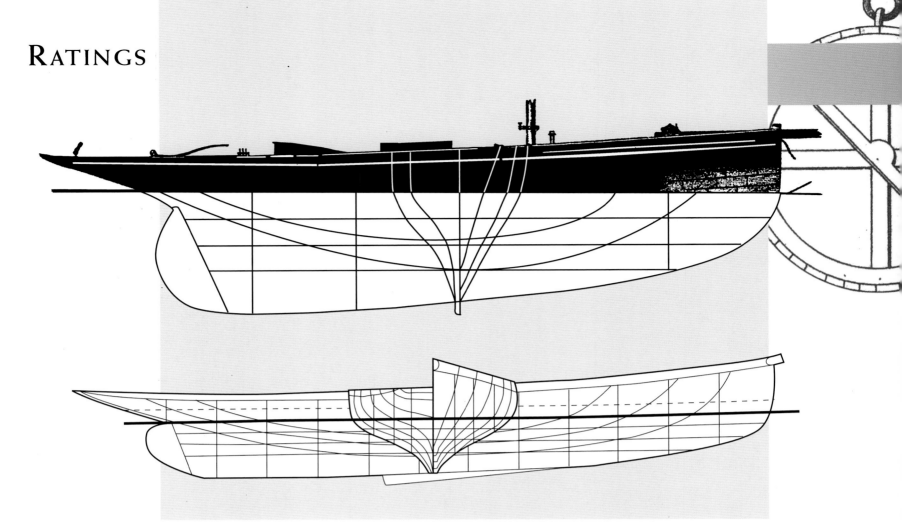

Anyone who has observed ships in a port, as I suspect we have all done at one time or another, will have noted that, like yachts, ships come in a host of different shapes and, above all, sizes. A 130-foot cargo vessel for coastal work is a ship, as is a 950-foot supertanker. Similarly, a 23-foot day cruiser is as much a yacht as a 165-foot floating gin palace.

Ever since the eighteenth century, this diversity of size has encouraged a search for a classification that allows us to picture a ship in relation to its size without actually seeing it. As at that time, and even more so today, such a classification was particularly important for cargo ships, a system was introduced that measured loading capacity. The original ratings were, in fact, a unit of measurement expressed in "tuns" which, roughly speaking, were the eighteenth century equivalents of modern-day containers. Thus "tunnage" actually had nothing to do with weight.

When man began to sail for pleasure and to build yachts of all kinds and sizes to this end, racing was an inevitable consequence (as we have seen the *Mary* was launched in 1660, and the first race between the *Catherine* and the *Anne* was staged in 1661). With it came the need to classify yachts in order to avoid unfortunate mismatches as the larger yacht almost always won.

The first ratings, adopted in order to classify and thus annul the dimensional differences between yachts, were based on existing marine classifications, the system of measurement employed for ships, to which was added a handicap attributed to the smaller yacht. The

44 top and bottom The first rating systems date from the early nineteenth century: the British formula penalized beam that was used as a multiplying factor of length. The outcome was increasingly narrow hulls. The drawing reproduces the master section and profiles of the Madge a typical "plank-on-edge" cutter, as was the Galatea seen in the photo.

44 center and 45 In a modified form of the Thames rating adopted by the British, the American reduced the significance in the formula of beam, B, and introduced displacement, that is to say the weight of the yacht, in place of the 1/2B. As a result the American designers tended to reduce ballast, in practice the only element of weight on which they could work in an era in which materials and constructional techniques were still primitive, and maintained stability by increasing the beam. The photo shows the Puritan, a late-nineteenth-century American yacht.

larger, more powerful boat may have been first over the line, but its time was then "corrected" on the basis of this handicap. The resulting finishing order could easily see a smaller yacht in first place, honors going not necessarily to the dimensionally larger but to the fastest or the better sailed boat.

Throughout almost the whole of the nineteenth century, yacht ratings were based, albeit with substantial differences, on tonnage. As we have already mentioned, in Britain the formulas for the definition of tonnage and therefore the rating took into consideration length and beam, ignoring draught. For this reason, very narrow hulls with a deep draught were developed. The formula for the Thames rating was a typical example: $(L-3/5B \times B \times 1/22B)/94$, where L = length and B = beam.

In America much importance was given to displacement: $(L-3/5B \times B \times D)/95$ where D = displacement, that is to say the effective weight of the boat. In order to reduce weight, the Americans favored stability of form, to the detriment of draught with the famous American "broad-and-shallow" hulls being created as a consequence.

Following the disasters of the broad-and-shallow *Mohawk* in America and the narrow-and-deep *Oona* in Britain, both countries adopted the formula that Dixon Kemp, a British architect, had developed in 1880: $(L \times SA)/6000$, where SA was the sail area. The Americans, reluctant to concede too much to their British rivals, modified the denominator, 4,000 instead of 6,000, not that this had any significance, as it had only been introduced to render the result of LxSA a reasonable number.

The diatribe between the two countries continues to the present day.

Early in the twentieth century, the British developed the first linear rating, thus eliminating the term tonnage from the yachting vocabulary. The result of the formula was a linear measurement and defined the class to which a yacht belonged. This formula was given international status, or more correctly European status given that no other country outside the Old Continent supported the British initiative, by the 1907 Paris conference and was defined as the "International Rule."

The formula is apparently complex: $R = (L+B+1/2G+3D+1/3VSA-F)/2$, but its validity is borne out by the fact that, albeit with certain substantial modifications, it still remains in force, has determined the form of America's Cup boats for forty years and is still the basis for extraordinary yachts being built today.

Out of the International Rule have come the meter classes: 23, 19, 15, 12 (the famous America's Cup 12-meter rating), 10, 8, 7, 6 and 5. 12-meter races are still staged today and 8- and 6-meter boats are still being built. The origins of the formula can be found in the late-

nineteenth century studies of the British mathematician William Froude whose "Froude number" was to have enormous influence on naval architecture, and in the efforts of Brooke Hackstall-Smith, father of all the English ratings between the end of the nineteenth and the start of the twentieth century. Hackstall-Smith was an extremely influential member of the Yacht Racing Association and later the International Yacht Racing Union, the body that still governs world-wide yachting. In the meantime, in 1883, the Seawanaka Yacht Club had abandoned tonnage in favor of a linear rating and had come up with the theoretical length for a yacht: Racing Length = $(L+VSA)/2$. The derivation from Dixon Kemp's formula is evident, but the root for the sail area renders the result a linear measurement.

Out of this formula came in turn one developed in 1903 by the great genius of American yachting, Nat Herreshoff, who was actually responsible for the introduction of the term "rating."

For Herreshoff the rating of a boat was a linear measurement deriving from: Rating = $(L \times VSA)/(5VD)$. He introduced the

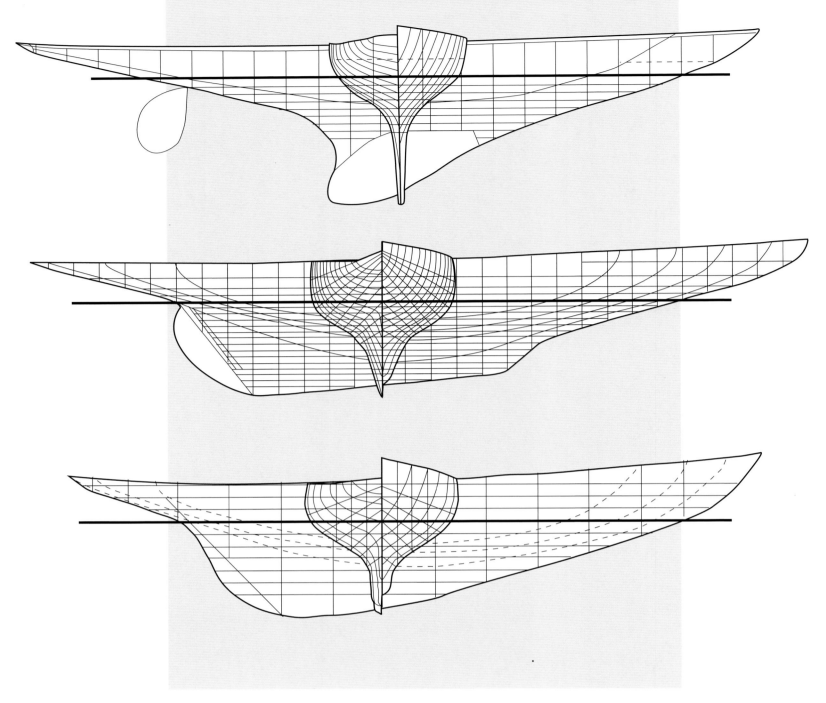

46 top and bottom In the late nineteenth century, Dixon Kemp developed a very simple formula that avoided the extremes of the British plank-on-edge designs and, when it was adopted with a minor modification to a coefficient by the Americans, of the New World's broad-and-shallow yachts. Sail area gained in importance and to reduce this much work was done on the wetted area and the weight of the boats as well as their length measured more or less at the waterline. Extremely attractive boats were designed with long overhangs and short keels that were similar on both sides of the Atlantic. The drawing depicts Dacia, designed by Charles Nicholson, while the photo portrays the great Reliance by the American Herreshoff.

factor dear to the Americans of displacement, no longer weighed but calculated, and correctly used as a denominator. Thus the higher the displacement, the lower the rating of the yacht and the greater the handicap.

With respects to handicaps, for many years, up until the end of the nineteenth century, the Americans and British yachting fraternities were actually in agreement for once: irrespective of the different rating formulas, they both used a handicap of 45 seconds per rating ton, a system developed in 1843 by a member of the Royal Thames Yacht Club, G. M. Ackers.

Subsequently, handicaps were, and still are, attributed on the basis of the various rating formulas adopted and, moreover, on times and/or the length of the course.

In agreement on the question of handicaps, the Americans and the British were continually divided by the ratings formula.

For the first half of the twentieth century Herreshoff's alternative, defined as the Universal Rule, stood in opposition to the International Rule. Thus boats were constructed to different standards according to the rating formula under which they were due to compete. It was not until 1970 that the two formulas were finally unified with the birth of the International Offshore Rule (I.O.R.) that replaced the R.O.R.C. and C.C.A. ratings.

Recreational sailing was at last a global phenomenon.

46, drawings center and bottom, and 47 The two formulas adopted in the early twentieth century were, despite formal differences, conceptually similar: they both tended to relate the volume of the hull, and thus its weight, to the sail area. Yachts built to the two ratings were in fact very similar and the British meter-class boats could easily be rated according to the Universal Rule. This was the case with the 23-and 24-meter boats which, without requiring any substantial modification, became J Class yachts. Both formulas are still valid today, but only the British International Rule is still applied. The two drawings compare the profiles and master sections of a J Class (bottom) and an International Rule 8-meter yacht (center). The photographs portray the 12-meter Tomahawk (bottom) and the J Class Ranger (top).

48-49 In the United States the most famous and most prestigious sailing association was undoubtedly the New York Yacht Club. Its intensive programs had a significant social impact and the prestige deriving from being a member led to veritable battles, complete with alliances and betrayals amongst the industrial and financial magnates of the nascent American nation. There is no doubt, however, that it was the club's sporting activities that determined its success. From the outset the annual regatta, originally conceived as a social occasion, was transformed into a highly competitive sporting event. A healthy crowd of distinguished gentlemen would watch the starting line maneuveres (required by the procedure of the day) of a number of classic American schooners.

48 top Like their counterparts in other countries, each American yacht club has its own pennant, an identifying symbol for yachts whose paths cross around the world. In this reproduction of a print from American Yachts by J. D. J. Kelley of 1884 can be seen at least fifty pennants, testimony to the spread of yachting in North America just forty years after the birth of the New York Yacht Club.

THE FIRST YACHT CLUBS

The term club apparently derives from the ancient Germanic word *Klumpe*, meaning a mass of metal, that in the 13th century became the English word club applied to the stick with a lump of metal at the end used to strike a sphere in what may considered to be the forerunner of golf. Over the centuries, it also came to be used for other sports and to indicate the place in which the players gathered. Naturally, Britain was the home of the first sailing clubs, even though it was not the birthplace of recreational sailing (we should not forget the fundamental role played by Holland).

The very first yacht club was, however, founded at the Irish port of Cork, far from the sport's spiritual home on the River Thames, and was known as the Water Club of Cork Harbour. This was in 1720, and sailing was by no means the principal activity of the members who met every fifteen days for the club dinner at which

be an association of true sailing enthusiasts, the great yachts of the British aristocracy and the royal family moved to the more distinguished port of Cowes on the Isle of Wight—the Thames was, after all, only a river—where the Yacht Club of Cowes was founded in 1815. In 1833, the club became the Royal Yacht Squadron, perhaps the world's most exclusive yacht club, then as now. The members were such snobs that the founders of the club felt obliged to amend its statute with a motion that permitted member to abandon etiquette in the case of real danger at sea: "although many members of this club do not know one another personally, it is to be hoped that in case of necessity they will offer mutual aid, even without having been introduced."

Yachting was slow to develop in other European countries, although the first yacht clubs were beginning to appear. The Royal Swedish Yacht Club was founded in 1830 and the first

the admiral, the present-day commodore, was responsible for the wine of each of the twenty-five members. Single-boat cruising was discouraged, whilst participation in the club's collective parades and displays mentioned in a previous chapter was obligatory.

It was a further fifty years before a British club was founded, at Starcross on Devon in 1770, while Thames sailing enthusiasts had their own five years later with the foundation of the famous Cumberland Fleet, subsequently to become one of the yachting world's most famous institutions, the Royal Thames Yacht Club.

While the Cumberland Fleet could be said to

French club, the *Société des Régates du Havre*, appeared in 1840, followed by the *Koninklijke Nederlandsche Jacht Club* of Rotterdam in Holland in 1846, the first imperial yacht club in Russia in the same year and the Konigsberg club in Germany in 1855.

Interest was also stirring in the British overseas territories with the Royal Hobart Regatta Association being founded in Tasmania in 1838 and the Royal Bermuda Yacht Club coming into being in 1844.

The other great event in the context of world-wide yachting was the foundation in 1844 of the first American sailing club, the New York Yacht Club.

49 *Sails loosened while awaiting the start of a race off Cowes, the Isle of Wight headquarters of the Royal Yacht Club on the South coast of England. The royal fleet soon moved from the crowded waters of the Thames to those of the Solent, with the castle at Cowes being adopted as the home of the most prestigious of yacht clubs. For centuries it has witnessed intensive racing programs and still today a shining battery of small cannons lined up on the grassy foreshore are fired to signal the start of the most important international sailing events, the Admiral's Cup above all.*

JOHN COX STEVENS

There are individuals and even whole families and dynasties with fundamental roles in the history of yachting, a history that in reality is based, something that is all too frequently forgotten, of the talent and labor of generations of craftsmen and boatbuilders who actually created the yachts.

One of the great figures was John Cox Stevens, a typical representative of the way of life deriving from the economic and social conditions of America. The Stevens family landed in the States, then a modest conglomeration of colonies, in 1669 and immediately amassed a small commercial fortune. By the middle of the following century the descendants of the original colonists were well established pillars of American society: another John (the father of the John in question), a colonel in the army of the new-born United States of America, became the treasurer of the State of New Jersey and plunged into the railroad business in which he was one of the pioneers. Among his six children, Edwin founded the Stevens Institute of Technology where the defenders of the America's Cup were all tank tested, while Robert, an engineer, followed in his father's footsteps by becoming one of the founders of the American railway system. Above all, however, he designed the *Onkaye* and the *Maria* which, as mentioned earlier, represented the points of departure for yachting in America. The third son, the dandy of the family, was John Cox Stevens. Initially, his consuming passion was the traditional English sport of cricket, which he introduced to America, and he was involved in a number of other sports, including what was to become the American national pastime, baseball. He then devoted himself to yachting. He was twenty-four years of age—careers were precocious in those years—when he commissioned his first boat, the 20-foot *Diver*. This was followed by the 52-foot 6-inch *Trouble*, another experimental yacht, a family vice, with the hull shape based on the canoes of the Caribbean island Indians. Then came *Double Trouble*, a catamaran of course, and lastly the extremely fast *Wave*, of which I have already made mention and with which Stevens raced along all the Atlantic coasts.

John Cox Stevens is, however, a major figure in the history of yachting for three particular episodes in which he was involved. On the 30th of July, 1844 he was aboard his latest yacht, the *Gimcrack*, anchored in New York Bay, together with 8 friends, all yacht owners. On that day the New York Yacht Club was founded, a milestone in the history of yachting. As the holder of the America's Cup the New York club was later to represent the hare everybody else was obliged to chase for over a hundred years.

The *Gimcrack* had been designed by George Steers, a specialist in the design of some of the fastest pilot boats on that coast. John Cox Stevens became the young designer's patron and when the question of a yacht with which to challenge the British, then considered to be the yachting elite, Steers was entrusted with designing its lines.

This resulting boat was none other than the schooner *America*, responsible for a true revolution in the field.

John Cox Stevens travelled to Cowes in England, fiefdom of the Royal Yacht Squadron and its aristocratic members, and won the Hundred Guinea Cup. This was the very trophy that eventually became known as the America's Cup and was put on display in the New York Yacht Club where it was to remain for almost fifty years.

51 top Sumptuous decor, representative of the economic and social success of the United States, sets off relics of the history of recreational sailing in the country. The club's great halls are adorned with majestic fireplaces that, now having lost their original function, remain as monuments to the sporting exploits of the members. In this image a large painting recalls the first transatlantic race disputed by Vesta, Henrietta and Fleetwing, three yachts belonging to members of the club, Mr. Pierre Lorillard, the Osgood brothers George and Franklin and Mr. Gordon Bennet Jr, who put up the vast sum of £90,000 for the winner. The New York Yacht Club is still today considered to be the most emblematic in the yachting world, despite not having the charisma and exclusiveness of the British clubs with royal connections.

51 bottom The building housing the New York Yacht Club is located on Manhattan's Fifth Avenue. It dates back to 1901 and was designed specifically for the club and built on a plot donated by the financier and then commodore of the club, J. P. Morgan. The style reflects the eclecticism of the time: the rich decoration features waves and marine animals while the windows of the first floor, those of the great halls, replicate the design of the transom stern of the eighteenth-century Dutch yachts that, not surprisingly, were the pride and joy of the wealthy commercial classes of that country. Certainly, there is one element missing from this headquarters, the sea. This "urban" clubhouse is, in fact, located at the center of the island with the greatest concentration of capital in the world. This fact takes nothing away, however, from the club's prestige. Today the chaotic traffic of the metropolis suffocates the façade and the galleon windows appear to be somewhat out of place but, beyond the threshold, a whole different world awaits.

yacht

In the nineteenth century, British yachting began to expand beyond the restricted confines of the royal court, and while with rare exceptions it remained an aristocratic sport, it did begin to assume a certain numerical significance. While early in the century there were around fifty yachts in the British Isles, by mid-century at least five hundred were sailing in British waters, and at the threshold of the twentieth century, yachts with a combined weight of 100,000 tons had been built in Britain accounting for a turnover of £5,000,000 that in present day terms would be something in the order of a billion pounds. In the second half of the century, Benjamin Nicholson, father of the founder of the famous Gosport boatyard Camper & Nicholson, was alone responsible for the design and construction large schooners with a combined weight of 2,500 tons as well as other kinds of yachts.

Racing had by then expanded with the establishment of clubs in many of the British coastal towns (there are now over seven hundred

and only finished when the boats got themselves untangled and the *Arrow* was able to continue and go on to win the race.

The two boats involved in this incident were no common-or-garden yachts; the *Arrow* being considered the fastest cutter on the coast. She was built in 1821 and raced successfully until 1844, when she was abandoned high and dry at Itcher. She was salvaged two years later and rebuilt, albeit with slightly modified lines, and continued to race against cutters that had in the meantime evolved towards ever more extreme examples of the "plank-on-edge" design philosophy, *Mosquito, Kriemhilda, Genesta* and *Spankadillo.*

As time passed the spirit of competition prevailed over the susceptibility of those gentlemen who in the eighteenth century let their swords do the talking, and a more scientific approach was taken towards yacht racing. It is interesting apropos of this development to read an 1872 report regarding the *Mosquito* (probably

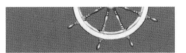

52 bottom The cutter sailing to windward in this painting is the Arrow, one of the most typical representatives of the British tradition and owned by Mr. Joseph Weld. Straight prow, long bowsprit, rounded lines to the bow and slimmer at the stern, for a two-decade period she was unbeatable. After being salvaged from the mud at Itchen and rebuilt with the same lines she remained competitive even when sailing against yachts such as the Mosquito representing the evolution towards more modern hull shapes. In 1851 she was at Cowes to compete against America and only an improvident shoal put an end to her race when she was in the lead.

53 top Together with the south coast of England, the Isle of Wight delimits the Solent, a stretch of water sheltered from the open sea but windswept and insidious due to the strong tidal currents. Since the end of the eighteenth century, Cowes has been the capital of European yachting as well as the island's major town. For centuries its seafront has been crowded with the sailing enthusiasts and nobility taking advantage of a unique setting from which to observe the regattas organized by the Royal Yacht Squadron.

THE FIRST GOLDEN AGE OF YACHTING

yacht clubs recognized by the Royal Yachting Association in the British Isles and the dominions, many of which were founded in the nineteenth century), even though the sport still reflected the eighteenth-century spirit when yachts were still armed with cannons. As late as the 1820s, if contemporary reports are to be believed, encounters at sea were still occasionally settled by physical conflict: during the Town Cup held off Cowes in 1826, the crew of the *Arrow,* owned by Joseph Weld, a great yachtsman (as was his father and as his son was to become), and that of the *Miranda,* came to blows when the former crossed in front of the latter and tangled her shrouds on the *Miranda's* bowsprit. A violent brawl broke out that even involved the *Miranda's* owner Sir James Jordan,

52-53 *The schooner rig was by no means unknown or even rare in Great Britain. The corresponding American craft would have had masts sloping much more steeply towards the stern, at most two foresails and, above all, the bases of the spankers reeved to the boom.*

The hull with its straight prow resembles those of the French lougres, eighteenth-century boats designed for chasing smugglers which already had well tapered lines at the prow deriving from Mediterranean models.

one of the most innovative cutters, being the first yacht to sport a steel hull and featuring lines that were no longer swollen like those of the 1830 *Alarm* that had in effect been the prototype of the cutter-yachts, marking the transition from the traditional pilot cutter to the true yacht). In preparation for a race "...the doors were at times disembarked; the drawers of the divans were taken out and placed on the floor; the equipment from the fore-cabin and the sail locker was taken to the centre cabin and the winch, the anchors and every heavy part of the equipment was placed below the cabin planking." These were of course all measures that would be taken by a modern crew.

In this climate, equipment was developed that was adopted by successive generations of yachts. The first galvanized cable shrouds were introduced in 1852 on the Fife-built *Cymba*, while in 1865 *Niobe* replaced the square-rigged sail used in following winds with a large,

almost hemispherical jib that was used successfully the following year on the *Sphinx*, and firstly called the "spin" and then "spinker" before finally becoming known as the "spinnaker."

All this took place in a precise geographical location, the Solent. By the end of the eighteenth century the focus of English yachting had shifted from the tranquil waters of the Thames and its estuary to Cowes, a small town on the Isle of Wight overlooking the Solent on the South coast of England.

It was no coincidence that the Yacht Squadron had chosen to locate its headquarters here, as the area had long been a pleasant vacation resort patronized by the royal family and the aristocracy. In 1540, two forts were built on opposing banks of the River Medina that still today divides the town of Cowes. Only one survives and, formerly the home of the governor of the island, has been restored. Lord Anglesey, the owner of the *Pearl*, a cutter from 1821 cited as one of the prototypes of the typical English cutter-yacht, was appointed as

governor of the island and tenant of the castle. On his death the Yacht Club, as the Royal Yacht Squadron had rather snobbishly become known, took over the lease and the castle became, and remains, its headquarters.

By the early nineteenth century, Cowes had become one of the world capitals of yachting. From 1826, the regular races and social events that were to develop into the Cowes Week were being organized on those waters under the patronage of the Royal Yacht Squadron, or that other mainstay of English nautical nobility, the Royal Thames Yacht Club, which had by then freed itself of its image of a somewhat "plebeian" club long associated with the Cumberland Fleet. Cowes Week is perhaps the most classical of all sailing events. Its appeal remains intact and from the period immediately after the Second World War it has been held in conjunction with the Admiral's Cup, widely regarded as ocean racing's World Championship.

Actually from 1999, the advertising and promotional demands that currently govern sailing (imagine the scandal that would have embroiled members of the R.Y.S. or the N.Y.Y.C. who sailed with commercial advertising on their hulls in the nineteenth century: it would surely have led to their immediate expulsion from their clubs), this joint event has been divided. The Admiral's Cup is still run from Cowes, but in July; while Cowes Week, stripped of its most prestigious race, is held in mid-August.

Nineteenth-century accounts describe a Cowes in which "steam-ships, boats of all kinds and yachts of all sizes lined the course for mile upon mile, a spectacle that not even the Adriatic in the glorious epoch of Venice has ever offered..."

in world yachting have taken place here, beginning with the summer of 1851, when the very formal and somewhat presumptuous members of the Yacht Club witnessed the arrival of the schooner *America*. For the first time in history, and 200 years after the appearance of the *Mary*, the British were forced to recognize that yachting had become an international phenomenon.

From that year onward, British yachts began to cross the Atlantic in order to race in the United States, whilst American boats sailed in the opposite direction. Among the most active of these trans-oceanic yachts was Lord Ashbury's *Cambria*, a 199-ton schooner designed and built at Cowes by Michael Ratsey between 1866 and 1870, that took part

54 left The 1851 race between America *and the British yachts at Cowes shook the world of yachting. Apart from numerous technical factors, for the first time yachts of different nationalities had met and raced, something that from then on was to encourage owners to abandon their home waters with increasing frequency. Lord Ashbury's* Cambria *crossed the Atlantic in 1870 to challenge the Americans and attempt to win back the America's Cup. The large Ratsey-designed schooner was, however, defeated by* Magic.

Nothing has changed since: I was there in 1975 when over 650 yachts took part in the Cowes Week events, crewed by around 4,000 sailors representing no less than nineteen nations, without taking into account the hundreds of English recreational sailors who simply took to sea to line the course and watch the racing close-up.

The social side of Cowes has always been important. For the British aristocracy, mid-August on the Solent crowned a cycle of obligatory society occasions that began with the Derby at Ascot. Contemporary reports perhaps pay more attention to the ladies' fashions than the rigs of the yachts.

Social aspects apart, the waters of Cowes have seen the most important boats from all eras and some of the most important episodes

in the Anglo-American race of 1851. On the same course, a circumnavigation of the Isle of Wight, *Cambria* won comfortably in 6 hours 12 minutes from three other British yachts, *Aline*, a 216-ton schooner, the 165-ton *Oiwara*, and the 135-ton cutter *Condor* which all finished within 12 minutes of each other. The only American entry, the large *Sappho*, a 381-ton schooner 118 feet long at the waterline, came home last as the British yachtsmen extracted revenge for the disgrace inflicted by *America*. The result was an exception, however. *Cambria* crossed the Atlantic in 1870 in order to bring the America's Cup back to Britain, but was sent unceremoniously packing by the American yacht *Magic*. Previously, Lord Ashbury had found the time to take *Cambria* to Egypt in 1869 for the opening of the Suez Canal.

54 right At the end of the nineteenth-century British yachting, to the clear disapproval of the traditional elements, was no longer the prerogative of the royal court and the aristocracy. The wealthy industrial and commercial bourgeoisie not only proved to be attracted by the sport, but were frequently among its leading figures. In the rarefied and conservative yachting club circles, Thomas Lipton was nick-named "the grocer", but five America's Cup challenges earned him the respect and admiration of his adversaries and a knighthood from his king.

55 Sappho was a large American schooner, 118 feet long at the waterline and displacing 380 tons, designed and constructed by the American Stueler. She crossed the Atlantic in 1868 and 1870 to race at Cowes. While not a technologically advanced design like America, her lines were similar to those of Steers' yacht. She was a boat conceived to carry to sea in appropriate luxury and to represent the social status of her owner, Mr. W. P. Douglas. Her great size also helped her to victory in the America's Cup.

Yachting had changed significantly since the era in which Charles II sailed on the Thames. Cowes was also the port of arrival (the finishing line was actually at Lizard Point, the extreme tip of Cornwall) of one of the first Trans-Atlantic races. The three American yachts that had challenged one another tied up in the Solent in 1866 (Henrietta, the winner, Vesta and Fleetwing, three typical American schooners all around 98 feet in length).

From the middle of the nineteenth century up until the outbreak of the First World War, the Solent saw the yachts of the first generation of great British designers.

The Jullanar of 1876, a yawl with a clipper-bow and canoe stern, was the first British yacht to assimilate the lesson taught by America and to abandon the stagnant canons of British yachting. The Jullanar was still fairly narrow, but very sharply tapered at the ends. The designer, a wealthy farmer, agricultural machinery constructor and, above all, dedicated yachtsman, E. H. Bentall, came to fame thanks to this yacht. The Satanita, designed by J. M. Soper, was instead rigged as a cutter, had an overall length of around 131 feet, 67 feet at the waterline, and a boom that was no less than 92 feet long. These remarkable dimensions (remarkable but nonetheless inferior to those of the Maria, the American sloop recognised as the world's largest single-masted yacht) corresponded to an extremely fast and very beautiful yacht. The Thistle, by Watson, one of the great names in British yacht design and responsible for a further two America's Cup challengers (the Thistle challenged, and lost needless to say, in 1887). Then there were the four Shamrocks commissioned by Sir Thomas Lipton from three different designers, G.L. Watson, C. E. Nicholson and William Fife, to whom we shall return shortly.

56 top The waters of the Solent were the setting for the challenges between the "Big Class" boats of the late nineteenth century; the dark blue hull of Britannia, the Prince of Wales' yacht designed by Watson in 1892, is just to leeward of the Valkyrie, another of the Scotsman's designs, this time owned by Lord Dunraven and protagonist of the eighth America's Cup challenge. The two yachts are racing on the Thames, just as in the era of Charles II.

56 bottom The Firth of Clyde is a deep Scottish inlet opening onto the North Channel between Northern Ireland and mainland Britain. These misty waters with strong winds and heavy seas have produced famous designers such as Watson and Fife and generations of excellent sailors. The racing season on the Clyde was as intensive as that of Cowes, but never enjoyed the same international standing. The social side, stimulated by the presence of the royal court and the Royal Yacht Squadron on the Isle of Wight, was missing.

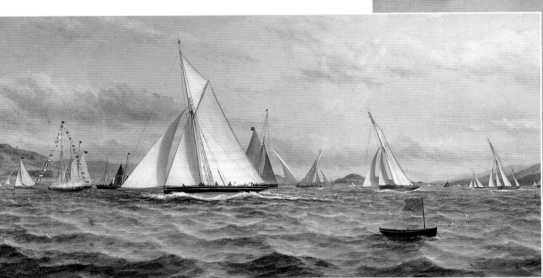

The Solent was, above all, the home of the royal yachts, above all the Britannia. Built in 1892 to the design of Watson for the Prince of Wales, the future King Edward III, she is considered to be one of the most representative British yachts thanks to her racing victories, the fact that she always flew the colors of the Royal Yacht Squadron and that on the request of the royal family she was scuttled off the Isle of Wight on the 10th of July, 1937.

Cowes was without doubt the social capital of European yachting and only there, perhaps, could an event such as Cowes Week have come into being thanks to the patronage of the royal family and the R.Y.S. However, while the Solent, with its sheltered waters and mild climate, was also the area with the greatest concentration of boatyards, and still today boasts an enviable range of boatbuilders, sailmakers, chandlers and marinas, it was not the only center of nineteenth-century British sailing. A second pole of attraction was the long Firth of Clyde in Scotland.

It was said that the best crewmen came from the Clyde, having been traditionally trained in fishing fleets that had to cope with the unpredictable waters of the North Atlantic on a daily basis. The Clyde also saw the rise of a group of talented yacht designers, including G. L. Watson, W. Fife, A. Mylne and McGruer, who were by no means overshadowed by the Solent school.

56-57 The western exit of the Solent is characterized by the white cliffs of the Needles, glimpsed in the background to the right. The racing yachts leave waters that are sheltered but turbulent due to the strong currents and enter the Channel. The Big Class schooners and cutters have today disappeared, but those waters still offer the spectacle of hundreds of racing yachts of all dimensions and classes. Cowes Week, the Admiral's Cup and the Whitbread Race are but a few of the international events still based on the Solent.

57 top The Big Class boats represented the evolution from the Thames rating that had produced the deep-and-narrow cutter to the Dixon Kemp formula. They were huge fin keel yachts with waterlines of around 85 feet and overhangs of at least 32 feet. Over ten thousand square feet of canvas were handled by crews of sixty seamen. Britannia is here seen chasing **White Heather** and **Ailsa**, an unusual situation in an 1893 season which saw her win no less than 11 out of 17 races.

57 center right The dead calm takes nothing away from the elegance and regality of the royal yacht Britannia, which was helmed firstly by Edward III and then by George V. After forty years of racing had taken their toll and undermined her competitiveness she was scuttled off the Isle of Wight.

58-59 With the abandonment of the Thames rating, the British cutter lost one of its most prominent characteristics, that of reduced width with respects to length. It nonetheless lost none of its appeal, and the less extreme forms that resulted were actually more harmonious. The bowsprit was still an important element, but was set axially as it was not generally withdrawn inboard given that the greater volumes and the bow overhang prevented it from dipping under with every wave. The boats were still rigged with three jibs, while the spanker was now reeved to the boom and the topsail was triangular. Petronella was designed and built in 1880 by Charles Nicholson in his yard at Gosport.

58 top It is difficult to imagine what Cowes Week would have been without the presence of crowned royalty and titled nobility, at sea and on the Solent foreshore. Certainly, the sporting aspects of the event would have been unchanged, but without doubt the social side has played a crucial part in its success. Much was made in contemporary reports of the costumes of the ladies and their lap-dogs, of who was in attendance and who was not. The crowds were certainly impressive for the era and unusual still today, except at Cowes.

59 top From the second half of the nineteenth century, Cowes and the Solent were the cradle not only of the sport of yachting itself, but also of designers, boatyards and a host of professional figures who achieved widespread recognition in the yachting world. Cowes, for example, was the home of the sailmakers Ratsey, and three generations of the Bekens family, photographers responsible for this 1895 image showing two of the yachts designed by Watson: the Caress (in the foreground) and the Marion Creole.

58 center The Solent is characterized by tidal currents, shallows and intensive commercial and ferry traffic; moreover, the racing courses are marked by the various beacons, lighthouses and towers punctuating the channel. When hundreds of boats are gathered for a regatta, sailing different courses and starting at intervals accidents are probable rather than possible. This was particularly true in the past when complicated rigs and heavy, unresponsive boats made maneuvering all the more difficult. Here Varuna is obliged to spill her wind to avoid running down the smaller Thalia.

59 bottom The first photographs which replaced the painted or engraved images of earlier times, record a new "intruder" alongside the sailing boats that were the regattas' raison d'être. Ownership of these steam yachts would once have been sufficient grounds for immediate expulsion from the Royal Thames or the Royal Yacht Squadron. Times were changing, however, and at the same time as photography steam power came to be accepted within yachting circles, at least as long as it did not produce smoke according to the R.Y.S.

The first yacht club to be established in the area was the Royal Northern Y.C. in 1824. It was founded by Scottish and Irish gentlemen, true sailing enthusiasts, and for a decade the club had a single headquarters, but two secretaries, one for each region. By the following year, Scottish and Irish boats were already racing on the Clyde. A fine contemporary painting shows the start of one of these races, with the committee boat, a crowded and beflagged cutter still featuring traditional rounded lines, firing the starting signal (the boat was still armed with a cannon, probably being a revenue cutter used to counter smuggling), while around fifteen cutters approach the line, sails to the shore, sailing close to the wind on opposing tacks. In the first half of the century competitive sailing

on the Clyde was probably an occasional activity. It was not until 1856 and the foundation of the Clyde Model Y.C. that regular weekly racing began to be organized. Once the club had earned "Royal" status, and in agreement with two other local clubs, the Royal Northern and the Mudhook Y.C., the annual Clyde Week was established that while never attracting great international attention, was in Britain second only to the similar regatta at Cowes.

Some of the most important British yachts of the turn of the century sailed on those waters reflecting the dark greens of the Scottish coasts, even though some of them were only completing sea trials after launching. The Clyde certainly saw Lord Dunraven's *Valkyries* and Sir Thomas Lipton's *Shamrocks* before they crossed the Atlantic and bravely but vainly challenged the Americans of the New York Yacht Club for the America's Cup. And then there were all the yachts built in a yard that, a family firm for four generations from 1791 to the post Second World War period, was to be a symbol of Clyde and a legend in world yachting, the Fife yard at Fairlie.

At that time, boatyards were little more than a shed on the beach, and the yard founded by William Fife I in the late eighteenth century was no exception. Initially Fife built small sailing yachts, to his own design, for the wealthy middle and upper classes of Glasgow and the surrounding area. These boats became increasingly ambitious, above all with William Fife II and his son William Fife III.

The singular lack of originality in the choice of family first names was compensated by a fertile imagination in the field of yacht design: at the end of the century, William Fife III was designing up to 50 yachts a year, half of which were built in his own yard, the others in Europe, America and Asia. The fame of the Fifes had, in fact, crossed the oceans and after it had appeared on the *Dragon*, the gilded dragon carved on the stringer at the prow was a feature of all their boats from 1889. The symbol distinguished yachts that were to become famous for their beauty if not necessarily their performance.

A NEW FORCE IN YACHTING:

GERMANY

60-61 *It is thought that Kaiser Wilhelm II's attitude to yachting was dictated by a genuine passion for sailing. Certainly we frequently see him portrayed aboard yachts during regattas, free of social connotations. In this he was very similar to his royal British cousins. Equally certain is that he commissioned no less than four very large yachts in a search for increased performance, but his interest was also motivated by a precise political strategy. He was eager to introduce Germany to the sea in order to prepare the nation for the construction and maintainance of a large naval fleet.*

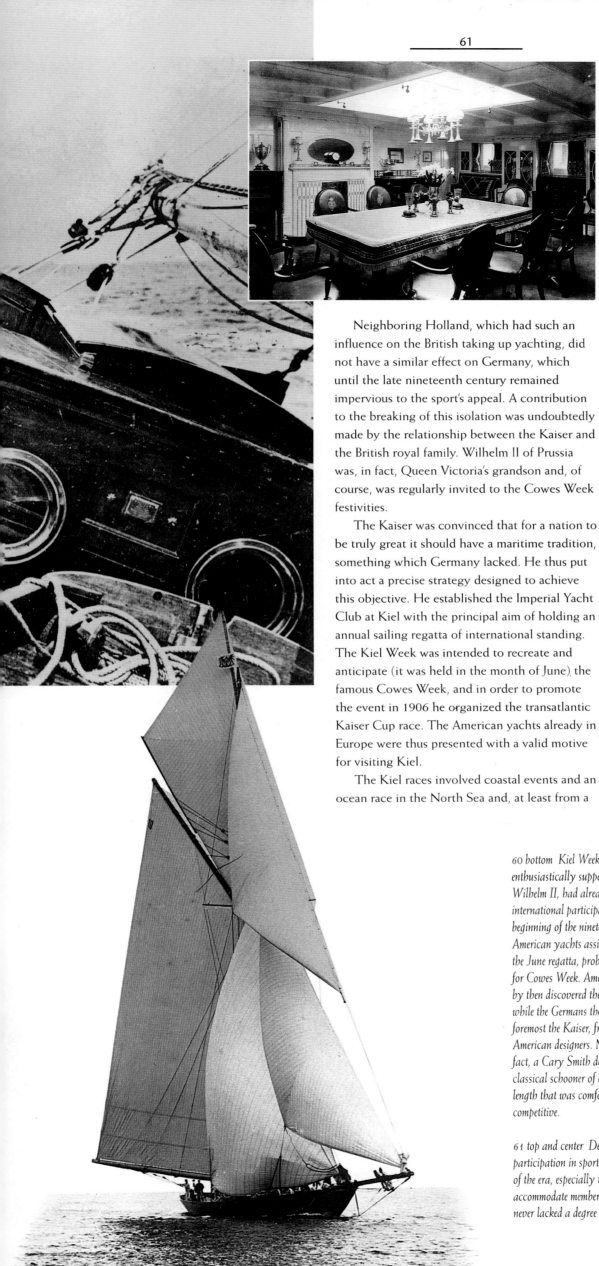

promotional point of view, provided a rich reward for the Kaiser's efforts. The Kiel Week came to be part of international circuit and, along with the Kaiser's large *Meteor IV* and the first schooners raced by a number of German industrialists, British, American, Italian, Norwegian, French and Spanish yachts all took part in the 1912 edition.

The Kaiser's brother, Prince Henry, once explained to his friend Brooke Heckstall-Smith, a reporter and well known yachtsman of the time (whom we have already encountered in connection with ratings), "The Germans are not

Neighboring Holland, which had such an influence on the British taking up yachting, did not have a similar effect on Germany, which until the late nineteenth century remained impervious to the sport's appeal. A contribution to the breaking of this isolation was undoubtedly made by the relationship between the Kaiser and the British royal family. Wilhelm II of Prussia was, in fact, Queen Victoria's grandson and, of course, was regularly invited to the Cowes Week festivities.

The Kaiser was convinced that for a nation to be truly great it should have a maritime tradition, something which Germany lacked. He thus put into act a precise strategy designed to achieve this objective. He established the Imperial Yacht Club at Kiel with the principal aim of holding an annual sailing regatta of international standing. The Kiel Week was intended to recreate and anticipate (it was held in the month of June) the famous Cowes Week, and in order to promote the event in 1906 he organized the transatlantic Kaiser Cup race. The American yachts already in Europe were thus presented with a valid motive for visiting Kiel.

The Kiel races involved coastal events and an ocean race in the North Sea and, at least from a

a population of navigators and many have never even seen the sea. But if they begin to sail on holiday and businessmen make efforts to practice this sport even just to please the Kaiser, then perhaps interest in maritime activities will develop and it will be possible to find the funds to build a fleet..."

Even though the emperor suffered from seasickness at the slightest breeze, he began to purchase yachts with Teutonic efficiency in order to further his strategic plan.

In truth, the true imperial yacht, the *Hohenzollern*, was more akin to a cruiser complete

60 bottom Kiel Week, an event enthusiastically supported by Kaiser Wilhelm II, had already attracted healthy international participation by the beginning of the nineteenth century. American yachts assiduously frequented the June regatta, probably in preparation for Cowes Week. American designers had by then discovered the German boatyards while the Germans themselves, first and foremost the Kaiser, frequently turned to American designers. Meteor III was, in fact, a Cary Smith design, a large, very classical schooner of over 130 feet in length that was comfortable but never competitive.

61 top and center Despite their participation in sporting events, the yachts of the era, especially those destined to accommodate members of the aristocracy, never lacked a degree of opulence in terms

of their interior fittings. The Kaiser's studio cabin and the salon aboard the Meteor III represent a classic layout on yachts of this size and era. The fireplace was not simply an eccentricity given that the yacht frequently sailed in cold, damp conditions; even British America's Cup challengers had them. During races the royal guests would even be served hot meals in the saloon.

61 bottom Kaiser Wilhelm II was one of the leading figures in what was a classic period for yachting on the threshold of the new century with the Big Class boats heralding new hull architecture dictated by the linear formula. His Meteor II, a Big Class yacht, was designed by Watson and replaced the old Meteor that had formerly challenged for the America's Cup as the Thistle and had been one of the great adversaries, with alternating fortunes of the Britannia.

62-63 Aboard the great yachts of the past, the handling of the sails depended exclusively on the physical strength and the size of the crew. There is no doubt that the crew members had excellent physical capabilities and that their numbers guaranteed a reasonable distribution of labor; however, those who are acquainted with the weights and forces involved in the handling of a large yacht well know that only perfect timing, the ability to act at precisely the right moment to execute a maneuver, allows a sheet or halyard to be employed correctly. Here the crew of the Meteor, sailing close-hauled, washboards dipped in the water, is concentrating hard, waiting for that moment and the orders from the helmsman at the stern.

with cannons and smoking funnels, around 384 feet in length and fitted with engines developing 9,500 hp. She was capable of 21 knots and was even larger than the *Victoria and Albert II*, the British state yacht.

This Prussian demonstration of strength aside, there were also four memorable sailing yachts, all named the *Meteor*, that Wilhelm II acquired while attempting to stimulate interest in seafaring matters.

Meteor I was none other than the old *Thistle*, designed in 1887 by G.L. Watson for the America's Cup. Like many yacht owners unsure as to the extent of their enthusiasm, the Kaiser initially turned to the second-hand market. In 1896, however, he commissioned Watson to design the new *Meteor II*.

The Kaiser's ambitions expanded at the turn of the century and, in America this time, at Shooter's Island, he commissioned a 412-ton schooner to the design of Cary Smith. The *Meteor III* was possibly the most famous of the Kaiser's yachts. This was in 1902.

The time was now ripe for the German boatbuilders to show what they were capable of. Built in the German boatyards at Kiel, *Meteor IV* was designed in 1908 by Max Oertz, who was to go on to become a famous designer of metre-class yachts.

In the meantime, just as Prince Henry had predicted, a number of German industrialists had bought schooners, mainly from abroad. Among them was the famous American yacht *Westward* designed by Nat Herreshoff in 1910 that was renamed as the *Hamburg II*. Others were responsible for the building of the *Germania* in 1911 at the Krupp yards. Wilhelm II's gamble had paid off.

62 bottom Wilhelm II's last yacht is something of a symbol of the achievement of his political aims: it was designed by a German, Max Oertz, who had by then gained considerable experience in the design of above all meter-class yachts, and built in a German yard at Kiel. Meteor IV was a fine boat launched in 1908, a yacht of 129 feet overall rigged as a schooner and undoubtedly inspired by American models (in those years the Germans had imported Herreshoff's Westward and Meteor III had been an American design). The crew, lined up here, welcomes the Kaiser aboard during Kiel Week in 1911.

63 top The German yacht racing beyond the sheltered waters of Kiel. Here we are far from the events of the Kiel Week where sport was diluted by the social aspects and, above all, far from the protected, almost lagoon-like conditions of the Kieler Bucht. Meteor IV, Wilhelm II's new yacht sailing close-hauled, all her canvas aloft and about to round the island of Helgoland in the North Sea, open to the fierce, cold northerly winds.

63 bottom Conditions aboard obliged even the high ranking guests to adopt clothing that while not particularly regal was at least efficient: Wilhelm II loved sailing and had a strong competitive spirit (he always felt that he was competing with his British cousins, sons of Queen Victoria) and hoped his example would encourage the German people to recognize the need to embrace the sea. Oilskins and sou'wester did little to conceal the emperor's proud bearing.

FRANCE AND THE MEDITERRANEAN

Like Germany, France came late to the sport of sailing. Nothing of note happened during the eighteenth century and only towards the middle of the nineteenth did yacht clubs begin to be established.

It is probable, however, that sailing boat races were held both in the Channel and the Mediterranean, disputed above all by fishing and pilot boats. The French "cotre" from Brittany was very similar to the British cutter and was widely used for both fishing and pilot duties. In the Mediterranean region, the "houaris" from Marseille were very similar, above all in terms of their rig, to the New York sloops. It was only logical therefore that, as happened in Britain and the United States, someone would have taken the initiative to organize races between local fishermen or pilots, and then decided that the sport would be of interest to gentleman sailors too. The birth of French yachting can be dated precisely to the 18th of August, 1839, the day of the opening of the *Hotel des Bains Frascati* at Le Havre, the occasion being marked by sailing races. Two years later the organisers of the regatta formed a club, the *Societé des Regates du Havre*, the first yacht club in France. From then on races were held and clubs were established throughout the country, the Mediterranean being the setting for regattas in the spring and the Channel and the Atlantic in the summer.

The *Yacht Club de France* was founded in 1867 under the patronage of Napoleon III, while the first French ocean race was disputed the following year from Ryde in England to Dieppe. Encouraging the arrival of foreign yachts in French ports was an effective way of promoting the sport in France. While British and American yachtsmen, for example, had long been cruising in the Mediterranean, visiting places of boundless romantic appeal such as Venice and Monte Carlo, a true apotheosis was achieved with the organization of races at Nice in 1880. Among the numerous yachts participating were the British *Ambrosia* and *Letonia* of 118 and 310 tons respectively and the 310-ton American boat *Sappho. Ailsa* and *Britannia* also took part in the 1895 edition. French sailing took a significant step forwards in 1900 when for the first time sailing was included among the sports in the Olympic Games held in France that year.

The first great French yachts began to appear in the second half of the nineteenth century with the Augustin Normand yards at Le

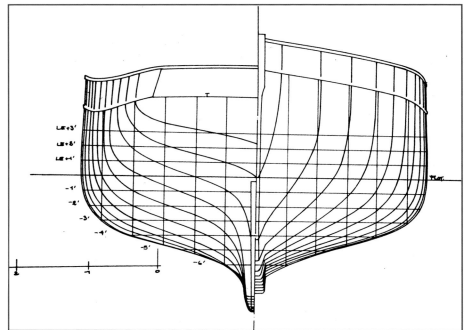

Havre launching the *Zemajteij* for the Russian Count Tyskiewicz. This 147-foot 6-inch schooner was subsequently to become well known in the Mediterranean under the name *Velox* after having passed into French hands. 1910 instead saw the launching of *La Resolue*, in reality a large mixed motor and sail yacht (at the turn of the century the French had great experience in, and were leading constructors of, commercial sailing ships, the famous wind-jammers, and *La Resolue* was probably inspired by these), 172 feet in length and rated at 840 tons. In 1915, on the eve of a tragic period in European history, the 225-ton schooner *La Korrigane* was launched for Count Etienne de Gannay and became a well known cruising yacht.

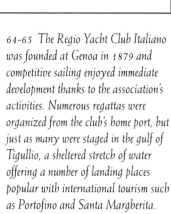

64-65 *The Regio Yacht Club Italiano was founded at Genoa in 1879 and competitive sailing enjoyed immediate development thanks to the association's activities. Numerous regattas were organized from the club's home port, but just as many were staged in the gulf of Tigullio, a sheltered stretch of water offering a number of landing places popular with international tourism such as Portofino and Santa Margherita.*

65 top right Ugo Costaguta's boatyard had all the features of a craft-based operation: wooden sheds on the beach, hoists and slipways. Yards throughout the world were similarly equipped. The launch of a yacht was a complex operation, dependent on the skill of the foreman, the number of men available (generally the whole village would lend a hand) and the caprices of the

sea. In 1902 the Costaguta yard launched the *Artica* a 10-ton yacht for the Duke of the Abruzzi, designed for the French Cup which it was to win from the holder, the French boat *Suzette*.

65 center right Races between yachts of the same class were widespread in the Mediterranean. There were continual challenges between France

and Italy, in a sequence of cups won and lost. The French Cup was disputed between yachts of the 10-ton class (still the era of the Thames rating, and the formulas that derived from this system). This type of racing also attracted German and even British yachts to the Mediterranean, however the events remained principally Italian and French affairs. The photo shows *Artica*, winner in 1902.

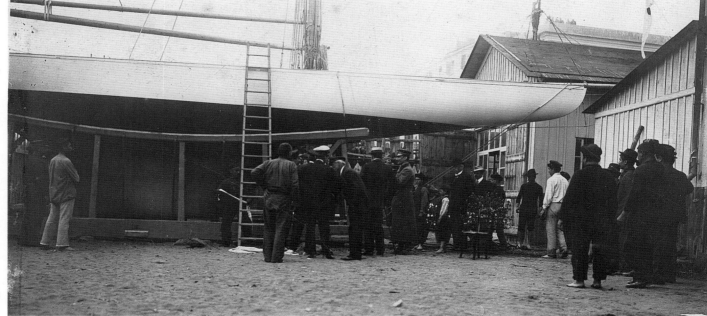

65 bottom In the second half of the nineteenth century there were numerous constructors and designers in Italy devoting themselves to the production of sailing yachts. Among these of particular note was Ugo Costaguta, the founder of a yard that was to be run by the family for almost a century. Its fame was never to progress beyond the Italian borders and its clientele consequently remained essentially Italian. However, Costaguta's boats were successful not only in the Mediterranean but also in Northern Europe. Ugo Costaguta was a designer and constructor above all of centerboard and formula yachts, the type of boats most popular in Italy in that period. The Duke of the Abruzzi soon recognized the design talent of Ugo Costaguta and entrusted him with the creation of numerous yachts. This photo shows the preparations for the launch of *Artica*.

Elsewhere in the Mediterranean, passion for sailing was restricted to a few notable sportsmen, of noble lineage of course. As usual, the example was set by the British. Early in the nineteenth century, two English poets sought inspiration in the atmosphere of profound romanticism evoked by the landscapes and mild climate of the Mediterranean, sailing their yachts along the coasts of Italy: Lord Byron in Tuscany with his *Bolivar* and Percy B. Shelley in Liguria who was lost at sea aboard the *Ariel*.

Among the Italian enthusiasts, it was the Duke of the Abruzzi, His Royal Highness Prince Amedeo, who took on the pioneering role, initially with yachts constructed abroad. His first boat was the 1-ton *Chechette*, designed and built in France by Guédon in 1897. She was later joined by the 5-ton *Fern*, designed by Fife and the large *Bona*, designed by Watson. The Duke

Yachts were also to be found at Austrian-controlled Trieste where the Regio Yacht Club Adriaco was founded in 1903. The small enclosed Adriatic Sea was the setting for the maritime exploits of Carlo Stefano, the Archduke of Austria. His first boat was the cutter *Nair*, 36 feet in length and rated at 25 tons, strangely constructed at Castellamare di Stabia, near Naples, the home of boatyards with long traditions of shipbuilding but little experience with yachts.

Subsequently, in 1888, the Archduke purchased an attractive schooner by Nicholson, the English designer-constructor from the Solent. This was the 80-ton, 88-foot 6-inch *Christa*, formerly the *Heather Belle*. The *Christa* was followed by another English yacht, a cutter of the same size built by J. Fay at Southampton in 1889, the *Valkyrie*.

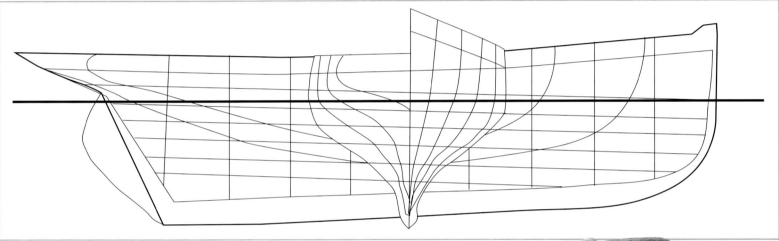

subsequently had a number of small yachts designed and constructed in Italy by Ugo Costaguta of Genoa. *Nella*, *Artica* and *Leda* all belonged to the 5- and 10-ton classes.

The Duke was a true sportsman and much preferred small yachts that he helmed personally. Before his time, Italian waters had been cruised by the great American yacht *Sappho*, a 121-foot schooner and veteran of numerous races on the Atlantic coasts that had been purchased in 1875 by Prince Matteo Sciarra Colonna. *Ailsa* and *Satanita* also found their way to Italy.

It was, however, another figure who was to influence the direction taken by the nascent Italian yachting movement. A certain Captain Enrico d'Albertis completed adventurous cruises in the Mediterranean and the Atlantic, effectively putting Italian yachting on the map with his yachts *Violante*, an 36-foot cutter considered to be the first yacht to be launched in Italy in 1875 (in reality the very first was probably the 8-ton *Black Tulip* commissioned by an Englishman, the consul Sir Yeats Brown), and *Corsaro*, a 71-foot boat from 1882, both built in the Briasco yard at Genoa to the designs of Luigi Ometo.

In the late nineteenth century, three Italian cities contended the status of cradle of the new sport: Naples where a sailing club was founded in 1873, with no less than 35 registered boats, Livorno (Leghorn) and Genoa where the Regio Yacht Club Italiano was founded in 1879.

66 top and bottom Among the enthusiastic Mediterranean yachtsmen, a place of honor has to go to Captain Enrico Alberto D'Albertis. Also a great navigator, he crossed the Atlantic on a number of occasions. A talented writer, he described his voyages in a number of books. The top photo shows the cover of one of his numerous travel stories: Crociera del Corsaro a San Salvador, la prima terra scoperta da Colombo from 1898, probably Captain D'Albertis' most interesting exploit aboard the Corsaro, departing from Huelva in Spain and retracing Columbus' voyage in search of the Indies.

66 center Captain Enrico Alberto D'Albertis, one of the promoters of the Regio Yacht Club Italiano, is famous for his numerous and adventurous exploits aboard his two boats, Violante and Corsaro. His first yacht was the Violante (drawing, center), a cutter 37 feet 6 inches long overall with a beam of 11 feet 6 inches and a draught of 8 feet 4 inches, designed by Luigi Oneto and built by Agostino Briasco. This may be considered to be the first yacht built as such in Italy and was inspired by contemporary British models.

67 Captain D'Albertis' second yacht was the Corsaro, a yawl this time and much larger at 71 feet long overall, with a beam of 15 feet 6 inches and a draught of 11' 6". By the same designer and builder, she was launched in 1882 and with her long bowsprit, vertical stempost and generous stern overhang she was still an essentially British design. Corsaro is known above all for her transatlantic cruises but enjoyed good racing results, participating in the first regattas at Nice at the dawn of yachting in the Mediterranean. The bottom photo shows Corsaro on the slipway of the Agostino Briasco yard where she was built to the designs of Luigi Oneto. The top photo shows Captain D'Albertis' second yacht on the occasion of her last voyage: a cruise to Kiel in 1895 for the inauguration of the navigable canal. During the leg from Kiel to Gosport, the boat was rammed and seriously damaged. It was not possible to repair her adequately and she was demolished at Portsmouth.

THE AMERICA'S CUP

In 1850, John Cox Stevens, who needs no further introduction, decided that American yachting was sufficiently mature and backed by adequate experience and financial and technological resources to provide definitive proof of its independence. This proof was to take the form of a challenge to the British yachtsmen, then rightly considered to be the masters of recreational sailing.

The design of the boat that was to carry American hopes was entrusted to George Steers, son of an English master carpenter who had emigrated to America from Devonshire. In the previous century the British had constructed

naval or commercial vessels in their overseas colonies, but always using yards provisionally installed on beaches and specialist workers who, once their task had been completed, were repatriated so as not to cede know-how to the colonies. This may well have been a reason why American boatbuilding, and therefore yachting, was slow to take off, but also one of the reasons why naval architecture in the States eventually developed in independent, innovative directions. John Steers' father probably escaped repatriation, which in hindsight was a grave mistake by the British!

George Steers was responsible for the design of the fastest pilot boats, three yachts for members of the N.Y.Y.C. and, above all, the schooner *Mary Taylor* for Captain Richard Brown, then considered to be extremely fast and innovative for its slim forward lines. The William Brown yard thus began work on a 101-foot 6-inch schooner to Steers' design, a boat that was to be named *America*. The yacht was completed in six months and immediately proved its worth

with a victory over Robert Livingstone Stevens' sloop, *Maria*. On the 21st of June, 1851, *America* commenced the transatlantic voyage that would take her to Cowes, the temple of the Royal Yacht Squadron, the secretary of which Lord Wilton had sent an invitation for the racing season to the N.Y.Y.C. *America* competed in the R.Y.S.'s Hundred Guinea Cup, the first non-British boat to do so, on the 22nd of August, 1851. The race was open to yachts of all kinds and consisted of a 53-mile circumnavigation of the Isle of Wight. At that time the starting gun was fired with the boats at anchor, and *America*, whose anchor fouled on the bottom, was delayed for some minutes after the other competitors had departed. At the end of the first leg of the course with a slight head-wind she was nonetheless on the heels of the British yachts.

Off the eastern tip of the island the Nab lightship marked a sandbank and the shallows between itself and the island. The regulations did not explicitly indicate whether the shallows should be left to starboard, partly because no yacht ever dared to take the inside line for safety reasons. *America* did so, however, and went into the lead thanks to this shortcut which saved a couple of miles. Weak and variable winds characterized the southern leg of the course, reducing the American schooner's lead but the strong tidal currents instead worked to her advantage. The cutter *Arrows* was pushed onto the beach by the currents, the *Alarm* stopped to lend assistance while *Freak* and *Volante* collided due to the difficult conditions. These were *America's* most dangerous opponents. Having rounded the Needles, very weak, variable winds from the West this time slowly blew *America* towards the

finishing line at Cowes. 10 hours and 37 minutes after starting; the American schooner was first across the line, followed home 18 minutes later by a small cutter, *Aurora*. *Brucchante* and *Eclipse* finished almost an hour and 70 minutes behind respectively, while *Brilliant* reached Cowes no less than five hours after *America*. The other yachts either retired or finished outside the maximum permitted time. A formal protest presented to the Race Committee because *America* had not rounded the Nab was rejected by the judges. Commodore John Cox Stevens received the Hundred Guinea Cup which he took back to his club where it remained until 1983, despite the 24 attempts to regain it. This marked the beginning of the America's Cup story, perhaps the most talked-about sailing event of all time, and certainly the one that has attracted the most money and concentrated the greatest efforts of designers and boatbuilders.

The Americans undoubtedly took a fine boat to

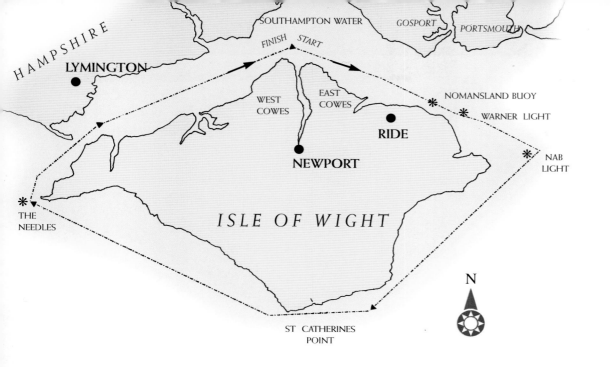

68-69 America was profoundly different with respects to her British rivals and the format of this illustration tends to highlight, perhaps excessively, one of the schooner's most unusual aspects: America was an extremely simple yacht, one conceived for pure performance in contrast with customary practice in Britain and elsewhere where heavy penalties were paid for the demands of appearance and luxury.

69 top The race that gave rise to the legendary America's Cup was a clockwise circumnavigation of the Isle of Wight.

69 bottom The designer of America, perhaps the most famous yacht in the history of sailing, never enjoyed the notoriety of his creation: George Steers is still, in fact, relatively unknown.

68 On the 22nd of August, 1851, the generally subdued English press had to report on an event quite extraordinary for the times: the participation in a race in British waters of a yacht from a foreign nation that had, moreover, only recently broken away from the control of the motherland. The schooner America had lined up for the start of the 100

Guineas Cup on that morning of weak and variable winds. A large crowd, certainly larger than usual thanks to the presence of the unexpected guest, can be seen lining the quay at Ryde: the boats had covered just a tenth of the full distance but America had already recovered much of the time lost due to a fumbled start.

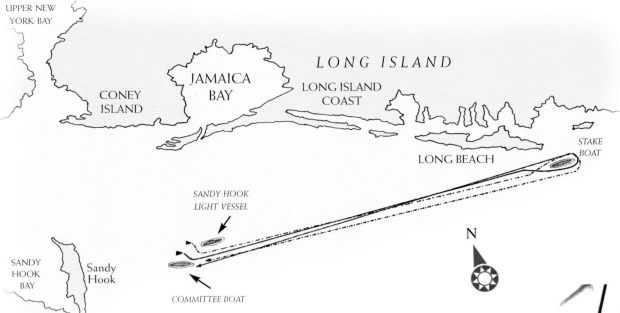

UPPER NEW
YORK BAY

CONEY
ISLAND

JAMAICA
BAY

LONG ISLAND

LONG ISLAND
COAST

STAKE
BOAT

LONG BEACH

SANDY HOOK
LIGHT VESSEL

N

SANDY
HOOK
BAY

Sandy
Hook

COMMITTEE BOAT

70 top left *The first editions of the America's Cup were staged on the sheltered waters of Long Island Sound, the long bay protected from the ocean waves and tipped by the city of New York. The first races had outward and homeward bound legs of 10, 15 and 20 miles depending on the wind conditions. This was a more technical course than the circumnavigation of the Isle of Wight in 1851.*

Cowes in 1851 and they won because they had a crew prepared for the race and an expert captain, Dick Brown, who was paid to win. They also won because they had machine-woven cotton sails reeved to the boom while their British adversaries were using very porous hand-woven canvas sails with a free base. They won because they had specifically designed a boat to win whilst the British, somewhat presumptuously, approached the race with traditional yachts that had never faced competition other than from similar boats and were laden with aristocratic and social symbols rather than technology. Most importantly, however, *America* won because she found a loophole in the regulations, the inside passage between the Nab and the island, and because she enjoyed considerable good fortune: light following winds when the British cutters were at their best in and accustomed to stronger head winds, and the tidal current that eliminated four of her most dangerous rivals. *America* won in real time, the small *Aurora* would not have beaten her even on compensated time, but only because after the arrival of the American schooner, the wind dropped almost completely and the British cutter had to struggle

across the finishing line. Compensation would have reduced the deficit to just two minutes, a period far shorter than that necessary to sail the two miles gained by *America* at the Nab. The true winner, however, was progress, which is no bad thing, and confirmation of the validity of the American victory was provided by the successive editions of the America's Cup in spite of the various controversial episodes that distinguished them.

1ST CHALLENGE - 1870

Disputed by the British challenger, Lord Ashbury's *Cambria*, designed and built at Cowes by Michael Ratsey, and a small fleet of 17 American yachts along the lines of the original race on the Solent nineteen years earlier. The race was won by the Loper-designed *Magic*. *Cambria* was a 199-ton schooner while *Magic* was also rigged as a schooner after having been launched as a sloop 13 years earlier for Franklin Osgood.

The race was held on a 38-mile course between Staten Island and Sandy Hook and back.

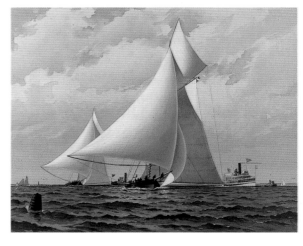

2ND CHALLENGE - 1871

The challenger was again Lord Ashbury with his new yacht, the *Livonia*, again a traditional schooner designed by Michael Ratsey. The Americans accepted to defend the cup with a single yacht, which would seem to me to be correct, and launched the *Columbia*, designed by J. B. Van Deusen. The Americans won 2-1, with one of their victories being hotly disputed and only won because Ashbury's protest was rejected. For the fourth race the Americans asked and were allowed to change their boat: they raced and won with *Sappho*, a large 118-foot schooner designed by R. Poillon for Mr W. P. Douglas.

3RD CHALLENGE - 1876

The challenger this time was a Canadian with a classic schooner, the *Countess of Dufferin*, designed by Alexander Cuthbert, an expert fishing hull designer. She was pitched against *Madeleine*, designed by David Kirby. The Canadians arrived in a precarious state, short of money, and were soundly beaten.

4TH CHALLENGE - 1881

Canadians again, and again a Cuthbert design, a cutter this time, the 70-foot *Atlanta*. The Americans agreed to modify the rules: from then on the America's Cup would be disputed by a sole "defender." The United States were represented by *Mischief* an unusual steel-hulled boat designed by Cary Smith that won easily.

5TH CHALLENGE - 1885

The British return: Sir Richard Sutton challenged the Americans with his J. B. Webb-designed cutter *Genesta*, a classic 90-foot, plank-on-edge yacht with a 15-foot beam. Edward Burgess' *Puritan* was chosen to defend the cup. The American yacht was 94 feet long, 23 wide and featured a centerboard. The Americans won the best-out-of-three series 2-0.

6TH CHALLENGE - 1885

Another traditional British cutter, again designed by Webb, the *Galatea*, owned by a Mr Hemm who lived aboard with his wife, dogs and a monkey in luxuriously appointed accommodation. With their customary pragmatism the Americans launched a yacht designed by E. Burgess, again exclusively for the regatta, the *Mayflower*. 2-0 again.

70 center A period of twenty years was to pass before a British yacht braved the Atlantic Ocean to attempt to regain the Hundred Guineas Cup, by then rebaptized as the America's Cup in honor of the 1851 winner. The first challenge was issued in 1870 by Lord Ashbury's Cambria, the cup being defended by no less than 17 American yachts. Among these was the Loper-designed Magic that was by no means as innovative as America but was nonetheless more advanced than the traditionally British Cambria.

70 bottom The 1881 challenge, once again issued by the British, marked the end of the large schooners, at least in the America's Cup. The two contenders that year were rigged as cutters with plenty of canvas but by the standards of their day were small yachts: Mischief was just 67 feet long overall with Atlanta just a little longer at 70 feet. Remarkably, the British yacht was owned, designed, built and helmed by the same person, Alexander Cuthbert

70-71 For many years the British entrusted their chances of regaining the America's Cup to yachts that were anything but purpose-built. The main deck of the Livonia was a perfect example of all that was required of a large cruising yacht, with elegant skylights, high topsides to protect guests and crew, all the rigging concentrated on the stringer and derricks for the yacht's dinghy. I believe that this is one of the first photographs to portray an America's Cup yacht and dates from 1887, sixteen years after Livonia's defeat by Sappho.

71 top Lord Ashbury was back on the waters of Long Island Sound in 1871, issuing another challenge to the New York Yacht Club with a yacht that while new replicated the concepts embodied by Cambria. It was no coincidence that the designer and constructor were the same, Michael Ratsey of Cowes. Livonia was a fabulous yacht for the cruises enjoyed by her owner, with the necessary seaworthiness to tackle an Atlantic crossing but penalised by the sheltered waters and light winds of the North American coast.

72 top left Thistle was one of the first British challengers to have a realistic chance of winning a race such as the America's Cup. She was designed by George L. Watson (portrayed top, right), entrusted to a professional skipper of great experience, John Barr (bottom) and financed by a syndicate headed by James Bell (top, left) of the Royal Clyde Yacht Club. She was therefore a Scottish yacht.
She enjoyed little luck in America, but overall her career was extremely successful and particularly long-lived; she was eventually sold to the Kaiser Wilhelm II of Germany and renamed as the Meteor.

72 top right In 1887 the America's Cup races were disputed by the British challenger Thistle and the New York Yacht Club defender Volunteer. The American yacht was almost the same length as the Thistle at the waterline, 85 feet 10 inches against 86 feet and 5 inches, but was considerably wider at 23 feet against 20, had a shallower draught at 10 feet against 18, but was above all 6% lighter and carried 4% more canvas. The Thistle was fast, but Volunteer was a winning yacht. The portraits show the owner, General Paine (top, left), the designer Edward Burgess (top, right) and Captain Stone (bottom).

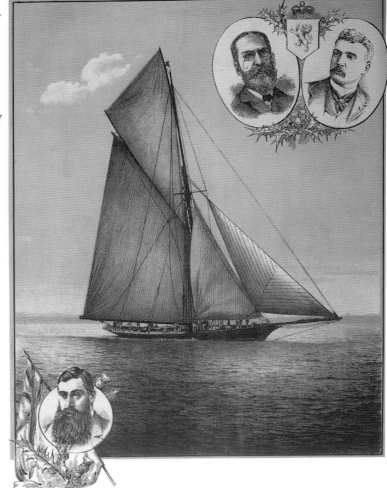

72 bottom While Burgess' design proved to be superior to that of the challenger, both yachts were part of the old guard, their lines reflecting consolidated concepts with the Americans relying on a centerboard and the British on the plank-on-edge model. Volunteer is seen passing in front of the judges' boat, gaining on the heavier Thistle in the light winds. Neither of these yachts would be competitive against the boats that disputed the successive edition of the race.

73 top left Lord Dunraven was one of the most ardent America's Cup competitors: in the United States they never learned to love his aggressive racing tactics, but it was this very competitiveness that perhaps first gave the defenders cause for concern. Dunraven's yacht Valkyrie II was designed by the Scotsman G. Watson, an engineer with a thorough technical background who created a hull with wooden planking over a steel frame. This feature benefited performance in that it lent greater rigidity to the yacht while saving weight.

7TH CHALLENGE - 1887

The British challenger was the Thistle designed by the Scotsman, G. L. Watson. This was, at last a "new" design, a broader cutter, with more gentle lines and a clipper bow. It was nonetheless defeated by the Volunteer, yet another Burgess design.

8TH CHALLENGE - 1893

Another boat by Watson who was no longer a designer bound by British conventions. Watson was an engineer and attempted, using the instruments available to him at the time, to apply scientific methods to yacht design. The Valkyrie II, owned by Lord Dunraven, was 117 feet long overall (87 at the waterline) and 24 feet 6 inches wide. This was no plank-on-edge design and was constructed with wood over a steel frame, a novelty for that period.

Once again the American defender was more up-to-date technologically. Designed by the "Wizard" Nat Herreshoff, she featured a steel structure and bronze plating. Another American victory.

73 top right The Vigilant heralded the opening of the era of Nat Herreshoff, the Wizard of Bristol, who for around twenty years was to contribute crucial chapters to the history of world yachting with his designs. Vigilant also inaugurated the era of the great "skimming dish" yachts that were ever longer and ever shallower, with enormous overhangs and huge sail areas. The rig was still traditional, but the hull was built in steel and bronze while the keel still featured a centerboard blade but with the ballast profile concentrated towards the center.

73 center Beating in a stiff wind, all sails aloft, the white hull of the Vigilant is leading to leeward by a few lengths. Valkyrie II failed to win any of the three races, but proved to be a worthy adversary for the defender whose victories were all very close. The two yachts were not dissimilar in terms of dimensions, having the same length at the waterline. The British boat was still narrower and deeper but not by much. They both had the same displacement while the American yacht carried a few square metre more canvas. The two schools of thought were drawing together thanks to advances in engineering.

73 bottom In the first race of the 1893 regatta, Valkyrie II found herself with a clear lead: the Americans were facing their first defeat in an America's Cup race. Unfortunately for the challenger the wind dropped and the race was annulled. In the second race the two yachts were evenly matched right from the start: the British yacht luffed below the committee boat, thus to windward, while the Vigilant started from the center and had already picked up speed. Valkyrie II was designed by the Scotsman George L. Watson who was responsible for four America's Cup challengers for four editions of the regatta.

9TH CHALLENGE - 1895

The players were the same, Lord Dunraven representing Britain with the *Valkyrie III* again a design by Watson. The Herreshoff-designed *Defender* was even more innovative with bronze skinning in the hull and aluminium topsides.

Defender won, but Lord Dunraven presented two protests, both rejected and was disqualified after the second race which he had won. A seriously tainted edition.

74-75 *Defender's mainsail had an area of 7,965 square feet and it took around twenty men to hoist it using a double halyard. Running rigging generally involved blocks and tackle with winches only being used for certain sheets.*

The Defender was commanded by a legendary figure, Captain Henry "Hank" Haff, one of the best professional skippers of the period. The crews of the America's Cup boats were all paid and generally recruited by the skipper himself.

75 top left *The ninth America's Cup challenge of 1895 was once again issued by Lord Dunraven who commissioned another Watson design, Valkyrie III. The Scottish designer ignored the dictates of British tradition in this case and for the first time a British yacht was wider than the American defender, 26 feet against 23.*

The draught and displacement were identical but Valkyrie III carried more canvas thanks to the greater stability provided by its breadth. The cup was to remain in the hands of the New York Yacht Club largely thanks to the judges: the aggressive Lord Dunraven presented two protests, both of which were rejected, at least one unfairly.

The America's Cup

75 top right The cup was then disputed over the best of 3 races, but the 1895 regatta was decided in the committee room rather than at sea. The Americans won the first race with an 8-minute advantage. In the second there was a collision between the two boats when the race was still balanced. Defender crossed the line first and Dunraven protested but the jury decided in favour of the Americans. In the third race Valkyrie III was impeded by the fleet of spectators' boats at the start: Dunraven retired and presented a protest. He was well within his rights but the jury decided against him: victory went to Defender and the cup remained in the club at New York.

75 bottom The yacht designed by Nat Herreshoff for the 1895 challenge earned a place in the history books thanks to its highly advanced specification. The frame was in steel with aeronautic-style ribs and crossmembers; the skinning of the bottom was in bronze while that of the topsides and the deck was in aluminium. A true racing machine designed to last the duration of the regatta. Before each race the yachts were taken out of the water to clean and polish the hulls. The depth of the keel is stunning: the yacht had a draught of 19 feet 8 inches!

76 top The last challenge of the 19th century was held in 1899 and brought into the limelight a figure who, with his five challenges and air of a self-made man, may not have won the America's Cup but certainly conquered the Americans: Sir Thomas Lipton, the English tea baron and the first of the event's great "gentleman drivers". His *Shamrock* designed by William Fife was without doubt a match for Herreshoff's *Columbia* but unfortunately he lacked a Charlie Barr, the great American helmsman.

76 bottom The America's Cup yachts were true racers and even the British challengers had eradicated the fireplaces, carpets and pet monkeys of old. Very stiff hulls, immense sail plans, metal masts which were lighter than wooden components but also more delicate given that steel production technology did not yet allow close control of tolerances. Scenes such as this, with *Columbia's* great metal mast broken and crumpled on the deck, were if not common then at least not infrequent during the America's Cup yachts' sea trials.

10TH CHALLENGE - 1899

The first of Sir Thomas Lipton's five attempts to regain the trophy for Britain. The first of the yachts entered by the "grocer" as Lipton was rather snobbishly nicknamed in reference to his tea-importing business, was designed by W. Fife and was a true racing machine. Bronze and aluminium skinning, steel frames: 128 feet long overall, 89 at the waterline, and thus enormous overhangs that she could exploit as buoyancy reserve whenever she heeled. *Shamrock* was the first of a series of boats to be so-named.

On the opposite side of the Atlantic, *Columbia* was another Herreshoff design, very similar to Fife's yacht, being just a little broader in the beam and another true racer.

For the first time a triangular course was adopted, windward-reach-leeward-leeward-reach-windward, that was destined to become the classic America's Cup format. *Columbia* won the series 3-0, but the two boats were evenly matched, the difference being made by the American skipper, Charlie Barr.

11TH CHALLENGE - 1901

For his second challenge Lipton chose a Watson yacht: the *Shamrock II* was a truly extreme design with an absolutely flat hull, huge overhangs and a very slim, deep keel. This was almost a fin keel design, around 137 feet in length plus a bowsprit.

Herreshoff designed a new yacht named *Defender* like its predecessor from 1895, but this boat was unconvincing during sea trials and the race was again disputed by *Columbia* with Charlie Barr at the helm.

The three races were hard fought, with the American yacht only winning the last on compensated time after the *Shamrock II* crossed the line 2 seconds ahead.

77 top left Sir Thomas Lipton changed designer for his Shamrock II, with Fife being succeeded by another Scotsman, George Watson, responsible for the design of three previous challengers. Watson had a more thorough technical grounding than the intuitive Fife and designed a truly extreme yacht in terms of form, while using a new alloy bronze with improved mechanical qualities for the skinning. The British challenger was truly on a par with the American defender and the difference was made once more by the expert helmsman Charlie Barr.

77 bottom left Shamrock II's sea trials were conducted in May, 1901, on the waters of the Solent. The new metal mast, subjected to the enormous stress imposed on the rigging by the sail area of 15,000 square feet, snapped cleanly. over 130 feet of mast and the boom of almost 100 feet crashed down onto the deck crowded with the at least thirty men required to handle this yacht.

77 right The Americans once again turned to Nat Herreshoff for the defender yacht in the 1901 challenge against Sir Thomas Lipton. The Wizard of Bristol's design was conditioned by the knowledge that the British were now close in terms of the performance of their yachts to the American vessels. A series of races in

which the "old" Columbia also took part were organised to decide which yacht would defend the cup. Herreshoff had no doubt that his 1899 design was still the best and it was chosen for the races against Shamrock II. This image shows Constitution, Columbia, and Independence shortly after the start of one of the elimination trials.

12ᵀᴴ CHALLENGE - 1903

Thomas Lipton was greatly encouraged by the fact that in the previous edition his boat had proved to be as good as the American defender but, with one of those decisions that are difficult to interpret but which at times affect the outcome of history, he entrusted the design of the new challenger to Fife when he should have kept faith with Watson. As was inevitable, Fife designed another cutting-edge boat, a fin keel design with a lead bulb and a hull in the new nickel-steel. *Shamrock III* was 134 feet long overall, 23 feet broad and carried 15,000 square feet of sail.

Herreshoff's new design, *Reliance*, was a monstrous boat, born to race and crammed with technical innovations: a hollow rudder that could be filled with oil in a following wind, a brake on the rudder pivot, winches mounted below decks and an adjustable mast step. She also featured an aeronautical-style structure with T-ribs in steel and tubular transverse tie-bars, bronze skinning, and cork-lined aluminium decks. Once again the British team had a good boat, but the American yacht was truly extraordinary and, moreover, had Charlie Barr at the helm. The result was yet again 3-0 to the Americans. Sir Thomas Lipton still had no intention of surrendering, however, but the New York Yacht Club, under pressure from the great Nat Herreshoff, felt that the entire America's Cup system needed overhauling. This was due on the one hand to the high costs of the boats and above all, the fact that they were now vessels conceived expressly for this one event, and on the other to the anomaly of racing with yachts of different types. When the Universal Rule and the International Rating came into being it seemed logical to adopt these formulas for the definition of an America's Cup boat. The problem was that the N.Y.Y.C. members' deliberations dragged on for to long and the next edition of the America's Cup was not staged until 1920.

78-79 The start-line maneuvers of the two protagonists of the 1903 challenge: tight circling in search of the best position with respects to the start-line at the moment in which the cannon was fired. Races started with the yachts at anchor were long past: over fifty years, in fact, when the schooner America was delayed by a fouled anchor off Cowes.

78 bottom In 1903 the Herreshoff yard at Bristol produced the most extreme racing machine ever seen. The America's Cup yachts were by now designed and produced to last the duration of a single regatta and had evolved into extreme forms based on previously unthinkable dimensions. Reliance was around 138 feet long, had over 52 feet of overhang and a draught of around 20 feet. A broad, flat hull that carried over 17,000 square feet of sail but weighing just 140 tons. Seeing her in the dry-dock is fascinating as she resembles a modern ultra-light bulb keel yacht.

79 top The British challenger was no less extreme in terms of her specification than the American yacht: she was built in nickel steel which was lighter for a given strength than bronze and had an external bulb in lead. This was the first British America's Cup yacht to have a wheel rather than a traditional tiller. The Americans had instead been using this feature for years as it allowed improved control as the forces on the blade increased.

79 bottom The British yacht entered by Sir Thomas Lipton for his third challenge was designed by Fife, like the first in the series. I do not know why Lipton entrusted the new boat to the designer from the Clyde rather than Watson after the fine showing of *Shamrock II* in 1901. In fact, Fife's design, while as up-to-date in terms of features and materials as Herreshoff's, did not prove to be as competitive as her predecessor and was comfortably beaten by *Reliance* in three uneventful races, despite the varying wind conditions.

80 top, center and bottom The emphasis on speed led to the institution of an annual regatta, the International Fisherman's Race, organized along the lines of the America's Cup between a defender and a challenger. Initially schooners built and actually used for fishing participated in the event. Subsequently, the Canadians of Halifax built the Bluenose specifically for this race and naturally emerged victorious. Bluenose retained the trophy for a period of twenty years and also proved her worth on the fishing grounds, actually being used for the activity for which this type of boat had originally been conceived. In the center photo, Bluenose, winner of the 1922 Fisherman's Race, is trailing Gertrude L. Thebaud, the Gloucester challenger, while below she is racing against Henry Ford.

The coasts of North America have two characteristics that have made them famous throughout the world: they are lined by outcrops of the continental shelf where the ocean floor forms shallow banks, and they are lapped by the cold waters of the Labrador Current. Excellent fishing areas are: from Nova Scotia in the Canadian Atlantic with its Grand Banks of Newfoundland, down to Portland, Gloucester and Provincetown for cod fishing and, further south, from Boston, with the George Bank, down to Baltimore for oysters and crustaceans. While all this may appear to have little to do with the subject of yachting, it serves to introduce a phenomenon that had a constant influence on American yachting and the work of the region's greatest yacht designers: racing between the fishing boats of North America.

80-81 The large American schooners of the early twentieth century all derived from the fisherman and pilot schooners. Great designers devoted themselves to these themes: Ingomar, seen here in pursuit of Elmina, was designed by Nat Herreshoff in 1903.

The contribution of naval architects with a solid technical grounding became all-important after the second half of the nineteenth century when a number of fisherman schooners were lost at sea due to their lack of stability and seaworthiness.

when it was fresh they simply wanted to get it to the salting houses before it rotted. In the early twentieth century this natural, spontaneous form of competition spawned an annual organized regatta for these boats, the International Fisherman's Race. The event was a kind of championship for fishing schooners, with a defender and challengers along the lines of the America's Cup that, in a certain sense, had inspired the race. The fishermen had, in fact, been scandalized to see the magnificent, technological and incredibly expensive America's Cup yachts trapped in harbor by winds of just 25 knots. They instead went out to sea and staged races amongst themselves.

From early that century to the 1940s, the racing fishermen continued to compete among themselves and organize their annual regatta. This induced the great designers of the time to make a contribution to the genre on the one hand while on the other drawing inspiration from it. The origins of this type of boat are to be found in the broad, flat New York pilot schooners equipped with centerboards and the better balanced Boston versions with the already mentioned *Hesper* as the winner. Both of these in turn derived from

There was nothing new about competition amongst working boats and we have already mentioned the Boston and New York pilots and the fishermen of the Long Island Sound and Chesapeake Bay. Those working sloops were to form the basis of the great American racing yachts. There were also, of course, the great clipper races from Australia and China to England: the first cargo, be it of wool or tea, to reach the docks would sell for up to twice the price attracted by the second boat home. Designers, boatyards and, above all, captains thus learned to crowd on the sail with increasingly well built hulls designed expressly to reduce the duration of ocean crossings, thus guaranteeing increased earnings for

the owner, glory and a gilded pennant to carry ashore for the captain and his clipper. Even though the times of the clippers were punctually reported in the newspapers of the era, and even though records were established and became the object of repeated challenges, and even though wagers in cash and kind stimulated competition, the clipper races were never organized and institutionalized as such and never became regularly scheduled events, as was the case with the American fishing schooners.

Initially the banks fishermen raced each other home from the fishing grounds, when their cargo of fish was already salted in order to obtain the best possible price on the market, but

the Baltimore schooner, the prototype American schooner. Out of this tradition was born the Gloucester fisherman boat used for fishing on the Newfoundland banks, where the need for speed outweighed considerations arising from the dangerous sea and wind conditions the boats had to face. Each year many vessels were lost and their crews with them, of course.

A famous designer of the era with various editions of the America's Cup to his credit was asked to design a fishing schooner that would be as safe as it was fast. Edward Burgess responded to this brief with the *Carrie E. Phillips* in 1886, which proved to be faster than the earlier pilot schooners and the yachts derived from them, and

was above all more seaworthy than the Banks fishing boats. Early in the twentieth century it was the turn of Nat Herreshoff to tackle the theme, beginning with the *Ingomar* of 1903. This schooner has actually been attributed to Thomas McManus, a fishmonger and enthusiastic yachtsman of Boston. McManus certainly did design numerous fishing vessels, some of which were famous for their speed such as the *Elsie*, which was chosen as the port of Gloucester's challenger boat and once managed to prevail over the all-conquering Halifax champion *Bluenose*. This last was a W. J. Howe design, expressly conceived and constructed for the International Fisherman's Race, which it in fact won and successfully defended for twenty years. Between one race and another, *Bluenose* regularly

went fishing and was almost always first home with her precious cargo.

Two reports of races between this kind of boat, from which the Americans were to spin a true tradition and gain immense experience in cruising and racing yacht design, are particularly indicative of the technical qualities of fishing schooners. The first dates from 1882 and describes the exploits of the *Harry Belden*, a 111-foot 6-inch Boston schooner that fished the George Bank, 150 miles out of the city. The *Harry Belden*, which held the record of exactly 10 hours for the trip home from the fishing grounds, participated in a fishing boat race out of Gloucester in winds blowing at 60 knots. The captain and crew refused to reduce sail—this was taken care of by the gales themselves as the *Harry Beldon* was stripped of four

foresails and two gaff topsails. She still went on to win the race.

The second report concerns the International Fisherman's Race, also held at Gloucester, and Uffa Fox, a British designer, technical expert and yachting historian. The race was between the American *Henry Ford* and the Canadian champion, *Bluenose*. The American won the first race in light winds while the Canadian took the next two in a stronger breeze. In the fourth and decisive race the wind was blowing at 30 knots and was won by *Bluenose*, which on the windward leg registered a constant speed of 13 and a half knots, under full sail, the leeward topside dipping below the waves and the whole of the crew, helmsman apart, on the opposite side by the foremast.

82 top In contrast with recreational yachts, working boats were frequently named after their owners, something that is still true today. The Henry Ford is a typical Gloucester fisherman schooners: very broad to ensure stability, given that ballast occupied valuable interior space or at least requires a certain draught that would have been an impediment to navigation in the shallow waters of the Grand Banks, a clear deck for fishing activities and a low freeboard. These very fast boats were entrusted to captains who would pile on the canvas in all conditions, whether homeward bound with a full load or because a wager had encouraged them to pit their boats against those of a rival.

82 bottom left Gloucester was the most important fishing and processing centre on the Atlantic coast of North America. The Elizabeth A. Howard was one of the many schooners fishing out of Gloucester that had no hesitation in racing against similar boats from other ports along the coast. Then again, the return home from the fishing grounds was always a race against the other crews.

82 bottom right The great mainsail of a 100-foot schooner might weigh a ton, complete with gaff and rigging, and had to be hoisted manually with the sole aid of blocks and tackle. While on a J Class this operation was performed by at least 20 crewmen, on a working boat 4 or 5 fishermen had to suffice. And the friction losses on a fishing schooner were undoubtedly far higher than on a sophisticated J Class!

83 top This shot of the helmsman of the Henry Ford, determined to make the most of a light breeze, shows all the tension of competitive sailing. The adversary, the Elizabeth A. Howard, is slightly ahead, but to leeward, and is making good headway. The situation is apparently incongruous for this type of boat, conceived not to race but to make profits on the fishing grounds, but competitiveness is a way of life for those who sail at sea.

83 bottom Races between the North American fishing schooners soon became extremely popular and attracted the attention not only of technical experts – famous designers in fact tackled this type of boat – but also figures who had achieved fame within the ambit of the America's Cup. In the photo Sir Thomas Lipton is portrayed during the prize-giving ceremony for the 1923 Fisherman Race.

OCEAN RACING

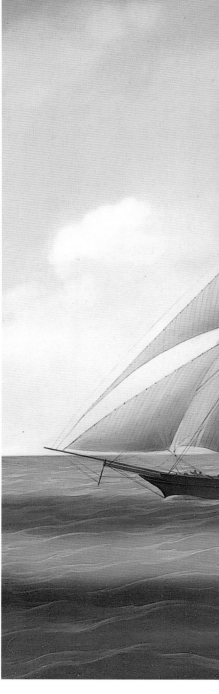

By the late nineteenth century, yachting had spread far beyond the British waters in which it had developed and was popular in the United States, in the Mediterranean, the Baltic Sea, Australia and New Zealand.

This spread had been stimulated and nurtured by ocean racing, that is to say, races staged outside the sheltered waters of the Solent, the Firth of Clyde or New York's Long Island Sound. While yachting had not taken long to spread beyond these confines, the first ocean races were few and far between and usually one-off events.

The first race in open water of which detailed accounts have survived was held on the 29th of August, 1771, between the Duke of Richmond and Sir Alexander Smith, with 1,000 pounds sterling at stake. Their yachts raced between Brighton and Beachy Head on the south coast of England; in the English Channel, therefore

rather than the ocean, but this was just the beginning. Following that modest exhibition, the next open sea event (again in the Channel) was not until 1834, a 130-mile race off the Isle of Wight between the brigantine *Waterwich* and the schooner *Galatea*. Around the same time, in 1838, on the other side of the globe albeit still in British territory, the Royal Hobart Regatta Association was founded and that same year organized a regatta in what were indubitably oceanic waters. In 1849, with the foundation of the Royal Bermuda Y.C., the first international ocean race was disputed in the Atlantic (although close in to the island) between the British *Pearl* and the American *Brenda*. The former won by a margin of just 55 seconds. Up to this point ocean racing was still in its infancy.

In 1851, *America* crossed the Atlantic to race in Britain; the time was ripe for a trans-oceanic

race. In 1866, three American schooners, the 105-foot *Vesta* of the tobacco magnate Pierre Lorillard, the 106-foot *Fleetwing* of the brothers George and Franklin Osgood and the 107-foot *Henrietta* of Gordon Bennet Jr., raced each other from Sandy Hook (New York) to Cowes. At stake was what was the vast sum (for the time) of 90,000 dollars. This prize went to the winner of the first trans-oceanic race that was, furthermore, held in the middle of winter with the three yachts crossing the starting line on the 11th of December. The boats had to cope with storms and snow, the *Henrietta* having to lie to and the *Fleetwing* losing 8 men overboard. This last yacht arrived at Cowes at midnight on Christmas day, preceding the *Vesta* by just 40 minutes after 3,000 miles of racing. The winner, however, was *Henrietta*, which had crossed the line at three o'clock in the afternoon after completing the

crossing in 13 days, 21 hours and 55 minutes. The ice had been well and truly broken. A second transatlantic race was held between the *Cambria* of Lord J. Ashbury and the *Dauntless* of J. Gordon Bennet, in the July of 1870, this time from East to West. *Cambria*, which had travelled to America in the vain hope of bringing home the America's Cup, was victorious in a race that was again marred by the loss of two men swept overboard by a wave. From that year on, Atlantic races were held with a certain regularity, frequently being motivated by the British challengers' participation in the America's Cup and their return voyages.

The American yachts taking part in Cowes Week and Kiel Week, rather than those simply interested in the social aspects of European waters and ports, frequently raced in the West-East direction.

84 top Transoceanic races were stimulated by the feats of America. Following the American yacht's victory at Cowes in the summer of 1851, the British were obliged to sail to the United States in order to try to regain the cup while, in the meantime, a number of boats flying the stars and stripes emulated America in sailing to the Solent. Among them were the Dauntless owned by J. G. Bennet and Lord Ashbury's Cambria. The Dauntless raced with little success in British waters and when she eventually returned home challenged Cambria which had crossed the Atlantic for the 1870 America's Cup.

84 bottom The three American schooners still hoisted the large square sail generally used in following winds on the foremast. This was an inheritance from the previous century and yachts such as America were already tending to use larger foresails when running before the wind than when beating. Henrietta, Vesta and Fleetwing left the American coast immediately after the departure from Sandy Hook, the extreme tip of Long Island Sound, the inlet leading to New York.

84-85 The inhospitable waters of the North Atlantic witnessed the first oceanic race in 1866. Three 100-foot schooners were owned by three friends who put up a considerable sum in prize money, something that was not unusual in that era when races also attracted by heavy betting. The race was extremely arduous due to the adverse wind and sea conditions. Fleetwing lost eight men overboard while Henrietta lay a'hull for two days.

PHOTOGRAPHS BY WEST, BEKEN, BROWN, BYRON, KIRK.

"AILSA" (YAWL); OWNER, MR. H. S. REDMOND.
English built, 80 ft. long, 15.3 ft. beam, draft 10.6 ft.

"HAMBURG" (SCHOONER); OWNER, GERMAN SYNDICATE.
English built, 116 ft. long, 17.6 ft. beam, draft 15 ft.

"ENDYMION" (AUX. SCHOONER); OWNER, MR. G. LAUDER.
American built, 101 ft. long, 21.4 ft. beam, draft 14 ft.

"FLEUR-DE-LYS" (SCHOONER); OWNER, MR. L. A. STIMSON.
American built, 86.3 ft. long, 21.2 ft. beam, draft 13 ft.

"VALHALLA" (AUX. SHIP); OWNER, LORD CRAWFORD.
English built, 240 ft. long, 37.2 ft. beam, draft 20 ft.

"HILDEGARDE" (SCHOONER); OWNER, MR. E. R. COLEMAN.
American built, 107.4 ft. long, 26 ft. beam, draft 16.9 ft.

LORD BRASSEY'S FAMOUS "SUNBEAM."
Auxiliary schooner, English built, 157.5 ft. long, 27.6 ft. beam, draft 17.9 ft.

"APACHE" (AUX. BARQUE); OWNER, MR. F. RANDOLPH.
English built, 136 ft. long, 28 ft. beam, draft 10.9 ft.

"ATLANTIC" (AUX. SCHOONER); OWNER, MR. W. MARSHALL.
American built, 135 ft. long, 29 ft. beam, draft 16.5 ft.

"THISTLE" (SCHOONER); OWNER, MR. R. T. TOD.
American built, 124 ft. long, 27.8 ft. beam, draft 14 ft.

"UTOWANA" (AUX. SCHOONER); OWNER, MR. A. V. ARMOUR.
American built, 135 ft. long, 27.8 ft. beam, draft 14.6 ft.

86 The race from Sandy Hook in the United States to Lizard Point in England in May 1905 attracted intensive coverage in the European press. The event had been promoted by Kaiser Wilhelm II, but the only participating boat from Germany, the large Hamburg was owned by a group of German industrialists. Up to then only "private" transoceanic races had been staged, personal duel between one owner and another. That of 1905 was the first official race and was to become a regular event, albeit not one with fixed dates.

87 top The 1905 Kaiser Cup was won by the American yacht Atlantic, a three-masted schooner with an overall length of 134 feet 6 inches and a beam of almost 30 feet. The design was by William Gardner and at the time was considered to be the most advanced vessel ever constructed for recreational sailing as well as the most sophisticated schooner. The owner, Wilson Marshall, enrolled Charlie Barr, the winner of a number of America's Cup regattas, as helmsman: his faith was rewarded as Atlantic won in a record time that was not to be bettered until 1980 by Erik Tabarly.

87 bottom The first transatlantic race from West to East was held in 1905 in very severe conditions; the yachts followed the Great Circle route that took them into northern waters where they sighted icebergs and were constantly dogged by storms. Fleur de Lys, one of the 11 participants, was a classic American schooner with an overall length of 86 feet owned by L. A. Stimson. In this photo the helmsman is securely roped to prevent him being washed overboard by the waves that crashed onto the deck as the yacht sailed at 14 knots.

Two sporting events of great significance were staged early in the twentieth century. In 1905, Kaiser Wilhelm II offered a cup (as part of the policy of promoting the development of a German seafaring tradition discussed earlier) to the winner of a race from Sandy Hook to Lizard Point in England. The departure, set for the 16th of May that year, was postponed by a day due to thick fog, a phenomenon anything but rare in that area. The following day a cannon was fired to start a fantastic race disputed by eleven boats, two three-masted schooners, five two-masted schooners, a yawl, a topsail schooner and two barques. Among them were the Fife-designed 128-foot yacht Ailsa, the American George Lauder's schooner Endymion, another "small" American boat, the 108-foot Fleur de Lys, the large 242-foot 6-inch British ship Valhalla and the beautiful three-masted schooner Atlantic by the American designer W. Gardner for Wilson Marshall. At the helm of this last was the famous Charlie Barr, the Scotsman who had skippered three America's Cup winners. The sole German entry was the Hamburg, formerly named the Westward, entered by friends of the Kaiser. The race enjoyed a constant stiff breeze which the Atlantic exploited to establish a lead from the second day. She covered no less than 340 miles in a single 24-hour period and when caught by a strong south-westerly kept a full set of canvas aloft, dumped her oil-sack ballast and sailed on for four days with Charlie Barr virtually lashed to the helm. The Atlantic won in a record time of 12 days and 4 hours, an average speed of over 10 knots, that was to stand until 1980. Whilst this extraordinary race was being held, early twentieth-century yachting was characterized by a series of initiatives promoted by the publisher and editor of the American periodical The Rudder. A race was organized in 1904 from Brooklyn (N.Y.) to Marblehead, Massachusetts, after having circumnavigated Long Island. The race was reserved for yachts of under 30 feet in length and attracted six entrants including the organiser Day's own 24-foot 6-inch Sea Bird, which actually finished last. This defeat did nothing to discourage Day from organizing the race the following year, this time over a reversed course from Brooklyn to Hampton Road in Virginia. The number of participants doubled to 12 and the race was actually won by Day himself.

In 1906 Day invited his readers to participate in a far more demanding race from Gravesend Bay (N.Y.) to Bermuda, 600 miles of ocean, crossing the Gulf Stream. Only three yachts started, the *Tamerlane*, Day's new yawl-rigged 37-foot 6-inch boat, another 39-foot yawl, *Lila*, owned by Richard Floyd, and an 28-foot sloop, the *Gauntlet*, owned by George Robinson. Shortly after the start *Lila* was demasted and escorted to Gravesend by Day, who thus lost almost two full days to the *Gauntlet* which, unaware of *Lila's* misfortune had continued. A squall caught Robinson's yacht just as it met the Gulf Stream and obliged him to bear up. Day's *Tamerlane* was thus able to win. In spite of the demanding nature of the event, no less than twelve yachts entered the following year. The Bermuda Race became one of the three classic ocean races that are still held to the present day and represent the dream of all sailors, the other two of course being the Fastnet off the English coast and the Sydney-Hobart. Ocean racing had come of age.

88 top *Following the New York Yacht Club, the American metropolis' second sailing association was founded in 1870: the Seawanhaka Yacht Club in the elegant Oyster Bay on Long Island. Among it members were J. P. Morgan, Vanderbilt and the President Roosevelt.*

88-89 *Sunbeam was a large three-masted schooner, a classic family yacht conceived to carry to sea restless Anglo-Saxon gentlemen whose home waters were already overly familiar in the late eighteenth century. We have already encountered Sunbeam at the start of the Kaiser Cup of 1905: I have no information as to how she fared in the race; undoubtedly in good company as apart from the decidedly more modern Atlantic, the four "small" schooners, Endymion, Thistle, Fleur de Lys and Hildegarde and the sporting Ailsa, the others in the field were large cruising yachts along the lines of the Sunbeam.*

There is a clearly identifiable evolution in yacht design influenced by the vessels' intended use. There is no doubt that the primary role of the yacht was originally as a representation of the status and power of the owner. The first yachts were, in fact, destined for royal families and the members of their courts and they were used for colorful maritime parades.

Subsequently, and this was a revolution that was not long in coming thanks to man's innate spirit of competition, yachts began to be used for racing: firstly on the narrow reaches of the Thames, then in the sheltered bays of England and the United States and finally on the open ocean. From that moment the recreational sailor enjoyed the possibility of travelling by sea to visit places and people.

Man had of course been navigating for centuries, and the impulse to cross the seas had always been stimulated by the desire to see with one's own eyes what lay beyond that headland or that island lying on the horizon. Previously, however, the motives behind the great voyages of exploration had been commercial or military, never pure pleasure and recreation. Ulysses was simply trying to return home to Ithaca and if it took him ten years it was only due to the technical inadequacy of the means of transport available to him. The Phoenicians passed the Columns of Hercules in order to open new markets and the Romans sailed to expand the confines of their empire.

By the end of the nineteenth century, yachting had matured in terms of experience and technical means to the point where its cycle of growth could be completed. The yacht was a means by which its owner demonstrated his social standing, let off his competitive steam and satisfied his curiosity as to what lay beyond the next horizon. This last aspect is open to diverse personal interpretations, be it a refusal of terrestrial conventions, a spirit of adventure or simply a passion for the sea. The first to move in this direction were the Americans. The nation was still young and recreational sailing was still a new phenomenon, but the distant horizon was already calling out to the indomitable pioneering spirit of a nascent people.

The *Union*, a yacht built in England in the mid-eighteenth century for Mr. Baptist May, was a typical English cutter of the Cumberland Fleet period. Forty years later she was sold in the United States and set sail from Newport with a crew of 23 young Americans in 1794. She was to return four years later after having circumnavigated the globe in a voyage with no commercial purpose and indeed with the sole aim of seeing other peoples and other lands by sea. This was the birth of cruising.

Some years later another American, George Crowinshield, commissioned the building of *Cleopatra's Barge* and only premature death prevented

him from sailing in all of the Seven Seas.

Towards the end of the nineteenth century, cruising had a precise social connotation, at least for the wealthy American owners who naturally began the season on home waters. They would meet aboard their yachts on Long Island Sound in late spring, frequenting the sumptuous Seawanhaka Yacht Club and cruising as far as Newport, the setting for regattas and gala evenings. The summer saw the yachts cross the Atlantic for two crucial social occasions, the Kiel and Cowes Weeks. Once the racing and festivities were over the fleet, as this collection of boats with average lengths of around 98 feet flying the stars and stripes and joined by a number of British vessels, must have appeared, left the Isle of Wight in search of milder autumn and

winter climates. The Mediterranean welcomed them with open arms from Monte Carlo to Venice. From here they sailed on to the Caribbean on the last leg of their annual cruise before heading back to the yards to prepare the yachts for the following season.

The "Grand Tour" of the American yachts had its European counterpart in a spirit of greater curiosity and desire for adventure. Lord and Lady Brassey, for example, set sail from Chatham in England on the 1st of July, 1876, with their children and a number of guests aboard, on the first leg of a memorable round-the-world cruise of 36,000 miles that was to take the best part of a year. Lady Anna Brassey has left us with a detailed account of the voyage in her *Around the World in the Yacht Sunbeam*.

The *Sunbeam* was one of those large schooners, in this case three-masted, built in both Britain and the United States in the last decades of the nineteenth and the early years of the twentieth centuries. She was specifically designed for recreational cruising, in antithesis to the ever more extreme yachts designed for the great regattas.

The *Sunbeam's* lines were the work of St. Claire Byrne, a British designer specializing in this kind of sailing vessel. She boasted an overall length of 175 feet 6 inches, a beam of 27 feet 4 inches and a draught of 13 feet 2 inches. Rated at 530 tons, she carried almost 10,000 square feet of canvas, a sail area that was subsequently reduced to 8,000 square feet.

This yacht had a teak over steel hull, a structural characteristic typical of the contemporary British boatyards (the Americans instead preferred all-steel hulls, not having those sources of tropical hardwoods, teak and mahogany above all, provided by the British colonies).

Various schooners of this type were built in Britain with St. Claire Byrne also designing the *Margaret* (400 tons), the *Gitana* (500 tons) and the *Saint George* (830 tons), while Nicholson designed and built the *Chazalie* (545 tons) and the *Czarina* (565 tons). These were just a few examples and all were built between 1875 and 1890!

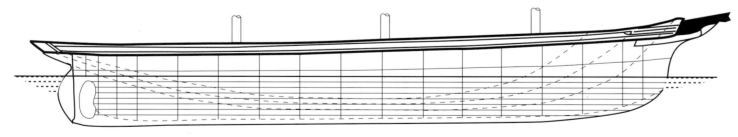

89 top The great sailing voyages, beyond the coastal waters and across the oceans, were heralded by the exploits of the yacht Union *that a group of four young Americans sailed around the globe in four years, departing from and returning to Newport. The* Union *was*

an old yacht, of the type we are accustomed to seeing racing on the Thames with the Cumberland Fleet: the free mainsail, the short peak, the curling foam at the prow revealing the voluminous lines of the hull that only with America in 1851 were to be called into question.

89 bottom The design of the Sunbeam *was certainly not that of a racing yacht. It did, however have one innovative feature, that of the well for a propeller, just in front of the rudder stock. Up until the mid-nineteenth century yachts were sailing yachts*

and nothing but. Many British clubs actually black-balled any prospective member whose boat was fitted with an engine. Many yachts similar to the Sunbeam *were built, extremely efficient on long cruises but also able to hold their own in ocean racing.*

CORINTHIANS

90 top and center The British army
captain John McGregor, having retired
from his military career, became one of
the earliest exponents of the nascent
practice of single-handed sailing. In the
second half of the nineteenth century he
was still a highly unusual figure. The
yacht with which he undertook his epic
voyages was equally unusual: a small
15-foot Eskimo kayak-style canoe
equipped with a single mast, a fore-and-
aft spanker and a jib.

The nineteenth century is seen as the century
of the great yachts, whether they were designed
for racing or, as we have described, for cruising.
Alongside this important movement, however,
there flourished a strictly amateur trend
privileging personal, romantic and somewhat
eccentric adventure. This attitude is well
represented by a quintessential British figure,
John "Rob Roy" McGregor. His early passion
was for Indian canoes and Eskimo kayaks and he
founded the Canoe Club in London for similarly
minded gentlemen, which soon found emulators
in the United States where the first American
club reserved exclusively for active owner-
sailors, the Seawanhaka Corinthian Yacht Club,
was founded. It is worth pointing out here that
the nineteenth-century yachtsman, whether he

R.Y.S., was offered the opportunity to "take the
helm" by the captain of his yacht Dryad. He
dryly replied that he "never took anything
between meals, thank you."

The enthusiasts, the "Corinthians", were
instead only too happy to take the helm and were
unwilling to allow "professional" sailors on their
boats. McGregor's initial enthusiasm for canoes
passed as he went on to develop a type of yacht
that would allow him to sail easily without the
help of a professional crew, a sailing canoe that
was sea-worthy and large enough to carry
provisions for two people for lengthy voyages. In
1870, he undertook the first of his adventures
aboard the Rob Roy, as he named the small 21-
foot sailing canoe that was to carry him
throughout the European seas from the Baltic to
the Mediterranean and even into the Red Sea.

McGregor was emulated by one Captain Voss
who completed long voyages aboard his sail-
driven Indian canoe, analyzing the foul weather
performance of a sea anchor and oil sacks; by
Frank Cowper who circumnavigated the British
Isles and explored the Channel coasts single-
handed, leaving us with enchanting accounts of
his experiences; by a certain McMullen who
sailed up and down the Channel aboard a heavy
lugre of French origins, with his wife aboard but
doing all the sailing himself.

Out of McGregor's experience came various
single-handed cruising yachts that could be
handled by a lone sailor. The Haze was one of the
first single-handers, just 18 feet long, rigged as a
yawl and featuring leeboards. The helmsman
could sail the boat from the cockpit while below
decks was all that served for life on board, a
bunk, a galley and a head. The boat was designed
for his own use by Linton Hope, a racing yacht
designer. The Aere Perennius, a Swedish design and
winner of a competition for single-handed
cruisers, was a more practical vessel in terms of
dimensions and her sloop rig. She featured a
central cockpit from which all sailing operations
could be completed, including the raising of the
anchor and the pumping of the bilges. As
designed the boat was 30 feet long and had a
displacement of 4 tons, although I do not know if
she was actually built. Cruising yachts frequently
replicated working boats. It could be said that the
same is true of racing yachts, but this is not quite
true as in this case the typical features of working
boats were developed for racing, while the
cruising "replica" was to all intents and purposes a
working boat with few modifications. The ease-
of-handling characteristic of a good working boat

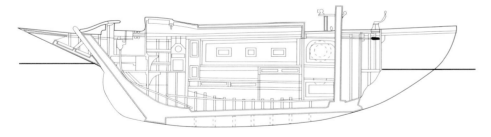

90 bottom Designers became aware of the
new trends: there was a need to design
yachts that could be handled not only by a
reduced crew but also by enthusiasts who
were not the professional seafarers who had
up until then monopolized the actual sailing
of yachts. Smaller yachts were created, and
rigs and deck layouts were conceived that
could be managed by a single man. Aere
Perennius, which as far as I know was
never actually built, represents this new
school of thought.

was aristocratic or just merely wealthy, treated
his boat with a certain detachment: this principle
is well illustrated in D. Bayes' portrait of the
owner of the Cambria and the Livonia, both
America's Cup challengers, Lord Ashbury,
aboard this second yacht. He is dressed in
jacket, waistcoat and tie, with impeccable white
spats above his shoes and is shown in a relaxed
pose at the stern of the yacht, with a telescope
on his arm and a tray of fruit, a silver claret jug, a
glass and a newspaper alongside him.

Equally indicative is the reported episode
when Lord Cardigan, a member of the exclusive

was, in fact, of vital importance to cruising yachts sailed with skeleton crews or even single-handed.

Moreover, the racing yacht was born out of the comparison of performance against a similar rival and thus evolved, while the cruising yacht "simply" had to satisfy its owner—no mean achievement—in a closed man-boat relationship.

Among the classic cruising yachts of the nineteenth century, the pilot cutter was the most common (they are still sailing today, especially off northern France and the British coasts). Thanks to its sea-worthiness the Bristol cutter was considered to be one of the very best of the breed. When working, these boats would quickly set sail in any weather to carry a pilot out to the ships that needed to be guided into port. They would then usually be sailed home by a single crewman.

Another classic type of cruising yacht much appreciated by those who had little interest in competitive sailing was the Colin Archer, also known as the "canoe" or "Norwegian" stern or the "double-ender." These vessels in fact derived from the Norwegian Viking boats from the first millennium that had sterns as finely tapered as the bows with no transom.

The original boat to which enthusiasts of this type, undoubtedly a sea-worthy design but no more so than others, is the Norwegian *reduings-skoite*, the rescue boat designed in 1892 by Colin Archer. Herein lies a fundamental

misunderstanding. The Norwegian rescue boat was specifically designed to aid the fishing fleets that rowed out of the fjords to fish in the open sea. In the case of strong winds the Colin Archer would tow them home. The boat therefore had to be heavy (like any other kind of tug) and needed to be able to cope with heavy seas while stationary, conditions in which a tapering stern is helpful. Once under sail, however, with the headway generated by the wind, the stern tends to dip, just like a tapering prow. The Colin Archer is an excellent boat for the task for which it was designed, but a Bristol cutter is the better cruiser. Significantly, this type of hull has never been particularly popular outside Norway, except as a rescue boat.

91 top The canoe stern has been aesthetically successful in very few yachts. Its origins lie the rescue boat, a type of vessel in which aesthetics were of no account (the British cutter was also derived from a type of boat, that of the pilots, that paid little attention to aesthetics, but in this the result was almost always of extreme elegance). Perhaps as a result of this origin, despite the fact that the concept of safety has frequently been interpreted in myopic fashion by the nautical community, the canoe stern, or Colin Archer, attracted a number of enthusiasts, especially among those who decided to sail single-handed.

91 bottom With the advent of the "Corinthians", owner-skippers, who came to sailing with a passion for the sport, a second era drew to a close: in the first the yachts had been owned by crowned heads of state and members of the royal families, *then came the great industrial and financial magnates whereas now it was the true sportsmen who took the helm. Lord Ashbury had owned firstly Cambria and then Livonia and had challenged the Americans for* *the America's Cup with both, and with both, he had cruised extensively and had even taken part in the parade marking the inauguration of the Suez Canal, but the hand on the wheel was never his.*

SINGLE-HANDED VOYAGERS

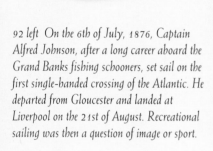

At the end of the nineteenth century, while large yachts were crossing the Atlantic from West to East and from East to West, with large, professional crews in the service of wealthy businessmen, expensive equipment and luxurious internal fittings, smaller boats had already been sailing in the same waters for some time. At the helm were solitary seamen whose spirit of adventure had led them out to the high seas.

The first single-handed Atlantic crossing was made in 1786 when Captain Josiah Shackford set sail from Bordeaux in France, heading for Dutch Guyana on the other side of the ocean. In truth, he did not set out with the intention of making the crossing alone, but lost his companion overboard mid-voyage.

Joshua Slocum was born in Nova Scotia in 1844 and had commanded and sailed ships throughout the seven seas before a friend mentioned a small sloop lying abandoned at Fairhaven, near New Bedford. Slocum went to Fairhaven hoping for a ship with which to revive his career. That the *Spray* as the sloop was named was semi-derelict was interpreted by Slocum as a sign of destiny; he took the boat to Boston where he had it rebuilt. There is a degree of resignation and fatalism in the words with which Joshua Slocum describes, in *Sailing Alone Around the World*, his departure from Boston on a voyage that was to last three years: "I had decided to sail around the world and, as on the morning of the 24th of April, 1895, the wind

92 left On the 6th of July, 1876, Captain Alfred Johnson, after a long career aboard the Grand Banks fishing schooners, set sail on the first single-handed crossing of the Atlantic. He departed from Gloucester and landed at Liverpool on the 21st of August. Recreational sailing was then a question of image or sport.

92 right Captain Johnson, a native of Denmark, acknowledged a great debt to his adopted homeland, the United States which had welcomed him as an immigrant and offered him good opportunities for work. He therefore dedicated his enterprise to the American nation, casting off in the year of the first centenary of its foundation and naming his boat Centennial, *a dory, the type of boat used for sea fishing after the schooners had dropped anchor.*

93 top right The first single-handed circumnavigation of the globe was completed at the end of the nineteenth century by Captain Joshua Slocum. An American, like all the pioneering solo sailors, Slocum had long sailed the seven seas at the command of sailing ships in search of loads to transport. The loss of his ship and, in the same period, that of his wife, left him in a state of deep depression that only the solitude of the open sea was able to alleviate. He was 51 years old when he set out on his epic voyage, an age, especially in that era, at which the spirit of adventure was generally appeased.

Officially, the first single-handed Atlantic crossing was made by the American Alfred Johnson, in part because Shackford's motivations were obscure while Johnson's were crystal clear: a spirit of adventure and a love of his homeland, the independence centennial of which he wished to celebrate in this manner. His crossing took 46 days aboard his 21-foot boat *Centennial*. The following year it was the turn of William Andreus with the *Nautilus*, and Captain Thomas Crapo aboard the *New Bedford*.

Like Johnson, both Andreus and Crapo, and indeed Shackford, were Americans, and single-handed sailing, pervaded by a typically "Yankee" sense of adventure, initiative and presumption, was for a time an American prerogative. Yet another citizen of the USA, Captain Joshua Slocum, undertook his own solitary voyage at the advanced age of 51, after two tragic events that had marked his life, the loss of his wife and his ship.

was favorable, I weighed anchor at midday, set sail and departed from Boston."

He was to return to Newport on the 27th of June, 1898, after having completed the first single-handed circumnavigation of the globe. The *Spray* was a typical New York sloop, a sailing boat built for fishing that was to have a profound influence on the design of American yachts. She was 37 feet 6 inches long overall, with a beam of 14 feet and a shallow draught. Apparently fragile and ill-suited to blue-water cruising, in her favor was the fact that she was extremely well balanced and once the sails were well trimmed would keep to her course without further adjustment, a factor of crucial importance to the lone yachtsman. This was further proof that the narrow-and-deep and broad-and-shallow concepts were less important than the distribution of volumes along the hull. Where the wind is concerned, anything goes except extremism.

93 center Joshua Slocum left the port of Boston on the 24th of April, 1895. He was to return to the United States three years later, on the 27th of June, 1898, at Newport, Rhode Island, after having crossed all the oceans. From Boston he headed to Gibraltar, and from there he sailed to South America, calling at Pernabuco, Rio de Janeiro and Montevideo. He then crossed the Strait of Magellan from East to West and traversed the Pacific, stopping at the Chilean archipelago of Juan Ferdnandez, the Samoan islands and Australia, from where he sailed directly to Cape Town. He crossed the Atlantic heading northwards and taking in St. Helena, Ascension, Grenada and Antigua before finally dropping anchor at Newport.

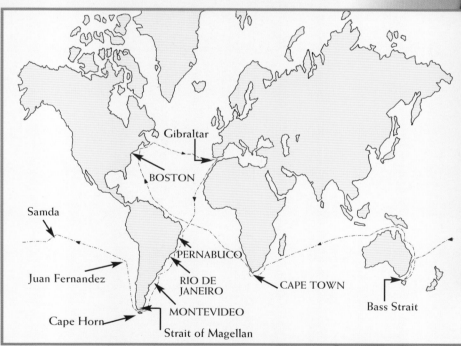

93 bottom The Spray, the yacht with which Joshua Slocum completed his circumnavigation, would hardly appear to be the most appropriate vessel in terms of her size, hull shape and rig for such a voyage. She was in fact a typical sloop from the bays of the Atlantic coast of the United States, a type of boat generally used for fishing. She had a good carrying capacity, a shallow draught and plenty of canvas. There was only one feature, albeit one of a certain weight, that favoured single-handed ocean sailing: the Spray held an extremely stable course under sail. The single-handed sailor could thus leave the tiller in order to tend to the sails at the mast or the prow without the yacht putting or luffing up.

THE GREAT THEORETICIANS

The science of naval architecture is generally conservative; still today if you ask any of the leading boatyards for anything out of the ordinary the most likely reply will be "can't be done." This is something I have heard all too often in thirty years' activity as a yacht designer.

In order to overcome this entrenched way of thinking there needed to be a concatenation of factors including a favorable economy, political stability and technological progress. In the second half of the nineteenth century, and in particular in the 1870s, such a concatenation occurred.

Four major nations, in particular the United Kingdom and the United States, but also France and Germany, were enjoying strong economic expansion, had a solid political structure and were witnessing remarkable scientific developments.

During this period yachts, which can be seen as a kind of socio-economic barometer, increased in number in the US from 400 to almost 700 in just three years, while at the same time in Britain the fleet of yachts of over 40 feet in length accounted for a combined 90,000 tons.

In those years, the diatribe between the supporters of the cutter and those of the sloop, between the deep-and-narrow and broad-and-shallow schools of thought was coming to a head. The 16-foot *Madge*, a typical small British cutter designed and constructed in 1879 by Watson in Scotland, was to win all the races staged in America against the American sloops, although this triumph should be seen in the context of the fact that the Madge was new, in perfect condition and equipped with lead ballast while the American boats were generally older, in relatively poor condition and frequently still carried stone ballast. Only *Shadow* managed to beat *Madge* once, but this was a Herreshoff design and an early signal of the innovations to come.

The dual tragedies of the *Mohawk* and the *Oona* helped stimulate technical thinking in a field that was ripe for development, due to the general conditions of the two countries concerned as well as certain old fashioned concepts that undoubtedly derived more from the deep, rough seas of Great Britain and the shallow, sheltered bays of New England than from scientific theories.

It is true that the British continued to be more conservative, indubitably as a consequence of having more deeply rooted traditions (they had, after all, been constructing and sailing yachts since the seventeenth century while their American cousins came to the sport a century later). Despite a series of defeats that began in 1851 with the schooner *America* and continued into the next two decades with 23 losses against

13 wins in head-to-head races, the British still came to the line in 1885 and 1886 with traditional narrow-and-deep cutters, the *Genesta* and the *Galatea*, that boasted club-like interior fittings (the *Galatea* had leopard skins, porcelain vases, fireplaces and raced with the wife of the owner and three dogs aboard). The British cutters were soundly beaten by the *Puritan* and the *Mayflower*, designs by the already innovative Edward Burgess. An American willing to work with the positive aspects of the two extremes, Edward Burgess was the first designer to recognize a need for change to put forward compromise solutions. He was, moreover, the first in the US to introduce engineering methodology to yacht design, the methodology on which Nat Herreshoff's genius was to be based.

The British response came from G. L. Watson, an engineer by trade and nature. Earlier still, in France in 1875, J. A. Normand had

designed and constructed the *Velox* (originally named the *Zemajtej* and mentioned earlier), a yacht that was without doubt more "scientific" than traditional. In order to gain a foothold in the yachting world, the revolutionary "scientific" approach inevitably required the development of a sound theoretical basis. As early as the eighteenth century, studies and research in the field of hydrodynamics had been conducted. The first great theoretician was probably Frederik Henrik af Chapman, a British naval architect in the service of the Swedish royal family who published the monumental *Architettura Navalis Morcatoria* in 1786. Chapman was the first to test models in a kind of prehistoric towing tank. However, these experiments did not result in any formal theories but rather a series of designs that actually replicated what had gone before.

Robert Livingstone Stevens, the designer of the revolutionary *Onkaye* and *Maria* also tested various models in a tank before defining the lines there was one kind of resistance at high speed whilst at low speed it was only the friction against the internal surface of the pipe that slowed the motion of the water. He therefore posited the theory of friction without which the intuitions of his predecessors, from Chapman to R. L. Stevens, Scott Russell and Beaufoy, could not be proved. However, it was not until 1874 (in that crucial decade), that another British hydraulic engineer, William Froude, developed something fundamental to hull design, the law of similitude. Froude, who had built a large towing tank 295 feet in length, 36 feet wide and almost 10 feet deep, the first true tank for testing model ships, identified the formula for scaling up the speed of a model to that of a full-size ship, and therefore the resistance of the model to that of the real vessel.

The law of similitude and Froude's Number became cornerstones of naval architecture, and therefore of yacht design, up until the advent of computers, which all but did away with towing tanks.

Other great theoreticians established their reputations in the second half of the nineteenth century, including Vanderdecken, the pseudonym of William Cooper. In reality he was a leading journalist who described in his 1873 book *Yachts and Yachting* different types of hulls, trying to interpret the performance characteristics of each (he also proposed a kind of hull with lines designed to take advantage of loopholes in the ratings rules that measured length from the stempost to the rudder axis by

94 and 95 Up to the advent of the "great theorists", yachts replicated the shapes and rigs of working boats while their fittings reflected the owner's terrestrial tastes. Performance was sought-after but there was no scientific study and it occurred to no one that foregoing paintings, furnishings and decorations might improve it. The British boat Galatea was to challenge for the America's Cup, but her owner never considered sacrificing her fine decor.

of his first yacht. In Britain a certain Scott Russell also tried to identify the influence of a the passage of water on a hull by hanging small colored spheres from a model. He noted that the passage of a body with a voluminous bow provoked a violent movement of the spheres, whilst tapering lines had a gentler effect with the spheres remaining attached to the model hull. Then there was Colonel Beaufoy, who towed a flat plate through the water (he never tested models of yachts or ships, only geometric solids) and intuited another resistance to forward motion, that of friction, as well as the effect of wave formation.

If Chapman is to be granted the honor of being the first great theoretician given the age in which he worked, the second was a Scotsman, W. MacQuorn of Glasgow. MacQuorn was an hydraulic engineer who in 1865 conducted experiments into the motion of fluids by running water through pipes (this was, in fact, his area of interest rather than yachts), demonstrating that

setting the rudder as far forwards as possible). In this respect, the Jullanar design by Bentall was of greater importance and was actually built. The rating question meant that the helm was set forwards while the hull had a cylindrical body and external ballast to reduce the wetted area.

Colin Archer, a naval architect of Norwegian residence but British birth, developed a type of hull later named after him and in 1877 theorized, with no scientific or experimental proof, that the problem of resistance should be considered in relation to the volumes rather than the lines. He was correct, at least in part. Lastly, there was Dixon Kemp, the secretary of the Yacht Racing Association of 1867, who made careful studies of hull shape and turned his hand, albeit without success, to yacht design.

Worthy of separate mention was Philip Marrett, who in 1850 wrote a booklet titled *Yacht Building* in which he explained his theories for the calculation and design of hulls without

recourse to three-dimensional models. These theories were put into practice for the first time by the American Cary Smith, the designer of the *Vindex* in 1870, a yacht that earned a place in the history books for this reason alone (although it was also the first iron hull built in the US but preceded by the British Mosquito from 1848). Until 1870, the start of the magical decade, yachts, like ships, were built from models, or rather a half-model of the hull. The designer would "sculpt" the shape following his instincts, using his eye and sense of touch to confer a certain form and line to the hull. Thus was born George Steers' *America* and this was how William Fife went about designing. The traditional system worked, but Marrett's method of drawing on paper was decidedly more scientific and guaranteed a certain result, irrespective of the genius of the designer even though the latter could continue to play the key role in the creation of a yacht.

NAT HERRESHOFF

96 top *Captain Nat was 72 years old in 1920 and most of his life had been spent in his studio, at home and at the family boatyard. By that time he had already designed and constructed the defenders for no less than six editions of the America's Cup, the quays of the most important American yacht clubs were lined with dozens of yachts built to the Universal Rule, the rating system he had developed early in the century. In those years, he decided to retire after having contributed priceless chapters to the history of yachting.*

The period that succeeded the fabulous 1870s, an era stretching from 1890 to 1920, can rightly be described as the era of "the Wizard of Bristol," Nathanael Greene Herreshoff, more familiarly known as "Captain Nat."

Between 1893 and 1920, Herreshoff designed all the America's Cup defenders, five yachts for six successful regattas against the trio of the greatest British designers of all time: Watson, Fife and Charles Nicholson. He invented the "Universal Rule," patented welded steel construction and designed the first metal masts, the mainsail track and bronze fittings. He was also the first designer of fast steam yachts.

Nat Herreshoff was born at Bristol, Rhode Island, in 1848 and immediately joined the boatyard founded at Bristol by his brother under the name "Herreshoff Manufacturing Company." Under his direction it was to become the world's largest boatyard and also the most modern, equipped with a slipway that descended directly from the construction shed; this in an era where yachts were usually built on an open beach.

Initially the young designer and his yard produced above all motor launches for the navies of America, Britain, France and other countries, occasionally branching out with large steam yachts.

It was the summer of 1891 when the *Gloriana* slipped into the water. This has to be considered one of the first modern racing yachts. There were no concessions to cruising, only a steel structure and double planking in pine to save weight and

96 bottom *When Gloriana was launched in 1891, she announced that the division between the typically British deep and narrow design and the contrasting American broad and shallow approach had been bridged. Gloriana was in fact wide enough to ensure stability of form, but carried a great deal of ballast, 60% of*

her total displacement, in a deep and narrow keel. The form of this ballasted keel heralded in fact what was to become a trend of the immediate future; the fin keel, a hull design in which the keel no longer traced an extended straight line from stem to stern, but was only long enough to carry the required ballast.

97 top left *The Bristol yard that produced the yachts designed by Nat Herreshoff, built under cover on slipways capable of being adapted to suit the new hull shapes specified by the designer. Until then hulls had conformed to the demands of the yards, with the long keel inclined with respects to the horizontal plane being*

a result of this. This "modernity" takes nothing away from the traditional appeal of the launch, the moment of the first encounter between a yacht and its natural element, the sea. In this photo from 1903, Reliance, an America's Cup defender and one of Herreshoff's most significant designs, can be seen.

enable 60% of the displacement to take the form of very short ballast set low down. Thanks in part to efficient stability of form, *Gloriana* carried more canvas than the other boats and as soon she began to heel her very pronounced overhangs at both stem and stern (45 feet 6 inches at the waterline, she had an overall length of over 70 feet!) dipped and increased buoyancy. As a consequence, in light winds and therefore at low speeds, the yacht had a very small wetted area but as the breeze rose the *Gloriana* would settle in the water, increasing the critical speed. Moreover, her overhangs served to provide

thrust at either end when sailing in a swell, dampening the pitching that has an adverse effect on the performance of a yacht. The *Gloriana* had stability of form but had the draught of a British cutter: this "compromise" won seven races out of seven in August, 1891. Three months later the Bristol yard launched the *Dilemma*, the world's first fin keel yacht.

Up until then, the hull of a yacht had been conceived in terms of performing three simultaneous functions: supporting the weight of the boat with a corresponding volume, countering leeway (the tendency to drift

97 bottom left Alpha *was built in 1892: the first modern centerboard yacht, a racing yacht or coastal day cruising, a form that was to become particularly common throughout the world after the Second World War. Yachts with centerboards had been constructed since the late eighteenth century, while the American coasts had already seen boats whose stability was entrusted to the weight of their crews. Both of these types were, however, constructed in response to external demands.* Alpha, *on the other hand, was specifically designed as a high performance, technologically advanced yacht.*

downwind) with a keel and balancing the heel induced by the wind on the sails with ballast.

All this was to be achieved with a single form. Herreshoff created an ideal hull, with a minimal wetted area and thus minimal friction, with the sole purpose of providing buoyancy. He then provided a sheet of steel to counter heeling and hung a torpedo-shaped bulb in lead from this as low as possible to act as ballast. Moreover, the *Dilemma* had the maximum permitted length at the waterline of 25 feet, but this increased enormously as the yacht heeled (the *Gloriana* effect). It goes without saying the *Dilemma* carried all before her, and became a model for yachts throughout the world; the fin-keel was here to stay.

The following year, 1892, it was the turn of the *Alpha*, the first centerboard yacht. A boat that carried no ballast, fairly wide and extremely light with a centerboard to counter heel and the crew hanging overboard to act as ballast whenever necessary. These three remarkable inventions in this three-year period were to influence yacht design for the next fifty years.

By the time the yard closed in 1946 it had launched 1,521 boats during a seventy-year period that spanned two world wars. Nat Herreshoff was a formidable worker; he worked at the drawingboard at home, in the evening inspected the yard and in the morning met with the workforce to communicate specifications and constructional details, twelve hours a day, Sunday included. He also adopted a working method that was revolutionary for the time: he would begin with drawings, tracing the waterlines, the master section, the wetted area and freeboard profiles and from these constructed a half-model to check progress and then once again transferred everything to drawings. He was an engineer and had absorbed Philip Marrett's lesson, adding his own profound knowledge of structural engineering and materials. His yachts always had, in fact, structures that were very advanced from a mechanical point of view and he always used innovative and above all appropriate materials.

In the 1920s, following the death of his brother, Captain Nat, now well over seventy years old, handed over the boatyard and responsibility for the design work to his son, Francis Sidney. While an earnest disciple, the son lacked his father's genius.

97 top right Herreshoff and his yard, the Herreshoff Manufacturing Company at Bristol, produced over 1,500 boats in over seventy years. The yard was not devoted solely to sailing yachts: its early fame in fact derived from the fast boats conceived initially for the navy and *subsequently for recreational use. In the last decade of the nineteenth century, sailing yachts began to be designed and produced, both racers and cruisers that were to consolidate the reputation of the yard and, above all, of Nat Herreshoff himself.*

98 top The 1930s saw the rise of the owner-sailor: the American magnate Harold Vanderbilt successfully defended the America's Cup in the three editions disputed with the J Class yachts at the helm of his own boats, aided by their technical superiority but demonstrating notable ability in the role. This was a new figure in yachting circles, one freed from the demands of ostentation that characterized the earlier period of yachting.

98 center The most tenacious British challenger, Sir Thomas Lipton, who competed in five editions of the America's Cup with his Shamrocks, the last being a J Class. Shamrock V never had any chance of victory against Vanderbilt's "mechanical yacht," and Lipton had to abandon a dream that had accompanied him for thirty years. The stubborn English "grocer" still belonged to the world of the past, not that of aristocratic yachting, but still that of the Royal Yacht Club, and he put a professional, Captain Heard (with him in the photo), at the helm of his yacht.

98 bottom The Big Class yachts frequently found themselves competing against J Class boats and the earlier British America's Cup challengers, and with their awe-inspiring sail areas they enlivened the waters of the Solent. This photo shows Lulworth, the Big Class yacht of Mr. Weld, leading close-hauled, just to leeward of Thomas Lipton's Shamrock III. Lulworth was to beat Lipton's Shamrock V, the last of the line, in a number of trials for the America's Cup of 1930, in spite of her fore-and-aft spanker rig.

World War I involved all the nations that had been protagonists in the history of yachting for three centuries. Just nine days after the armistice of the 11th of November, however, the Sailing Committee met in London and hoped that on "the Thames or in any other place a sailing regatta would be held by the end of 1919."

Sailing was no longer a sport confined to the elite clubs and, wars permitting, by the twentieth century was destined to become part of the collective heritage, in terms of image at least if not in practice, as it could never said to be truly "popular." Up until the nineteenth century, recreational sailing had been the prerogative of aristocratic boat-owners, but with the dawn of the twentieth century, skippers, crews, designers and constructors came to the forefront and even owners began to take the helm. Vanderbilt and Lipton inaugurated the era of the "owner-driver,"

and the yachts themselves underwent a radical metamorphosis. Earlier, in the nineteenth century, there had been a simple change of use regarding working boats, but now these vessels began to be subjected to modifications. In the century of modernity, the yacht became identified as the recreational boat par excellence, acquiring a formal and substantial autonomy of design and construction, while all other craft were either ships or boats.

While at the end of the nineteenth century it had been the science of hydrodynamics that laid the basis for a scientific approach to hull design, by the twentieth century aerodynamics made a decisive contribution to a field still reliant on the inventiveness of individual geniuses, who intuited efficient forms by observing the shape of a model roughed out by hand. New materials such as Duralumin, a light alloy of aluminium

and magnesium, or special steels were available to create lighter hulls and structures capable of absorbing the stresses imposed by the first great revolution in the field of sails, the disappearance of the gaff topsail and the adoption of triangular mainsails. These new spankers were known as Bermudian or Marconi rigs because the new masts—reinforced with a system of shrouds that no longer had the sole task of keeping them upright but also of conferring form and rigidity—resembled the antennas that launched Marconi's radio messages into the ether.

At the bow appeared a large overlapping foresail, that is to say a sail of which the foot extended beyond the mast and was superimposed over the mainsail, the genoa. This sail was named after the Italian city on the waters of which it was first used. The genoa replaced with greater aerodynamic efficiency the three foresails previously carried before the masts on many yachts. The use of this new type of foresail was also to lead to the disappearance of the bowsprit. At the same time, mechanical equipment began to be introduced to facilitate the handling of the new sails. The winches used to adjust the sheets were a development of devices already used aboard eighteenth-century ships, but were also early evidence of mechanical aids being employed on yachts for the first time.

New materials, new rigs and new technology: a complete engineering-based system at the service of a new generation of yacht designers.

$\mathcal{T}$HE INTER-WAR DECADES

6

99 In the waters of the Solent, magnificent giants whose origins lay far distant in the previous century continued to race in the inter-war period: Britannia, Satanita, Meteor, Lulworth (in the photo), the "Big Class" boats. These yachts maintained a tradition that was above all British, that of the large aristocratic yacht with luxurious interiors that derived its performance from an enormous area of canvas and the numerous crew needed to handle it. Lulworth belonged to Mr. Weld, a member of a family present in the history of British yachting from the late eighteenth century.

THE BIG CLASS ERA IN BRITAIN

Testifying to British conservatism but also to the underlying technical validity of their designs, two pre-war yachts, the *Britannia* and the *Satanita*, continued to dominate the Solent regattas held immediately after the First World War. Both large cutters and launched in 1893, and were designed by Watson and Soper, respectively. Their presence on the Solent and their racing success did not, however, impede the establishment of a new name of the first order in the yachting firmament, Charles E. Nicholson.

The boatyard founded by Nicholson's father had already in the previous century launched a great number of schooners, a category of cruising yachts the son was never to disdain. However, the Thirties saw the consecration of C. E. Nicholson as a designer of racing yachts, above all meter-class boats, yachts built to the International Rule, approved by the European countries and amended early in the 1920s with contributions from Nicholson himself and others.

The Gosport yard, then on the opposite bank of the Itchen in respect to its present location, was above all responsible for the 78-foot 6-inch

Candida and the 23-meter I.R. *Astra*. Launched in 1928, *Astra* was almost 115 feet long, 19 feet 6 inches broad and carried 7,158 square feet of sail. *Candida*, which took to the water the following year, was built to practically the same design as the *Astra* but carried more canvas (7,448 square feet), thanks in part to a short bowsprit at a time when this type of rig had all but disappeared, at least on racing yachts.

Both yachts featured composite construction, with steel frames and wooden planking, a technique very much in vogue in that period, especially in Britain. They were also both used as development "hacks" in the fine-tuning of the British America's Cup challenger in 1930. Today, still in perfect condition, they sail in the Mediterranean where they replicate, with unaltered competitive zeal, the epic encounters of sixty years earlier.

101 bottom The most spectacular racing yachts of the inter-war period were the Big Class craft. Britannia, designed by Watson, is seen here with her original fore-and-aft spanker rig and leading the group. This photo, taken by Frank William Beken with the assistance of his son Alfred Keith in 1926, shortly after the start of the annual social regatta organised at Cowes by the Royal Yacht Squadron, is a remarkable image in terms of its subject matter and its technical qualities.

102-103 Charles E. Nicholson at the helm of Candida, the 23-meter International Rule yacht he designed and later converted to J Class specifications. Nicholson belonged to a dynasty of constructors that still has a boatyard at Gosport in England operating under the same name. All the

British J Class yachts, other America's Cup challengers and many of the yachts that have written the history of British yachting, came from the Nicholson yard.
Charles E. Nicholson frequently sailed aboard his creations, being a competent and enthusiastic sailor.

102 bottom Nicholson established his reputation as a designer and constructor of large cruising yachts in the late nineteenth century. Following the First World War, he found success with racing yachts designed for the America's Cup. He tackled numerous meter-class designs, for example that of Candida an International Rule 23-Meter from 1929.

103 top Nicholson was the only British designer to pen a J Class yacht, the category defined by Nat Herreshoff's Universal Rule with which the America's Cup regattas were disputed in the 1930s. The first of the series was Shamrock V designed for Sir Thomas Lipton. Shamrock V is seen here before crossing the ocean to the United States.

103 center Candida at full speed, all sails aloft (including the spinnaker) and the crew shifted towards the cockpit in order to optimise the weight distribution for this point of sailing. Candida was never a true match winner: only with the first of the two Endeavours did the British designer manage to create a yacht "to beat," unfortunately she had to compete against the race committee of the New York Yacht Club.

In that period C. E. Nicholson designed a number of 6-meter, 8-meter and above all 12-meter boats to the International Rule. Two yachts from the 12-meter class launched in 1939 are worthy of particular mention: *Evaine*, which would still be used for development work on the American defenders of the America's Cup in the post-war years (after the 1950s it was decided to race with 12-metre rather than the overly demanding J Class boats); and *Tomahawk*, unbeatable on the Solent in those last months of peace, at least until the appearance of the technologically more advanced American

12-meter, Vim. Nicholson had designed *Tomahawk* for Sir Thomas Octave Murdoch Sopwith, an heroic pilot during the war, an aircraft constructor and well known in yachting circles for his America's Cup challenges of 1934 and 1937. C. E. Nicholson was a true America's Cup protagonist, designing all the British J Class challengers. In 1920, he had designed Sir Thomas Lipton's fourth challenger, *Shamrock IV*, succeeding Fife and Watson, who had been responsible for the owner's previous three boats. In 1930, he was also responsible for the design of the last yacht, that of the fifth challenge put up by the stubborn, indomitable "grocer", *Shamrock V*.

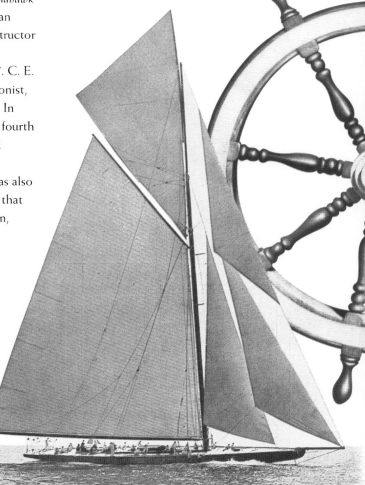

103 bottom In 1914 Nicholson designed and constructed Sir Thomas Lipton's fourth America's Cup challenger, Shamrock IV. *This was probably the British designer's masterpiece, a yacht of unusual form and very light construction but aesthetically unappealing, earning the nick-name "ugly duckling." The First*

World War confined her to a shed in Brooklyn while awaiting the opportunity to challenge Resolute *that, in the meantime, was practicing on home waters. Once the regatta got under way, Nicholson's "ugly duckling" immediately proved to be highly competitive and only a little ill luck prevented her from beating Herreshoff's defender.*

104 top The 1934 edition of the America's Cup could have been designer Charles E. Nicholson's big chance: his Shamrock IV had already come close to success and his new yacht, Endeavour had proved to be very fast during practice. However, on the eve of the regatta, the professional crew struck over demands for a 5 pounds raise. Sopwith sacked them all and took on an amateur crew, entrusting his wife with the delicate task of timing the starts.

104 bottom left The British yachts designed for the America's Cup rarely had competitive rivals against which they could be matched when fine tuning: the first Endeavour, designed by Nicholson for Tom Sopwith, is seen here racing against the old Britannia, launched thirty years earlier, a yacht that was undoubtedly a fast and efficient boat, but not an appropriate match for a racing machine such as a J Class yacht. However, Nicholson's J Class was a match for the defender and, according to many observers, actually faster.

104-105 and 105 bottom right Endeavour II, the last J Class designed by Nicholson, was not as successful as her predecessor, perhaps because she found herself up against what is universally recognised as the fastest of all the J Class

yachts, Starling Burgess' Ranger. In recompense, Endeavour II, originally designed for Tom Sopwith, is perhaps the most beautiful yacht of her class and has amply justified the attentions of her present owner, who has subjected her to a complete restoration, albeit with numerous concessions to modern developments in terms of rigging and interior fittings. Today, with the power of her hull and the immense sail area carried by her mast, Nicholson's 1937 yacht testifies to the highest expression of racing yacht design achieved seventy years ago.

Nicholson's masterpiece was, however, *Endeavour*, designed for Tom Sopwith in 1934. This was the only yacht before Australia in 1984 to be a match for the Americans in the America's Cup. The regatta was won by the representatives of the United States 3-2, but all observers agreed that the *Endeavour* was the faster boat and was only defeated due to a controversial interpretation of the racing rules. Even the American newspapers admitted as much, with one running the famous headline, "Britannia rules the waves but America waives the rules." The British designer was also responsible for Tom Sopwith's next challenger *Endeavour II* but this time met with less success because she was competing against *Ranger*, undoubtedly the greatest J Class yacht ever built and the first to benefit from truly efficient tank testing.

105 top The Camper & Nicholson yard soon achieved considerable importance, also in terms of the size of the yachts it was commissioned to build. It was no longer a craft-based enterprise with boats built directly on the beach and in the open, as was still the case with many yards in the late nineteenth century, Fife included. From the outset, the Southampton yard (which moved to Gosport after the Second World War) boasted covered slipways and efficient launch equipment. This photo shows the launch of Endeavour, the first British J Class with a steel hull.

As well as the two *Shamrocks* and the two *Endeavours*, Nicholson also designed the *Velsheda*, which never challenged for the America's Cup but was used as a development "hack." Decidedly advanced in his thinking, although never as innovative as the Americans in the design of racing hulls, meter- or J Class as they may have been, Nicholson was more conservative in the field of cruising yacht design. In the twenty-year period between the two wars, he designed innumerable yachts of this type, but all drew in one way or another on tradition. The *Patience* for example, launched in 1931, replicated the *Flame*, an attractive cutter from the early twentieth century: the same overhangs, the same straight, very elongated stern and the same short, slightly spoon-shaped prow,

and *Flame* in '33 were beaten by the same American boat, a yacht that was innovative in conpcet if not in her lines, Olin Stephens' *Dorade*. C. E. Nicholson derived three famous boats constructed in the second half of the 1930s, from the *Patience*, the *Foxhound*, the *Bloodhound* and the *Striana*, still traditional yachts with the same lines as their predecessor. These were narrow, seaworthy boats with good beating characteristics. Only on deck and in terms of the rig did one notice the changing times, with the tiller helm, more sensitive than a wheel with rack and pinion transmission, the doghouse replaced by a small rounded deckhouse, a Marconi-type rig and, finally, no bowsprit. *Bloodhound*, in particular, continued to race with a degree of success into

ketch-rigged but retained traditional superstructures with a doghouse, a bowsprit and a generally late-nineteenth century appearance. Mylne also tackled meter-class designs, signing-off a number of 12-meter yachts that never enjoyed any significant competition success. One of his 12-meter boats, the *Veronica* from 1937, was converted to cruising and rigged as a yawl. Frederick Shepard was an even more deeply-rooted conservative. His 1930 *Lexia* was virtually a copy of one of his own designs from the beginning of the century. Shepard built cruising yachts and saw no need to experiment with new features to gain an extra half a knot in maximum speed or a few degrees when sailing close to the wind at the expense of owners whose only desire was to sail in comfort and safety.

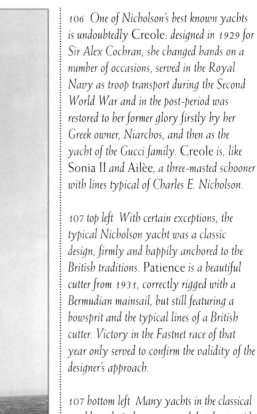

106 One of Nicholson's best known yachts is undoubtedly Creole: designed in 1929 for Sir Alex Cochran, she changed hands on a number of occasions, served in the Royal Navy as troop transport during the Second World War and in the post-period was restored to her former glory firstly by her Greek owner, Niarchos, and then as the yacht of the Gucci family. Creole is, like Sonia II and Ailèe, a three-masted schooner with lines typical of Charles E. Nicholson.

107 top left With certain exceptions, the typical Nicholson yacht was a classic design, firmly and happily anchored to the British traditions. Patience is a beautiful cutter from 1931, correctly rigged with a Bermudian mainsail, but still featuring a bowsprit and the typical lines of a British cutter. Victory in the Fastnet race of that year only served to confirm the validity of the designer's approach.

107 bottom left Many yachts in the classical mould—relatively narrow and deep boats with excellent sea-going qualities capable of providing comfortable cruising and respectable performance in the many races organized around the British coastline—were still being built in Britain in the Thirties. Thendara is a fine representative of the species and was designed by Alfred Mylne in 1935.

107 right The spread of events reserved for classic boats has brought many yachts of the past back to the sea: today we are able to admire some of the great designs that have marked the history of yachting, and a number of owners and many sailors and simple enthusiasts have enjoyed a sailing experience denied to modern yachtsmen in which the relationship with the rig is more direct and the materials of the hull have more character. Creole today sails with her original lines and sail plan as designed by Charles E. Nicholson in 1929.

the same very slim lines. The internal partitioning was also shared with a small doghouse almost amidships from which one descended to reach the aft stateroom and the forward saloon. The rig was instead different, the *Flame* being rigged as a yawl with fore-and-aft spanker, the *Patience* as a cutter with a Bermudian mainsail. She did, however, retain a bowsprit, a feature that at the time was already in decline.

C. E. Nicholson was conservative because the results he achieved gave him no reason to change, at least in the field of ocean racing where boats designed exclusively as racers tended find themselves in difficulty. *Patience* won the Fastnet the year she was launched, while the *Flame*, despite her age, actually won it in 1933 after having been re-rigged as a Marconi cutter. The British cutter derived from the Bristol pilot boats was still proving its worth! It has to be said, however, with regards to that period, that ocean racing tended to reward the ability of the crew and the seakindliness of the boats rather than pure hull speed and, in any case, on compensated time both *Patience* in 1931

the post-war period and as late as the 1960s. Through the inter-war years, the designer and his yard continued to design and construct large cruising schooners. The 187-foot *Ailée* was launched in 1928 for the French yachtswoman Virginie Hériot, the 190-foot *Creole* in 1929 for Sir Alex Cochran and the 180-foot 6-inch *Sonia II* for Miss Betty Carstairs, a pioneer of power boating. All three featured composite construction with teak planking over steel frames, and all three were rigged as three-masted schooners with Bermudan mainsails on the mizzenmast, boomed jibs and stay sails between the masts. While not particularly efficient in terms of speed, this configuration was well suited to cruising. The three schooners were, of course, all fitted with bowsprits.

Other traditionalist designers working in Britain in that period included Mylne, Shepard and Fife. Alfred Mylne was responsible above all for the design of large cruising yachts along the lines of British yachts from the end of the previous century, with only the rig being changed. The *Albyn* from 1934 and the *Thendara* from 1935 were

The transom was sharply cut and vertical while the sheer lacked the traditional saddle, which was actually inverted with a reverse curve in the bow section. The deckhouses had new shapes and details, Clark's being long and low with numerous small rectangular portholes while Giles' were just as long but with a raised section and round portholes. Both boats were rigged as cutters, with a large genoa before the mast which had to be both stiff and light. The mast was therefore hollow with a rectangular section to resist the tension of the forestay rigged from the large genoa. The racing yacht was still tied to the demands of cruising, but was beginning to seek out lightness to the detriment of this aspect. Robert Clark and Laurent Giles were the first British designers to pick up on the lead set by the pioneers on the other side of the Atlantic.

William Fife III is worthy of special mention. He was not a true conservative, as he always sought out new features and his boats rarely resembled one another except for the fact that they were all aesthetically exceptional. Having little faith in the scientific approach, he preferred to continue to design yachts of the basis of half models, but the unmistakable elegance of his designs was frequently accompanied by good performance. A particularly beautiful Fife-designed yacht from this period is the *Latifa*. I use the present tense here because the *Latifa*, launched in 1936 for M. Mason, the Commodore of the R.O.C.R. is still sailing in perfect condition. Still rigged as a yawl when this configuration had started to give way to the less elegant ketch, with a bowsprit and Marconi mainsail, she is 69 feet 8 inches long overall, 52 feet 2 inches at the waterline and 13 feet 6 inches broad. She is not one of the classic British narrow yachts, her sections at the prow being fairly full while flattening out a little towards the stern, but the overall lines have great harmony and elegance.

Fife's yachts always managed to combine the elegance of classic lines with innovative ideas. In 1922, he was the first designer to produce a 12-meter yacht to the new formula (revised in 1921), the *Vanity*, and in 1926 he was probably the first British designer to employ a Bermudian mainsail on the stunning *Halloween*, designed according to the 15-meter ratings but in reality a compromise between this type of yacht and an ocean racer.

Towards the end of the 1930s, designers began to emerge in Britain who were capable of freeing themselves of tradition and putting forward new ideas. Their boats were to become popular in the post-war period with only the outbreak of the global conflict preventing them from enjoying immediate success. Two 1937 yachts, *Ortac* and *Maid of Malham*, penned by the young designers Robert Clark and Laurent Giles, respectively, began to dominate regattas and continued to do so in the years immediately after the war. Neither had the deep sections of the classic British cutter and the keel profile was concentrated at the center of the boat. While *Ortac* retained the topsides overhangs and sheer of classic designs, *Maid of Malham* was revolutionary in this sense too.

108 top Fife designed Halloween *in 1926. This was one of the first yachts to adopt a Bermudian mainsail, that is to say lacking the gaff and gaff topsail that had always characterized the sail abaft the mast. The hull was designed with the meter classes in mind; in particular* Halloween *could have been rated as a 15-meter boat. She had all the elegance of the Fife yachts and was extremely efficient: I have had the opportunity of seeing her at a number of classic boat regattas and she has always impressed me with her speed.*

108 center It is difficult to select a yacht that is representative of the Fife output as a whole, but Latifa *is generally considered to be typical of the Fairlie designer's work. A yawl of around 69 feet in length designed in 1936, she is rigged with Bermudian mainsails, has a small bowsprit and features a characteristic canoe stern that Fife adopted, for this design only, as an aesthetic solution to the stern overhang. An extremely elegant yacht, there is more to* Latifa *than fine lines: it is frequently said that a good boat is a beautiful boat and this is quite true in the case of* Latifa. *The fact is demonstrated in this photo where she is shown close-hauled and even more so by her long career composed of voyages throughout the world which began with her first owner, the Commodore of the R.O.R.C., Mr. Michael Mason, and continues today with her present Italian owner.*

108 bottom New directions in yacht design were sought out in the late Thirties, even in conservative Britain. Certain designers and yachts marked this new trend: Robert Clark designed Ortac, a match winner in the seasons following 1937 and in the post-war period, despite having very little in common with traditional British hulls, of which she retained only the formal elegance of the topsides.

108-109 The large schooner was by no means an exclusively American prerogative: Camper & Nicholson constructed numerous examples between the nineteenth and twentieth centuries and William Fife designed one that is still sailing, perfectly restored, today. Like all the Scotsman's designs she is, above all

beautiful, but also boasts excellent sailing qualities. Altair is a yacht with an overall length of around 130 feet, designed and constructed at Fife's Fairlie yard in 1931.

109 bottom The grandfather of the Fife dynasty, William, began by designing and constructing, at the time one and same thing, working boats. The father, another William, continued the activity and built the first small yachts on the slipways of the family boatyard, in reality a shed on the beach at Fairlie on the Firth of Clyde in Scotland. Lastly, William Fife III, after having learnt the art of yacht design from Watson, conquered the fame and honors still recognized today. There was a fourth, the son of a sister, but he was no Fife, in name or talent, and the dynasty was extinguished

yacht

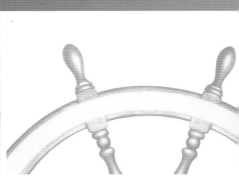

Recreational sailing in the United States was dominated by the America's Cup exploits of the J Class boats, the pure racing yachts built to the Universal Rule, developed by Nat Herreshoff early in the twentieth century, that represented veritable floating laboratories for materials and equipment.

The J Class apart, American sailing in the period between the two wars was actually characterized by a degree of inventive stasis.

Just as in Great Britain the cutter form had already been perfected, and was thus never questioned, in America, Herreshoff alone had over the preceding thirty years defined the perfect racing and cruising yachts.

The first in six successful defences of the America's Cup, and the second by starting out with the nineteenth fishing schooner and honing its lines and rig from 1900 onwards.

Moreover, as we have already seen, Herreshoff contributed to the regulation of racing classes with the Universal Rule, created the New York single-class cruising racers of 30, 50 and 70 feet and had developed the open centerboard yacht as a sporting craft designed for pure fun. In short, he had set in place all that was necessary and sufficient for the American yachtsman.

It was only logical, therefore, that the period between the 1920s and 1940s, straddling the Great Depression which had social consequences in the United States even greater than those of the two World Wars, was for the American designers a period of reflection rather than innovative research.

The great names of yacht design in this period were thus associated with consolidated type forms. In the 1920s and 1930s, John Alden designed numerous schooners, deriving both the lines of their hulls and their rigs from the countless similar boats penned by Herreshoff earlier that century.

110 top left If Herreshoff characterized the first two decades of the century, American sailing in the inter-war period was marked by the yachts of John Alden. A versatile but above all fertile designer, he penned a great number of schooners to the point where his name was used to define the type. Malabar IV, owned by the designer himself, was in a sense the prototype of the "Alden schooner:" she won a Bermuda Race and was also a leading Fastnet contender in that period.

110 top right In 1927, a schooner designed by John Alden gave rise to one of the most hard-fought editions of the Fastnet in the history of the race; after six days of tempestuous weather, just two boats crossed the finishing line separated by less than an hour. The British Tally Ho, a classic cutter and the American La Goleta, an Alden design rigged as a schooner. La Goleta, like Malabar IV, was a traditional yacht and drew on the classic fisherman boats of the Atlantic coast of the United States that John Alden successfully raised to the status of yacht.

THE UNITED STATES OF AMERICA: FROM THE LARGE SCHOONERS TO THE MODERN YACHT

110 bottom For Alden the large yacht should be schooner-rigged. Puritan is perhaps the American designer's most famous yacht: around 100 feet long overall with a centerboard in the best East Coast traditions and a steel hull with riveted plates by the Electrical Boat Co., a yard specializing in military vessels, submarines in particular. This was a medium-sized cruising yacht for that era,

and not only in America. Her 100 feet appeared to be an ideal compromise between the comfort they offered aboard and the difficulty in handling associated with the size of the boat. The schooner rig is undoubtedly favorable with regards to this last aspect, even though it lacks some of the efficiency and above all elegance of the ketch rig.

111 Like Puritan, Lelantina too is still sailing today in the Mediterranean, a beautiful reminder of the American schooner derived from the traditional nineteenth-century models. These are yachts of traditional appearance, deriving from the rig rather than from the lines of the hull that has all the power and agility of modern yachts. Lelantina is smaller than Puritan

with an overall length of just 82 feet and was built in 1937 by a European yard that had in that period been discovered by the American designers and was respected for the quality of its work in steel: Abeking and Rasmussen in Germany. Lelantina is a "heavy" yacht at almost seventy tons and her 4,300 square feet of canvas are all required to get her up to speed, even in a fresh breeze.

In 1923, three schooners designed by Alden lined up for the start of the Bermuda Race alongside numerous other boats of all kinds. Alden's designs had no innovative features if not their size, all three being under 65 feet in overall length. All three finished the race in the first five positions, with *Malabar IV,* owned by the Boston designer himself, coming home first. That type of yacht became known as the "Alden schooner" and others he designed took part in the successive editions of the Fastnet, *Primrose* finishing second in 1926 and *La Goletta* emulating her feat the following year.

All these races had been characterized by very strong winds and extreme conditions in which that type of rig with the total area of canvas divided amongst a number of small sails evidently enjoyed a significant advantage. John Alden kept faith with the schooner rig even when he was commissioned to design larger yachts.

In 1931, he was responsible for the design of the *Puritan,* 101 feet 6 inches long overall with an all-steel hull and a centerboard, built by the Electric Boat Company, a yard specializing in military vessels. Another famous schooner by Alden dates from 1937, the 82-foot *Lelantina* built by Abeking & Rasmussen in Germany. I mention these two yachts because they are both still sailing in perfect condition. They participate in all the most important European classic boat events where they testify to a genre of yachts that was typical of the American coasts for over 100 years.

John Alden first came to fame, however, with the *Svaap,* a small 32-foot ketch designed in 1925 that, three years later, set sail on a circumnavigation of the globe. William A. Robinson was at the helm and recounted his voyage in the book *Deep Water and Shoals.*

112-113 Royono is one of Alden's most beautiful yachts, a 72-foot yawl built in 1936 by the Herreshoff yard at Bristol. With Royono and Karenita, to cite two yachts that are well known because both are still sailing, the American designer can be compared with Fife in that he seems to privilege beauty as the basis for the lines of his yachts. Certainly the two designers are differentiated by the traditional ratios of length and breadth, always below 5 for Alden and over 6 for the Scotsman.

113 bottom John Alden did not by any means restrict himself to the schooner rig, and while it is true that his reputation was made with this type of boat, his most beautiful designs were rigged differently and suffered from no preconceptions. Karenita is certainly more attractive than the designer's schooners and certainly more efficient at all points of sailing, except perhaps in very strong winds. She is a ketch with Bermudian mainsails and an overall length of around 75 feet built in 1929.

Another two beautiful Alden yachts that exalt the schooner form are the 75-foot 6-inch *Karenita*, a Marconi-ketch from 1929 and the *Royono*, a 68-foot 8-inch Marconi-yawl from 1926. Both are cruising yachts whose efficient rigs make them fast enough to hold their own in racing. Fortunately both have found enthusiastic owners who have kept them sailing to the present day.

Francis Herreshoff, son of the great Nat, was himself a fairly versatile designer. He established his reputation in the same fields as his father, designing yachts to the Universal Rule such as *Istalena*, an M Class from 1930 with a canoe stern

sections and even flatter at the stern with respects to *Landfall* which was built to the meter-class specifications while *Tioga II* was designed for fast sailing in free winds. The yacht enjoyed considerable success in ocean racing and, like *Landfall*, is still sailing today. *Landfall* and *Ticonderoga* are two somewhat unusual boats in terms of the American sailing scene of their day and thus of particular interest even though neither could be said to have influenced the history of yachting.

that in truth had little of the elegance of *Latifa*, designed by Fife four years earlier, but was reproposed on the J Class yacht, *Whirlwind* (the subdivision into classes according to the Universal Rule was identified with letters of the alphabet according to length at the waterline: from A to E for ketch-rigged yachts, from M to Q for other rigs). These were boats that never enjoyed particularly successful racing careers, the canoe stern deriving from their formulaic design rather than from any happy intuition or scientific concept.

The fame of Francis Herreshoff is tied above all to his glorious surname and to a book, *Sensible Cruising Design*, in which he included details and drawings of a number of his boats and which is still used today for the reconstruction of boats from that period. Among these, worthy of particular mention is the *Landfall* of 1931, a large 72-foot 2-inch ketch with Bermudian mainsails, a bowsprit and an external rudder on a large transom that cuts off the stern overhang. The *Landfall* cannot be said to be a beautiful boat with her doghouse and round portholes lacking the elegance of the contemporary *Patience*, and her rather flattened sections towards the stern and sharply tapering at the prow. She participated in the 1931 Transatlantic Race, coming home second behind *Dorade* and being classified sixth out of ten on compensated time.

Tioga II, now named the *Ticonderoga*, was built in 1935. Rigged as a ketch with the addition of a wishbone to fly a staysail (something the rating did not take into account), she is more or less the same length as *Landfall* but a very different boat: a clipper bow, a transom stern like those of the classic American schooners, more powerful in her bow

yacht

114 top left The Herreshoff family boatyard at Bristol represents the first example of an industrial yard dedicated almost exclusively to the production of recreational boats. Large brick-built sheds, covered slipways, pre-fabrication areas, fitting-out quays with derricks for the mounting of fittings and rigging. Only the height of the J Class mast in the foreground appears to down-scale the industrial complex, or perhaps it is the mast itself that is abnormally huge!

114 top center After the death of Nat, the Herreshoff Manufacturing Co. continued working under the guidance of his son, Francis. Yachts penned by the leading American designers continued to be launched from its slipways up until the post-war period. This photo shows the launch of Istalena, a Francis Herreshoff design from 1930. In full view is the canoe stern, a feature that exploits the ratings and carries the attachment of the stay running to the head of the mast well astern. A price is paid, however, in terms of the weight of this part of the hull.

114 top right The great Captain Nat left the yard and the design work in the hands of his son, Francis. In fact, the genius and fame died with the Wizard of Bristol. Francis always lacked that extra something that would take him to the heights reached by his father in terms of both inventiveness and engineering expertise. Nonetheless, he was responsible for the irreplaceable collection of his father's designs, a number of books of plans that are still being built and a number of good yachts.

114 bottom Istalena is an M Class, a yacht therefore built to the Universal Rule like the larger J Class. This was an intermediate class between the giants, the J Class and 23-Meter yachts, with lengths at the waterline of around 85 feet, and the very popular 12-meters which had lengths at the waterline of around 44 feet. The M Class had a waterline of around 54 feet, somewhere between the International Rule 15- and 19-meter boats. Like these last two classes it was never developed, neither in the United States nor in Europe.

114-115 Francis Herreshoff designed Landfall to fill any eventual loopholes in the rating system; in the case of Ticonderoga, however, he seems to have been thinking about American traditions, at least in terms of the shape of the hull. Stem and stern recall the early Alden schooners and thus the fisherman traditions. He introduced an innovation to the sail plan, however, with the addition of a wishbone staysail, a few square feet of canvas not measured in the rating.

115 bottom The original ideas of Nat Herreshoff displayed genius backed-up by in-depth technical knowledge. Those of Francis appear instead to be casual attempts to change something. Landfall, a 72-foot ketch from 1931, is a strange yacht with out of scale small boat features, such as an external rudder and an old-style dog house with atypical round portholes. She is not a particularly attractive boat and never demonstrated any particular racing qualities. She does, however, have the merit, although this can hardly be attributed to the designer, of continuing to sail and satisfy her owner today.

yacht

something of a bible not only for those who had or wanted to design or improve the rig of a boat, but also those who want to race to win; for the first time race tactics had a theoretical footing rather than being left up to the "nose" of the likes of Charlie Barr.

Davids had an assistant in his work at the Stevens Institute towing tank, one Olin Stephens, no less. The young designer discussed the new methods with Harold Vanderbilt, then still under the effect of the near-defeat of his *Rainbow* against the British America's Cup challenger *Endeavour*, an event that shook the complacent Americans to the core.

Vanderbilt thus instructed Starling Burgess, apparently meeting with little opposition, to

121 right The towing tank as a means of determining the resistance of a model ship dated back to the eighteenth century. What was missing was, on the one hand, the knowledge of the ratio necessary to interpret the difference in scale between the model and the full-size vessel (resolved in the nineteenth century by the Briton Froude), and on the other the notion of the ratio between real thrust and that to apply to the model in the tank. Davidson was to supply this last element, together with the fundamental law of the boundary layer, that "coating" of water that both the ship and the model drag with them as they move. The photos show two different tank testing sessions of the hull of Ranger.

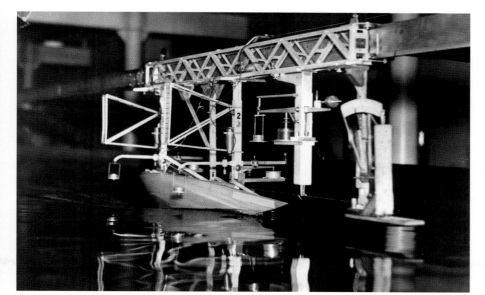

Davidson found a way of calculating the effect of the boundary layer on models and thus of rendering testing data compatible with what actually happened with a full-size hull. Moreover, Davidson also developed a system for analyzing the thrust provided by sails and the coefficients necessary to calculate the amount of force to be used to tow the models in the tank. In this work, he was helped greatly by studies being conducted in a new scientific field, that of aerodynamics.

A prophet in his own field, and thus worthy of a place in the Pantheon of great theorists, Manfred Curry was an enthusiastic and talented yachtsman (in one season he won 43 of the 45 races he started) and pioneer aerodynamicist. His book *The Aerodynamics of Sails and the Art of Winning Regattas*, published in 1925, became

take on the young Stephens with all his scientific Stevens Institute baggage when designing the next defender. The pairing came up with the *Ranger* (Burgess again taking credit for the lines), which comfortably beat *Endeavour II*.

122 top In the Thirties, Kenneth Davidson worked with the Stevens Institute of Technology, founded by Edwin Stephens, the brother of Robert and John Cox, in the late

eighteenth century at Hoboken opposite Manhattan.
The tank seen in the photo in front of Davidson was used to tow scale models of hulls.

122 bottom Olin Stephens at 29 years of age watching the launch of Ranger. In 1929, together with his brother Rod, he joined the yacht broker Mr. Sparkman in forming Sparkman & Stephens, a company that is still in existence.

118 bottom Dorade *is a yawl with an overall length of around 52 feet, pronounced overhangs, especially at the stern, and a very narrow, deep hull revealed in this photo as, now perfectly restored, she heels hard in a light breeze. While the forms may be traditional, the ratio between length and displacement is less so. We are below a ton per yard, an important figure that some years later Clark and Giles were to take up.*

118-119 and 119 top Dorade *was the most traditional yacht to have the most influence on the development of yachting; Olin Stephens designed a narrow boat, a traditional British cutter, gave her an absolutely conservative yawl rig and yet went on to win all there was to win. The reason for his success lay in his methods: the designer no longer restricted himself to conceiving a form, but followed the construction of the boat, its fine tuning and how it was raced.*

In 1901, *Shamrock II*, designed on the basis of tank testing at Glasgow, was easily beaten by Herreshoff's *Columbia* and the designer C. L. Watson was said to have declared disconsolately, "I wish Herreshoff had had a testing tank."

The "someone" who was make the scientific approach a reality was Kenneth S. M. Davidson, who worked at the Stevens Institute (founded by the Stevens family of Onkaye, Maria and the schooner America fame) and intuited that the unreliability of towing tank data was down to the fact that the model yacht did not provide a true scale replica of the "boundary layer," the sheath of water that a body carries with it when it moves through a liquid medium and which increases the weight of the body and its drag.

120 top left In the construction of the 1937 defender, considerable economic resources were invested in the design phase and in testing models in a towing tank. Vanderbilt, who financed the enterprise, as he had in the previous two editions, found himself in difficulties. It was the boatyard in Bath, Maine, that offered him a way out by constructing a hull at particularly advantageous terms. Moreover, the yard's workers excelled themselves and Ranger proved to be a perfect boat.

120 bottom left Around 70% of the displacement of a J Class, and Ranger was no exception, took the form of lead ballast, an indispensable ratio given that expanse of canvas the yachts were required to carry. Ranger weighed 166

tons, her ballast 110. In the yard at Bath, as elsewhere, the positioning of the lead casting on the slipway was an operation of particular delicacy to be performed with great care.

120-121 The launch of what was to be the best but also the last of the J Class yachts from the slipways of the Bath Iron Works. After the war the America's Cup was to be disputed by the less demanding International Rule 12-meter boats. Ranger was launched with her mast lying on the deck: it was to be rigged once the yacht was in the water, a gesture of recognition on the part of Vanderbilt to the craftsmen of the yard at Bath. A gesture that was to cost him dearly as the mast broke in two as the yacht was being towed.

122-123 *In order to rig* Ranger, *Vanderbilt cannibalized the other American J Class boats.* Yankee, Weetamoe *and* Rainbow *all sacrificed part of their rigs in favour of the latest defender. In spite of this* somewhat improvised fitting out, the superiority of Burgess' design in competition was never in doubt. For once it was undeniable that the greater speed of a yacht depended exclusively on the lines of her wetted surface, a victory for the testing tank and Kenneth Davidson. Vanderbilt is seen here at the helm with Ranger close-hauled. The wind is light but the boat has developed impressive headway. Her shape is new, with her very rounded stemhead. Any one who watched the America's 'Cup races in February 2000 between Black Magic *and* Luna Rossa *could hardly help noticing a certain similarity in the way* Ranger *and the New Zealanders' boat attacked the water.*

The design work began in 1935 (while the regatta itself was staged in 1937) and in my opinion marks the birth of modern yachting. The British cutters and American schooners could safely be consigned to the history books. Science was to guide the hand of the designers from then on rather than intuition based on the stereotypes of tradition.

From 1935, in fact, Stephens finally began to design all-new boats with precise pointers to the future and no significant ties with the past. The first truly modern design was that of *Stormy Weather*. 53 feet 8 inches long overall with a beam of 12 feet 6 inches meters, *Stormy Weather* was rigged as a yawl like *Dorade*, but was 20% broader and only 5% longer. With similar dimensions, she could hardly be classified as a deep and narrow boat, but neither was she a classic American broad and shallow design. The compromise was born not out of time-honored concepts handed down from one generation to another, but rather theoretical studies and experimentation. *Stormy Weather* was to be as successful as *Dorade* (winning the 1935 Transatlantic and Fastnet races, the Bermuda Race in '36 and so on), but above all she was a boat that while free of historical references was visibly "right" in every aspect. In 1939, another Stephens design was seen in the waters of the Solent. The 12-meter International Rule *Vim* was radically different to all the other 12-meter yachts designed by Nicholson, Anker, Fife or Giles. The hull was lighter and stiffer thanks to double longitudinal planking and could thus carry more ballast and more canvas, her lines had a new equilibrium of form, more powerful with no loss of agility and her rig was nothing short of revolutionary with a light alloy mast, aerodynamic section wire shrouds and coffee-grinder winches on deck. *Vim* had no rivals.

124 top In 1934, four years after Dorade, *Stephens designed* Stormy Weather: *this was finally a truly new boat as were the British yachts of that year,* Ortac *and* Maid of Malham. *Wider but just a little heavier per foot of length than* Dorade, Stormy Weather *was not as broad as a classic American yacht but much more so than the traditional British model. This was the compromise between the two schools, which drew on the best features of both while being free of preconceptions.*

124 bottom left The ocean races of the first half of the twentieth century saw boats with rigs of all types. At the start of the 1935 Transatlantic race that was to be won by Stormy Weather *a large schooner and a yawl act as a backdrop to* Vamarie *the wishbone ketch of Cox and Stevens.*

124 bottom right Vim *was built to race in Europe: while they were popular in American waters, races for this class attracted huge entries on the Solent and the British tended to consider the category their own. As usual, Vanderbilt applied all the rigor and methods that had guaranteed him success in business to the boat's tuning and organization.* Vim *with the Stephens brothers aboard was a perfect racing machine when she set out to cross the ocean.*

124-125 Stormy Weather *has recently returned to the high seas: a perfect restoration blessed by a visit from the ninety-year-old Olin Stephens allows us to see today a yacht that has influenced the shape of racing boats since the immediate post-war period. The American yacht was built by the Henry B. Nevins yard at City Island, New York, for Mr. Philip LeBoutillier. Rigged as a yawl, with a bumpkin on the transom stern for the mizzen stay and sheet,* Stormy Weather *had an overall length of 53 feet 10 inches, 39 feet 6 inches at the waterline, a beam of 12 feet 6 inches, a displacement of 20 tons and a sail area of 1,290 square feet. During her career, she won ocean races and Olympic triangle events, her skipper in the early seasons being Rod Stephens. For the Transatlantic Race of 1935, won by* Stormy Weather, *Rod was joined aboard by Kenneth Davidson on his first ocean race.*

125 bottom The experience with the testing tank at the Stevens Institute and his work with Kenneth Davidson allowed Olin Stephens not only to make an important contribution to the design of the J Class Ranger, but above all to verify the new "compromise" ideas that were to underlie the design of Stormy Weather. In spite of the scientific element, the hand of the designer is still evident. There was still a search for beauty in the conviction that what looks good is good.

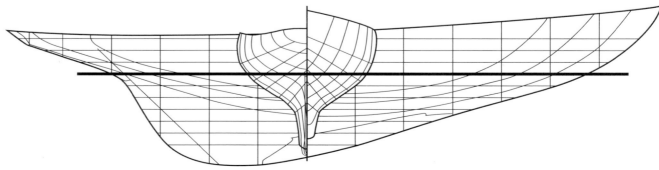

OFFSHORE YACHTS IN NORTHERN EUROPE

With rare exceptions to the rule, yachting in the inter-war period continued to be dominated by Britain and America. Things were stirring, however, in the countries of Northern Europe following the efforts of Kaiser Wilhelm II and thanks to the proximity of Britain. Germany in particular had by now adopted that attitude towards the sea so eagerly promoted by the emperor, and in 1910 the German designer Max Oertz had been responsible for the creation of his last yacht, the *Meteor IV*. In the period after the First World War, Oertz was to specialize in the design of meter-class yachts, in particular 8- and 10-meter boats that together with the 6-meter class were particularly popular in Europe, partly because they had been chosen as Olympic classes.

In the late 1930s, a number of successful yachts were built by another German designer, Henry Gruber, who had worked in the studio of Starling Burgess, clearly absorbing his teachings and methods. One of his boats was the *Roland Von Bremen* of 1936, designed for the transatlantic race planned for that year on the Bermuda-Cuxhaven route, with a cup provided by the Führer at stake. The *Roland Von Bremen*, which drew on the American "compromise" school, finished first. She was to all intents and purposes a copy of *Stormy Weather*, although a little larger with an overall length of 59 feet, a beam of 13 feet 6 inches and 1,453 square feet of canvas. She was an attractive boat, just like *Stormy Weather*, in fact.

I have had the opportunity of seeing another yacht by the same designer, *Nordwind*, at a number of classic boat regattas. This is a much larger craft at 85 feet in overall length but is also extremely attractive. She was designed in 1938, the year in which Europe was plunged into the horrors of war.

Johan Anker was an extremely successful Norwegian designer responsible for numerous meter-class boats and one of the first American 12-meter yachts, the *Magda XI*. His designs are frequently encountered in British waters while in Italy, I have seen *Eva Maria*, a large American-style 78-foot 6-inch schooner, and the *Lasse*, a 59-foot 8-inch sloop designed in 1940 and clearly inspired by the meter-class ratings.

Other designers active in the seas of Northern Europe were generally associated with particular boatyards such as Rasmussen in Germany, De Vries Lentsch in Holland and Lindblom (responsible for the beautiful *Marjatta* a 59-foot Marconi yacht from 1943) in Finland.

Nonetheless, we had to wait until after the Second World War before a true tradition in terms of boat-building rather than design developed to the point where it could rival those of Britain and the United States.

126 *top With the passing of the years, Henry Gruber broke away from the American school, apparently in favour of the British tradition: Nordwind, a large 85-foot 4-inch ketch designed in 1938 and launched by the Burmester yard at Bremen in Germany the following year, had more classical lines than the Roland Von Bremen. The ratio between length and breadth is once again close to 5 against the approximately 4 of the earlier boat, and she had a very deep draught of 13 feet.*

126 *bottom One of the few German ocean racing yacht of the inter-war period was the Roland Von Bremen, an 59-foot yawl just a little larger than Stormy Weather, designed two years earlier and a clear influence on the German boat. The two yachts resemble one another closely with the same lines, the same dimensional ratios and the same rig. Roland Von Bremen is an attractive boat, as was Stephens' design of course, and won the Transatlantic Race in 1936 with the great Sherman Hoyt aboard.*

METRE CLASSES IN THE MEDITERRANEAN

The Mediterranean in the years between the two wars saw the rapid development of yachting in the smaller meter-classes.

Although Italian constructors and designers were responsible for a number of large cruising yachts, boats built to the International Rule were to represent the bulk of the national output.

From the second half of the nineteenth century, a number of boatyards had been established, particularly on the Ligurian coast. These were generally run by master carpenters who alternated the building of commercial vessels with that of recreational craft. As was normal at that time, the boats were actually built on the beaches.

Among these yards were a number that were to achieve international recognition: Beltrami, Baglietto and Costaguta. Others produced, with less success, recreational craft at La Spezia, Leghorn and Castellamare di Stabia (near Naples).

The development of the meter classes in the Mediterranean, the 6- and 8-meters in particular, is linked to the interest aroused in the era by two sporting events: the Italian Cup, initially reserved for yachts rated at up to 5 tons, and the French Cup for yachts of up to 10 tons. The first was soon contested by 6-meter class boats while the latter was reserved for 8-meter craft. French and Italian victories followed in an alternation that stimulated progress in terms of design and the spread of these classes.

This last was confirmed by the participation of *Mebi* in the 6-meter class in the Olympic

127 top left Prince Amedeo Umberto of Savoia, the Duke of Aosta, was the president of the Yacht Club Italiano from 1933 to 1942. He participated enthusiastically in Italian regattas, racing above all in the Star class. In this photo he is seen with the designer and owner Francesco Giovannelli aboard the 6-meter Bambetta. *Among his yachts was the large 85-foot 4-inch schooner* Amrita, *built in 1933 at Lussinpiccolo.*

127 bottom left Francesco Giovanelli was an atypical figure in the yachting world, an amateur designer specializing in the meter classes in much the same way as the American Clinton Crane. Among his designs was Cheta, *an 8-meter built by Baglietto in 1925: she was to win the Italian Cup, beating Madame Virginie Hériot's* Aile IV.

127 top right and bottom Vittorio Baglietto was the other great Italian designer-builder. His Bona, *an International Rule 8-meter seen sailing in the top photo, won the French Cup in 1938. She was built in 1936 for Prince Eugenio of Savoia, who can be seen in the bottom photo together with Baglietto on the day of the launch.*

Games of 1924 and *Cheta* in the 8-meter class at Cowes in 1925. Both boats were designed by Giovannelli and built by Baglietto.

In the meantime, a technical "invention" had been introduced that has continued to influence international yachting to the present day, the Genoa jib. Up to 1925, small foresails of various shapes were rigged in front of the mast of yachts of all kinds: generally foresail, jib and flying jib when beating, a spinnaker when running before the wind.

It was actually Giovannelli, aboard *Cheta* in races at Genoa in 1925, who first tried beating with a spinnaker too. The form of the sail restricted the boat's ability to pinch the wind somewhat, but saved time that would otherwise be wasted changing the foresails when passing the marker for the windward leg.

The following winter a sailmaking skipper, Raimondo Panario, designed and made a flatter form of spinnaker and also correctly modified, on the basis of a personal intuition later confirmed by Manfred Curry, the shape of the spanker in order to favor the interaction of the two sails that overlapped one another when beating.

The 1926 season saw this type of sail successful in regattas held at Genoa and from then onwards yachts began to hoist a single large foresail that appropriately became known as a "Genoa".

The diffusion of coastal regattas, of which the Italian and French Cups were but the best known international events, perhaps prevented the development of ocean racing (the first ocean race from Cannes to Barcelona, with markers at Marseilles and Palma de Mallorca, was not held until 1929, despite the fact that open sea navigation had had a precursor and literary proselyte in the form of D'Albertis and his yachts *Violante* and *Corsaro*, in the second half of the nineteenth century), and consequently the construction of large yachts: between 1919 and 1939 no less than 87 meter-class yachts were launched by Italian yards compared with just 17 cruising or ocean racing yachts which in that era were the same thing. Most of the latter were built by two yards at Lussinpiccolo on the Istrian peninsula near Trieste. One of these, the Martinolich yard, built a number of important yachts including the *Croce del Sud* of 1931, a three-masted schooner rated at 210 tons with an overall length of 123 feet 6 inches and a steel hull. She is still today one of the most beautiful yachts sailing in the Mediterranean and, an unusual fact that is worth underlining, is still owned by the family that launched her. The *Emilia*, a schooner designed and constructed by

Costaguta in 1929, and the *Popi*, now named the *Niña Luisita*, designed by C. E. Nicholson and built in the same year by Baglietto, are also still sailing in the Mediterranean.

The aforementioned Francesco Giovanelli was an atypical figure on the Italian yachting scene. He owned, and above all designed, exclusively 6- and 8-meter-class yachts, achieving consistently excellent results in competition (four Italian Cups won between 1924 and 1930 as well as races throughout Europe, from Kiel to Cowes) at the helm of his boats (his boats in the sense that he owned them, but above all because he actually designed them too). Giovanelli also wrote two books, *Le Barche a Vela Vanno a Vela* and *La Regata e la Sua Legge*, veritable compendia of his theories and passions. From a historical point of view, he can be considered as the first true Italian yacht designer and he established himself at a time when the field was dominated by master carpenters with their baggage of experience and intuition and the "British" model. So strong was the influence of the latter that it is said that even into the late nineteenth century in Italy a popular nick-name for a yacht was a "Lordino," a diminutive of the title borne by many British yachtsmen. In the same period, the yacht builder Luigi Onesto was nick-named "Ingleise," or "Englishman" in the Ligurian dialect.

128-129 Prior to the Second World War, the production of yachts in the Mediterranean basin concentrated almost exclusively on boats destined for coastal racing and cruising. Emilia is one the exceptions: she was originally laid down in the Costaguta yard in 1929 as a 12-meter yacht, but during the course of her construction she changed owner and vocation: she was rigged as a schooner destined for cruising as we see her today.

129 top Attilio Costaguta was famous not only as a boatbuilder but also as a designer. This photo shows the launch on the 26th of June, 1936, of the International Rule 8-meter Italia which was to win its class in the Olympics at Kiel in 1936. The launch of a yacht is a ceremony that always involves the owner, the boatyard workers, and the crew as well as the inhabitants of the town, all gathered on the beach to follow the slow descent of the hull on the blocks.

129 bottom Charles II in England, Wilhelm II in Germany, Alfonso XIII in Spain: sailing seems to have aroused curiosity and passion in many crowned heads of state. Yachting did not exist in Spain prior to the reign of Alfonso XIII, but was well established by the time of his death. This photo shows one of the few I. R. 15-meter boats, Hispania, designed by William Fife who was interested in the class, and launched in 1908 at Santander by the Karpara yard for King Alfonso XIII. The 15-meter class, like the 19- and 10-meters, never achieved widespread popularity, perhaps because it fell between the 12-meters of which it shared the vices and virtues, and the 23-meters that could race against the new J Class and classic Big Class boats.

NOBILITY AND YACHTING IN SPAIN

The origins of Spanish yachting are inextricably linked with the figure of King Alfonso XII, already an enthusiastic yachtsman when he acceded to the throne. As was more generally the case in Italy, the king privileged the meter classes, opening his increasingly intensive racing career with an International Rule 6-meter boat.

However, his best-loved yacht was perhaps the International Rule 10-meter Tonino. This class was never particularly popular, perhaps because it was overshadowed by the international success of the 8-meter class early in the twentieth century and the 12-meter boats from the 1920s.

Tonino was built to the designs of William Fife by Astilleros de Nervion, one of the first Spanish yards to flank its traditional activities with the construction of recreational craft in order to satisfy King Alfonso XIII's yachting ambitions.

The 15-meter Hispania was built a few years earlier by the Karpara yard of Santander, again for the king. This was another class that aroused little interest elsewhere but enjoyed a certain popularity in Spain in that period with four yachts being launched. Apart from the Hispania, there was the Tuiga owned by the Duke of Medinaceli, the great friend and sailing rival of the king; Encarnita owned by the Marquis of Cuba and Slec, acquired by a consortium of members of the Real Club Nautico de Barcelona when she was named the Shimmi. All of the above mentioned yachts were designed by Fife, with the last three also being built in his yard.

In the years between the two wars, the example set by Alfonso XIII encouraged a number of wealthy and aristocratic members of Spanish society to take up yachting, and in 1930 the pennant of the Barcelona club, the oldest in Spain having been founded in 1873, was flown by thirty sailing yachts. The previous year, the Catalan club had organized its first ocean race, a cross between a cruise and a race, in fact, in collaboration with the Yacht Club Italiano (which that year had organized its first open sea regatta) and the French, with legs from Genoa to Pollenza, from Marseilles to Pollenza, from Barcelona to Pollenza and lastly from Pollenza to Barcelona. A total of 39 yachts took part.

Alfonso XIII will also be remembered for having organized the 1928 Transatlantic Race from New York to Santander, which saw the first victory to be recorded by Burgess' schooner Niña which was to continue to dominate the Atlantic races after the Second World War. On her arrival, she was met at sea by the king himself with the cry, "Bravi! Congratulations! I am the King of Spain."

THE PIONEERS OF YACHTING IN FRANCE

130 top France successfully exported numerous cultural and social models but, at least until the period after the Second World War, not its ideas regarding yachts and yachting. This was despite the presence of a number of interesting figures such as Gustave Caillebotte, a painter of the Impressionist school, an excellent helmsman and a theorist of the new-born nautical sciences. He was a nineteenth-century man but his ideas, while never spreading beyond the national boundaries, influenced French yachting throughout the early twentieth century. As a helmsman, he was a French champion three years running, but as a designer he never enjoyed similar success.

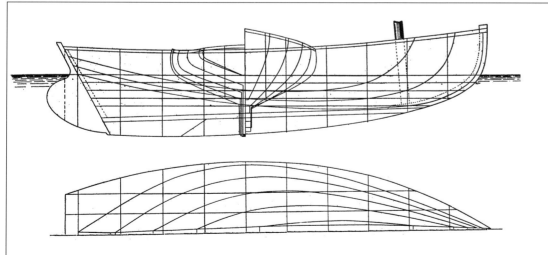

130 bottom Caillebotte, good painter that he was, adopted the theories of Marrett in designing yachts and was one of the first to set down the lines of the hull on paper before beginning construction. Seen here is the lines plan of Vol au Vent.

130-131 This photo, like others in the archive relating to Caillebotte, carries no relevant information, but it is not difficult to recognize in the yacht under construction a small cutter like those Caillebotte helmed successfully in competition. The framing of the yacht has already been completed and the master carpenters have put in place the main elements of the planking. These will be followed in an extremely precise procedure by the others that should fit snugly between the first.

In the late nineteenth and early twentieth centuries, France saw the emergence of a number of figures who might have played significant roles in the history of yachting, were it not for the dominance of the British and American schools.

Gustave Caillebotte is probably better known for his Impressionist paintings, but was also an excellent competitive sailor and an amateur designer. He influenced the early designs of Chevreux, who at that time was a competent naval architect, convincing him to design a yacht, the Thomas, on the basis of a compromise between the British and American models. With Caillebotte at the helm, Thomas won the national title three years in succession and would perhaps have achieved greater fame were it not for the fact that, like French yachting in general, she never left home waters.

Despite Caillebotte's relative obscurity in yachting terms, he was the father of a rating system which the Yacht Club de France promoted on a national level and was responsible for the Arriett, an extremely advanced design even when

compared with international contemporaries. Unfortunately, the design never got further than the drawing board. Caillebotte could at least be credited with being among the first to apply Marrett's methods, having drawn the lines of *Arriett's* hull when a half-model was still the preferred approach to yacht design. He was an artist after all!

Godinet was an almost identical figure who also developed a rating system that was among the first to take into account all three hull dimensions as well as the sail area, and was the first to receive international recognition (being adopted by the Swiss, Russians, Belgians and Spanish; the first using it until 1920). In 1893, Godinet also designed and constructed the *Vendenesse*, which featured the world's first aluminium hull. France, however, failed to take advantage of these innovations, with *Vendenesse* proving to be a disaster at sea and the Germans taking a lead in the use of aluminium by constructing four yachts in the material by the end of the century, with the irrepressible Herreshoff hard on their heels of course. The Godinet rating system failed to make further progress due to the British and American hegemony in the yachting world. Between the two world wars, France found herself with a well developed fleet of centerboard and fin-keel boats but nothing more and, like Italy, directed her attention to meter-class racing. The nautical history of the two neighboring countries in this period was in fact very similar.

131 bottom left All of Gustave Caillebotte's projects proved to be too advanced for their time. The available materials and constructional technologies did not allow the yachts that were built to maintain the promises held out by the drawings. *Vendenesse* in particular, with her aluminium hull, the world's first, suffered technical problems both during her construction and at sea.

131 bottom right Thomas *was a small Chevreux-designed cutter. It should be noted that* Thomas *may be considered as the first "compromise" between the British and American schools, a yacht that was well balanced in terms of the ratios between length, breadth and displacement. Caillebotte, enthusiastic about the performance of* Thomas, *drew up plans according to the theories of Marrett of the* Arriett, *a yacht that would have been modern even in 1930. Unfortunately she was never built.*

FRANCE

There was one figure, however, who achieved world-wide fame in the sport of sailing, thanks to her exploits at sea and, above all, because she was a woman, Madame Virginie Hériot. Long before feminism and even earlier than the suffragette movement, Virginie Hériot was a symbol in France far beyond the restricted circles of yachting. She was by no means the only woman sailor; others, in the main Americans, had preceded her or were her contemporaries. But in a period in which sailing clubs did not look kindly on applications for membership from the gentle sex, or even expressly forbade them, Madame Hériot was truly remarkable for her authentic passion and technical skill: she it was who held the tiller and raced the yacht.

Born in 1890, Virginie Hériot was the heir to the owners of the Le Printemps department stores and therefore benefited from an immense fortune that allowed her to devote herself to satisfying her passion. She lived in that inter-war period in which for France, and for many other European countries, the spread of sailing was associated with yachts built to the International Rule of 1906. Virginie Hériot possessed no less than thirteen yachts of this type: a 10-meter, acquired in 1912 to take part in the French Cup which was then staged for yachts of this class; seven 8-meter boats acquired between 1922 and 1931, which were perhaps her favorites and all of which she named *Ailée*, from *I* through to *VII* (she won the gold medal at the Amsterdam Olympics of 1928 at the helm of *Ailée VI*), and five 6-meter boats all named *Petit Ailée*, for the One Ton Cup and the Italian Cup. Neither did she ignore ocean sailing, undertaking cruises in the Atlantic and the northern seas as well as her home waters of the Channel and the Mediterranean, and racking up a total of almost 150,000 miles.

In 1924, Madame Hériot purchased *Ailée I*, the former *Meteor IV* designed by Max Oertz and built by the Krupp yard in 1909 for Kaiser Wilhelm II, while in 1928 she commissioned C. E. Nicholson to design and build *Ailée II*, a 187-foot, three-masted schooner. She sailed this last yacht in a number of ocean racing, repeating the success she had enjoyed in the "small" meter-classes.

The success achieved by Virginie Hériot proved that she had the talent to match her undoubted ambition and she received official

recognition of the fact when nominated as a knight of the Legion of Honor and a Quartermaster of the French navy.

On the 27th of August, 1932, while already ill, she insisted on starting a race at Arcachons at the helm of the last of her 6-meter boats. For the first time, an *Ailée* had to retire during the course of a regatta due to the indisposition of her helmswoman. Virginie Hériot died the following morning. During her lifetime, she spoke at no less than 54 conferences on her favorite subject, the sea, and wrote more than ten books. She said of sailing that, "There is no more beautiful, more thrilling, more stirring sport than the Sport of Sailing. The slim, gently swelling lines of a racing hull are joy to the eyes; the white lightness of the sails, the fineness of the mast

132 top and bottom Virginie Hériot had no peers in any of the countries that at that time were far more advanced in the sport of sailing. Mrs. Vanderbilt and Mrs. Lipton accompanied their husbands in the cockpits of the J Class boats, but neither ever took the helm in a race as Virginie did, and neither covered as many miles at sea as the French woman with her Ailée I, in the bottom photo, and Ailée II.

soaring towards the sky and that of the rigging form an incomparable composition of harmonious grace and beauty. Under the thrust of the wind this dormant beauty awakens, is animate, shivers and vibrates under the hand of the helmsman, surges onto the blue swell snorting like a living steed, but one ever faithful to the call of the helm and ever obedient. And all around extends the moving blue sea, the breeze that plays its joyful tune through the rigging and the bracing air that embraces you in its pure and inebriating caress. And then there is the struggle, at times difficult and tenacious, against the natural elements, the courteous yet intense encounters of the regattas where the competitors demonstrate knowledge, skill, cunning and daring, disdaining fatigue and danger. Add to this the attention to the sails

throughout the race, the heart-stopping anxiety of rounding the last marker and the joy and exaltation of victory, sportingly obtained, magnificent to the highest degree in the case of a National triumph. This is the Sport of Sailing!"

Little remains of that period apart from the meter-classes: the *Resolue*, a large sail and motor schooner of 52 meters was converted into a cargo vessel after the war, while the *Ailée* has disappeared.

Two large ketches, *Hygie* and *L'Iliade et L'Odyssée*, the first of 78 feet 6 inches and built by Le Marchand to the designs of Severi in 1930, the second of 73 feet 10 inches and built by Lamarie to the designs of Camatte in 1935, are both still sailing, testimony to a little known yacht building industry.

132-133 Virginie Hériot of France was one of the first yachtswomen, the first to win an Olympic gold medal, in 1928 in the International Rule 8-meter class. She can be seen in this photo at the helm of her first Ailée, the large schooner designed and launched as the Meteor IV by Max Oertz for Wilhelm II of Germany, who accompanied her to various regattas. Madame Hériot alternated meter-class racing with long voyages aboard this large yacht.

133 bottom While on the northern coasts French yachting dallied with the typical fishermen's cotres and the futuristic ventures of designers such as Caillebotte, in the Mediterranean Madame Hériot showed remarkable tenacity in racing, frequently winning, some times being defeated, for prestigious and by now traditional trophies. The photo shows her Ailée IV racing against the Italian Catina IV in the Italian Cup: the fresh breeze and the waves crashing against the breakwater of the port of Genoa provide a stern test for the two 8-meter yachts.

THE AMERICA'S CUP AND THE J CLASS BOATS

It is frequently the case that the size rather than the quality of a given object attracts the collective imagination. It is also frequently the case that people will gather on a quay to watch the docking of a yacht simply because it is "big," failing to notice the small but perfectly formed boat tied up alongside.

Big is not necessarily "beautiful," "important" or "attractive," but in the history of yachting it just so happens that it worked out that way; the largest racing yachts ever constructed were also the most beautiful—the boats built to the American Universal Rule and the European International Rule. The fabulous lines of these yachts were not distorted by rating systems in which, if I might be forgiven a technical simplification, the dimensional restrictions concerned above all volumes and surface areas with linear measurements being consequential, and their appeal actually increased with size. An American S Class, rated at 17 feet, thus has the same lines and is thus just as attractive as a J Class rated at 76 feet, but the "grandeur" of the latter makes it all the more impressive.

The same is true of an International Rule 6-meter compared with a 23-meter yacht built to the same formula. The British 23-meter boats were actually re-rated on the basis of the more or less equivalent American system, thus becoming J Class yachts, in accordance with an international agreement reached immediately after the First World War whereby the Universal Rule was used for yachts of the 15-meter class and upwards and the International Rule for the smaller classes.

This preface serves to introduce a type of yacht that was actually built in very restricted numbers, within a period of just a little over two decades and was used for just a handful of regattas. Today, nobody would dream of building such monsters, and yet the J Class boats are still considered to be the most beautiful as well as the largest yachts ever seen.

At this point a brief note regarding the Universal Rule would be helpful.

As described earlier, the formula was developed in 1903 by the wizard of American yachting, Nat Herreshoff, in response to the New York Yacht Club's request for a system allowing yachts to race against one another without having to make recourse to compensation to establish a realistic finishing order. They wanted to compete in real time, with the first boat home winning the race.

The formula expressed a rating, and according to this rating the yachts were subdivided into classes, each identified by a letter of the alphabet: S Class for the 17-footers, R for 20', P for 31', N for 38', M for 46' and lastly J for boats rated at 76 feet.

The formula used to determine the rating of a yacht was:

"Eighteen percent of length at the waterline multiplied by the square root of the sail area and divided by the cube root of the displacement."

A series of instructions established how the dimensions used in the formula were to be measured.

Everything was apparently very simple: in order to increase the length at the waterline, a factor determinant for the speed of a yacht,

134 top and bottom The yachts that were most representative of the sport of sailing were in reality only a fleeting presence: less than two decades were illuminated by the highest expressions of yachting technology and aesthetics, quite literally with masts over 160 feet tall. Remarkably, this presence was seen in only two places that are rightly considered to be centers of world yachting: the waters of Newport, Rhode Island, in the United States, and the traditional Solent off Cowes, the home of the prestigious Royal Yacht Squadron. In those waters, both sheltered but sufficiently breezy, the J Class boats staged epic duels for the world's most sought-after sailing trophy, the America's Cup and, as a corollary, attracted mass regattas of the club members. In the two photos J Class boats are seen on the waters of the Solent: Velsheda, Shamrock V *and* Endeavour I, *joined by the former 23-meter* Candida *and the glorious* Britannia, *both rated according to the International Rule.*

134-135 *Following the last edition of the America's Cup disputed by the J Class boats, that of 1937, five boats raced for the New York Yacht Club Cup* at Buzzard's Bay, between Newport and Marthas Vineyard: from the left, Endeavour I, Rainbow, Ranger, Endeavour II *and* Yankee.

either the sail area had to be decreased or the weight of the vessel increased.

In the case of a J Class, the length at the waterline had to be between 73 and 87 feet. History was to prove that maximum length at the waterline, irrespective of the reduction in sail area or the increase in displacement, would provide the best results: *Ranger*, the last J Class built, was exactly the maximum permitted 87 feet long at the waterline. On average a J Class was 131 feet long overall, with a waterline of around 85 feet, a beam of around 21 feet 4 inches , a draught of 14 feet 6 inches and a displacement in the order of 150 tons; a yacht therefore that featured long overhangs and was fairly narrow and heavy, but the weight of which was strongly conditioned by the ballast it carried—around 110 tons of lead! She would be rigged with a Marconi mainsail and at most two jibs. The average sail area was over 7,500 square feet, a vast quantity of canvas therefore, carried by a single mast that towered up to 150 feet above the deck, around 165 feet from the water, or the equivalent of a 16-storey building. The J Class yachts had a certain propensity to being demasted, partly because they frequently adopted futuristic approaches to mast design.

The mainsail of *Ranger*, to take one example, had a surface area of 5,060 square feet, was made of Egyptian cotton and weighed almost a ton: sixteen men were required on the halyard to hoist it. All the running rigging was assisted by winches and blocks, but a very large crew was required nonetheless and around forty people would be carried by a J Class yacht during a race. This is put into perspective when you consider that every tack required at least three sheets to be adjusted for the foresails, the two flying jib sheets and the mainsail sheet while the curvature of the mast and that of the boom also had to be adjusted. All this just to change tack, while rounding a marker required the sails to be changed, the spinnaker being hoisted in place of the jibs which must have resulted in some frenetic on-deck activity! Moreover, the J Class boats, like all the meter and Universal Rule classes, were not fitted with rails.

The J Class boats were built essentially for the America's Cup which adopted them following the 1920 edition, but they did actually participate in other events, including fleet regattas (the America's Cup was, and still is, a match race series, with two boats competing head-to-head) both in

England and America. In 1937, for the very last time the Solent saw no less than seven J Class yachts racing together: six British boats and the *Yankee* that had crossed the Atlantic from America especially for the regatta (just for the record, in eighteen days escorted by *Atlantic*, the seasoned ocean voyaging schooner owned by William Gardner).

The previous year five J Classes, the two British *Endeavours* and the Americans *Rainbow*, *Ranger* and the omnipresent *Yankee* had taken part in the New York Yacht Club Cruise, a superb annual regatta along the North American coastline between New York and Boston. They raced together after what was to be the last edition of the America's Cup to be disputed by the J Class.

Only two countries built yachts of this class, and they could hardly be other than the two countries that, at least up until the Second World War, dominated the yachting scene, Britain and the United States. The first constructed four, to which have to be added the 23-meter and Big Class yachts re-rated as J Class boats, while the second built six.

Resolute and *Shamrock IV* which disputed the 1920 edition of the America's Cup were not true J Class yachts even though their dimensions were comparable and they deserve mention in this section. *Resolute* was a Nat Herreshoff design from 1913 that contested with William Gardner's *Vanity* the honor of defending the cup that year in the fourth challenge issued by Sir Thomas Lipton. The winds of war blowing through Europe led to the regatta being postponed until 1920.

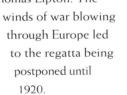

136 bottom Ranger was the first yacht to be a true product of the testing tank as the work carried out at the Stevens Institute and the contribution of Professor Kenneth Davidson were fundamental to her design. In particular, the tank allowed the efficiency of Endeavour I which had demonstrated her superiority to Rainbow to be verified and compared with that of the other American J Classes. This provided a solid basis for the design work of Starling Burgess and his young assistant Olin Stephens.

136-137 Even though the scientific approach now dominated the design of the America's Cup boats, and despite the diffusion of mechanical sail handling aids, the role of a J Class crew was always physically gruelling. All hands were needed to hoist Ranger's great mainsail, a ton of canvas to be hauled aloft, fortunately on the occasion of this photo in light winds and with a dead calm sea!

Resolute was a little smaller than the British challenger and received a small amount of compensated time. However, she had a steel frame, bronze skinning and decks in cork-covered aluminium panels, a true racer like her predecessor *Reliance*. Both boats being constructed for a single regatta, the America's Cup and were subsequently demolished; a very American, very pragmatic (but winning) approach to competitive sailing.

Shamrock IV, the British challenger owned by Sir Thomas Lipton, was also fairly innovative, but only in relation to the conservative British standards. She was designed by Nicholson, with three-ply planking, a layer of cedar, one of spruce and the last of mahogany over spruce longitudinal elements and ply frames: a very light system that however produced a rather inelegant hull. The yacht was in fact nick-named "Ugly Duckling." Both yachts were still rigged with a gaff mainsail and a bowsprit, and while they were not J Class boats, neither did they belong to the era of the giant cutters with over 13,000 square feet of canvas seen in the previous editions.

For the record, the regatta was of course won by *Resolute*, albeit not without having to put up a fight.

The first race was in fact won by *Shamrock IV* when *Resolute* retired with a broken topmast and the challenger also took the second race, this time fair and square and by a decent margin. In the third race it was again *Shamrock IV* that crossed the finishing line ahead, but her 19 seconds advantage were not sufficient to overcome the handicap imposed by compensated time; at this point it was 2-1 to the British boat. The fourth race was a clear-cut victory for the Americans, while the fifth and decisive round disputed in variable winds was again won by the Americans thanks to a healthy dose of good fortune. For the first time the challenger had come close to snatching the America's Cup from the halls of the New York Yacht Club.

From this point onwards, the J Class boats became the true protagonists of the America's

138 bottom left The J Class boats were derived from the large cutters, or sloops according to the Americans, which themselves developed from the first fin keel yachts of the nineteenth century. These were the so-called "skimming dishes," immense yachts with long overhangs and broad, shallow hulls. Resolute, designed by Herreshoff for the 1920 edition of the America's Cup, was the last of the line.

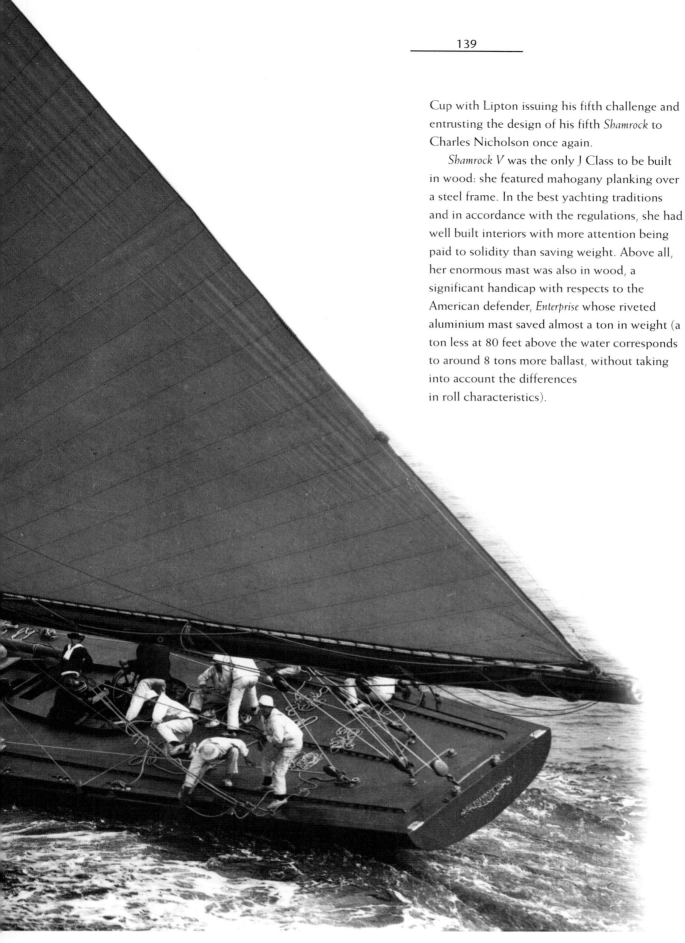

Cup with Lipton issuing his fifth challenge and entrusting the design of his fifth *Shamrock* to Charles Nicholson once again.

Shamrock V was the only J Class to be built in wood: she featured mahogany planking over a steel frame. In the best yachting traditions and in accordance with the regulations, she had well built interiors with more attention being paid to solidity than saving weight. Above all, her enormous mast was also in wood, a significant handicap with respects to the American defender, *Enterprise* whose riveted aluminium mast saved almost a ton in weight (a ton less at 80 feet above the water corresponds to around 8 tons more ballast, without taking into account the differences in roll characteristics).

138-139 Shamrock IV, the "Ugly Duckling", raced during the J Class era but belonged to the past. She was designed by Charles Nicholson in 1913, perhaps the great Solent boatbuilder's most innovative boat. The Great War meant she spent seven years in a shed in the port of New York. Shamrock IV, like all Thomas Lipton's yachts, raced for the yacht club of Cork in Ireland and it would be more correct to speak of Irish rather than British challengers.

138 bottom right Thomas Lipton issued his second America's Cup challenge in 1913, proposing to dispute the regatta with a J Class in the belief that he was thus acting in accordance with a resolution of the New York Yacht Club committee. After considerable hesitation, however, the committee decided to postpone the debut of the class and Lipton unwillingly launched the last British fin keel challenger, Shamrock II.

139 bottom left Nothing superfluous, just rigging on the decks of these large racing yachts. While the J Classes had great helmsmen, professionals generally recruited from the fishing fleets, the crew members who dealt with the rigging had to be equally proficient: generations of anonymous but highly skilled seamen capable of acting with perfect timing in often difficult conditions.

139 bottom right The British America's Cup challengers, at least those of the Twenties and Thirties, frequently started with a serious handicap: they rarely had competitive yachts against which to race while fine-tuning the rig and training the crew. The last Shamrock, the 5th of the line, is seen beating with the Big Class Cambria in attendance. This was hardly a valid test given the technical qualities of the American defenders in that period.

The 1930 edition of the America's Cup was disputed on a best out of four basis with compensated time no longer being applied. The event was moved from the heavily trafficked Long Island Sound to the waters off Newport, Rhode Island, which was to remain the home of the America's Cup until 1983.

The races were uneventful with *Enterprise* strolling to a 4-0 victory.

The Americans had launched no less than 4 J Class yachts for the defence in 1930: *Weetamoe*, designed by a formula yachts specialist Clinton Crane and considered to be particularly fast (she was still being used as a "hare" in 1934, when she was almost selected in place of *Rainbow*, and in 1937); *Whirlwind*, a rather unusual design featuring a canoe stern by Francis Herreshoff who never lived up to the reputation of his father; *Yankee* by Starling Burgess, the most long-lived of the American J Class yachts (after having participated in the elimination trials of 1930, '34 and '37 she was still racing in the waters off Newport in 1939 before being cannibalized, like *Weetamoe*, to fit out *Ranger*); and lastly *Enterprise*, another Starling Burgess design and the boat eventually selected to defend the cup.

Enterprise had a number of innovative features in her rig and came to be known as the "mechanical yacht." Apart from the mast in riveted Duralumin mentioned above, she had a boom with an extremely wide upper section, the so-called Park Avenue boom, that was equipped with transverse rails allowing the shape of the mainsail to be adjusted. No less than 24 winches were fitted for the halyards and sheets, most of them located below deck level so as not to have the weight of the crew too high. She was also equipped with two centerboards, one for beating and another smaller one for use in following winds. *Enterprise* won all her races comfortably, but she was so extreme and expensive that the Americans themselves introduced modifications of the regulations to outlaw, at least in part, her mechanical features.

That 1930 edition introduced two men who were to become legendary figures in America's Cup and J Class history: the designer Starling Burgess, whose father had already designed the three defenders of the 1880s, and Harold Vanderbilt, the owner of the three American defenders of the 1930s.

In the light of his 1930 experience, Nicholson used steel for both the frames and skinning of his next three J Class boats: the two *Endeavours* for Sir Thomas Octave Murdoch Sopwith and *Velsheda*, which acted as sparring partner for *Endeavour II*.

The mast of *Endeavour* also abandoned wood

140-141 No less than four J Class boats were launched in the United States in 1930: Enterprise and Yankee by Starling Burgess, Whirlwind by Francis Herreshoff and Weetamoe by Clinton Crane. The photo shows this last close-hauled in a stiff breeze and slight swell during the elimination trials for the 1930 edition of the America's Cup. Weetamoe was consistently competitive but was unable to overcome Burgess' yachts: Enterprise in 1930, Rainbow in '34 and Ranger in '37.

140 bottom Yankee, a Starling Burgess design from 1930. This yacht never participated in the America's Cup but she was nonetheless one of the strongest J Class boats: in the 1934 elimination trials she won at least 10 races against Rainbow, essentially chosen as the defender because she had a more up-to-date rig. Yankee is also the only American J Class to have crossed the Atlantic to race on the Solent, repaying the courtesy shown by so many British J Classes that had had to make the reverse journey.

141 bottom Shamrock V leading Enterprise, the "mechanical yacht", a boat on which everything could be adjusted mechanically and that was so technical that even the New York Yacht Club committee agreed to restrictions being imposed for the next edition. In the meantime, however, the hugely long so-called "Park Avenue boom" fitted to Enterprise together with transverse rails allowed the shape of the mainsail to be controlled perfectly, a factor that was alone sufficient to ensure that Shamrock had no hope of victory.

in favour of steel with the plates riveted longitudinally and welded on the horizontal joints. The boom in the same material had a circular section that was very flexible in all directions and therefore difficult to adjust. It was replaced prior to the regatta by a version with a triangular section.

Numerous new jib designs were tried on *Endeavour* with double and triple clews: this last feature was abandoned due to adjustment difficulties whilst the first gave a significant advantage. The sailmaker that provided the canvas for *Endeavour* and so many other British boats, Ratsey & Lapthorn of Cowes, was a true yachting institution. The firm's sail loft, still in

Rainbow for the 1934 edition: regulations no longer permitted the mechanical aids employed aboard *Enterprise* and prescribed a minimum weight for the internal fittings of seven tons. While Nicholson created true interiors, Burgess destined two of those seven tons to the batteries needed to power the on-board equipment and instrumentation and then located them in the bilge. Nonetheless, *Endeavour* was the faster boat and *Rainbow* only won thanks to the efficiency of her crew and, as mentioned earlier, a certain stretching of the rules.

The first two races went to the challenger and *Endeavour* was again leading in the third a few miles from home. At this point the

disconsolate Vanderbilt, convinced he had lost the America's Cup, left the helm in favor of Sherman Hoyt, his second in command. Hoyt's masterful tactics drew *Endeavour* into a soft spot and *Rainbow* went on to win—it was now 2-1. The Americans also won the fourth race. The British boat lodged a valid protest after *Rainbow* failed to give way but the Race Committee disallowed it on a technicality. It was two-all going into the fifth race.

The last two races were won by the Americans who thus retained the cup. On this occasion, *Endeavour* had proved to be superior to *Rainbow* while Lipton had demonstrated that he was a match for Vanderbilt at the helm. The cup was actually won by the (American) Race Committee.

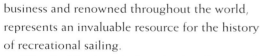

business and renowned throughout the world, represents an invaluable resource for the history of recreational sailing.

The double-clewed jibs, which unfortunately for the British were copied in time and thus also used by the American defender, provided four tons of extra thrust under certain conditions compared with the traditional system. However, this meant that under load the sheet blocks failed and had to be replaced rapidly.

Frank Murdoch, an engineer employed in the T.O.M. Sopwith aircraft factory, was a key figure in the development of the yacht, devising a system of tension gauges for the shrouds, the stays and the other rigging.

Starling Burgess instead came up with

142 top left The historic sailmaking firm of Ratsey & Lapthorn is still in business at Cowes. There can hardly be a yacht among those flying the Union Jack whose sail plan has not been sent to the firm for an estimate. Here on the immense wooden floor the sailmaker's entire workforce is gathered round the mainsail cut and sewed for Endeavour, *5,000 square feet of Egyptian cotton in bolts 17.7 inches wide.*

142 top right One of the few photos of the interior of a J Class yacht: the sail locker of the Charles E. Nicholson-designed Endeavour, the most competitive British challenger.

142 center Endeavour I was more than a match for the American boat Rainbow. Nicholson had no hesitation in acquiescing to the New York Yacht Club's request for plans of the boat which were immediately sent to the Stevens Institute testing tank and were used to optimize the lines of Ranger.

142 bottom The success of the Enterprise convinced Vanderbilt to entrust the design of the 1930 defender to Starling Burgess once again. In spite of Endeavour's best efforts, Rainbow was victorious and Starling went on to design Ranger.

143 The owner, Thomas Octave Murdoch Sopwith and his wife at the helm of the J Class Endeavour I. The photo is clearly posed with the crew kept well out of the photographer's way, but it is also true that the owner's wife was a constant presence aboard the America's Cup yachts of the Thirties: Vanderbilt's wife in fact accompanied her husband and was entrusted with the task of promptly signalling the maneuvers of the adversary.

The next challenger, again owned by Lipton, was *Endeavour II*, which had no particularly innovative features and was modified only in terms of the lines of her hull and her dimensions. She came up against *Ranger*, the greatest J Class ever built, and the result was practically a foregone conclusion.

In order to prepare *Endeavour II*, the British had also launched the Nicholson-designed *Velsheda*, their fourth J Class and one very similar to the old *Endeavour*. In the trials, *Endeavour II* proved to be consistently superior, but we should take into account the fact that the sparring partner was frequently crewed by less experienced hands and

never had such up-to-date equipment as the number one boat.

For the 1937 edition of the America's Cup, the Americans launched what was to be their last J Class yacht, *Ranger*. Starling Burgess was assisted in the design of the boat by Olin Stephens and drew on the work carried out in the testing tank of the Stevens Institute in Hoboken, New Jersey. The tank was used to test a model of *Endeavour* after C. E. Nicholson very sportingly sent the original drawings of his boat to Burgess. *Ranger* did not win as a result of her rig, the materials of which she was constructed or the regulations; she simply had superior lines to *Endeavour II* and was thus much

faster. The challenge between *Endeavour II* and *Ranger* was the sixteenth edition of the America's Cup and drew the curtain on the J Class era, as after the Second World War the event was to be disputed by the International Rule 12-meter boats.

Prior to the J Class yachts, the British had built a number of 23-meter yachts to the International Rule that regularly raced in the Solent amongst themselves and on compensated time against the Big Class yachts: *Astra* and *Candida*, both designed by Nicholson; *Cambria* and *Shamrock* (the first of Lipton's family of yachts) designed by Fife and *White Heather* were among the first group, while *Britannia* owned by the royal family and *Lulworth*, the renowned Big

144 top There is an air of deflation and perhaps resignation in this photo. Certainly the faces of the Sopwiths express all the bitterness that comes with the collapse of a dream. With the defeat of Endeavour II in 1937, the British aircraft manufacturer's hopes of bringing the America's Cup home to Britain that had been reinforced by Endeavour's performance in 1934 were finally dashed.

144 bottom Starling Burgess' design demonstrated a clear superiority with respects to the British challenger. Vanderbilt always started in the lead and, leg by leg, constantly increased his advantage. In contrast, in the previous edition the British boat, while faster, and taking into account the weight of the committee decisions, never gave the impression of being capable of winning easily. The technical qualities and experience of the American crew was decisive.

Class cutter owned by Mr. Herbert Weld (descendent of the famous Joseph Weld, owner of the English cutters *Alarm* and *Arrow*, both of which competed against *America* at Cowes in 1851) were among the second. These yachts were re-rated according to the Universal Rule in order to race in real time against the America's Cup J Class boats.

The J Class will also be associated with two figures in particular, one British, the other American, who with their passion, competence and competitive spirit enlivened what was perhaps the most significant decade in the history of the America's Cup, Thomas Octave Murdoch Sopwith and Harold S. "Mike" Vanderbilt. Both were also representatives

of a new breed, that of the owner-skipper; they were skilled helmsmen and the battles between their yachts were also personal duels between their own technical and tactical abilities. Thomas Sopwith was known in both sailing and social circles by his initials, T.O.M. or Tom. An aeronautical engineer and flying pioneer, he designed and built in his factory military aircraft such as the famous First World War Sopwith Camel. After flying, his great passion was sailing and he became Britain's leading amateur helmsman. He had also raced in America and was familiar with the waters off Newport where the America's Cup regattas were staged. All he lacked to bring the

trophy home to Britain was a suitable crew; in fact he trusted only his wife, who was a constant presence in the cockpit, with timekeeping duties. Sopwith's great adversary was Harold Vanderbilt. The heir of a shipbuilding and railroad dynasty, he was, like his British rival, a great yachting enthusiast, dividing his free time between sailing and his other great passion, bridge. As well as a fine helmsman, he was an astute businessman and brought his logistical and organizational talents to his America's Cup campaigns and his cockpit. The members of his crew were always perfectly trained and knew exactly what they had to do at any given moment.

The inter-war decades

144-145 *Ranger's victory was ensured in the testing tank of the Stevens Institute, but the excellence of the boat's after guard also made a vital contribution: Rod Stephens, brother of the designer Olin, oversaw the rig and its handling, Olin himself was aboard as assistant helmsman, Professor Zenas Bliss was the navigator, Gertrude Vanderbilt, the observer, of the adversary that is, and Arthur Knapp was responsible for the trimming of the sails.*

145 *The sails hoisted by America in 1851 were undoubtedly one of her most powerful weapons: Sails continued to be the yachts' "engine", an element fundamental to their performance. In 1934, Endeavour I presented this spinnaker with a series of apertures at the center: they were intended to be used to reduce the turbulence caused by the perpendicular impact of the wind against the sail and therefore increase the pressure on the canvas and improve its stability.*

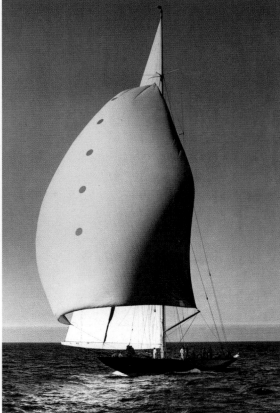

THE GREAT OCEAN RACES

The J Class yachts only raced in winds under 21 knots; they were racing machines as delicate as they were fast, as beautiful as they were limited in what they could do—somewhat like the Formula 1 cars of today that could never compete in a rally.

There were yachts, however, that competed in the sailing world's equivalent of rallies, the ocean races. The fishermen of Gloucester were scandalized when they saw that the J Class boats remained in port when the wind was blowing at 25 knots and went out in their schooners, all sails aloft, to race among themselves. They were mistaken, however, if they thought that it was the amateur yachtsmen who were afraid of the wind and sea conditions.

This was demonstrated in that period by the growing interest in ocean racing. The first editions of the Bermuda and the great Transatlantic Race were held in the early twentieth century and became regular events between the two wars.

The Bermuda Race was revived in 1923, with no less than 23 yachts at the start, including a great number of schooners of the type designed by Alden and based on the Gloucester fishing schooner model. By 1930, they had become a fleet of 42 boats despite the economic crisis. The event was a great success albeit exclusively "American," with the first foreign yacht only taking part in the period following the Second World War.

Ocean racing also found enthusiasts on the Pacific coast of North America as California began to establish itself as one of the wealthiest states.

146-147 1923 saw the revival of the Bermuda Race after the end of the Great War. As is frequently the case, the waters of Newport, Rhode Island, from where the race started, were characterized by calms and banks of fog.

147 top From Newport to Bermuda, in the middle of the Atlantic, over 600 miles traversed by the Gulf Stream, a current of relatively warm water that provokes local fogs and depressions and makes keeping to a correct course all the more difficult thanks to the speed of the current and the effect it has on wave patterns. When the wind blows against the direction of the current, short, sharp waves are raised that impede forward sailing, place enormous stress on rigging and make life uncomfortable for the crew.

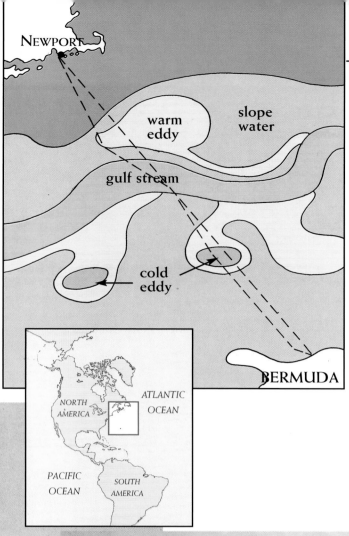

A year after the Transatlantic Race promoted by the Kaiser in 1906, the first Transpacific was staged between San Francisco and Honolulu, capital of the Hawaiian Islands—2,300 miles of open ocean that in reality was far less demanding than the 660 miles of the Bermuda Race, with its Gulf Stream, fogs and sudden squalls.

On the San Francisco-Honolulu route, once clear of the American coast, the yachts found themselves riding the Northeast Trade Wind that carried them directly to the finishing line to the Southeast without ever blowing hard or falling away completely. It was a long, pleasant, relaxing cruise with a favourable wind.

Ten editions of the Transpacific were staged after that first edition and prior to the outbreak of the Second World War. From 1936, it was decided to hold the event biannually, alternating with the Bermuda Race so as to allow boats and crews to participate in both.

147 center Meteorological conditions have always influenced the Bermuda Race. Fog was a feature of the start of the 1923 edition: the yachts circled the committee boat like phantoms propelled by a light breeze. These conditions are determined by the Gulf Stream, a current of warm water that generates instability and sudden changes in the weather with small local squalls

147 bottom The Bermuda Race was revived in 1923: 23 yachts lined up for the start including numerous so-called "Alden schooners." One in particular, the famous Malabar IV, owned by John Alden himself, was to win the race. Up to the Second World War, or rather until the appearance in the late 30s of Stephens yachts such as Dorade or Stormy Weather, ocean racing appeared to be the preserve of yachts that were particularly robust and seaworthy rather than fast, such as Malabar IV.

The center of American yachting was, however, the Atlantic coast, in particular that stretch of sea from the sheltered Long Island Sound, at one extremity of which sits New York, up to Massachusetts Bay and the city of Boston. Those waters, generally windy but rarely bothered by storms, at least in the summer, and rimmed by green coastlines and long sandy beaches where the East Coast aristocracy built their prestigious summer homes, were the protected by Block Island. Having reached the Brenton Reef lightship off Newport, Rhode Island, a resort for the wealthy cream of American society, the fleet heads to Martha's Vineyard, Cape Cod and finally Marblehead, near Boston. The Cruise is still today considered to be an unmissable event for the members and their yachts.

Returning to the periphery of the vast territory of the United States, and to bear brief

setting for the most significant sailing events, above all the America's Cup.

Since the founding of the New York Yacht Club in 1844, a cruise-cum-regatta has been staged between New London (on Long Island Sound) and Marblehead. The event, the New York Yacht Club Cruise, represents the social pinnacle for American sailing enthusiasts.

The 1844 edition saw the participation of eight yachts: the *Gimcrack* of Commodore John Cox Stevens, aboard which the club itself had been founded that year, the *Spray*, the *Coquille*, the *Cygnet*, the *Dream*, the *Minna*, the *Petrel* and the *Mist*. The eight yachts alternated short cruises between the many anchorages offered by the area with races and pleasant social occasions.

The cruise became an annual event and initially lasted a week, but it was subsequently extended to ten days and was held in August. The yachts departed from the sheltered waters of Long Island Sound, which the previously cited Heckstall-Smith, English yachtsman and acute observer of the yachting world, described as "... the ideal place for any kind of yacht up to the 300 ton schooners. It is a magnificent stretch of deep sea, protected by the surrounding land, with a surface area of 10 miles by twenty..." In reality the sound is ten miles wide only off New Haven at about halfway along its length, and from New York to its mouth on the open sea it is over fifty miles long. Upon leaving Long Island Sound, the fleet of N.Y.Y.C.C. yachts tackles a stretch of sea that while relatively exposed is nonetheless

testimony to the rapid spread of yachting in the country, it is here appropriate to mention another ocean race (if we may use the term) that is unusual in that it is probably the longest of those staged on inland fresh water lakes: the Chicago-Mackinac, 330 miles on Lake Michigan whose vastness makes the term "ocean" appropriate. This is also the oldest of the long distance races, the first edition dating back to 1898 when it was disputed by five yachts from Chicago and was an amateur and improvised event. Since 1904, it has been organized on an annual basis by the Chicago Yacht Club. It is now the world's most famous fresh water race and is frequently staged in difficult conditions, above all because Lake Michigan is subject to unpredictable lulls and violent squalls that have often provoked accidents.

The 1911 edition saw eleven yachts start the race, leaving the Chicago shore on a light breeze. A sudden wind with gusts of 80 knots obliged part of the fleet to seek refuge in the bays along the shore, and the large sloop *Vencedor* went aground on the rocks. Only seven yachts finished the race, which was won by *Amorita*, a 98-foot 6-inch schooner, in 31 hours and 11 minutes, a record that still stands today.

The British, despite leading the way in many areas of yachting and actually being the inventors of the sport, waited until 1925 before staging their first ocean race: a 615-mile voyage departing, of course, from Cowes on the Solent

148 In the late nineteenth century, racing was still a marginal activity in the yachting world where the demands of status and a desire for the "good life" were paramount. The annual regatta-cruise, an unmissable event for the members of the New York Yacht Club provided pleasant stop-overs in bays such as the one at Newport, Rhode Island (seen here), that were the occasion for meetings, parties and gala evenings.

148-149 In the early twentieth century the most important event in club's calendar had already assumed more sporting connotations. There was no lack of dances and receptions, but at sea the sailing was taken seriously and between one leg and the next the members' yachts, subdivided into classes, raced enthusiastically. In this photo, Petrel is leading the fleet shortly after the start of the 1900 edition. Year by year, the numbers increased and the event continues to be staged up to the present day.

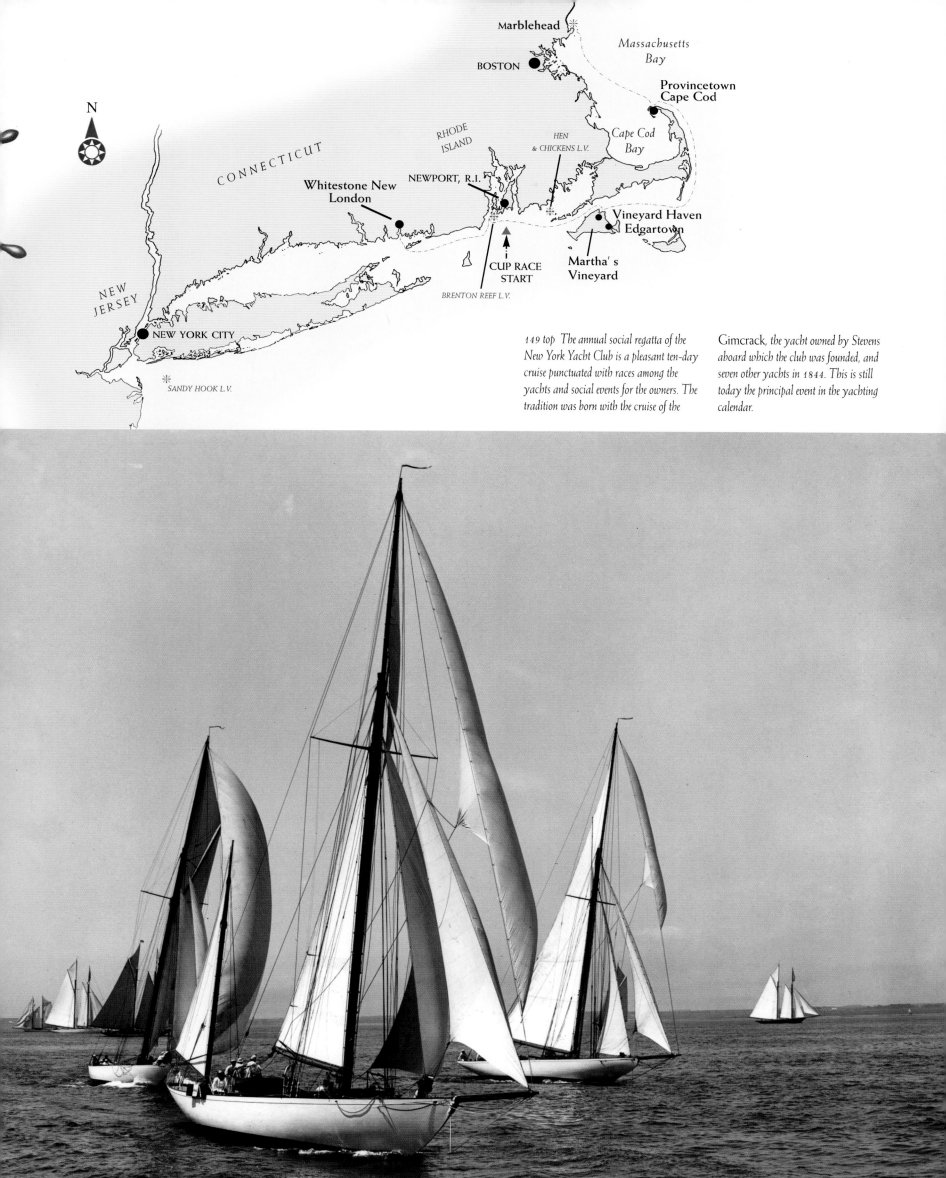

Marblehead

BOSTON

Massachusetts Bay

Provincetown Cape Cod

N

CONNECTICUT

RHODE ISLAND

HEN & CHICKENS L.V.

Cape Cod Bay

Whitestone New London

NEWPORT, R.I.

Vineyard Haven Edgartown

CUP RACE START

Martha's Vineyard

BRENTON REEF L.V.

NEW JERSEY

NEW YORK CITY

SANDY HOOK L.V.

149 top The annual social regatta of the New York Yacht Club is a pleasant ten-day cruise punctuated with races among the yachts and social events for the owners. The tradition was born with the cruise of the Gimcrack, *the yacht owned by Stevens aboard which the club was founded, and seven other yachts in 1844. This is still today the principal event in the yachting calendar.*

and proceding to the Fastnet Rock off the southern coast of Ireland, before finishing at Plymouth in Devon after having rounded Land's End and the Isles of Scilly, an insidious group of rocks and small islands, mute witnesses to numerous tragic shipwrecks. This is a race that covers less than 200 miles of true ocean but which is without doubt one of the most difficult events in the sailing world due to the severe conditions that are frequently encountered. Strong currents, frequent squalls, fog and rain storms, seas with oceanic wave patterns that become steep and sharp as they meet the continental shelf—all this on a route lined by shallows and rocks. Of my first Fastnet, I remember a gruelling windward leg against a sea

The first edition of the Fastnet Race was held in 1925 with just seven boats lining up for the start. It was won by the *Jolie Brise*, a pilot cutter built at Le Havre and converted into a yacht. She had more in common with the traditional British cutters of the early nineteenth century than with contemporary recreational sailing boats, and her adversaries were of the same mould: there was one yacht, designed by Shepard and as usual very dated, two Bristol pilot cutters, a Colin Archer and a working boat from the Highlands.

The *Jolie Brise*, owned by E. G. Martin, won the Fastnet again in 1929 and '30, achieving legendary status and putting forward a formidable argument in favor of the supporters of the British cutter.

British cutter owned by Lord Stalybridge, and *La Goleta*, owned by Mr. R. Peverhy, a typical American Alden schooner, were left in the race. *Tally Ho* won on corrected time, reaching Plymouth just 52 minutes after the American boat. On two consecutive occasions, the century-old duel between the British and American schools had seen victory go to the conservatism of the latter. The following year, however, was to see this verdict overturned with the race being won by *Niña*, the Starling Burgess schooner with a Marconi mainsail and a modified rig compared with the classical Alden layout deriving from the old Gloucester fishing schooners. The yacht, designed by Burgess for two American businessmen, Paul Hammond and

made vertical by the strong adverse current. There followed a dead calm that obliged us to drop anchor so as not to be pushed back by the tidal current that had in the meantime changed direction (the wind had left the sea so short and violent, before it was flattened by the current, that one boat was demasted in the bay due to the violent pitching). The first night at sea was again to windward with banks of fog and rain, followed after the rounding of the Fastnet by a 45-knot following wind and oceanic waves swamping the cockpit. After a second night at sea, there followed a morning calm and a dawn finish at Plymouth in fog and rain with a lookout at the bow to spot, before it was too late, the numerous buoys with their lugubrious bells marking the entrance channel.

Much has already been said and written about my second Fastnet, both at the time and in the years that followed: 303 yachts started, 85 finished and 15 men were lost at sea.

The 1926 edition already had an international flavor with the participation of *Primrose IV*, one of those Alden schooners that dominated the Bermuda Race. That year's Fastnet was won by *Ilex*, designed by Nicholson in 1899: she was to be third in 1929 and again in '30. It perhaps goes without saying, but the quality of the traditional British yachts never ceases to surprise.

The third edition of 1927 was like the previous two, characterized by bad weather. In 1925, a storm had forced all the boats to seek refuge in the last part of the race with the exception of *Jolie Brise* which had already passed through the area. In 1926, instead, the storm caught the boats just as they were rounding Fastnet Rock; one yacht was deliberately beached in order to avoid sinking after suffering a severe beating from the waves.

The 1927 race was, however, even worse. Of the fifteen participants, nine had been obliged to retire even before they had left the Solent and after having rounded Land's End only *Tally Ho*, the

Elihu Root Jr., had been built for the King's and Queen's Cup (the king being Alfonso XIII of Spain while the queen was Victoria of England), the 1928 Transatlantic Race, by the dinghy and cat-boat builder Reuben Bigelow of Buzzard's Bay, Massachusetts. He took just four months, a time unthinkable today for an 60-foot yacht, but not exceptional in those years when labor was plentiful and the working week was far longer than the present-day 40 hours. Moreover, yachts were much simpler then: once the hull, interior and rig were completed the boat could be launched as there were no systems, machinery and accessories to install as on modern yachts. *Niña* won the Transatlantic race and, with this as her calling card, started the Fastnet on the 15th of August, 1928. Aboard as helmsman and tactician was Sherman Hoyt, already considered to be one of the finest American yachtsmen even before the stroke of genius that saved the 1934 America's Cup. She went on to triumph in the Fastnet too.

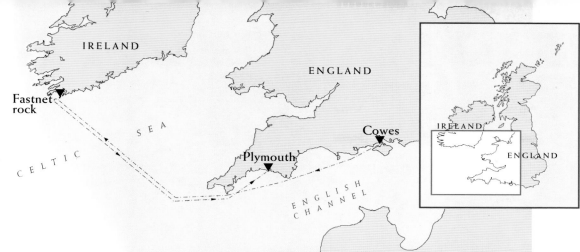

151 bottom right The schooner designed by Starling Burgess tackling the short, sharp waves of the Bermuda Race. These are uncomfortable conditions mentioned earlier and those in which Niña comes into her own. Perfectly trimmed sails, the large mainsail hauled very taut keeps the head up and provides plenty of thrust which the staysail and jibs are very flat. This is an ocean race and Niña is a yacht designed for the open sea.

150 left La Goleta *flew the stars and stripes in the Fastnet of 1927, the third edition and a race that centred around the duel between this boat and* Tally Ho, *a typical British cutter. In this case, there is no sense in taking the cutter's victory as evidence of this type of yacht's supremacy with respects to the American schooner: a six-day race in stormy conditions testifies only to the skill of the crews that made it to the finish.*

150 right The early editions of the Fastnet race saw the participation and victory of yachts, built for their seaworthiness rather than pure speed. Jolie Brise *won the inaugural race in 1925 and twice repeated the exploit in 1929 and 1930. She was actually a converted Le Havre pilot boat, a type of boat common throughout the Channel. Still sailing today, it is always a pleasure to see her.*

151 top left The most classic of all ocean races starts from Cowes, on the waters in front of the headquarters of the Royal Yacht Squadron, and heads west from the mouth of the Solent. The yachts follow the coastline of southern England, round the Isles of Scilly and head for the lighthouse on Fastnet Rock, Ireland on a north-north-westerly route. Having rounded the lighthouse they head back towards the Isles of Scilly and finish at Plymouth.

151 bottom left Like Jolie Brise, Tally Ho *is a former pilot cutter converted into a yacht by Albert Strange and became an attractive and highly effective Fastnet contender: she won an epic duel with* La Goleta *in 1927 on corrected time, thanks to the handicapping that allowed her to make up the 52-minutes difference at the finish.*

152 top left In the early post-war period, France pursued a policy of democratizing and developing recreational sailing: designers invented economical methods of construction. Philippe Viannay promoted a sailing school in Brittany that introduced enthusiastic youngsters to the sport. Jean Jacques Herbulot designed dual or single chine boats to be made in plywood. The illustration shows the "cotre des Glénans," the Breton school that was to be a point of reference in Europe.

152 center left Vito Dumas set sail for a voyage around the world: he was to be the first single-handed sailor to round the Cape of Good Hope, Cape Horn and Cape Leeuwin. This was an extreme voyage, especially for those times: rigging was heavy, communications systems were non-existent and there was no one to worry about a lone sailor wandering the oceans.

TOWARDS A REVIVAL: A NEW YACHTING

The Second World War had a devastating effect on the nations involved and recreational sailing was naturally the last thing on peoples' minds. However, even in the darkest years of the conflict traces of the sport that had been so popular in certain countries were still to be found.

The enormous quantities of lead used for the ballast of the great yachts of the Thirties were requisitioned to make ammunition (this is the reason why, still today, when old hulls are salvaged, especially in Great Britain, ballast in the form of ingots of cast iron, concrete or an iron-concrete agglomerate may be found). The large yachts, above all the "floating gin palaces" were converted into cargo carriers, hospital ships or troop transports. The vast spinnakers, generally made of pure silk, the most recent perhaps in synthetic silk, were sacrificed to make shirts, parachutes, tents and so on.

Mentioning only some of the best known names, the men who had dedicated their talent to allowing the magnates of industry and the Old World aristocracy to race at sea under sail also put their skills at the service of the warring nations. Olin Stephens followed up *Dorade* and *Ranger* with a design for an amphibious vehicle that was widely used in the Normandy landings, while the ingenious Uffa Fox transformed one of his sailing dinghies, making it unsinkable. He equipped it with a watertight canvas cover, two short masts, each with its own sail, and a set of instructions on how to use the boat. This was the first air-sea rescue dinghy. Built in countless numbers, it was dropped into the sea by the search and rescue planes looking for the bomber crews who ditched in the Channel and was responsible for saving hundreds of airmen.

Yachting was also used as a form of

humanitarian support for the prisoners of war locked in camps in Germany. The French were responsible for founding the Stalag 1 S Yacht Club that organized regattas for the models built by the prisoners within the camp. For the British prisoners, the Royal Ocean Racing Club organized a competition for the design of a yacht of between 30 and 35 feet in length, providing entrants with paper, pencils and drawing instruments.

Somewhat ironically, the war favored the process whereby democracy came to the world of yachting. Pétain's provisional government in

France encouraged the development of recreational sailing practiced with dinghies and single-class boats and, as a consequence, the nation entered the post-war period with a fleet that was actually larger than that of the Thirties. Jean Jacques Herbulot designed the *Vaurien*, a small dinghy mass produced in plywood, followed by the *Corsair*. Both enjoyed widespread success in what were extremely difficult economic conditions.

During the war, the seed of a passion had been sown; a new way of going to sea that broke away from the traditional mould and was now being provided with appropriate and affordable boats. It is true that initially the *Vaurien* cost as much as a bicycle at a time when a bicycle cost much the same as a small apartment, but nonetheless France, which as a nation spent 40% of its income on

food, had no less than 2,300 dinghies and single-class boats afloat in 1947.

In the meantime, in the post-war years the thrust towards the "minor" classes, established by the Pétain government and irrespective of ideologies and party politics, found an apostle in Philippe Viannay who founded a sailing school for young people at Glénans that preached a spartan, sporting and popular approach to yachting. This school was to leave a significant and indubitably positive mark on post-war sailing, and not only in France. What a difference compared with the great Uffa Fox, the personal sailing instructor of the Prince of Wales!

Britain also adapted to the changing times, and in 1947 the *Daily Mirror* launched a dinghy that was intended to be produced industrially and thus at low cost. Industrial-scale production,

together with improved welding techniques, were among the very few positive things to come out of the war. As soon as the conflict drew to a close, yachtsmen began to take to the sea once again and as early as the summer of 1945, what was probably the first post-war race was organized from Cowes to Dinard. There were only nine participants but it was at least a beginning.

Britain had not forgotten its pioneering role in the development of yachting and, thanks to the initiative of Captain John H. Illingworth, a man who was to make a major contribution to international sailing, the Royal Ocean Racing Club was soon up and running once again. By 1947, Illingworth was racing at the helm of his *Myth of Malham*.

In the United States, the Stephens brothers, Olin and Rod, had immediately returned to their yachting careers and, when the Bermuda Race was revived in 1946, the New York designers participated with their latest boat. During the war one man had searched at sea for the peace he was unable to find ashore. The Argentine Vito Dumas with his ketch *Legh II*, designed by the naval architect Manuel Campos and based on the Colin Archer hulls he favored, departed on a round-the-word voyage on the 1st of July, 1942. He completed his circumnavigation by way of the three capes, the first time the feat had been performed.

152 center right Competitive sailing was revived from as early as 1946. In the United States, it was again the Bermuda Race that attracted the attention of the yachtsmen. This photo shows the start of that year's edition of the race. Latifa, the beautiful yawl designed by William Fife III in 1936, is leading the fleet, well to windward, her prow showing well. In the center is Sunbeam, a boat I am not familiar with, and the famous Burgess-designed Niña to leeward and bearing away. Niña won in 1929 and was to repeat the feat in 1962.

152 bottom The Legh II, the yacht with which Vito Dumas sailed round the world, was a classic Colin Archer, a boat with a canoe stern, a so-called "double-ender." Thanks to this unusual form it was considered to be a safe and particularly seaworthy boat. The misunderstanding arose from its origins as a boat designed to rescue Norwegian fishermen and thus to lay-to in heavy seas and to be capable of towing other boats in difficulty. Using it as a cruising boat is another matter, but Dumas successfully completed his voyage.

152-153 The start of the 1946 Bermuda Race B Class reserved for smaller yachts and thus particularly popular. The first editions of the American race were frequented by boats with lengths of under 32 feet, despite the fact that it involved ocean sailing and was notoriously demanding due to the frequently adverse weather conditions.

153 right Niña has picked up a good head of speed and, above all, she is putting up well: she does not appear to be penalized by her schooner rig even in comparison with her direct rival,

Gesture, an Olin Stephens design from that year, an attractive sloop of around 56 feet. The modification made by Burgess to the traditional schooner sail plan with the elimination of the spanker staysail in favor of a jib made a significant improvement when beating. Gesture nonetheless won the Bermuda Race that year.

THE NEW YACHT

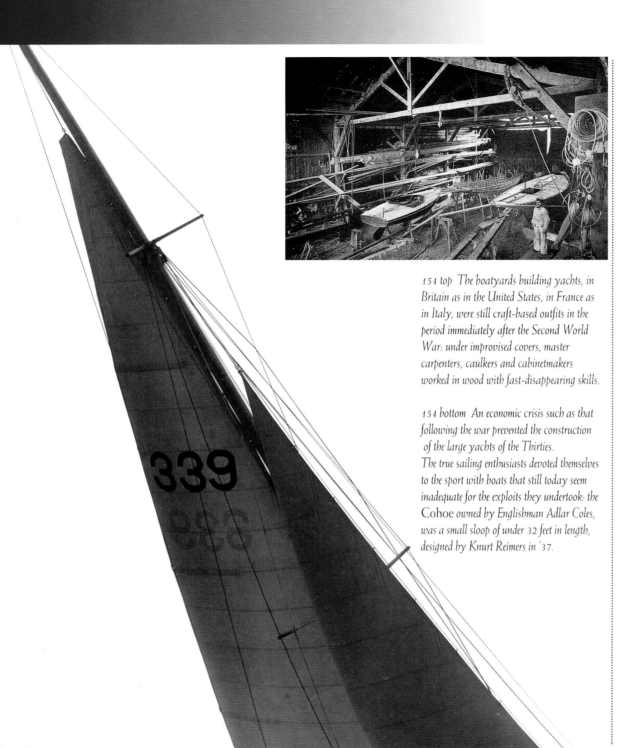

154 top The boatyards building yachts, in Britain as in the United States, in France as in Italy, were still craft-based outfits in the period immediately after the Second World War: under improvised covers, master carpenters, caulkers and cabinetmakers worked in wood with fast-disappearing skills.

154 bottom An economic crisis such as that following the war prevented the construction of the large yachts of the Thirties. The true sailing enthusiasts devoted themselves to the sport with boats that still today seem inadequate for the exploits they undertook: the Cohoe owned by Englishman Adlar Coles, was a small sloop of under 32 feet in length, designed by Knurt Reimers in '37.

In the post-war period the world found itself facing economic problems of such magnitude that all the available resources had to be used in the reconstruction of housing and factories and the supply of primary necessities. Yachts were hardly a necessity. Moreover, the war had had a levelling effect on society and introduced new concepts of democracy.

This does not mean that yachting disappeared, and we have already seen how, when peace arrived, there were those who, despite the unfavorable economic climate, immediately began hoisting canvas aloft. And they were by no means captains of industry, financial giants or members of the aristocracy who had either been swept away or had more pressing matters to attend to. They were genuine enthusiasts, true yachtsmen, those who in the late Thirties had quietly begun to replace the followers of social fashion.

Post-war yachting thus had to tackle new problems: yachts cost too much for the pockets of those wishing to purchase them.

The war itself had provided answers to this particular problem. The industrial processes adopted for the construction of ships and aircraft in response to ever more urgent demands for the means of destruction had brought to light new materials and new technologies and, above all, had led to the development of systems of serial construction.

Obviously, yachting in the early post-war years was not yet ready for this: in order to start serial production there must be a demand for sufficient "units" to justify the investments necessary to industrialize the production process. That demand was absent partly because yachts were too expensive.

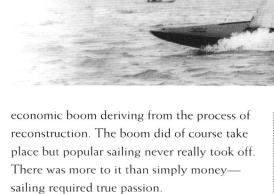

The solution was already in the air: the boats had to be smaller. The yachts of the post-war period, especially the first to be produced, were relatively small. And in order for a small yacht to provide satisfactory performance it had to be light.

As the war drew to a close, a British sailing enthusiast by the name of Colonel Hasler examined the alternatives to satisfy his passion. All he could find was a Swedish "30 m²" formula yacht from 1934, an inland sea boat and by no means a "yacht" in the traditional sense. In the years around 1945, however, you had to be grateful for what you could find.

Hasler made certain modifications to the rig so as to bring his new boat into line with the R.O.R.C. rating system, restored the interiors and deck so as to obtain at least minimum standards of comfort and safety, and started racing the following season, 1946. His *Tre Sang*, proved to be a winner and was immediately copied by another well known British yachtsman, Adlard Coles who also bought a Swedish boat, the *Cohoe*, designed by Knut Reimers in 1937. She was a racing boat but designed, like Hasler's *Tre Sang*, for the sheltered waters of the Scandinavian fjords. The slightly modified *Cohoe* also proved to be a successful boat, winning the first post-war Transatlantic Race no less, from Bermuda to Plymouth.

Tre Sang was 27 feet 4 inches LOA and had a displacement of 6,172 pounds; *Cohoe* was slightly larger at 32 feet 2 inches overall and 7,716 pounds. They demonstrated their worth by racing against and beating the yachts of twenty years earlier; the difference between them and their rivals was that they were smaller and lighter. And were therefore less expensive.

If yachts were cheaper, there would be more potential purchasers, and more orders would justify the industrialization of production methods, which in turn would drive prices further down and stimulate a further growth in demand.

All this pointed to an explosion in the popularity of sailing as the world enjoyed an

economic boom deriving from the process of reconstruction. The boom did of course take place but popular sailing never really took off. There was more to it than simply money— sailing required true passion.

Returning to the early post-war years, the conditions were ripe for the introduction of industrial methods. What the yachting world proved to be ready to accept immediately were the new materials and the new construction techniques. Certain processes, that at the outbreak of the war were experimental, had been transformed into reliable and above all readily available technology by the experience gained during the conflict.

In metalworking, welding had replaced riveting as it was much faster, safer and cheaper. Wooden structures for the aeronautical industry (at that time many components were still in wood as aluminium alloys had yet to be developed) were fashioned from plywood, a number of thin layers of wood bonded one to another with the grain running in alternate directions. There were no waterproof glues before the war and only certain internal elements for boats could be made with plywood (*Flica II*, an International Rule 12-meter designed by L. Giles, was a forerunner of the later lightweight boats built in the Fife yard in 1933. She had internal bulkheads in plywood composed of two external layers of mahogany and an internal core of balsa, an extremely light but very soft wood.

156-157 Among the British designers, who even prior to 1940 had been interested in light displacement boats, Laurent Giles was without doubt one of the most innovative. His designs were characterized by a search for technical features that reduced weight: Flica II is an International Rule 12-meter yacht designed in 1938 and launched from the Fife yard at Fairlie the following year. Inside Flica II, all the bulkheads were composed of two light sheets of wood bonded to a balsa core, an extremely light wood. This was a forerunner of the sandwich construction technique used for modern racing boats.

During the war, a number of synthetic phenolic or resorcinol glues were developed that had the great advantage of being waterproof. From this moment onwards, plywood, which was quicker to work with, did not require such specialized labor as traditional planking and overcame the difficulties in sourcing high quality timber, allowed the production of cheap hulls.

There was, however, one small drawback: the hulls could not be sculpted and had to be designed with sharp edges and angles. They worked just as well but were "ugly" and, as is well known, beauty has always been a fundamental quality in a yacht.

Boatbuilders thus concentrated on another technology that to some extent is a more aristocratic relation of plywood construction, "bois moulé" or moulded wood. In reality, this was already a well known technique and cabinet makers would give rounded forms to furniture by gluing, one on top of another, thin layers of wood that were flexible, especially when wet. Before the outbreak of the war, the technique had even been used to construct large yachts, albeit at an impossible price. As glues could not be used (because they dissolved in water), thousands of small copper nails were employed to bond the various layers after oil-drenched silk had been placed between them. The new synthetic glues were not the complete answer to the problem, as to be truly efficient the layers of wood that were to be bonded had to be subjected to great pressure and high temperatures.

The heat could be supplied by a simple stove but the pressure was a different matter. The solution was to make recourse once again to metal tacks, this time applying them over a strip of fabric that was subsequently removed, pulling away the nails with it when the glue had begun to set. The system is rather complicated but effective and not particularly expensive and on occasion it is still used today. The boats in moulded wood were lighter, simpler and quicker to build, in a word cheaper.

In the meantime, progress was being made with another lightweight material, aluminium. The aluminium alloy (the basic mineral from which aluminium is produced is bauxite and thus all commercial aluminium is an alloy) was modified with the addition of magnesium, in varying percentages depending on the use to which it to be put, thus preventing oxidation. The metal had of course already been used in the skinning of a number of J Class yachts, but these were boats deliberately built not to last. In the late nineteenth century, *Vendenesse* in France and *Defender* in the United States were built in aluminium but the material was then very much experimental and was not taken further because the necessary technology was simply not available. Once Duralumin had been developed, however, new horizons opened up. As early as 1944, aeronautical experience was put to use in the construction of a small light alloy sloop in the United States and years later Olin Stephens designed and had built in the material another yacht of 37 feet 6 inches, the *Wind Call*. However, both of these boats still featured riveted joins in the skinning as still used on aircraft today. Aluminium welding was a later development.

158 *The nineteenth-century experiments such as* Vendenesse *in France and* Defender *in the United States were not followed up: aluminium tended to oxidize in contact with water and therefore corrode. Only in the 1930s did the Aluminium Company of America develop a light alloy based on aluminium, manganese and magnesium, capable of resisting oxidation, and ask*

Starling Burgess to design and construct a half hull in the material. It was retrieved after 6 months immersion in salt water with no signs of oxidation. The first boat constructed in the material was a sloop of around 30 feet LOA, built with a double chine in 1944 by Geerd Hendel in the United States. It was, however, the inevitable Olin Stephens who launched the first true aluminium

yacht in 1946: Wind Call *seen in this photo, was a sloop of 38 feet LOA. Her skinning was composed of sheets of light alloy with watertight riveted joints, a method evidently deriving from aeronautical practice. Welding would arrive later to complete a constructional system that enjoyed great success in the Seventies and Eighties.*

159 top Like the Herreshoff Manufacturing Company in the United States, in Britain recreational sailing had a major boatyard organized on industrial lines: in the post-war period the new Camper & Nicholson yard was founded at Gosport, on the other side of the estuary to Portsmouth. The firm had nineteenth-century roots but had lost its original premises during the war. The new yard was built according to new criteria, but even the old yard had had little in common with the usual craft-based establishments.

Work was also in progress on the development of the material of the future: a combination of a synthetic resin derived from hydrocarbons and a strong fiber.

Many objects were already being made with resins, Bakelite having been introduced in 1907 (in my youth many household objects were made of Bakelite, a material that was attractive, easily mouldable but delicate—if it was dropped it shattered).

There were also tough fibers available, both the natural fibers such as sisal, jute, hemp, linen and cotton and, from as early as 1836, glass fiber. For use with this last fiber a polyester resin was

that would be cut to standard sizes and shapes between one job and the next. It should be remembered in this respect, that in the eighteenth century and into the nineteenth, timber could be pre-shaped by training the growth of the trees to certain curvatures. In short, the yards could count on a stock of relatively standardized planking, beams and ribs that suited the approximate nature of naval architecture.

Following the Second World War, materials were scarce and, quite rightly, the workforce no longer came cheaply and was not prepared to work for 70 or more hours per week. The yards thus had to equip themselves for the

new technologies and the demand for economical constructional methods.

The first modern boatyard was probably that of Herreshoff at Bristol; it was to disappear with the outbreak of the war, but was to provide the inspiration for those that followed with their covered sheds and slipways that allowed yachts to be built irrespective of the weather conditions, and with a smaller workforce and more machinery.

In reality, however, the boatyards were to remain essentially craft-based enterprises until the advent of mass production in the 1960s.

A forerunner of the mass produced yacht and the smaller craft with blue water cruising and racing capabilities was actually presented as early as 1935 by the most innovative of the British designers of the era, Laurent Giles. *Andrillot* a 25-foot gaff cutter was the prototype of the "Vertue" class that, with minor modifications in respect to the original, was to be produced in series after the war.

developed and composite materials, in this case fiberglass, a combination of resin and glass fibers, were born.

The first fiberglass yacht was presented at the 1948 New York Boat Show. It was still a prototype as yachting was not yet ready to adopt a product that needed to be mass produced to be economical.

The boatyards were, however, undergoing a process of transformation. In the nineteenth century, yachts were still being built on beaches or, at best, on rudimentary slipways and always in the open.

If the yards were capable of building boats quickly, this was due to the availability of plentiful cheap labor, long working hours and the possibility of storing large quantities of timber

159 center Working conditions in the recreational boatyards were frequently precarious. The shoring up of the hulls was rather haphazard, something that as well as being dangerous for the workers also made it more difficult to ensure precise control over the dimensions of the work in progress (left). With this kind of equipment the casting of large quantities of lead ballast was undoubtedly a perilous and imprecise process.

159 bottom Laurent Giles' Vertue can be considered as the first series-built yacht. Initially built in wood, it is still in production today in fiberglass. Designed in 1935, she is 25 feet 6 inches long overall with a beam of 7 feet 10 inches and a displacement of 4 tons. The interior provides 2 berths, a comfortable saloon, a small galley and a concealed bathroom.

160 top Stormvogel was created in 1961 by Van de Stadt, the Dutch designer who had come to prominence with Zeevalk, a light displacement double chine boat (ugly but impressively fast) in marine ply. Laurent Giles (structure) and John Illingworth (sail plan and deck layout) collaborated on the design. Although Stormvogel is not an attractive boat, she has a highly respectable honor roll: in the Sixties she won practically every race in which she took part. She planed easily in strong following winds, while Illingworth's sail plan with a yankee and staysail (clearly seen in this photo) gave her remarkable power when beating, backed up by a light displacement that allowed the hull to maintain speed even in a swell. After years of "small" boats in Europe, Stormvogel marked a return to full-size yachts.

Her overall length of 74 feet 6 inches is misleading as she has no overhangs which means she is comparable with a 78-foot boat of some years earlier.

160 bottom Captain John Illingworth made a significant contribution to offshore racing of which he was an active enthusiast; his racing experience allowed him to develop a rig that was extremely efficient, particularly in the stiff breezes frequently encountered in the areas where he usually sailed. His collaboration with Laurent Giles was particularly fertile; the British high priest of the light displacement met the great advocate of the fractionated rig: a small mainsail, a yankee and a staysail at the prow. Maid of Malham was born out this collaboration.

161 Other significant yachts based on the ideas of John Illingworth: Mouse of Malham, *bottom, is a small yawl, a RORC Class III, which won the Fastnet in 1955. This was confirmation of the validity of the light displacement concept and* marked the definitive demise of the classic yacht. Racing boats were now built to exploit the regulations and optimize performance. The light displacement placed less strain on the rig and hull structure and the boats were faster and more reliable. Outlaw, *seen in the top photo, is perhaps still today the best known British design: 36 feet LOA, a very characteristic reversed sheerline, the cockpit in front of the winches, beautiful exposed cedar planking over cold bonded laminate.*

In the meantime, in the wake of the success of *Tre Sang* and *Cohoe*, naval architects concentrated on reducing displacement.

Laurent Giles was again at the forefront of developments, thanks in part to his successful partnership with that fine yachtsman Captain John Holden Illingworth, one of those typically British figures whose passion for the sea and sailing led him to devote his entire life to both, as had Uffa Fox, and as is still the case with Henry Spencer. A yachtsman from a very early age and subsequently a naval officer, in 1937 Illingworth commissioned the *Maid of Malham* and actively assisted Laurent Giles in her design. At the helm of this yacht, he won the British ocean racing championship the following season. He probably had little influence over the structure or the lines of the hull, but Illingworth certainly had much to say with regard to the rigging. The deck was his realm and he brought to this area an unmatched ability in fine tuning, handling and race tactics. The collaboration between Giles and Illingworth resulted in the *Myth of Malham* of 1947, the first true British "light displacement" yacht and a two-time winner of the Fastnet, and lastly the *Mouse of Malham*.

At this point it is worth making specific mention of John Illingworth and the role he played in post-war sailing, not only in Britain. In 1945, with the war barely over and while serving in Australia, Illingworth organized, launched and won with the yacht *Rani*, the Sydney-Hobart race. In 1950, he was elected as Commodore of the Royal Ocean Racing Club, which was to become the world's premier ocean racing

organization. In those years, together with Angus Primrose, he also opened a naval architecture studio, designing yachts that were absolutely original and instantly recognizable as well as regular race winners. The 48-foot 6-inch *Outlaw* from 1963 is still today a supremely beautiful racing machine. She sits low in the water, the reverse sheer highly accentuated, extremely light with her crossed planking in exposed cedar and above all her cutter rig with a yankee jib and staysail at the prow, something of an Illingworth signature. He also made a significant contribution to what is rightly considered to be one of the key designs of the Sixties, *Stormvogel*, born out of the collaboration between Van de Stadt for the lines and Giles for the structure. This was a large boat, especially for the era, a light displacement yacht of 74 feet 6 inches LOA, that planes like a dinghy. She was a consistent winner during the Sixties and now tours the world as a charter yacht.

Illingworth's last design dated from 1966 and was none other than Sir Francis Chichester's *Gypsy Moth IV*. In the meantime, he had been a major figure as technical advisor (it might be said that more attention should have been paid to his advice) in the two editions of the America's Cup in the post-war period. One of the best features of the British challengers had been their spinnakers, which were lighter than the American equivalents and, designed and manufactured by the French firm Herbulot, were adopted at Illingworth's insistence. It was strange that an Englishman should show a preference for French things, but thererein lies Illingworth's greatness.

When advancing years suggested a more tranquil occupation than hopping from one part the deck of a racing yacht to another, he turned to writing—about sailing naturally. His *Offshore, Further Offshore*, and *Twenty Challengers for the America's Cup* are works whereby the voice of Captain John Illingworth is still heard in the world of yachting today.

Returning to the work of Laurent Giles, it is important to examine the *Myth of Malham* design. This was a brand-new yacht: she had virtually no overhangs, her ballast keel was very short and she sat fairly flat in the water, well balanced between stem and stern. The sheerline was reversed (moving towards the prow, the toerail line rises amidships before descending again); the sail plan had unheard of aspect ratios while the prow triangle was divided into a number of small sails. *Myth of Malham* was above all light: 8 tons for 37 feet 8 inches LOA, four of those tons being ballast.

The influence of aeronautical engineering was clear: Giles' design featured double skinning crossed at 45° over a reticular frame composed of thin, closely spaced ribs and longitudinal members.

While in the case of the *Jolie Brise*, the winner of the Fastnet only 20 years earlier, the ratio between displacement and length was 5:1, in the case of *Dorade*, the winner 15 years earlier, it had dropped to 3:1, and in the case of the *Myth*, the ratio was further reduced to 2:1 and she was all-conquering between 1947 and '50.

In 1949, Giles went even further, creating an all-alloy hull for the 55-foot LOA *Gulvain*, which had a displacement of 15 tons, the same as the meter-longer *Dorade*.

A Dutch designer, Van de Stadt, was working along the same lines and, while relatively unknown at the time, was to become one of the most prolific designers in the years to come. His *Zeevalk* was even lighter than Giles' yachts: 41 feet LOA for a displacement of 4.8 tons. The hull was in plywood with structural bulkheads, hollow at the extremities, and was an angular design. These were boats designed to be inexpensive, but after an initial period in which they enjoyed a certain popularity they became

162 In Great Britain, the late Thirties with Giles and Clark saw a significant shift towards light displacement boats. The trend was to be confirmed in the post-war period with a series of extreme yachts, at least in relation to the standards of the day, in the United States, which usually preceded Britain in terms of innovation. The Stephens brothers, after the success of Dorade *and* Stormy Weather, *continued in the same direction: a yacht that represented a compromise between the old British and American schools, with displacement attention being paid to displacement. A Stephens yacht was solid and traditionally built. The question of weight entailed its distribution rather than its reduction.* Loki, *seen in the top photo, was designed in 1949, 15 years after* Stormy Weather *but is more conservative.* Argyll, *bottom, is only larger and has the same rig, interior layouts and typically Stephens lines. The Stephens yachts were successful, winning just as much as the contemporary British yachts of Giles and Illingworth, and when the two schools met, honors were shared.*

increasingly rare. As I have already said, ugliness does not pay.

It was only logical that the trio of Illingworth, Giles and Van de Stadt should come together at some point. The occasion was the design of the *Stormvogel*.

Strangely, in the United States, which prior to the outbreak of the war had countered with traditional British cutters with lighter hulls, the light displacement extremes of certain European designers failed to take hold.

With occasional exceptions, the Americans designed "compromise" yachts, following the trail blazed by Stephens with *Stormy Weather*. For example, *Argyll* and *Loki*, were "classic" yachts, reasonable developments based on what had gone before: when they came up against the European light displacement boats they proved to be winning designs.

163 Myth of Malham is worthy of close attention. She was the prototype British light displacement yacht of the early post-war period from which all the light yachts that were to win races in the Fifties and Sixties, especially in Europe, were to derive. She cannot be said to be attractive and was built to the rating formula. Within the minimum size, John Illingworth and Laurent Giles managed to create an extremely powerful racing machine. The structure conceived by the designer clearly derives from aeronautical practice with a framework of longitudinal members and transverse elements over which lies a "structural" skin composed of three-ply diagonally superimposed laths. This skinning is very stiff and thus helps the frame, something that traditional planking does not do, or not to same degree. The deck layout was designed by John Illingworth with the helmsman's cockpit separate from the men working the winches, while the deckhouse allows the necessary central interior headroom but is narrow to allow the gangways either side to be clear for handling the rig. The sail plan is very elongated, absolutely unique at the time, with a small mainsail and multiple jibs at the prow—a large number of small sails to ensure a constantly well balanced boat. The interiors are spare and concentrated amidships; Myth's extremities are light, with no overhangs and thus no volume to set on the water. The design dates from 1949, the same year as Loki and Argyll. She is a completely different boat and won the Fastnet in severe conditions when the others were winning the Bermuda Race.

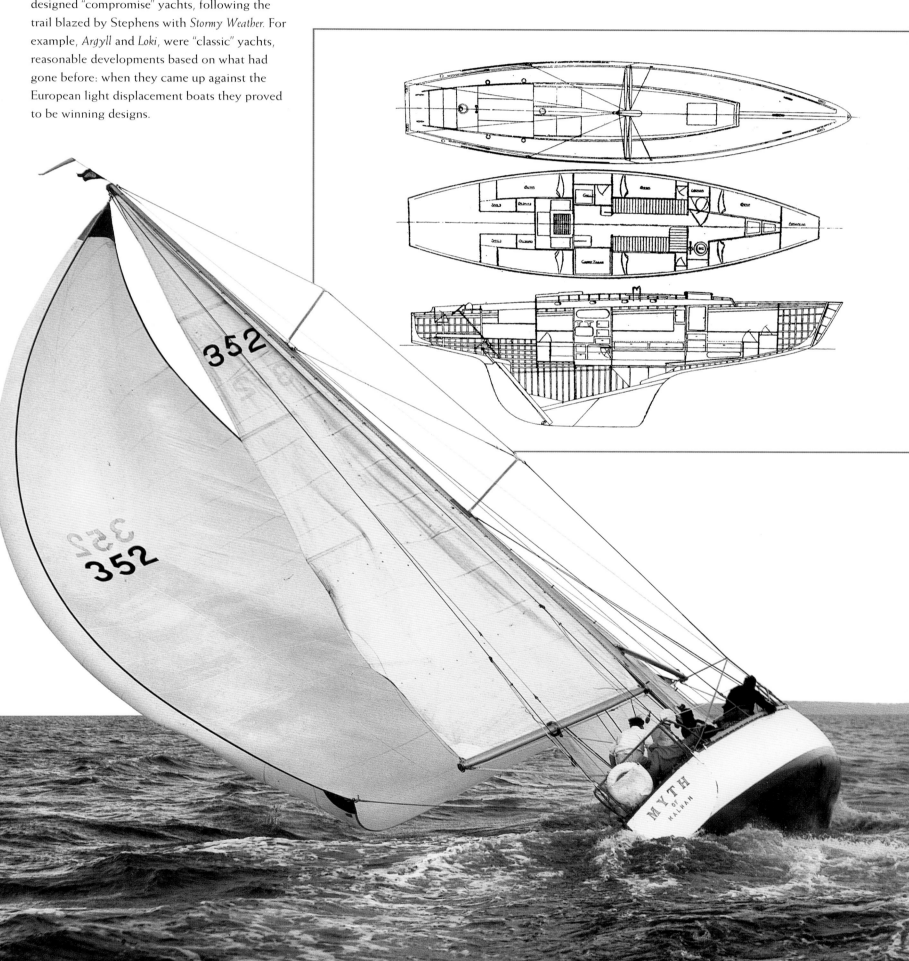

THE SINGLE-HANDED YACHTSMEN

The yachting of the past—the post-war years are part of the modern period despite the rapidity with which changes occur today—was cloaked in romanticism and aristocratic exhibitionism. Pure sporting passion had already made its appearance in the Thirties, but it was still the prerogative of a restricted circle of people and was easily confused with snobbery.

The post-war and thus the modern period (even though the most recent episodes have tended to obscure the fact), was to bring new motivations, and alongside the spread of the sport in general a new phenomenon emerged. While there were those, and they were in the majority of course, who wholeheartedly embraced the process of reconstruction, dedicating themselves to reviving the economic infrastructure, there were also those who remained attached to a romantic image, those who found themselves addicted to the adrenaline stimulated by the war and those who were unable to rediscover the values that had encouraged them to accept and participate in progress.

From the late Fifties onwards, there was a choice to be made: either join the race towards economic success or find alternative routes to self-fulfillment. One of these alternatives was to be single-handed ocean sailing.

The history of yachting had already featured this type of sailing and as early as the nineteenth century there had been yachtsmen prepared to cross the oceans alone. But these had always been marginal episodes of no broader significance, individual, self-contained feats. Instead the Sixties were to see the development of a true specialization within the vast world of

yachting and the consumer society was to seize on the phenomenon and exploit it to its own contrary ends.

It perhaps hardly needs to be said that the impetus was provided by a Briton, Herbert G. "Blondie" Hasler. During the war, Colonel Hasler had been a part of a commando regiment and had conceived and carried out a night attack in winter on the German fleet stationed at Bordeaux in occupied France. His group actually entered the French port in kayaks and went on to sink seven ships!

In the post-war period, the enthusiastic yachtsman raced, as we have seen, with his *Tre Sang* and also plunged into single-handed sailing. He designed and fitted a junk rig to his *Jester*, a modified Folkboat which he sailed in single-handed races during the Sixties. As well being remembered as one of the pioneers of this type

164 top The Folkboat responded to the demands of the post-war yachting market for boats that were inexpensive, reliable in bad weather and capable of offering decent cruising and respectable racing performance. The type became common on the south coast of England and justifiably still has its fans today. Colonel Hasler rigged an example for single-handed sailing. He reinforced the superstructure to increase interior space and provide protection in the case of capsizing. Above all, he modified the rigging with a form of junk rig that was as strange as it was efficient in its simplicity: easy to adjust, easy to shorten. Perhaps not fast but that was not its raison d'être.

164 bottom Herbert Hasler opened the way for single-handed Transatlantic racing. His example led to a busy series of events that are still very popular.

165 top left Francis Chichester's Gypsy Moth IV *off Cape Horn, the extreme southerly tip of the American continent and a legendary passage in yachting history. Chichester was involved in the first single-hand round-the-world*

challenge in 1966. The British sailor was to take 226 days to return to his point of departure, making a single stop at Sydney. Gypsy Moth IV *was a 52-foot 6-inch ketch, the largest boat to be sailed single-handed up to that time.*

165 top right The Frenchman Alain Gerbault, an aircraft pilot and tennis champion, completed a single-handed round-the-world voyage between 1923 and 1929, a feat that received wide coverage in the French press.

165 bottom After the completion of his 1966 single-handed voyage, Chichester received a knighthood from Queen Elizabeth II, becoming Sir Francis Chichester. This was in recognition of the sporting achievement of a man who had made adventure a way of life. He had fought a life-threatening illness and in 1930 had already attempted a single-handed circumnavigation of the globe, but by plane. Departing from England, he had reached Australia and then New Zealand before his flight ended when he crashed into electricity cables. He was fortunate to escape with his life. In 1960 he won the first single-handed Transatlantic race and was second to Tabarly in the 1964 edition. He participated in his last Transat in 1968 aboard his new Gypsy Moth V.

of sailing, Hasler's name will also remain associated with the invention of self-steering gear that once set would automatically sail the yacht according to the direction of the wind.

Evidently dissatisfied with a monotonous and tranquil civilian life after his war-time exploits, in 1958 "Blondie" Hasler posted details of a single-handed race across the Atlantic on the notice-board of the Royal Ocean Racing Club in London. He had to wait two years before Francis Chichester replied to his yellowing announcement. A pioneer aviator and heroic solo flier, after having survived a crash in his float-plane, Chichester had to struggle against and defeat serious illness before taking the helm of his *Gypsy Moth III* and winning the first Solo Transatlantic race in 1960.

Colonel Hasler aboard his small *Jester* and Francis Chichester, who was to finish second were again present at the start of the second edition of the single-handed Transatlantic in 1964. The race was won, however, by a young Frenchman by the name of Eric Tabarly who had, and was to continue to have, only two passions in his life, sailing and the family yacht, the *Pen Duick*, an old gaff cutter built by Fife in 1898.

In the meantime another Frenchman, Bernard Moitessier, was wandering the seas in search life's meaning after the Indochina debacle, unwilling to plunge into that race towards the new prosperity. He was a yachtsman of a new breed, hostile to the terrestrial world and enamoured of the great oceanic spaces. For him a yacht was only a means to this end. Whether it was seakindly or fast, graceful or ugly was of no importance. All that he required was something that floated and aboard which he could sail the seas as far from the coast as possible. His first boat was a kind of junk he designed and built himself on a beach, with no notions of naval architecture or boatbuilding practice. His second, this time built in a boatyard, had a steel hull but was fitted out with whatever came to hand: the masts in fact were two telegraph poles. Moitessier was a kind of seafaring gypsy, a solitary hero whose books were essential reading for decades.

In 1966, Francis Chichester set sail aboard

167 top left A young Tabarly aboard Pen Duick *while taking a bearing on a landmark, already a scene from bygone times.*

167 top right and center Eric Tabarly continued to name his boats Pen Duick*; from the first, the 1898 cutter that belonged to his father, seen top right in perfectly restored condition sailing off Saint Tropez, to the second, in the center, a 46-foot ketch with which he won the 1964 Transatlantic, the third, a RORC-rated schooner with equal height masts with which he raced in numerous regattas throughout the world, including the 1967 Admiral's Cup, through to* Pen Duick VI*, a 72-foot ketch.*

167 bottom Bernard Moitessier represents the single-handed sailor bewitched by the irresistible call of the sea rather than one driven by dissatisfaction with life on dry land. A philosopher rather than a navigator, a sailor rather than a racer, when he took part in the 1968 non-stop round-the-world, after having completed almost the entire circumnavigation, he headed out into the ocean again in the direction of the Pacific islands, then the furthest he could get from "civilization."

166 Pen Duick was an old cutter built at Cork in Ireland in 1898 to the design of William Fife III. She belonged to the father of Eric Tabarly. In the post-war period, Eric persuaded his father to give him the boat and used his savings to begin a slow restoration of the hull that, in the meantime, had fallen victim to an enforced lack of maintenance during the war and was in very poor condition. Tabarly died falling overboard from Pen Duick during the night of the 12th of June, 1998, while sailing in the Irish Sea.

his new *Gypsy Moth IV* on the first single-handed circumnavigation of the world, passing by way of the three capes (the Cape of Good Hope, Cape Leeuwin and Cape Horn were to become renowned as the "marker buoys" of marathon single-handed racing). He was to return to England in 1967 after having made a single stop at Sydney.

That single stop-over was perhaps what stimulated the spirit of adventure of these men. Chichester had no sooner returned home than the *Sunday Times* was promoting a non-stop single-handed race around the world, passing by way of the three capes in an anti-clockwise direction; that is to say, against the prevailing winds.

Eight lone yachtsmen set out; only Robin Knox-Johnston, another former Royal Navy officer, was to complete the voyage. Four retired after the gigantic waves of the southern oceans had capsized their yachts; one, after having seen his trimaran disintegrate, was to commit suicide shortly afterwards; another went out of his mind in the middle of the Atlantic and was lost at sea. Bernard Moitessier, who had already completed the circumnavigation, decided not to stop at the

finish, not to cross the line in fact. Rejected by civilization, he went halfway round the world again before finding a place appropriate to his ideals in Polynesia.

The single-handed round the world race was repeated in 1970 and was won by Chay Blyth, a British former parachutist. The British single-handed yachtsmen were stimulated by a spirit of adventure, a search for intense emotions; almost all of them had military backgrounds and were adrenaline driven. The French instead had existential motivations.

However, the civilized world, if we can make the distinction between single-handed sailing and the civilized world, was about to absorb the presumed rebels. As early as 1968, the participation of the eventual winner of the Transatlantic, Geoffrey William, was economically dependent on a commercial sponsor, Lipton. The tea company founded in the nineteenth century by Thomas Lipton, famous for his five America's Cup challenges, financed the construction of William's boat, the *Sir Thomas Lipton*. In the 1970, the Whitbread company, which had already "sponsored" Francis Chichester's 1966 round-

the-world voyage, launched under its own name what was to become the world's longest and most important ocean race, the Whitbread Round The World; this time for crewed yachts.

Sponsorship was another of the new aspects that had begun to enter the world of yachting. For the purists of the sport it is seen as unwelcome, but today nothing takes place without financial backing from industry.

Yachting owes much to the spirit of the single-handed sailors: their contribution to stimulating interest in the sport is demonstrated by the fact that while Italy and Germany had no single-handed yachtsmen of the stature of Tabarly or Moitessier and recreational sailing struggled to take hold, it flourished in France. 3,800 recreational boats were built in Italy in 1963, against the 28,400 built in France. This state of affairs was helped by the coverage devoted by the media to the exploits of Eric Tabarly.

The economic support of industry for promotional purposes was both an inevitable consequence of the sport's popularity and a vital aid to its further development.

168 right Sir Francis Chichester set sail in 1968 on his third and last single-handed race aboard Gypsy Moth V. She was a schooner with equal height masts, a rig very common in the Sixties after it had been used by the single-handed sailors, firstly Moitessier, then Tabarly and finally Chichester. It had the great advantage of evenly distributing the sail area along the length of the hull while allowing the use of small sails that were easier to handle single-handed. In this photo the sixty-year-old Chichester appears to have no problems climbing the shrouds.

168 left Gypsy Moth IV under sail during her 1966 circumnavigation. The ketch-rigged yacht is powered by two twin jibs at the prow with a mizzen staysail hoisted on the mizzenmast and the windward side. This is a classic sail plan for single-handed sailing in light winds. The two boomed jibs at the prow held the boat to her route; when the hull started to bear away the windward jib spilled while the other brought her round to the weather and vice-versa. In very stiff breezes the very high foot of the two jibs prevented the boom from dipping.

169 top Single-handed races were stimulated in the Seventies by companies who recognized the promotional potential of such events. The first was Lipton Tea, a name already familiar to the yachting world thanks to five America's Cup challenges of the firm's founder, Sir Thomas Lipton. The British company financed the yacht of Geoffrey William, naming her Sir Thomas Lipton. This was a fairly timid initial approach compared with the amount of advertizing carried by today's boats. At the helm of Sir Thomas Lipton, Geoffrey William was to win the 1970 edition of the single-handed transatlantic race, now a regular four-yearly event.

169 bottom left Chay Blyth's British Steel in the Solent for the start of the non-stop single-handed round-the-world. This was in 1970 and British Steel was clearly a sponsored boat. She was a large 60-foot ketch with a steel hull demanded by the industry financing her and approved by her skipper. She was taking part in the event that two years earlier had caused such problems for eight single-handed yachtsmen, including Blyth himself; of the nine who started, only one managed to complete the race for motives that were more or less tragic. The British former parachuter gained his revenge by completing an anti-clockwise circumnavigation against the prevailing winds.

169 bottom right Robin Knox-Johnston with Ocean Spirit; in 1968 he was the only competitor to complete the single-handed round-the-world promoted by the Sunday Times. In the Nineties, he was to win the Jules Verne trophy by completing a circumnavigation of the globe in less than 80 days.

POST-WAR RACING:
THE REVIVAL

The spectators watching the racing from the green lawns lapped by the waters of the Solent during Cowes Week in 1953 immediately noticed that something was missing: the immense sails of the likes of *Britannia, Lulworth,* and the J Class and 23-meter International Rule boats were conspicuous by their absence. At most there were a few, very few in truth, International Rule 12-meter yachts that actually only appeared to be truly large in comparison with the mass of smaller sails. They were in reality 8-meter boats.

They were accompanied by dozens of

28 days aboard their *Sopranino,* again designed by Giles; Ann Davidson became the first woman to cross the Atlantic single-handed with her *Felicity Ann* of just 23 feet; Eric Hiscock took his two *Wanderers,* the second of 24 feet, the third of 30 feet, both designed by Laurent Giles, cruising to the Azores and around the world respectively. This list contains only those navigators who have left us with published accounts of their voyages with which they undoubtedly contributed to the success of small yachts in regattas.

Today all this may appear surprising: even

smaller yachts, generally open such as the Swallow class, or half-decked such as those of the X class and the Swedish 30 m² class, along with a few International Rule 6-meter boats and the Dragons. This should have come as no surprise given that in 1950 the first post-war transatlantic race from Bermuda to Plymouth had seen only yachts of under 65 feet 6 inches LOA at the start line, while early in the century the smallest participant in the Kaiser Cup was the 108-foot *Fleur de Lys* and the largest, the 242-foot 6-inch *Valhalla.*

It is remarkable how many ocean cruises were undertaken in the post-war period with yachts of under 39 feet 6 inches in length: Lennon Goldsmith headed for Bermuda and the Bahamas aboard the 30-foot gaff cutter *Diotima;* Humphrey Burton sailed from Falmouth to New York aboard the Laurent Giles-designed 26-foot *Vertue XXXV;* Patrick Ellam and Colin Mudie covered 2,680 miles in

the big yachts such as the IOR Class I or the Class A boats race on Olympic triangle courses and in 1999 the Fastnet has been replaced in the Admiral's Cup by a shorter race that does not venture into the Atlantic.

Who today would head out into the ocean to participate in the Bermuda Race or to cross the Atlantic aboard a 30-foot yacht, such as *Cohoe* or a former fin keel such as *Tre Sang?* In those years, however, it was the done thing. A few summers ago I was in Cowes, invited to dinner by the remarkable Henry Spencer, a wooden mast and traditional rigging maker as well as a great yachtsman and so enamoured of the sea as to personally assist yachts or small ships in difficulties with his own small tug (on my behalf he salvaged from the mud in which it had lain for forty years, the hull of *Lulworth,* a Big Class no less, filling it with air bags before towing it to Camper & Nicholson; he also rebuilt Lulworth's mast to the original

specifications and was of invaluable help to me in rerigging *Flica II* and *Trivia.* He received a knighthood from the Queen for his services and is now Sir Henry Spencer). Illustrating his story with photographs he had taken at time, Henry recounted how he had delivered by sea and naturally under sail (given that the yacht was not equipped with an engine), the pre-war Nicholson-designed International Rule 12-meter *Evaine* from Gosport to Newport, Rhode Island. And he recalled the episode as if it was nothing out of the ordinary, by no means an adventure. I have sailed on enough International Rule 12-meter boats to know that they are very narrow yachts, with a 88-foot mast and no rails—two-foot waves and you are already reaching for boots and oilskins. An International Rule 12-meter was a big boat for the regattas of the 1950s.

In Britain, the match winners of the era were the boats of Laurent Giles.

170 and 170-171 In the Fifties, Europe saw the spread of fixed-keel racing classes, that is to say boats lacking the centerboard that was to enjoy greater popularity in more recent times, thanks to the fact that they were frequently selected as Olympic classes. They descended from the smaller meter-classes such as the 6-meter boats and from the American inventions of Nat Herreshoff such as Dilemma from fifty years earlier. In effect in the United States, yachting practised in boats without cabins or without decks had always been popular. Races were staged for the "sand-baggers" and other small boats generally derived from those by the fishermen in the bays and internal waters of the Atlantic coastline. In contrast, European sailing was associated with the concept of the ocean-going yacht. In these photos, the first post-war races in the Solent of Cowes feature, left, yachts of the X.O.D. Class beating in a stiff breeze, and on the right, the Swallow Class boats caught out by a shifting wind to which K 46 is the first to react.

171 bottom left Wanderer III was designed by Laurent Giles in 1952 for the Hiscocks; slightly larger than her 1937 predecessor by the same designer, she was to permit a long, three-year cruise around the world. A yacht of around 30 feet in length, she was a perfect example of the new breed of cruising boat: inexpensive, extremely reliable and fitted out to a standard that today would only be considered acceptable for a 24-foot day cruiser.

171 bottom right We have already mentioned the Giles Vertue series: number 35, seen here, was to achieve fame thanks to Humphrey Burton's single-handed transatlantic crossing. This 26-foot yacht has been built in hundreds of examples all descending from a 1935 prototype, Andrillot which featured a gaff rig and a small and very low deckhouse. Giles modified the rig and designed a well balanced superstructure to give greater internal headroom. She is still an attractive yacht to see sailing today.

Following his success with *Myth of Malham* in 1947, '48 and '49, the English designer, as ever in collaboration with Illingworth, designed *Mouse of Malham*, another light displacement boat, an RORC Class III that was to win the Fastnet in 1955. Another of his designs, *Lutine*, won Class I in 1953 and 1955, and his reputation and yachts began to attract attention further afield.

In Italy, post-war reconstruction with economic support from the United States and the craft traditions of the boatyards on the Ligurian beaches led to development of the sport of sailing. The designs of Laurent Giles were among the first to reach boatbuilders who were to achieve widespread fame in the years to come. Sangermani built *Artica II* and *Tapineer*, while Beltrami was responsible for *Niña V.*

Robert Clark was less innovative and unwilling to adopt the light displacement formula. He continued to design boats along the lines of *Ortac*, with which he had enjoyed a

certain success in the late Thirties. His yachts presented classic forms with rounded prows and very pronounced stern overhangs. A short but fairly tall deckhouse recalled the dog houses of thirty years earlier. However, in 1951, his *Jocasta* won the larger class in the Fastnet race (this was a sloop of around 55 feet LOA) and in 1953 *Favona* won Class III in the same race. This last was a yacht designed in response to a precise brief compiled by the British Sailing Committee for an economical boat to be built in series with a length at the waterline of no more than 24 feet. Clark designed *Favona* while Giles responded with the famous *Samuel Pepys*, the winner of the 1950 Transatlantic Race and the prototype of a series for the Royal Navy, the R.N.S.A. 24. Another traditional yacht was Charles Nicholson's *Foxhound*, one of three yachts that descended directly from *Patience* of 1931, the others being *Bloodhound*, the winner in 1949, and *Stiarna*.

172 top right A classic Laurent Giles design from the Fifties: Lutine, a yawl-rigged RORC Class I yacht won the Fastnet two years running, in 1953 and '55, beating Clark's Jocasta in '53 on both real and corrected time. In '55 corrected time gave her the edge over Nicholson's Foxhound. She was back for the Fastnet in '57, although not the Admiral's Cup, and was beaten by the American boat, Carina.

173 Two beautiful designs by Charles Nicholson that belonged to the past—they are from 1935 and '36—but which still proved their worth in post-war racing: Bloodhound, bottom, is a large yawl of almost 65 feet which won the 1936 Channel Race and the Fastnet in both 1939 and 1949. In the post-war years she also took part in the 1952 Bermuda Race, finishing second in class. She continued to race successfully into the Sixties under the ownership of the British royal family. Foxhound, top, was one of a group of 3 boats designed by Nicholson in succession. She differed in terms of her rig with respects to Bloodhound, which had benefited from the contribution of Stephens to her sail plan: Foxhound was rigged as a sloop with a 7/8 forestay, as was to be the last of the series, Stiarna.

172 top left Jocasta is an RORC Class I yacht designed by Robert Clark which was part of the British team selected for the first edition of the Admiral's Cup in 1957. She was by no means the king-pin of the team, finishing fifth of six in the Channel Race and last in the two Olympic triangle races, but saved face in the Fastnet with a fine third place. The British victory in that edition was down to the first place recorded by Myth of Malham.

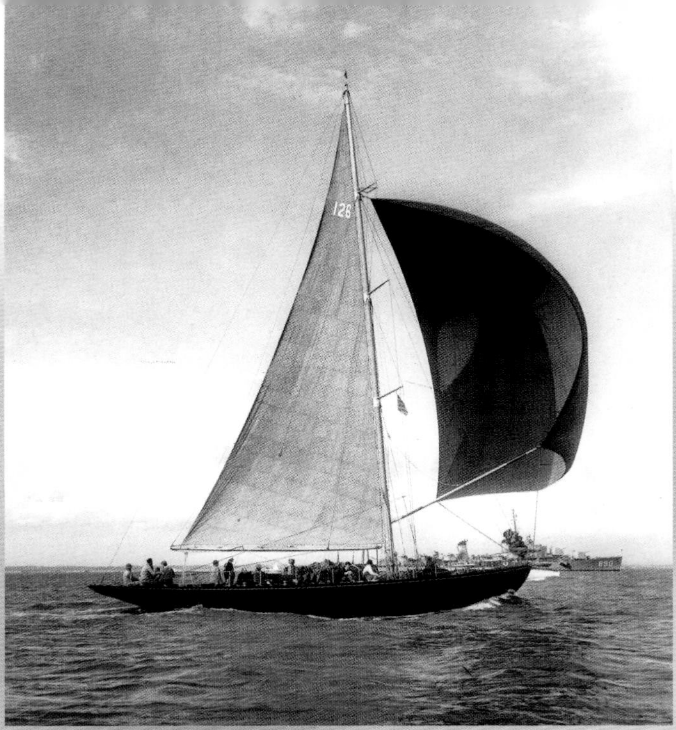
126

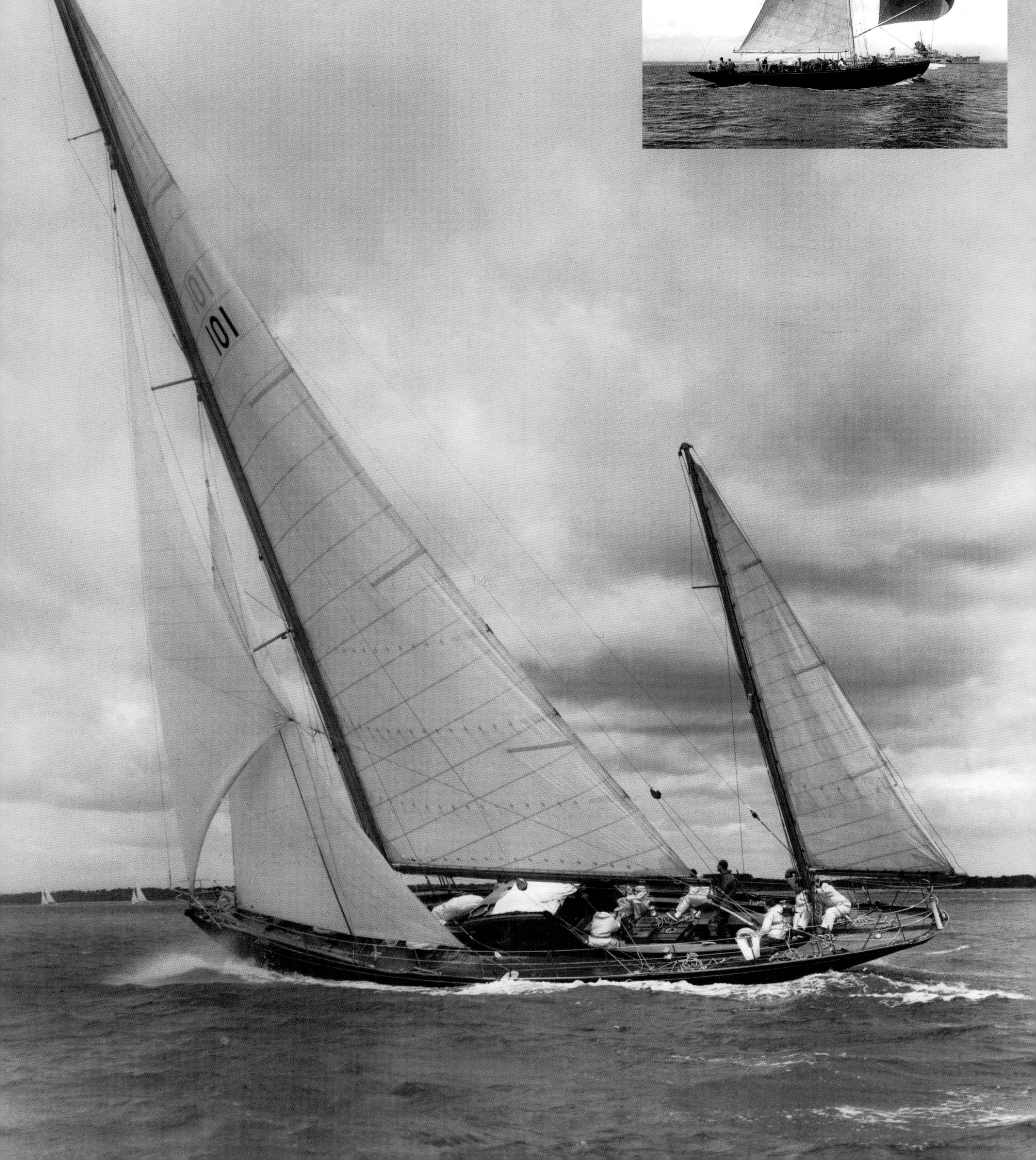
101
101

The American designers, Olin and Rod Stephens and Philip Rhodes, attempted to provide opposition for the British boats. The Rhodes-designed *Carina* is a beautiful yacht with pronounced although not excessive overhangs. She was around 10% wider than the average British yacht and, more importantly, had a more central midship section which conferred a more balanced appearance. The deckhouse was small but rounded, with none of the hard lines of Clark's designs. *Carina* was fitted with a centerboard, a single blade for sailing to windward, stability being guaranteed by her beam and the fact that no less than 45% of her

Stephens brothers had to be content with second places. In recompense, *Bolero* and *Argyll* won the premier class in the Bermuda Race while *Loki* took the Class III, defeating the British yachts in the process.

Bolero was the first large yacht of the post-war period at 73 feet 6 inches LOA with a beam of 15 feet 6 inches. *Argyll* was a little smaller at 57 feet 6 inches LOA while *Loki* was a Class III yacht with an overall length of 38 feet that won the Bermuda Race against Giles' light displacement boats but lost against his and Clark's Twenty-fours in the Fastnet. There is always an advantage in sailing in "home" waters.

With the Solent out of commission and Kiel being identified with the Nazis, the Americans tried to establish an offshore championship in their own waters. As Newport Bay was already the home of the America's Cup and the Pacific still too remote, Florida was chosen as the home of the Southern Ocean Racing Conference, the SORC as it was to become known. The event featured a combination of windward-leeward and offshore races as at Cowes, in waters that were already oceanic and, above all, traversed by the insidious Gulf Stream.

The first edition was held in 1941, clearly in

displacement was accounted for by ballast. She would appear to be a boat designed for following winds but won the 1955 edition of the Fastnet sailed in testing conditions to windward. The fact is that ballast that is not set too low makes for a sweeter yacht when breasting waves and pitching and a well designed centerboard can have a greater effect than a long keel integrated with the hull. The result is a yacht that is faster to leeward and beats better.

Following the remarkable success of Dorade and Stormy Weather, the yachts designed by the

Like those of Giles, the American designs were also built in the boatyards of continental Europe, Abeking & Rasmussen in Germany becoming the favorite yard of the Stephens brothers and Rhodes while Baglietto and Sangermani in Italy were also chosen by the former.

The United States were involved in the Second World War for a shorter period than the European countries, and most importantly the conflict did not have a direct impact on the national territory.

the absence of the European nations. As it was an all-American affair, there were no problems in applying the Cruising Club of America (CCA) ratings rather than the RORC system of the European boats. In the post-war period the European designers would either have to produce RORC yachts that were penalized by the American system, or compromise boats. One of the latter was *Lutine*, already mentioned as a winner of the Fastnet, that Laurent Giles designed with the two formulas in mind. *Lutine*, however, was a winner only in Europe, while the

American yachts were in turn generally successful in their home waters, the rating systems always affecting the performance of the yachts.

The SORC became an international event from 1952 onwards, but only in the 1970s with the unification of the ratings did it achieve significant world-wide status.

The same was true of the Sydney-Hobart, the first edition of which was held in 1945. Along with the Fastnet and the Bermuda, the Sydney-Hobart is now one of the three classic 600-mile offshore races. The 630 miles between Sydney in Australia and Hobart, the capital of Tasmania, are covered during the Australian winter (the most favourable season), crossing the Roaring Forties, that band of ocean to the south of the fortieth parallel famous for its almost constant westerly winds that can blow with great intensity and raise huge waves that encounter no land to break their momentum as they roll around the world. The race is considered by some to be the world's most demanding, although I would personally still bestow this honor on the Fastnet.

What is certain is that since the Seventies, it has been the most popular race in the southern hemisphere despite being difficult for the European yachts to reach.

174 Carina was the yacht which stunned Europe on her arrival in the 1950s: an RORC Class II designed by Philip Rhodes which won the Fastnet in '55 and '57 when she was a member of the American Admiral's Cup team. She was a typically "American" yacht, with a greater beam than her contemporaries and a centerboard. She appeared to mark a return to the past compared with the Stephens "compromise" designs. Her crew perhaps paid a crucial part in her success.

175 top Up until 1970, the sailing world had been split in two by the ratings: the Americans raced with the CCA system, the Europeans with that of the RORC. The designers therefore had to decide on which formula to base their projects according to the client's programs. Alternatively, they could design a hull and rig that took both systems into account as Giles did with Lutine whose owner wanted to race in both Europe and America. Lutine was particularly successful in British waters. In the US it was perhaps a lack of familiarity with the waters that was more influential rather than the ratings.

175 bottom One of Stephens' most attractive designs from the Forties and Fifties was that of Bolero, a large yawl of over 72 feet LOA, with the same lines as Stormy Weather from 10 years earlier. The American designer was conservative; his boats were successful and widely admired— why change? Bolero was nick-named "Miss America" and could even carry a horizontally rigged tall boy on the 1954 New York Yacht Club Cruise.

yacht

176 top Ocean racing at times obliges yachts to tackle severe wind and sea conditions, with the waves subjecting the hull structure to violent poundings, especially when beating. A good design and skillful handling can render the enormous stresses on the planking and rig tolerable, but occasionally critical conditions are encountered: during the '55 Fastnet Carina began to take on water at the bow after two days of difficult beating. She still managed to finish and actually win the race thanks to the crew's labors on the pumps. In the '79 edition of the Fastnet, 24 yachts were abandoned by their crews following structural failures and 15 men were lost at sea.

176 bottom The start of the Fastnet, more so than the other Solent races, was an unmissable spectacle for the enthusiasts and tourists who crowded the coasts of the Isle of Wight. This is Outlaw leading a small group of yachts as they brave the shallows to one side of the channel where the current is weaker: sailing close hauled in a series of short tacks on the side chosen on the basis of experience and faith in good luck. Outlaw is ready to go about, as is the yacht to leeward of the group, evidently short of room for maneuver. The yacht designed by Illingworth, not part of the Admiral's Cup team, is leading the Nicholson-designed Quiver IV and Clark's old Ortac. Half-hidden is Musketeer, another Nicholson design.

The 1979 storm had above all caught out the smaller yachts during their outward beat towards the Fastnet Rock. The larger yachts had already rounded the lighthouse and took the wind from the stern, far more favorable conditions. Demasting was one of the most frequent incidents on that occasion and many crews abandoned their yachts following the breaking of the mast, thus rendering the boat impossible to govern. Coping on board in those conditions is by no means easy; they would have had to try and hoist an emergency rig and use it to lie to. Something that is far easier to suggest in the comfort of a yacht club saloon than it is to put into practice.

In the post-war period, the traditional European sailing events began to be revived, albeit with the changes that have been mentioned earlier. No less than forty yachts started the 1953 edition of the Fastnet, a record, but what was more important were the nationalities of the boats. Along with the British boats there were also participants from America, Belgium, Holland, Germany, Ireland and France; in eight years yachting had managed to overcome the hatred engendered by the war.

For the first time that year, the RORC accepted entries from "small" Class III boats, those yachts of 32-36 feet that had demonstrated their reliability by sailing throughout the world. This policy came into question after the tragic Fastnet

of 1979 in which 15 people were killed, all of them sailing on yachts from the minor classes.

The polemics that followed the episode have never been satisfactorily resolved, but what emerged is that many of the victims were among those who had abandoned their yachts, that many boats, irrespective of their size, were poorly equipped and commanded by inexpert skippers and that, lastly, the larger yachts had no problems simply because being faster they were already safely in port when the storm was at its height.

177 bottom left The rescue services were immediately alerted by the organizers of the tragic 1979 Fastnet: this photo shows one of the lifeboats that went to the yachts' aid from the Isles of Scilly, a group of perilous rocks and small islands at the extreme western tip of England, long the site of desperate marine tragedies. This type of vessel is unsinkable and self-righting should it capsize.

177 bottom right Helicopter assistance is vital in cases such as the terrible storm that struck the fleet during the 1979 Fastnet. Many lives were saved by the air-sea rescue teams that managed to pick up crews who had abandoned their yachts and those who had sent out SOS signals because they were unable to control their boats. The photo shows the rescue of the crew of the Camargue: it is not easy to decide to jump into the sea to grab the cable with the harness lowered from the helicopter. The Camargue does not appear to have suffered significant damage, you would need to be aboard to decide what had to be done!

FROM THE FASTNET TO THE ADMIRAL'S CUP

From 1957, the Fastnet was included among the races of a new event organized by the RORC, the Admiral's Cup, a kind of world offshore racing championship for national teams of three yachts. The Cup was disputed every two years, like the Fastnet, during Cowes Week. Two Olympic triangle races were held in the Solent, the technically demanding offshore Channel Race of 220 miles with its currents and variable winds and lastly the Fastnet. Only two teams participated in the first edition of the Admiral's Cup, Britain and America with the British emerging victorious with *Myth of Malham*, *Jocasta* and *Uomie*.

In 1959, the original two teams were joined by France with *Eloise II*, *Marie-Christine II* and *St. Francois* and Holland with *Zeevalk*, *Zwerver* and *Olivier van Noort*. Britain won again but the in following edition, which saw the debut of Sweden, the American team of *Figaro*, *Cyane* and *Windrose* triumphed; they had clearly been studying the home waters of their rivals.

The number of participating teams rose gradually with seven starting in 1963 (a third win for Great Britain), eight in '65 and nine in the '67 edition won by Australia. 1969 saw the participation of the Latin countries of Spain, Italy and Argentina, while from the 1970s onwards the Admiral's Cup became a true offshore world championship with an average of 15 nations taking part in each edition, the yachts being selected by their respective federations. In that decade, yachting ceased to be a pastime for aristocrats or the exclusive obsession of a wealthy few and became a true sport .

The '60s had already seen the first signs of the importance of the Admiral's Cup which, in contrast with the SORC, had always had an international character. These were the years of Eric Tabarly's *Pen Duick III* and those of Dick Carter, an American designer who had begun to threaten the supremacy of the Stephens. As early as 1965 *Rabbit*, a RORC Class III designed by Carter, won the Fastnet

178 top left Noryema, *the tenth of a series often seen in the Solent was a 46-foot design by German Frers: along with* Battlecry *and* Yeoman XX *she was part of the British team that won the 1975 Admiral's Cup. The British yacht won the Channel Race and placed well in the other events. A well reefed mainsail and a Genoa 2: a good sail plan for beating in stiff breezes and calm seas and, in effect, the yacht seems very well balanced.*

178 center left *The American team from 1977 featured three decidedly avant-garde boats, all designed by architects of the new generation.* Bay Bea *was a Britton Chance design with a centerboard and built in laminate by Palmer & Johnson. This was not the team's lead boat, as she was unhappy in the currents of the Channel Race where she was relegated to 44th place.*

178 center right *Australia won the Admiral's Cup for the second time in 1979 with a team that included Police Car III, a decidedly innovative yacht by a young British designer, Edward Dubois. This semi-planing boat was very light and featured a seven-eighths rig that was to become very popular. She was extremely fast, above all*

downhill: she finished seventh in the first coastal race, second in the subsequent sheltered waters round and seventh in the Channel Race. She made a hash of the second coastal race, finishing fourteenth after incurring a twenty percent penalty, but finished third in the Fastnet to make a vital contribution to the team's overall victory.

178 bottom In 1977, the Admiral's Cup was enriched with a third inshore race: this was felt to improve the technical side of the event, given that the weighting previously given to the two offshore races had frequently determined the final placings. That year the British won again, perhaps due to their greater familiarity with the local Solent currents. The Australian team included Syd Fisher's Class I Ragamuffin: she was in the team again in '79 and the owner was also to be involved in the America's Cup.

179 The Admiral's Cup regattas brought up to sixty yachts to the Solent, to which should be added those participating in the Cowes Week events, the enthusiasts' boats, those of the press, the commercial shipping and the ferries and hovercraft that cross it; a unique spectacle. The regatta revolves around a cup donated in 1957 by the Commodore of RORC, Admiral Myles Wyatt.

180 top 1979 will be remembered as the year of the storm that cost the lives of fifteen yachtsmen during the Fastnet. It was also the year the Italian team achieved a third place in the Admiral's Cup with Vanina designed by Gary Mull, RoseSelavy (in the photo), the former Moonshine from the British team of the previous year, and the new Yena, both designed by Doug Peterson. The cup was won by the Australians who were at their ease in the strong winds, with the Americans second. Britain had to be content with sixth place.

180 bottom Aries, a medium-sized yacht rated at 36 feet, was designed by the New Zealander, Ron Holland but raced in the American team that finished second to the Australians. The '79 Admiral's Cup was characterised by strong winds. Aries is seen here approaching a buoy, one of the many fixed seamarks positioned in the Solent channel. She is sailing at full speed with a spinnaker and a reefed mainsail. A storm jib is already bent to the stay – the next beat will be tough!

again in 1979, after which they concentrated their efforts on wresting the America's Cup from the grasp of the New York Yacht Club.

The Seventies had seen the evolution of hulls conditioned by the application of IOR regulations. The classic yachts had given way to light displacement boats with considerable width at the midships section, load bearing stern exits and hulls flat under the keel—the boats of Carter firstly and then the French with Finot and his *Revolution* and lastly the New Zealanders such as Farr with his *Gerontius*. The search for speed through lightness had created hulls that were nonetheless seaworthy but which had breakage points where it was difficult to predict that structural forces would be concentrated. It was perhaps this that led to one of sailing's greatest tragedies. The 1979 edition of the Fastnet, the fifth round of the Admiral's Cup, unfortunately saw 15 men lost at sea and 24 yachts abandoned while only 85 of the over 300 that started finished the race. A severe depression with winds of 70 knots had caught part of the fleet as it was beating towards the Fastnet; the yachts that had already rounded the lighthouse on the southern coast of Ireland rode home on a fast and demanding following wind, while the others had to head into the terrible oncoming weather. All the yachts involved in the Admiral's Cup, and thus presumably those which were the most technically extreme, survived the storm. The lives lost were above all among those who abandoned their boats, placing their faith in self-inflating life-rafts. In that edition, the large American maxi yacht *Condor* established a new Fastnet record while among the Admiral's Cup boats the race was won by the British Doug Peterson-designed 30-foot IOR *Eclipse* from the French *Jubilèe VI* and the Australian *Impetuous*, a light alloy replica of Ron Holland's *Imp*.

outright, even though she was not an Admiral's Cup competitor. In 1966, another of the designer's Class III yachts, the *Tina*, built in steel by Franz Maas in Holland, won the One Ton Cup. For the 1967 edition of the Admiral's Cup, Dick Carter designed *Rabbit II*, a Class II boat selected as a member of the American team, again built in steel by Maas. She was to return the best results of the American team despite a disqualification in the first inshore race. In spite of the performance demonstrated by *Rabbit* it was the Australian who went on to win, even though their boats were by no means exceptional: *Mercedes* was at last an Australian design, by Bob Miller (who was to change his name to Ben Lexcen – bear this in mind for the America's Cup), and was to finish third in the Fastnet. *Balandra* was a sistership of the British yacht *Noryema*, designed by Nicholson, and was to finish fourth while the latter was only eighth. Lastly, the "old" *Caprice of Huon*, a Robert Clark design from 15 years earlier, was to beat all the British boats and two Americans in the Fastnet! The Aussies were the world offshore sailing champions. They were to win

180-181 Imp, designed for the American team by Ron Holland, had already impressed two years earlier when winning the SORC and finishing first amongst the American Admiral's Cup boats in '77 when she won the Fastnet and an inshore race. In '79 she was again the best of the US boats. At 40 feet LOA, 33 feet LWL, and with a beam of 12 feet 5 inches she is a small yacht. It was her structure that rendered her unbeatable and some years in advance of her rivals. The skinning is in a polyester-balsa sandwich, with carbonfiber inserts at the ends, laid over a spaceframe of H-section light alloy profiles. Imp was built by the Californian yard Kiwi Yachts and drew on Ron Holland's 1971 experience aboard the red yacht Improbable when he was assistant to her designer Gary Mull. Improbable had caused a sensation among the participants in the Admiral's Cup (she was racing out of competition) for her lines with an external transom-mounted rudder and very broad stern with no overhangs and above all her speed: she was timed at sixteen knots and was the first yacht of that size to plane.

181 top The Admiral's Cup regulations, which called for 3 yachts per nation, frequently led to the exclusion of competitive boats. The yachts not selected were often "offered" to other nations: it was much easier for the British to take advantage of this having the Commonwealth countries to draw on. Vanguard, an Ed Dubois design, joined La Panthera and White Rabbit in the Hong Kong team for the '77 edition, finishing third.

THE WHITBREAD "ROUND-THE-WORLD" RACE

The media took a grip on sailing in the Seventies with, as I have already mentioned, sponsors entering the scene. One of them organized the world's longest race, the Whitbread Round the World Race, 27,100 miles by way of the capes and stopping over at Cape Town, Sydney and Rio de Janeiro. 17 yachts ranging from the 50-foot *Copernicus*, which also attracted attention for her provenance in Poland, then behind the Iron Curtain, and the large British *Burton Cutter* of 80 feet, set sail from Portsmouth, on the Solent naturally, on the 8th of September, 1973.

The first leg saw the early retirements of the *Burton Cutter* and the hot favourite, Eric Tabarly's *Pen Duick VI*. The second and third legs were the most dramatic with three men lost at sea in the high southern latitudes of the Roaring Forties. At the end of the fourth leg, the first yacht across the finishing line at Portsmouth was *Great Britain II*, whose crew of parachutists was led with cast-iron discipline by the ocean veteran Chay Blyth. The race was won on compensated time, however, by *Sayula II*, the Swann 65' of the Mexican Ramon Carlin: throughout the race, to the great envy of Blyth's paras, he had had his entire family aboard, together with large stocks of wine, vodka and caviar! The Whitbread too was to become one of the classic ocean racing events.

In the mid-Fifties, with the process of

182 and 183 center right Eric Tabarly was determined to win the '73 Whitbread and had prepared an ambitious yacht: designed by Andrè Mauric, one of the leading French architects, she was built in light alloy at Brest and was 72 feet LOA, 61' 6" LWL and displaced 32 tons, of which just over 14 and a half were ballast. Rigged as a ketch with very elongated spankers, her weakness lay in her masts: during the race she was demasted twice due to breakages or overloading.

183 top The first back to Portsmouth, the point of departure for the race in September of '73, was the British yacht Great Britain II commanded by Chay Blyth: she had taken 144 days to complete the 27,000 miles. Sayula, Carlin's Swann, was to finish six days later, a difference that Great Britain II's handicap was unable to absorb. In this photo, the yacht captained by Blyth with his crew of British parachuters is seen at the start, with a spinnaker hoisted to carry her quickly beyond the confines of the Channel.

183 center left The yacht owned by the Mexican Carlin, winner of the first race sponsored by Whitbread, was a standard Swann 65' built by the Finnish Nautor yard to the designs of Stephens.

183 bottom This photo shows Pen Duick VI at speed, close hauled in a stiff breeze. A yankee and mizzen staysail hoisted forward and the spankers reefed. She is a powerful yacht, well suited to ocean racing. The masts were stepped on the deck rather than passing through it, a feature typical of the French school but favored by few others and not something I like either: perhaps this was not why she twice lost a mast, but the doubt remains. Mauric wanted a boat that would perform especially well in strong winds and thus distributed volume the length of the waterline, practically as far as the transom stern and incorporating the rudder, the top of the blade being faired into the exit lines of the bottom. The tiller was once a common feature but today on a boat of this size is extremely unusual.

184 top right Another protagonist on the world racing stage in the Seventies was War Baby, the former American Eagle, an International Rule 12-meter designed by Luders in 1964 for a syndicate led by Dupont that certainly could not be said to have had financial problems. She was not selected for the America's Cup, being defeated in the trials by Stephens' Constellation, but gained revenge when, transformed and re-rated according to the RORC system, she won the 1971 Fastnet in a record time and the Sydney-Hobart on real and corrected time in 1972. An effective demonstration of the technical validity of the old meter-class yachts.

184 left The Seventies appeared to be witnessing a return of large boats: with the unification of the ratings under the IOR formula, a racing class was created for those boats that exceeded the Class I dimensions, the A Class. Kialoa, a large A Class of 80 feet LOA designed by Stephens, won the Transatlantic in record time in 1975, sailed in the Fastnet, out of competition and transferred to the Southern hemisphere to win the Sydney-Hobart, again in a record time.

184 bottom right The post-war period saw a revival of the tradition of transatlantic races which were, after all, a good way of reaching European regattas. Robin, seen here, took part in and won on corrected time the 1975 Transatlantic. She was designed by the sailmaker Ted Hood, and built in polyester and Kevlar, a new synthetic fiber by the yard established by the designer himself. Ted Hood, a major figure in American sailing, was also the helmsman aboard Robin and was a leading player in the America's Cup in those years.

185 Kialoa participated in the dramatic 1979 Fastnet, being the first to round the Irish lighthouse. She was eventually beaten on real time by the other Class A yacht, Condor of Bermuda, which set the Fastnet record. That same year she was to provide her owner with the consolation of winning the Sydney-Hobart again. Kialoa, was one of the protagonists in the era of the Maxi yachts, the heirs to the Big Class of the early twentieth century.

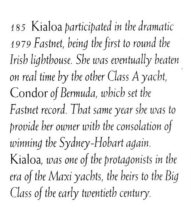

reconstruction in France and Italy and a boom in recreational sailing well under way, the Mediterranean also saw the launch of offshore sailing with a medium-length race of 240 miles departing alternately from France or Italy and arriving in the other country after having rounded the Giraglia Rock off Corsica.

22 boats from the 3 RORC classes took part in the first edition of the Giraglia Race as it was known. Among the protagonists in that era were two yachts designed by international masters, Stephens' *Mait II* and Giles' *Miranda IV*, both built by Baglietto.

Mait II was to be one of the first Mediterranean yachts to leave home waters and

race in the home of yachting when she took part in the 1955 Fastnet. She was back in England in 1959 and then participated in the 1962 Buenos Aires-Rio de Janeiro race.

Ocean races continued to exert an irresistible attraction into the Seventies and in 1975 a Transatlantic Race was organized from Brenton Reef off Newport, Rhode Island, the historic America's Cup "turning buoy," to Nab Tower in the Solent, mute witness to the hazardous "inside passage" effected by the schooner America in 1851.

Twelve yachts representing the United States, Great Britain, France, Italy, Austria and Bermuda lined up for the start. The first yacht

home was the 80-foot ketch *Kialoa*, while victory on compensated time went to the 40-foot sloop *Robin*. Both yachts were American, the first designed by S & S, the second designed, built and helmed by Ted Hood, sailmaker and great American yachtsman.

Among the competitors there was also *War Baby*, formerly known as the American Eagle, an International Rule 12-meter prepared for the America's Cup defender trials in 1964. Shortly after the start, she was demasted and had to retire. Fitted with a new mast she eventually completed the crossing and in 1977 participated in the Fastnet and set a new race record.

DEVELOPING FORMULAS

In the 1970s, the IOR rating born out of the laborious fusion of the American CCA and the British RORC systems seemed to have put an end to the problems of boats of different types and sizes racing together. It was, and still is, a well designed, comprehensive formula that avoided the excesses generated by earlier systems, although it was to have a shorter life-span. It failed to take into account one particular factor: the captain of a boat finishing first in real time is never happy to be beaten by a yacht that arrived when he and his crew had already showered, while the crew winning on compensated time always feels a degree of indebtedness to an adversary beaten in this manner. In short, what really counts in a sailing race is being first home. Had *America* won on compensated time, her victory would not have had such a profound effect on the history of yachting, and had a British yacht beaten her on compensated time we would still today be arguing over the validity of the formula and not the sailing and technical qualities of the yachts involved. This was exactly what happened in the 1970s. The formula was technically irreproachable, but offshore racing on compensated time lost much of its appeal. The were attempts to introduce other formulas, the IMS and CHS for example, in order to give everyone the chance of racing and winning, but the direction taken with these efforts was mistaken. Races between boats with similar characteristics was a spontaneous and significant development, initially the Level Classes and today the one-design classes. The Level Classes (the One Tonners, 3rd Class IOR yachts rated at 27.5 feet, Two, Three Quarter, Half, Quarter and the latest addition the Mini Tonners) re-invented a concept that had already been tested early in the twentieth century. Reference was made to a rating system (the IOR in this case) and yachts with the same rating raced against one another. The Level Classes dominated regattas for a decade, a situation which led to the evolution of two distinct types of yacht, racing and cruising boats. In 1967, *Pen Duick III* won the Fastnet; while she was no cruising yacht neither was she yet a pure racer. As the Seventies progressed, yachts began to appear that were designed solely for racing aboard which no one would ever go cruising: the hulls featured flush decks (with no deckhouse) in light alloy finished with a non-slip paint (teak was just unnecessary weight), while the waterlines were drawn on the basis of the ratings formula alone. *Revolution*, designed by Finot and built in light alloy by Huismann, was in effect the prototype specialist yacht. With the advent of the Level Classes, this evolution received official recognition. A One Tonner is a racing boat, a similar yacht of more or less the same dimensions with an IOR rating perhaps only slightly superior or inferior may still be a cruising boat capable of taking part in certain offshore races.

186 top A change in the shape of yachts had occurred in the late '30s with the designs of Stephens in the USA and Giles in Great Britain. A second evolution took place in the '70s, with the French designers and those of the Oceania this time having something new to say. At the 1973 Admiral's Cup the French unveiled Revolution, a Jean Marie Finot design built in light alloy by the Huismann yard: she was a light displacement boat with a broad stern, a long waterline and a flush deck. Revolution *was a new yacht: she took the theories of Carter regarding stability of form to extremes and appropriated the ideas of the New Zealanders regarding light displacement and took them to extremes too.* Revolution *was part of the French* Admiral's Cup team in '73, '75 and '77, while with the addition of another O to her name she also participated as Revoolution in 1979! She won the RORC championship in the 4 years mentioned and the Channel Race in '73 and '75. In '78 she won 4 regattas on the RORC circuit, the Cervantes Trophy, the Guingand Bowl, the Morgan Cup and the Channel Race.*

186 bottom When yachts such as Revolution, Improbable *and* Ginko *appeared on the scene, most racing yachts were still classical in appearance and substance. They were fine yachts, capable of good performance and still offering excellent cruising space and comfort. Typical of the breed was the Stephens-designed and Sangermani-built* Mabelle *seen here, a member of the Italian Admiral's Cup team in 1971 and 1973. They were not winners but at least made up numbers.*

MODERN RATINGS

In spite of the spread of increasingly international events, post-war yachting was still split in two. On the one hand were the Americans with their Cruising Club of America or CCA rating, while on the other were the Europeans with the Royal Ocean Racing Club or RORC system. The situation mirrored that of the early twentieth century, when it was Herreshoff's Universal Rule developed for the New York Yacht Club and the International Rule of the Paris conference that were in opposition, and even earlier when the American formulas that favored broad and shallow designs faced the British

187 top left THE CCA FORMULA
In 1932 the Cruising Club of America had developed a ratings formula that was to determine the form of American yachts and discriminate against European boats designed and raced in accordance with the RORC system. The CCA formula was complex to apply because it took into consideration values that were clearly difficult to measure, such as displacement and the displacement/ballast ratio. Either the yacht had to be weighed or its volume calculated or the drawings had to be

trusted. *The CCA yachts had full shapes, especially at the stern, a shallow draught and thus frequently a centerboard, and a high displacement. A degree of liberty was nonetheless left to the designer as the individual values were related to one another, in a way similar to the meter-class formula.*

187 top right THE RORC FORMULA
The RORC launched its rating system in 1931. It was soon adopted throughout the world except in the United States (apart from certain isolated cases), thanks to its

simplicity. *It replaced displacement with the product of two dimensions that were easily verifiable with the yacht in the water: breadth and depth measured within the hull. This formula led to excesses such as the section that narrowed at the deck (a form typical of the RORC yachts giving a lower B value) or reduced overhangs as was the case with* Myth of Malham. *The formula was subjected to an infinite series of modifications with the rating officials closing the loopholes the designers consistently managed to find.*

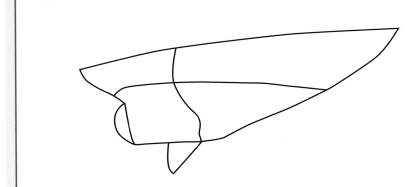
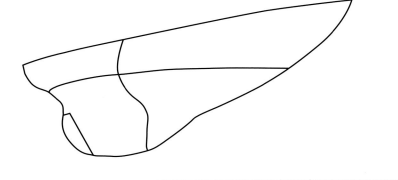

alternatives responsible for the classic plank-on-edge yachts. In truth, the RORC and CCA ratings were not so dissimilar, and some boats were actually designed and rated according to the two formulas, both of which were conceived for offshore yachts. The American formula was introduced in 1932 and was a linear measurement defining a "rated length" on the basis of which handicaps were applied.
RATED LENGTH = 0.95 x (L ± B ± D ± DISPL ± S ± F) x CE x FE. Where L = length, B = beam, D = draught, Displ = displacement, S = sail area, F = freeboard, C is a coefficient of stability and FE is a factor taking into account the propeller. The dimensions are a function of the measured length while the displacement is obtained from the design specifications or by weighing the yacht. This last factor, like the coefficient of stability, was difficult to calculate objectively. The European RORC system was introduced at practically the same time, in 1931, and was also a linear measurement: MEASURED RATING = 0.15 x + 0.2 (L + ÷ S). At first sight this system appeared to be simpler, with L = length, B = beam, D = depth and S = sail area, while neither stability nor the displacement needed to be calculated or weighed. The system was expressly designed to provide a simple means of rating yachts from diverse origins and with owners who were perhaps not in possession of the full technical specifications of their boats. This was also why the system spread throughout the world with the exception of the United States. Neither of the two formulas actually defined the form of a recognizable yacht, just as it is difficult to distinguish a J Class

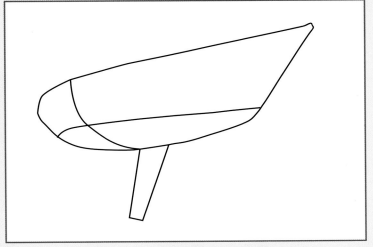

from an International Rule 23-meter. However, the American formula did favor broad, heavy hulls and the mainsail carried relatively little weighting and was therefore large, while the opposite could be said of the British system. The spread of international regattas from the mid-Fifties soon demanded that the question be resolved. In 1968, the international Yacht Racing Union, then as now the highest authority in international sailing, established an International Technical Committee entrusted with the task of defining a rating formula that took over the heritage of both the CCA and RORC systems. Two American designers, Olin Stephens and Dick Carter, two European designers, Ricus Vandestadt and Gustav Plym, and two international ratings officials with experience of the two formulas, Robin Glover and David Fayle, were appointed to the committee. After a period of gestation lasting almost two years, the

187 bottom THE IOR FORMULA
American yachts were coming to race in Europe ever more frequently and vice-versa, and it was soon clear that a single rating system had to be developed. The IOR formula is only apparently more complicated than the other two. It eliminates the measurement problems of the American system but is not as inflexible as the old RORC rule. It is in fact an effective formula and the IOR yachts were not so easily identifiable as such compared with those built to one or other of the earlier systems. If it is considered to be obsolete today it is only because, as ever, it is irritating not to win a race after taking line honors.

International Offshore Rule or IOR became official on the 1st of January, 1970, and was to govern ocean racing throughout the world from that date onwards. The formula defining the IOR rating is: RATING = (0.13 x + 0.25 L + 0.2 ÷ S + DC + FC) x EPF x CGF x MAF. Here L, B, D and S are the factors already mentioned in connection with the earlier systems, while EPF takes into account engines and propellers, CGF the stability and MAF eventual centerboards or other mobile appendages. It is a complex formula that includes parts of both the RORC and the CCA systems. It is sufficiently comprehensive to avoid leaving loopholes that would otherwise have a determinant effect on hull shape. This was therefore a ratings system appropriately conceived to allow the design of modern yachts suited to both Olympic triangle and offshore races.

THE EVOLUTION
OF RACING BOATS

In much the same way that the early
twentieth century could be defined as the
Herreshoff era, the early Seventies were still
dominated by a single great designer, Olin
Stephens.

As early as 1966, however, Dick Carter had
won the One Ton Cup with *Tina*, a boat that
was broader and lighter than those of Stephens,
with a rudder set well back, a feature that was to
become widely adopted on the leading yachts
of the following decade.

At Cowes and the Fastnet in 1971, particular
interest was aroused by a design by the young
American Gary Mull. *Improbable* actually had her
rudder set on the stern transom, was very light
and planed like a dinghy. That year Carter
raced *Gitana V*, an enlarged version of *Tina*, in
the Admiral's Cup. Stephens still emerged
victorious, but one of his pupils, German Frers,
attracted attention with his *Matrero*. Frers was to
be the continuator of the "classic" school, and
there is an identifiable thread linking the
Stephens' boats of the Sixties with those still
being designed by Frers in the Nineties:
equilibrium of form, no distortion of the lines or
the overhangs, boats that were always
attractive.

The Frers-designed *Recluta* of 1970 could
easily have been designed 10 years earlier or 10
years later; Bob Miller's *Ginko* instead could only
have come from that time with her external
rudder, flush deck and flat bottom, like Gary
Mull's *Improbable*.

The regattas therefore featured designs that
followed a coherent evolutionary line, like those
of Stephens and Frers, even when new materials
were adopted (*Charisma*, for example, was built
by Huismann in light alloy). But there were also
boats from the new school inspired by Carter
and his *Tina*, with broad load bearing sterns and
structures that were as light as possible. The
Frenchmen Jean Marie Finot and Michel Joubert
belonged to this new school and with their
Revolution and *Subversion* they brought Carter's
ideas to full fruition and were the forerunners of
the New Zealand school.

A different approach was taken by Gary
Mull, his pupil Ron Holland and the Australian
Bob Miller who favored maximum length at the
waterline and plenty of canvas.

In the early Seventies, the rigs also changed
with the appearance of the first Kevlar sails.
They ripped very quickly but were extremely
impressive while they lasted (it was soon
realized that Kevlar had to be blended with

*188 top and 189 bottom For some
years, in the wake of Tina's victory,
Carter's designs dominated regattas. In
fact, the American designer, who in '68
was, along with Stephens, Van de Stadt
and Plym, was a member of the
committee devising a new ratings
formula (which itself is evidence of his
importance in the field of yacht design),*
*restricted himself to indicating a direction
others were to successfully develop. His
Gitana V, part of the French team in
1971, was once again a classic boat,
apparently ignoring the success of Red
Rooster at Cowes two years earlier
with her ballast keel entirely within the
hull and her external rudder on the
transom stern.*

188 bottom Contrasting with the new
racing yachts, boats with classic lines
and built with traditional methods
continued to hold their own and even
win against more extreme designs in
ocean races. The Argentine German
Frers had served his apprenticeship at
Sparkman & Stephens, as had Gary
Mull, but while the latter rebelled
against his master, Frers adopted his
philosophy. Matrero helped Argentina
to a surprising fourth place in 1971.

189 top The Australians picked up on
Dick Carter's ideas regarding a new
way of designing a racing yacht: in
1971 the waters of the Solent saw for
the first time an ocean racing yacht
planing at 16 knots: Improbable,
designed by Gary Mull with the
assistance of the young Ron Holland.
This light displacement boat had no
interior fittings: the racing yacht was
forgetting its origins as a vessel that
took sailing enthusiasts to sea. Form
then on there would be a clear division
between racers and cruisers, boats
designed for outright performance and
those that privileged comfort

another fiber to avoid fragility); at the prow were
hollow stays with double slots to allow the jibs to
be changed more quickly as there was no need to
lower one before hoisting the other: no more
frantic grinding to hoist a jib, tearing up cold wet
fingers! The halyards were directed to the
cockpit, passing below decks, and the winches
were twinned so that two could work on a single
sheet. This was America's Cup experience talking.

Interior fittings disappeared from stem and
stern, and prior to a race everything possible was
removed from the boat as weight had to be
reduced and concentrated in the center so as to
reduce the effect of pitching.

At each tack the crew was sent windward and
to the center. A Class III weighed 13,227 pounds
and, with the crew representing between 5 and
10% of total displacement, its positioning was
crucial.

The confusion, in a quantitative rather than
qualitative sense, of design ideas appeared to be

refined when Doug Peterson appeared on the scene in the mid-Seventies. The *Ganbare* is a One Tonner from 1973; clearly the fastest boat in the fleet, she only failed to win that year's edition of the cup because she touched a buoy in the last race. Peterson was to win the One Ton Cup in '74 with *Gumboots* and the Half Ton that same year with *North Star*. In 1975 he was to win the SORC with *Stinger* while *Yeoman XX* was among the best of the Admiral's Cup yachts.

Doug Peterson combined the concepts of the Californian school with those of Bob Miller/Ben Lexcen and disciples. He built light boats that were a little narrower than those of Carter and long at the waterline. They were above all very simple as he eliminated all superfluous elements,

the rudder skeg above all. Ron Holland was to prove to be on the same wavelength.

In 1975, the designers contending outright victory had grown in number to represent a small crowd. Stephens was still around (of the fifty-seven yachts entered for the Admiral's Cup that year no less than twenty-four had been designed by the New York studio!), but German Frers was present with seven designs, the Dutchman Franz Maas (who was designing and building in fiberglass in his own yard) was continuing the Van de Stadt tradition, although his were "middle-of-the-road" yachts with an eye on serial production (the *Standfast 40*, for example) and had four boats in the Solent; then there were designs by Nicholson, Carter, Cuthbertson & Cassian (Canadian designers and serial builders of fiberglass yachts), Elvström (the great Danish helmsman also devoted himself to designing and later, albeit less successfully, to building fiberglass yachts) Finot, Hood, et al. Fiberglass yachts stormed the world of racing in 1975 with the series-built Swanns by Nautor, the Baltics, and the Camper & Nicholsons. Yachts were still being built in wood, but many now featured light alloy hulls by Huismann in Holland, Derecktor in the United States and, above all, a number of small French yards, while many more were already in fiberglass: at the Admiral's Cup there were fourteen wooden hulls, fourteen in light alloy

and twenty-seven in fiberglass. The race towards lightness imposed structural evolutions.

In 1976, the SORC was won by a Ron Holland yacht built by Kiwimagic in New Zealand, the RORC Class II *Imp*. This boat featured a sandwich skin with two layers of fiberglass reinforced with carbonfiber and a balsa core over a spaceframe structure of aluminium tubes.

The One Ton Cup of that year was won by a yacht designed by Britton Chance and fitted with a centerboard. But it was the extremely light boats of another young designer, the New Zealander Bruce Farr, that really impressed. In the Admiral's Cup all eyes were on another Doug Peterson design, *Moonshine*, a development of

190 top Doug Peterson, who may be considered as one the most conservative figures of the new generation, also produced a design that attracted attention, not so much for its forms that only developed the concepts of Ganbare, as for the construction that used materials destined to become, twenty years later, the most commonly employed in recreational sailing: the exotic fibers first seen together with wood on Imp and combined with a light alloy frame on Improbable. These exotic fibers were Kevlar and carbon, and on Moonshine they were used for the hull plating and frame, impregnated with epoxy resin.

190 bottom Two years after Moonshine, Peterson designed Eclipse which was selected as part of the British America's Cup team. The yacht was built by Jeremy Rogers in composite materials with exotic fibers: vacuum construction methods made their nautical debut, albeit after already being employed in the automotive field

for Formula 1 cars. The fibers, be they glass, Kevlar or carbon, were impregnated with resin in a vacuum, thus achieving a better, more even distribution and above all a saving in weight given that the use of the resin is optimised. Eclipse was to be the first home of the Admiral's Cup boats in the terrible Fastnet of 1979.

Yeoman XX, a composite structure with a sandwich of Kevlar and carbonfiber.

In the late Seventies, the designs of Bruce Farr and (at last) a British designer, Ed Dubois, came to the fore. Lightweight hulls, planing lines and a fractionated rig. The forestay did not reach the masthead but only 7/8 of the length of the mast, thus allowing it to flex better and release the fall of the mainsail. In those years the first vacuum-bagged construction methods were used to produce the hull of *Eclipse*, designed by Doug Petersen. Vacuum bagging is employed to improve the distribution of the resin during the stratification of fibers be they glass, Kevlar or carbon. An optimum resin/fiber ratio is crucial as too much resin means superfluous weight while

too little results in the delamination of the strata.

The 1980s also saw the organization of a world championship for maxi boats. These were large yachts of around 78 feet LOA, rated as Class A according to the IOR system, that is to say above what was the limit for the Class I rating. The championship was devoted to boats that were true racing machines crewed by 20-30 men and rigged like racing one-tonners, and comprised a series of regattas held around the world and thus required significant logistical investments. There are very few people in the world with the wherewithal to maintain boats such as *Helisara*, *Ondine* or *Kialoa* and the championship was confined to that remarkable decade in which it appeared any financial folly could be justified.

190-191 The development of recreational sailing in the post-war period culminated with the revival of races for large yachts. It was since the 1930s that yachts of over 65 feet LOA had not been seen in racing and the large Class A boats, the Maxi yachts, harked back to that period. Kialoa, a name present on the yachting circuit since the 1960s, reintroduced a forgotten spectacle: in sailing, size is, however, an aesthetic element and a crew of thirty men increases the sensation of power of these yachts.

AMERICA'S CUP

The long interval due to the Second World War had by no means dampened British desire for revenge: it was now a hundred years since the victory of the schooner *America* and the Hundred Guinea Cup was still sitting in the halls of the New York Yacht Club. The rapid revival of racing from the early years of the post-war period convinced both the Americans and the British that there was no reason not to revive the challenges for the America's Cup too, even though the general economic situation was such as to dissuade any one from building a vastly expensive J Class yacht. The challenge was feasible, but only with a different, less expensive kind of yacht.

Initially, the RORC in particular held out for a small but seaworthy yacht that, once the regatta had been completed, could be put to new uses, perhaps ocean cruising, a solution that was very much in the spirit of the RORC.

However, it was the philosophy espoused by the Royal Yacht Squadron that prevailed: the America's Cup could be disputed with a yacht smaller than the gigantic and exclusive J Class that served that sole purpose, but the new craft too should be a pure racing yacht, attractive and unmistakable, a pedigree America's Cup boat in short.

The choice, approved by the New York Yacht Club and introduced to the America's Cup regulations, fell on the International Rule 12-meter, in effect a junior version of the J Class given that the International Rule J Class equivalent was the 23-meter.

Although the 12-meters are smaller than the J Class racers, they are nonetheless large boats with an overall length of around 69 feet. The hull has long overhangs, the length at the waterline not exceeding 46 feet, with a draught restricted to a maximum of 8 feet 10 inches. At around 27 tons, a 12-meter is a fairly heavy yacht even though its interior is almost empty, it has no engine, it features relatively lightweight construction and much of its displacement is accounted for by ballast. A 12-meter carries a very large sail area at just under 2,150 square feet, with a sloop rig and a mast towering around 88 feet above the deck. A true racing machine, an Olympic triangle yacht with the superior dimensions and performance of a medium-sized offshore boat. The sharp bow dips easily under the water and the lack of a rail and pulpit makes any activity in this area precarious. In any case, a 12-meter is beautiful, a sailing yacht as it should be designed and, as mentioned above with repsects to the J Class, still a big boat. All of the America's Cup challenges since the Second World War have been disputed by yachts of this type.

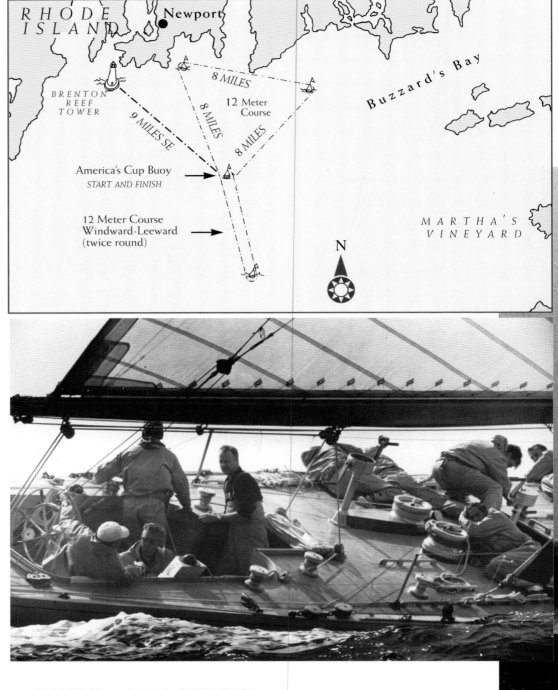

THE FIRST 12-METER CHALLENGE

The first post-war edition was held in 1958 with David Boyd's *Sceptre* challenging the American Olin Stephen's *Columbia*. Both the defenders and the challengers had approached the regatta with the utmost dedication. The British had tank-tested eight designs, two each from David Boyd, Charles Nicholson, Art Robb and James McGruer. The design eventually selected was one of Boyd's, but the British found themselves in trouble while fine-tuning the boat, as the only available sparring partner was Nicholson's old *Evaine*, a boat that was hardly at the cutting edge and which in any case was never well rigged and lacked a competitive crew. Unfortunately for the British, the only real weakness in their challenge proved to be the detail development of the boat.

The Americans instead launched three

192 top *The America's Cup waters from 1930 to the late 1960s: off Newport, Rhode Island, a little to the north of New York. The J Class yachts raced on the large triangle, 10 miles to each leg, and on the 15-mile leeward-windward course; for the 12-meter boats the triangle is 8 miles per leg and the leeward-windward 6. The Brenton Reef lighthouse dominates the setting.*

192 center *The International Rule 12-meter yachts were very technical boats: Columbia's deck gear today appears antiquated, the wooden blocks apparently belonging to the ships of the nineteenth century. In reality, the gear and the rigging were already very sophisticated. Here the crew is training, as shown by the presence of stanchions. Under racing conditions a toe hold was all that prevented the crew from sliding overboard.*

192 bottom *The Hundred Guineas Cup, named after the price paid to a London jeweller in 1851, is an ugly silver jug; yachts of all nations have competed for it for a hundred and fifty years.*

193 top *Sails have always represented a fundamental aspect of America's Cup research. The Americans were always at the forefront in this field, from the era of America up to the advent of the Australians and the New Zealanders who rapidly closed the gap. Here Columbia is slamming over the short Newport waves and displaying a radial Genoa: the shape was immediately copied by the British challengers.*

193 bottom *1958: the 17th challenge. The British yacht Sceptre, a David Boyd design, raced against the Stephens-designed American defender Columbia. The British yacht, short on development due to a lack of valid sparring partners, was unhappy in the waters of Newport and was never competitive. The cup remained in the halls of the New York Yacht Club, Columbia winning 4-0.*

new boats, the Stephens-designed *Columbia*, Phil Rhodes' *Weatherly* and Ray Hunt's *Easterner*. They also restored to competitive condition Stephens' *Vim* of 1939 that had easily beaten all the British 12-meter yachts before the outbreak of the war. She was entrusted to "Bus" Mosbacher who was to earn a reputation as one of the most able 12-meter and America's Cup helmsmen. *Vim* in particular proved to be a worthy adversary for *Columbia* although after a hundred or so match races between the four boats, this last was eventually selected. After such exhaustive fine tuning, the regatta against *Sceptre* was a breeze, the defender taking the series 4-0.

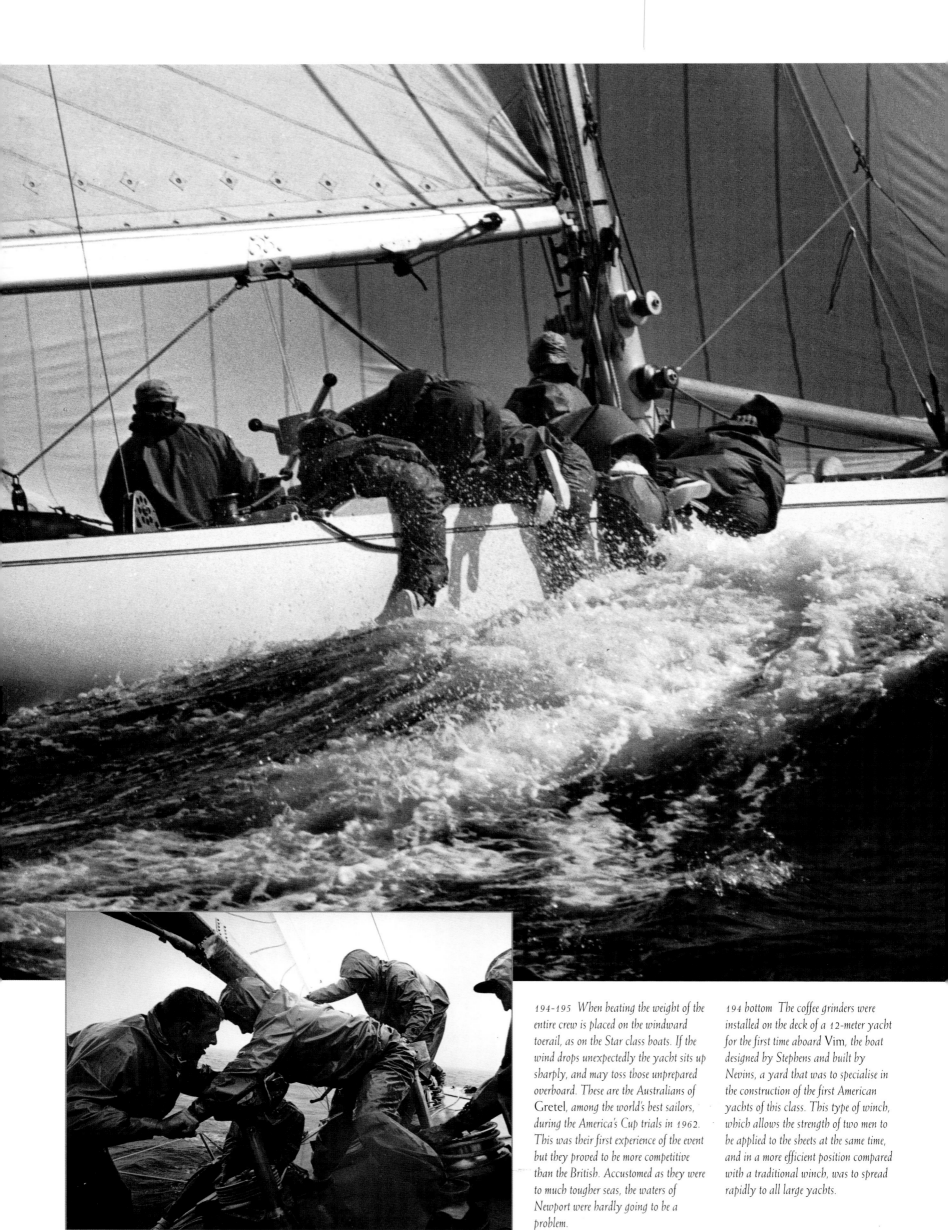

194-195 When beating the weight of the entire crew is placed on the windward toerail, as on the Star class boats. If the wind drops unexpectedly the yacht sits up sharply, and may toss those unprepared overboard. These are the Australians of *Gretel*, among the world's best sailors, during the America's Cup trials in 1962. This was their first experience of the event but they proved to be more competitive than the British. Accustomed as they were to much tougher seas, the waters of Newport were hardly going to be a problem.

194 bottom The coffee grinders were installed on the deck of a 12-meter yacht for the first time aboard *Vim*, the boat designed by Stephens and built by Nevins, a yard that was to specialise in the construction of the first American yachts of this class. This type of winch, which allows the strength of two men to be applied to the sheets at the same time, and in a more efficient position compared with a traditional winch, was to spread rapidly to all large yachts.

195 top *Changing a foresail has always been a tricky job on any yacht, all the more so on a 12-meter which has a sharply tapering bow, no stanchions and tends to dip into the wave. On* Gretel *a small pulpit has been installed to give the crew some support but the maneuver is nonetheless precarious. Today the changing of a foresail is greatly facilitated by the hollow forestay with a double groove in one side of which the jib aloft is bent while the luff cord of the new jib is inserted in the other. Slides were infernal devices, hard to open, especially with wet hands, just like those of* Gretel *undoubtedly will be. On the other hand, the speed of the maneuver was often crucial to the outcome of a race: a yacht without a Genoa aloft is running on two cylinders even though in the case of a 12-meter, the spanker does play a large part in its performance.*

THE AUSTRALIAN DEBUT

The second post-war challenge was issued by a country that, while it had no particular sailing tradition, clearly had the sport in its blood, Australia. The challenger team started out on the right footing by acquiring *Vim* as a sparring partner while its new boat, *Gretel*, designed by Alan Payne, was conceived and developed using Vim as a point of departure.

A new 12-meter was launched in America, the Hood-designed *Nefertiti* while *Columbia*, *Easterner* and *Weatherly* were modified and rerigged. Rhodes' yacht again proved to be the best and successfully defended the cup against *Gretel*. This last, and her crew, proved to be the most dangerous opponents since the days of *Endeavour*, but the Americans had Bus Mosbacher at the helm.

195 center *Weatherly was a good boat, especially in the light winds that prevail off Newport. Moreover, Mosbacher, seen from behind in his inevitable cap at the helm of the Rhodes-designed 12-meter, knew those waters very well and was at his ease in light breezes.* Gretel, *on the other hand, was extremely fast downhill: Payne had designed a hull with an unusually flat and very buoyant stern exit. In the second race* Gretel *planed several times with maximum speeds of 12 knots.*

195 bottom *The eighteenth America's Cup challenge saw a boat from Australia for the first time. The Americans had selected a new boat for the defence,* Weatherly, *designed by Phil Rhodes, and they had entrusted her to "Bus" Mosbacher, one of the greatest cup helmsmen.* Gretel, *the Australian challenger, was designed by Alan Payne, who had had at his disposition the old but still competitive* Vim *as a point of departure.* Weatherly *won the cup, but only after a hard-fought series of races, the second of which had been won by the challengers.*

Yacht

THE LAST BRITISH CHALLENGE

Another British challenge was mounted in 1964 with Sovereign, again designed by David Boyd, sailing against the American defender *Constellation*, a new Stephens design. This was another uneventful series, with *Constellation* displaying crushing superiority as she took the series 4-0.

196-197 *For the 1964 challenge, the New York Yacht Club again entrusted the design of their boat to Stephens who came up with a 12-meter to oppose the yacht of a second syndicate proposing to defend the cup led by the Dupont corporation.* Constellation, *Stephens' yacht, found a worthy adversary in* American Eagle, *the 12-meter designed by Luders and only prevailed after the helm was handed over to Bob Bavier.* American Eagle *made up for the disappointment by going on to win RORC races around the world.* Constellation *is seen here during a training run under a gust of wind from the northeast: note the mast, always a delicate element in the rig of these boats.*

197 top Sovereign, the British challenger yacht, was also designed by David Boyd: once again a good boat, but no where near the standard set by Stephens' design that itself was nothing extraordinary, given that it had been put under severe pressure by American Eagle and beaten on a number of occasions by the old Columbia. The latter herself had almost been beaten by Vim, a design from 1939 that had in her time comfortably beaten the British 12-meters. Constellation easily beat the challenger by record breaking margins: 5 minutes in the first race, 20 (!) in the second, 6 in the third and 15 in the fourth.

197 center left The America's Cup boats from the USA, and others but to a lesser degree, continued to race after the event. Constellation broke her mast during a coastal race from New London to Block Island in December, 1964. It was winter in those latitudes and the 12-meters were very wet yachts and by no stretch of the imagination comfortable.

America's Cup

197 bottom left A sail in the water during a change of canvas signifies the loss of a number of seconds. Fortunately this was a training run otherwise it could have been a costly mistake, especially in the light winds, almost non-existent I would say, of this hot day.

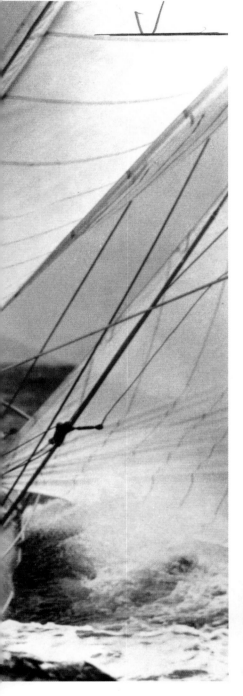

196 bottom Eleven crew members plus an observer in the stern: helmsman, tactician and navigator in the cockpit, then the men responsible for trimming the sails, one for the spanker, two, one either side, for the Genoa, three at the mast and two bowmen. With the occasional minor difference this was the distribution of roles on the America's Cup 12-meter boats. The preparation of the rigging crew was as important as the skill of the afterguard and the sail trimmers. It could be said that the quality of the crew was just as important to performance as the quality of the boat itself. Then there were the sails and the regulations, or rather the New York Yacht Club's Race Committee's interpretation of them which was often crucial.

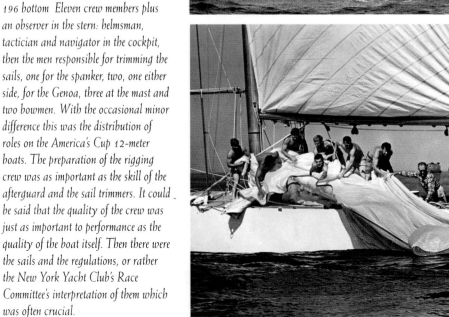

197 right From 1964 the America's Cup was disputed over a new course, as always off Brenton Reef: windward, reach, reach, leeward, windward, for a total of 24 miles.
198 top Intrepid is the 12-meter designed by Stephens for the 1967 challenge. She is seen in this photo during what is generally a delicate moment following the rounding of the reach buoy: the large Genoa is coming down and the spinnaker has to fill.

198-199 In 1970 the Australians found themselves, for the first time in the history of the event, having to win elimination trials in order to acquire the right to challenge the Americans. From then on the elimination trials disputed by the challengers were increasingly important, given that the pretenders were ever more numerous. This probably helped the challengers overcome the lack of experience that had always been their great weakness. In the event, Gretel II, the new design by Alan Payne, easily overcame France.

198 top Intrepid is the 12-meter yacht designed by Stephens for the 1967 challenge. She is seen in this photo during what is generally a delicate moment following the rounding of the reach buoy: the large genoa is coming down and the spinnaker has to fill.

198 center The 20th America's Cup challenge saw the first of a series of Australian attempts that ultimately concluded with victory some twenty years later. Dame Pattie, designed by Warwich Hood, formerly employed in the Alan Payne studio at the time of the design of Gretel, was longer at the waterline than Intrepid and according to the regulations thus had to have a smaller sail area. Hood had planned for strong winds like those in this photo, but they were, however, rare during the actual regatta.

198 bottom Intrepid leads to windward from Dame Pattie: the Australian boat proved to be at her ease in strong winds but was decisively inferior to Intrepid, perhaps one of the best of the 12-meter yachts designed by Stephens, in light breezes. Moreover, Intrepid was helmed by the great Bus Mosbacher, who never put a foot wrong during a regatta, in contrast with Jock Sturrock, the Australian helmsman who had already with Gretel in 1962 attempted to bridge the gap separating him from his rival with risky tactics that unfortunately for him never paid off.

THE AUSTRALIAN CYCLE

In 1967, it was again the turn of the Australians to carry the challenge to the Americans, but this time their *Dame Pattie*, designed by Warwich Hood, one of Payne's assistants, was unable to repeat the performance of *Gretel* and was defeated 4-0 by Stephens' new boat *Intrepid*.

MULTIPLE PRETENDERS

The Seventies brought a series of significant innovations to the America's Cup.

The decade opened with the New York Yacht Club receiving a number of challenges and for once it felt that it could not claim the right to decide on whom to face. The hopeful teams would have to compete amongst themselves in a series of races to decide the official challenger.

The Australians were once again in the water, this time with a new design from Alan Payne, *Gretel*

II. They came up against a French team, led by a figure destined to revive the splendors of his illustrious predecessors, Baron Bich, the rich and powerful industrialist who had already invaded Europe with his Bic ball-point pens and was determined to repeat his success in America too. The Baron provided the French challenge with apparently bottomless pockets, acquiring firstly *Sovereign*, the British 1964 challenger, and then the American defender that had beaten her, *Constellation*. Moreover, he commissioned a new 12-meter, *Chancegger*, designed by Britton Chance and built by Egger of Switzerland, hence the rather awkward name. All this was intended simply as a means of acquiring experience. He then entrusted the design of the challenger, *France*, to Andrè Mauric.

The French went into the challenger series with enviable resources: they had a set of twenty-seven mainsails and fifteen spinnakers, two training boats, various support yachts, two cooks and a

cellar-full of French wines. *Gretel*, however, won the series and went on to challenge the Americans, who approached the defence of the Cup with the "old" *Intrepid*. The hard-fought series saw an undeserved disqualification for the Australians in the second race after they had already lost the first. They squared the series with victories in the next two but in the end *Intrepid*, with Bill Ficker at the helm, prevailed.

....

199 top In 1970 the Americans again defended the cup with Intrepid, *Stephens' best 12-meter yacht: they won 4-2 in a series of races that repeated the close-fought battle between Rainbow and Endeavour. The two yachts were evenly matched, as were the skippers, Bill Ficker aboard* Intrepid *and Jim Hardy with* Gretel II. *The second race was, in effect, won by the Committee with a highly debatable decision in favor of the Americans. But then, this was the America's Cup.*

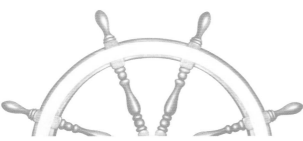

ALAN BOND'S FIRST TWO CAMPAIGNS

History repeated itself in 1974 when no less than eight nations issued challenges, but only France and Australia actually took part in the elimination trials. The French were again led by Baron Bich with a new yacht, *France II*, again designed by Andrè Mauric.

The Australians were instead led by a wealthy, impulsive and easy-going businessman, Alan Bond, by no means the type of man to appeal to the conservative members of the New York Yacht Club. Bond entrusted the design of *Southern Cross* to Bob Miller. The new Australian boat was significantly different, above all in her keel appendages, a hint of things to come ten years later when the same designer, working under a different name, penned a fin that was revolutionary enough to actually win the America's Cup.

The challenger series was again dominated by the Australians, while in the United States the preoccupation aroused by the closeness of the previous regatta led to the up-dating of the defender. Two new designs by Britton Chance, *Mariner* and *Valiant* were launched, along with the latest design by Olin Stephens, *Courageous*. Only this last proved to be a match for the glorious *Intrepid* and despite myriad doubts was eventually selected. It proved to be a well judged decision as she defeated *Southern Cross* four races to nil.

Three years later, Alan Bond's Australian team were back with a new boat, *Australia*, again designed by Bob Miller, this time assisted by John Valentijn.

The result, however, was the same disappointing 4-0 defeat, further testifying to the superiority of American sailing in the America's Cup context. The Americans had not even taken the trouble to build a new boat, *Courageous* winning her second edition.

200 bottom Southern Cross *was one of the new generation 12-meter boats: built in light alloy, she featured a fin distinctly separate from the bottom of the hull, with none of the fairings that had lined earlier versions with the past. Miller designed his 12-meter along the same lines as he designed IOR boats, paying close attention to weight: Southern Cross was lightened wherever possible, even the deck had an opening in the plating in the area corresponding to the stern overhang where the weight is unwanted.*

201 top Stephens *too designed a modern defender, built in light alloy by Minneford, with all the gear shifted below decks and two large apertures allowing weight to be saved on the stern overhang.* Courageous, *however, was still traditional below the waterline; Stephens had always produced winners and saw no reason to change now. His latest yacht was simply much lighter.*

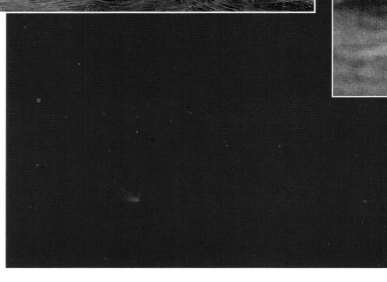

201 bottom Like the previous defenders, Courageous was only selected after a long series of elimination trials. Two new 12-meters were launched, Ted Hood's Independence and the other great sailmaker Lovell North's Enterprise, which were joined by the two 1970 Chance designs, Mariner and Valiant, which were useful in early testing. This photo, which refers to the 1974 edition, shows Courageous which had Ted Turner at the helm, as she crosses the path of another 12-meter during the elimination trials to select the defender.

202 *The 1980 edition of the America's Cup saw four nations contesting the right to challenge the New York Yacht Club: Alan Bond was back with Australia, as was Baron Bich with France, while Sweden presented a heavily revised Sverige. Above all, Britain returned to the scene after a 16-year absence. This photo shows one of the elimination trials with the yellow Swedish boat designed by Pelle Peterson leading Australia, Alan Bond's new 12-meter designed by Bob Miller, who in the meantime had changed his name to Ben Lexcen.*

203 *left Baron Bich's third America's Cup campaign was disputed with a new France, again designed by Andrè Mauric. She met Bond's yacht in the final and found the path to the America's Cup proper barred once more. Baron Bich was the last of the great owners who were not adverse to taking the helm themselves: this memorable image portrays him with his yellow leather gloves at the helm of his last France.*

FOUR NATIONS – FOUR CHALLENGES

The 1980s saw the return of the Americans' traditional adversary, Great Britain, to the waters of Newport. The British challenger had first to tackle intense competition from Swedish, French and, inevitably, Australian boats.

Sweden was represented by Pelle Peterson's *Sverige*, the French in their third attempt by *France III* owned by the extremely popular Baron Bich (his ball-point pens had by then conquered America too, meaning he had won his own personal cup!) while the British had launched *Lionheart*, featuring a remarkable banana-like curving mast; the top section above the stay grommet curved sharply sternwards, thus allowing the area of the last third of the mainsail to be increased by almost 10%. Alan Bond instead presented a significantly modified *Australia*.

The elimination trials were won comfortably by the Australian yacht, which this time went into the America's Cup proper holding a very strong hand. The defenders had in the meantime launched two new boats, *Freedom* by

Olin Stephens, *Clipper* by David Pedrick and the glorious *Courageous*.

Freedom helmed by Dennis Conner, won thirty-seven of the forty races in which she took part.

Australia, like *Gretel II* ten years earlier, managed to win a single race, but yet again the series was marred by the disqualification of the

challenger—for not having shown a red light when, for the first time in the history of the America's Cup, one of the races had finished after sundown.

The defeat was particularly hard on Alan Bond, as this was his third unsuccessful attempt, but the arrogant attitude once again displayed by the Race Committee perhaps helped to harden the Australians' resolve.

Three years later they were back in force with no less than three syndicates involved in the challenger series.

203 *top right The 1980 America's Cup was disputed between* Freedom, *the last 12-meter designed by Stephens and* Australia, *designed by Ben Lexcen and Johan Valentijn.* Australia *was disqualified from the second race, which finished after sunset due to light winds, for having delayed switching on her running lights.* Freedom *won the cup, but Alan Bond returned to* Australia *determined to gain revenge.*

203 *bottom right The British attempt to return to the America's Cup fold failed in the first series of elimination trials against* France. *The British yacht, and perhaps the entire project, were never a match for her rivals.* Lionheart *was notable only for her mast, the upper part of which curved towards the stern in an attempt to gain a few square feet of sail area.*

204 top 1983 marked the end of an era and the first year of a cycle of challenger races that developed into a true trophy within a trophy: winning what is today the Vuitton Cup, was itself a considerable feat. The Italians debuted with Andrea Vallicelli's Azzurra which, together with the British yacht Victory '83, a Jan Howlett design, progressed to the challenger semi-finals.

204 center left The Australians struggled to beat a worthy British rival Victory '83 in the challenger final, but made it through to America's Cup proper where she met Liberty, a new 12-meter designed by the former assistant of Ben Lexcen, Johan Valentijn and helmed by Dennis Conner, now considered to be the best America's Cup helmsman. The photo shows the two boats circling before the start of a race.

THE END OF A DOMINION

This was the first edition of a new-look America's Cup. While previously regattas had been held to select the challenger, never as in 1983 had they been so competitive and never had they seen such a large number of participants. From Australia came Alan Bond's fourth challenge, this time with a brand-new and top secret design from Ben Lexcen (the designer formerly known as Bob Miller!), as well as *Challenge 12* and *Advance*. Great Britain returned with the Jan Howlett-designed *Victory '83*, while Canada made her first appearance for over a century with *Canada I*. The French, bereft of Baron Rich, were nonetheless present with *France III*, while Italy made her debut with *Azzurra*, a Vallicelli design that was to put up a respectable showing.

The elimination trials held in three rounds eventually saw victory go to *Australia II* which defeated the British boat *Victory '83* in the final.

For the first time the Americans appeared to have financial difficulties; perhaps after a hundred and thirty years of consecutive and relatively comfortable victories, motivation was becoming a problem. In fact, two of the three syndicates proved to be unprepared and only Dennis Conner with his new *Liberty*, a design by Valentijn, the designer who had collaborated with Bob Miller/Ben Lexcen seven years earlier, was in an acceptable condition. He was faced with an Alan Bond made all the more aggressive by three frustrated attempts and equipped with a boat and crew that was finely honed after completing the long and demanding challenger series. It was essentially a mirror image of the situation found in so many previous editions when the solitary challengers arrived ill-equipped to face American boats that already completed an impressive number of races against one another. Moreover, *Australia II* was truly innovative: she had a keel with reversed geometry and two lead wings on the lower section; the hull had volumes concentrated in the center and a reduced wetted surface, given that it lacked major joints. This was a decidedly more modern boat, lighter by 2 tons (out of 28), with the same stability but improved maneuverability and acceleration, qualities fundamental in match racing. In spite of the clear superiority of the Australian hull, the experience of Dennis Conner enabled the Americans to go into the final race all square at 3-3. The seventh race was taken by *Australia II* and the Hundred Guineas Cup, won by the schooner *America* in 1851 at Cowes against the British yachting fleet, left the halls of the New York Yacht Club. A new era had begun.

towards a revival: a new yachting

204 center right Only at the end of the regatta was Australia II's secret revealed: a ballast fin of an unusual design which above all guaranteed greater speed when tacking, an important aspect in a match race between two boats of virtually identical performance that have to tack on innumerable occasions. Australia II's fin was developed in collaboration with Van Oossanen in the testing tank at Wageningen in Holland.

204 bottom After one hundred and thirty-two years the Hundred Guineas Cup finally left the halls of the New York Yacht Club: Australia II won the America's Cup, beating Dennis Conner and Liberty 4-3. John Bertrand, the skipper of the Australian boat, on the left, is seen celebrating victory with Alan Bond. This was Bond's third challenge and made up for having been defeated at Newport three years earlier due to a controversial disqualification..

205 Australia II was at last a truly new 12-meter: after 1983 all the boats in this class were to have hull bottoms and, especially, keel appendages inspired by those of the Australian yacht. Ben Lexcen had followed his innovator's instincts honed in the IOR classes, while the Americans had for some time been sitting on their laurels after a series of comfortable victories. Australia II, apart from her more efficient appendages, was 10% lighter and had much smaller wetted surfaces than any other 12-meter.

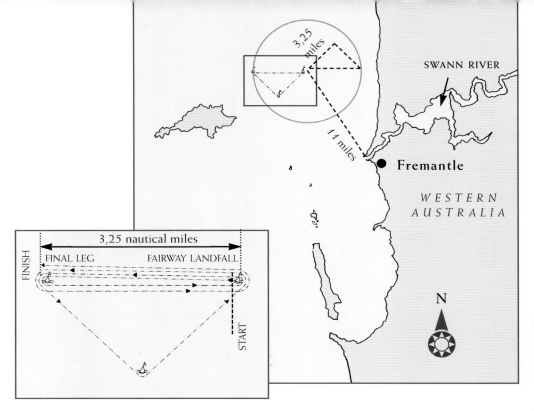

3,25 miles

SWANN RIVER

● **Fremantle**

WESTERN
AUSTRALIA

11 miles

N

3,25 nautical miles

FINISH | FINAL LEG | FAIRWAY LANDFALL

START

THE FIRST AMERICA'S CUP REGATTA OUTSIDE AMERICA

In 1987, the America's Cup would be staged outside American waters for the first time. The city of Freemantle near Perth in Western Australia, with its typical oceanic sea conditions, was to play host to the next edition. Six American syndicates participated in the challenger series which was increasingly an event within an event: Dennis Conner with *Stars and Stripes*, and *America II*, *American Eagle*, *U.S.A.*, *Heart of America* and the old *Courageous*. They were joined by two French boats, *French Kiss* and *Challenge France*, Peter de Savary's British boat *White Crusader* and the Canadians with *Canada II*. There were also two Italian consortia, testimony to a growth that was to bear significant fruit in the years to come: *Azzurra*, a new Vallicelli design, and *Italia*, designed by Giorgetti & Magrini.

Lastly, New Zealand made its debut on the America's

Cup stage, with *New Zealand*. This was not to be the last we heard of the team from Oceania.

The challenger series lasted no less than three months and saw *Stars and Stripes* helmed by Dennis Conner, thirsting for revenge, emerge victorious in the final against *New Zealand*.

The Australians devoted notable technical and financial resources to this, their first defence of the cup. Alan Bond's syndicate launched two boats and eventually selected *Australia IV*, but was defeated in the elimination trials by *Kookaburra III*. The challenger, an American for the first time in one hundred and thirty-six years, won comfortably 4-0 and carried the cup home in triumph. "Home" was not, however, the New York Yacht Club, as Dennis Conner's challenge had actually been sponsored by the less aristocratic and somewhat younger San Diego Yacht Club of California. It is fair to say that an era really had drawn to a close.

206 Taking into account the 1851 race won by the schooner America *at Cowes, for only the second time in history the Hundred Guineas Cup was competed for outside the generally calm waters of the bays beyond New York in 1987. Since 1983, the America's Cup had in fact been in the possession of the Royal Perth Yacht Club and the regatta was to be* staged in the oceanic waters off Freemantle, a town on the west coast of Australia. French Kiss, *representing the Société de regates Rochelaises designed by Philippe Briand, with Marc Pajot at the helm, chasing the Chicago Yacht Club's* Heart of America, *designed by Graham & Schlageter and helmed by the veteran Bud Melges.*

207 top left The America's Cup course at Freemantle was located in open waters. The Australians were determined to claim all the advantages reserved for the defenders and the fact that they were accustomed to conditions that were generally much more severe than those off Newport, should have made things all the more difficult for the challengers. The course was an Olympic triangle located 11 miles out of Freemantle with two reaches, three leeward and three windward legs for a total of 24 miles.

207 top right The Americans came to Perth with revenge uppermost in their minds. The 1983 defeat had dented their national pride. The Vuitton Cup to select the 1987 challenger had been staged at the end of the previous year and had seen no less than 6 American syndicates presenting boats, including one entered by the San Diego Yacht Club and helmed by Dennis Conner; the New York Yacht Club had yet to forgive the helmsman for the defeat against Australia II. In this photo, the French challenger French Kiss, *crosses* U.S.A. *on a starboard tack.*

207 center The challengers also included the New Zealanders, who presented a significant innovation; they were, in fact, the first to build hulls in fiberglass which proved to be extremely strong. New Zealand, *a Bruce Farr design in collaboration with Davidson and Holland, was helmed by Chris Dickson and represented the Royal New Zealand Yacht Squadron.*

207 bottom In the wake of the relative success of Azzurra in 1983, the Italians were present with two syndicates: that of the Yacht Club Costa Smeralda with Azzurra II, *again designed by Vallicelli and the Conzorzio Italia on behalf of the Yacht Club Italiano, with* Italia, *a design by Giorgetti & Magrini.*

208 top Stars & Stripes *rounding the mark ahead of* Heart of America. *These were two of the six American challengers participating in the Vuitton Cup. The others were* U.S.A., Eagle, *a Valentijn design with Rod Davis at the helm, the old* Courageous, *updated by John Marshall, and* America II. *Only* Star & Stripes *and* America II *qualified for the semi-finals. The latter, designed by Langan with the collaboration of Sparkman and Stephens, was the representative of the New York Yacht Club and carried most hopes of bringing the cup back to the United States.*

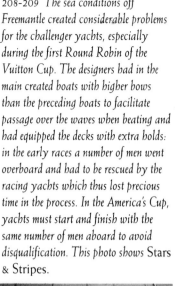

208-209 *The sea conditions off Freemantle created considerable problems for the challenger yachts, especially during the first Round Robin of the Vuitton Cup. The designers had in the main created boats with higher bows than the preceding boats to facilitate passage over the waves when beating and had equipped the decks with extra holds: in the early races a number of men went overboard and had to be rescued by the racing yachts which thus lost precious time in the process. In the America's Cup, yachts must start and finish with the same number of men aboard to avoid disqualification. This photo shows Stars & Stripes.*

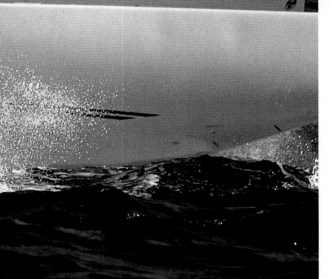

209 top *Stars & Stripes, the San Diego Yacht Club boat with Dennis Conner at the helm. In order to prepare for the event, Conner had no less than four boats built, all bearing the same name. His syndicate was considered from the outset to be one of the best equipped America's Cup challengers.*

209 bottom *The New Zealanders came to this edition of the America's Cup with excellent credentials.*
Their yacht had in fact won the world championship for its class that year, again at Freemantle, and their "kiwi plastics" as

the New Zealander boats in fiberglass were nick-named, had impressed observers during training. The 1987 edition was to be only the first in a series of participations that were to continue with successive improvements and eventual victory.

210 top right *The Australians had no less than four syndicates competing to defend the cup: that of Alan Bond, the winner at Newport, with two new yachts,* Australia III *and* Australia IV, *a second led by Kevin Parry that had built three yachts,* Kookaburra I, II *and* III *and another two with* Steak and Kidney *and* South Australia.

210 center *The Ben Lexcen-designed* Australia IV *appears to be suffering in the Freemantle waves. She failed to beat* Kookaburra III, *the new yacht designed by Scott Kaufmann and Jan Murray in collaboration with Swebrick that was to qualify to defend the America's Cup. Neither, however, was a match for either* Stars & Stripes *or* New Zealand.

210 bottom left *The final of the Vuitton Cup was much closer than the 1987 America's Cup series:* Stars & Stripes *struggled to overcome* New Zealand *which was in effect probably the better boat.*

210 bottom right *Dennis Conner, all smiles after the tears of Newport, lifts the famous Hundred Guinea Cup. His* Stars & Stripes *had easily beaten the Australian* Kookaburra III *in the America's Cup series: four-nil to the Americans — just like old times. Conner won at Freemantle thanks to his great experience in this type of competition. His yacht was by no means as superior as* Australia II *had been at Newport four years earlier, and the American helmsman can take much of the credit for the overall victory.*

211 Kookaburra III *leading* Australia *to windward. The Australians staged around a hundred races to select the defender and, to the very end, the boats of the two syndicates proved to be well matched.* Kookaburra *was eventually selected but she was no match for* Stars & Stripes.

towards a revival: a new yachting

212 *This replica of the historic schooner* America *can be seen sailing in the same waters as modern carbonfiber yachts: yachting today is more articulated than in the past with numerous different models responding to multiple demands. Seeing* America *under sail and appreciating her qualities despite the relatively limited performance and features she offers signifies, however, a rediscovery of the values that have underpinned yachting since its origin.*

213 *The America's Cup* 2000 *provided confirmation of the global nature of yachting. Challengers for the trophy arrived from every continents with the exception of Africa (and this last gap could well be filled in the future by South Africa which among the African natures is the one most involved in the sport). The event is representative of the trends and evolution of yachting in general: here the women of Mighty Mary, the first potential defender with an all-female crew, challenge the legendary Dennis Conner's* Stars & Stripes.

history. In the 1970s, industrial production went through a difficult period triggered by the energy crisis and the end of the dream of "popular" sailing. The *coup de grâce* was provided by a sequence of economic factors. The use of wood as a material was becoming problematic not so much for technical motives as because the specialized labor it required was scarce; there was a lack of apprentices learning the trade who could replace the master carpenters approaching retirement. Moreover, the timber itself, especially that of the highest quality, was increasingly difficult to source. On the other hand, fiberglass, which had appeared to be the natural replacement for wood, was beginning to be called into question on technical (the problem of osmosis, for example) and economic grounds. Good fiberglass construction is expensive and requires specialized premises and rigid quality control.

REGATTAS AT THE END OF THE MILLENNIUM

After departing from the origins of yachting we have now reached the present day which is where things become more difficult for the chronicler of what is a complex story. While its beginning may have been uncertain, there was at least a certain consistency of chronology, location and action; as time progressed, however, the locations and events multiplied exponentially.

Herein lies the first obstacle: including everything would be, if not impossible for the chronicler, undoubtedly tedious for the reader. Eliminating locations and deeds is embarrassing and in any case subjective. The second problem is that, while up to this point we have been talking about events concluded in the past and therefore objectively describable on the basis of historical facts, the arguments treated in this chapter concern on-going processes and people that are still actively involved in them: rather than reporting it is now a question of opinion. Only one thing is certain, and that is what it is not. Yachting is no longer an exclusive pursuit; it has definitely broken the thread tying it to spare time and, via wealth, to the dominant class. Today yachting has something of everything: sport, recreation and business. It is an end for those bitten by the bug, but also a means, for example as a promotional vehicle. In the past it was unheard of for gaff-rigged yachts of the

nineteenth century to be seen sailing with carbonfiber yachts sporting electronically controlled centerboards, cruising yachts of the Sixties together with the last surviving representative of the J Class. Now, however, it is an annual occurrence at the Saint Tropez Nioulargue. Once upon a time there was the British cutter on one side of the world and the American sloop on the other: but sailing, or yachting, had the same motives and rituals on both sides of the Atlantic. There were, it is true, those who privileged cruising and those who were devoted to racing; but both had a common passion, that of sailing, and when a cruiser encountered another yacht he could not help throwing down a gauntlet just as the devoted racer always took pleasure in cruising. This was true up to the 1960s. A sailing yacht was a sailing yacht. After the Fastnet some crew members would disembark while the wives of those who remained would take their place and one cruised back to the Mediterranean aboard the same boat.

Uffa Fox once said "The best ocean racer is the best ocean cruiser." It would seem that this is no longer true. What is the sailing yacht of today? We go cruising with a long-keeled yacht or with one equipped with winglets, but neither would be suitable for racing just as no contemporary racing boat is suitable for cruising. This said, we shall return to our

Moreover, the process pollutes and is hardly compatible with the environments in which boatyards are traditionally located, such as beaches, town centers and tourist resorts.

For centuries, American boat-owners commissioned their yachts from American yards and British owners from British yards. Other nations then began to appear on the scene, Germany, France, Canada and Italy, for example, but the principle of the owner and boatyard from the same country remained and tradition continued to be associated with quality in relation to boatbuilders. The 1980s and 90s were to be the years of globalization. While wealth can hardly be said to be evenly distributed, there were at least pockets of wealth on all continents and the mass media helped the spread of behavioral models throughout the world. The year 2000 edition of the America's Cup saw the participation of boats from four of the five continents, only Africa being absent. Freed from the need for the support of consolidated traditions, boatyards were established where labor costs were lower and the social and environmental problems were less significant. There remain a number of historic centers where the deep-rooted traditions have led to the development of highly specialized sectors that manage to offset the effects of higher costs compared with other markets.

YACHT DESIGN

The yacht has clearly undergone a profound process of evolution: today it has specific features that owe nothing to the traditions of the past. Differences that once existed and that allowed British and American yachts to be instantly identified when they were the only two types in existence have now been eliminated.

Today we only differentiate between racing and cruising yachts. The first has a deck devoted entirely to the rigging and gear, its layout being designed in relation to the handling of the boat. The deckhouse, where fitted, is small and low with the minimum openings necessary for the ventilation of the interiors which themselves are reduced to virtually empty shells, hammocks with tubular frames and canvas, an exposed W.C. and a minimal galley. Nobody actually sleeps or lives aboard; ocean races have all but disappeared and during regattas the crews sleep in hotels.

Above all, however, it is the hull that has evolved. Non-existent overhangs, an almost vertical stempost, broad, shallow sections: today the yacht slides over the water, the bottom being shaped to plane, a factor that has

overturned all the old theories regarding how a hull should be shaped to pass through water.

Great stability of form and the weight of the crew used as ballast, much in the same way as the American sand baggers, but with the addition of a blade keel and a lead bulb attached to the bottom. The sails are reinforced with Kevlar or carbon fibers and the masts themselves are made with the same materials, the entire complex being adjusted with hydraulic systems.

The new technologies, the new materials and above all systems of structural calculation that are far more precise than in the past allow designers to create far stiffer yachts that carry far more canvas and thus provide greater performance: today speeds of around ten knots are the norm while the logs of the Seventies showed such rates at the end of the scale.

The cruising yacht has clearly benefited from the advances made with racing hulls which are, in fact, frequently the commercial vehicles used to launch new production boats. Hull shapes are less extreme but they contain the principles with the result that they too are stiff and responsive. Great stability of form, in fact, leads to a less extensive but more sudden roll and the flat bottom tends to bounce on the wave and pitch. The modern cruising boats are less comfortable than those of the past but not necessarily faster because they generally lack the crew needed to get the utmost performance out them when there is wind and when conditions are still engines tend to be used.

However, what surprises me most about cruising boats is the deck: in order to provide interior space the deck house has to be very long and wide, while the gear such as winches, rails and so on is almost as extensive and complex as that on a racing boat (helping to justify elevated purchase prices while when cruising one actually uses only fifty per cent of such equipment). Consequently the deck is virtually unusable and one can only sit in the

214 top left With none of the characteristics of a traditional craft-based boatyard, the Cookson yard in New Zealand is the home of modern advanced technology yacht building. Composites are worked in three main phases: the first, the design phase, defines the materials and techniques to be used; the second, that of lamination, still features a manual, craftsman-like aspect; the third, lastly, involves the thermal and vacuum treating of the moldings in which quality control and methodology are all important.

214 center right Such is the importance attached to keels today that they are jealously concealed from the inquisitive eyes of rivals behind tarpaulins. The hull is, on the other hand, felt to be relatively uninfluential and thus exposed to the gaze of one and all. In effect, the lightweight boat has little below the waterline as she tends to slide over the top of the water, while the appendages, apart from righting the boat and correcting heel, are crucial to its performance. This photo shows America One, the American boat that disputed the final of the 2000 Louis Vuitton Cup.

214 bottom Lamination today replaces what was once the realm of the master carpenter: the skinning is constructed by overlaying in the mold successive strata of resistant materials, glass or more exotic fibers such as carbon or Kevlar, which are then impregnated with resin. The most sophisticated designs require a composite construction of two such "skins" sandwiching a layer of a very light material, balsa as seen in this photo, or another synthetic substance.

215 left The function of a modern yacht is immediately obvious: while Cambria could have been, and indeed was, a good cruising yacht as well as an America's Cup challenger, OneAustralia, *an America's Cup Class yacht from 1999, is unquestionably a pure racer. Moreover, she was built to last the duration of a single America's Cup regatta, a factor also true of the unforgettable J Class yachts.*

215 right *The mold has to be built with extreme care: its shape reflects the eventual form of the finished hull. Today molds are built from a CNC machined plug capable of translating the designer's digitally converted drawings into a three-dimensional form. The surfaces of the mold, on which the hull will be laminated, are mirror finished and are waxed to facilitate the extraction of the molded sections.*

216 left The yacht of the past was heavy, its displacement requiring notable hull volumes, and had appendages that, in order to be faired into the hull, were also voluminous: under sail she would displace large quantities of water and generate a clearly visible wave. Sixième Sens, a French America's Cup Class from 1999, has a very slim ballast fin creating no wave which can be glimpsed through the water in this photo.

216 right and 217 bottom The great design revolution was stimulated by the success of Australia over Liberty in 1983. Since then all the designers have recognised that yachts' appendages, the rudder and the ballast fin, could and should be redesigned from scratch. For years they had proceeded to employ minor and unscientific variations of the models and profiles created in the United States in the Fifties by NACA (eventually to become NASA and to concentrate on rather different

fields, but had in the meantime developed a series of different aerodynamic profiles that were employed in diverse roles from helicopter rotors to rudders, to propellers and anything else that had to move in a fluid). The yacht designers had remained attached to these models largely because of the inadequacy of the materials available to them. After 1983, a lesson taught by Herreshoff back in the late nineteenth century with Dilemma was revived: ballast is best employed as low as possible and therefore the ideal solution would be to link it to the hull via a blade as compact and slim as possible. At that time the results were conditioned by the materials used. Today, almost all sailing yachts, including rather unecessarily cruisers, have elliptical rudders and ballast keels composed of a blade hung with a lead bulb acting as the ballast. The designers have gone to town on this theme, as demonstrated by this series of photos of the ballast fins of Italia II (top right) which participated in the 1987 America's Cup, Stars & Stripes (bottom left) and OneAustralia (bottom center), America's Cup protagonists in 1995, and Courageous (bottom right) from the '87 edition of the America's Cup.

cockpit as it is impossible to lie and read a book or sunbathe anywhere else.

While differences between racing and cruising yachts are apparent, geographical differences have disappeared. For this reason when speaking about world-wide serial production, no mention is made of the forms and technical characteristics of the yachts. Wherever you go, from New Zealand to France, they are the same. Differences have been ironed out just as they have in fashion and social customs. The world of today is uniform and yachting has been unable to avoid following suit. This trend is determined principally by two factors. Above all, information is today a global commodity and experience and data are easily despatched from one end of the world to the other: once upon a time the British raced on the Thames and the Americans off New York. The voyage of the schooner *America* was a one-off episode and, in fact, was not followed up for fifty years, both countries continuing to build boats in their own way. International regattas spread in the twentieth century, but it was only from the Sixties onwards that yachtsmen began to compete throughout the world.

While the capitals of yachting could once be identified as the Solent, Rhode Island and, perhaps, Kiel, the present day geography is much more extensive. Florida and San Diego in the United States, Auckland and Sydney in Ocean, Palma, the Côte d'Azure and Porto Cervo in Europe are all, together with the traditional centers, established ports of call on yachting's "grand tour." The racing season sees boats and crews transported (no racing yacht ever attempts an ocean crossing now, except in

the hold of a ship!) from one event to the next. Nowadays, when one can fly from one continent to another in a matter of hours, an Argentine designer may just as easily build in the United States or Europe, with the same being true of a New Zealander, and both may even change their passports to meet the market demands. It is hardly surprising, therefore, that yachts are all the same.

The second reason for this homogenization is technical. At one time the design of a yacht was born out of the intuition a single person drawing on his or her own experience which, as we have already said, tended to be local. A

George Steers design could not therefore, except by accident, resemble one by the Englishman Michael Ratsey.

The differences diminished as objective science began to make inroads into yacht design.

The information provided by the early testing tanks was unreliable, the data having to be interpreted intuitively by the designer or engineer, and it was not until Davidson developed systematic testing in the Stevens Institute tank that something radical happened. But this was not until 1935!

The shape of the yacht began to be determined in a scientific fashion, with the designer's intuition increasingly playing a secondary role. Into the post-war period, therefore, the availability of an efficient tank

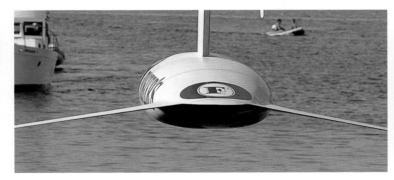

was of vital importance.

The Americans, especially in the America's Cup, enjoyed the significant advantage of being able to use the facilities of the Stevens Institute which were considerably more advanced than those of similar institutions in other countries. Only in the 1980s did designers from other nations have the opportunity of testing at Wageningen in Holland where there was a tank as sophicticated as those of the Americans. It was hardly a coincidence, in fact, that the Americans finally lost the cup in 1984.

The true revolution, however, the one that was to determine the present day situation of universal

standards, was to come with the introduction and widespread adoption of computers: information technology can, for example, be used to visualize the pressures induced by motion on individual parts of the hull and consequently optimum shapes can be established; similarly, forces can be simulated and evaluated to allow precise structural calculations to be made. Computing power allows a vast number of permutations to be experimented at a very low cost: in the 1980s a tank testing cycle to evaluate five models could cost around fifty thousand dollars. Today one hundred configurations can be analyzed with a two-thousand-dollar PC.

The information derived from computer-aided design can be sent throughout the world in real time: I can work on a design that is

217 top Extreme solutions were adopted in the search for outright performance: the Swiss 2000 America's Cup challenger, Be Happy, boasted two ballasted rudders, one at the bow, one at the stern. The system did not provide the hoped for performance, but the designers had great faith in a feature which might simply need further development and testing.

visualized contemporaneously on my monitor and the one my assistant is looking at in a boatyard thousands of miles away. This has led to a homogeneous diffusion of experience. Plank-on-edge on one side of the Atlantic and broad-and-shallow on the other is a thing of the past. A small margin of mystery does still remain because a sailing yacht is still such a complex system operating in such a variable environment that something will always be entrusted to the intuition of some one, be they a designer or a yachtsman.

In the meantime, yachts have also become more complex; previously there were either no on-board systems or they were at best rudimentary (I well remember sailing on yachts of even 65 feet which at the time were big, with no electronics whatsoever, just a pair of batteries, no pressurised hot water—what there was had to be pumped manually); the instrumentation was restricted to a compass, a chronometer and a patent log (a luxury) while the engine really was "auxiliary" and the deck

gear was limited and simple. Even the materials used in the construction were few in number, just wood, steel and light alloy.

The build process was also simpler. Boatyards were close to home and their experience played its part in the design phase, whilst today they are scattered throughout the world and are frequently companies specialising in one phase of the process that have to be co-ordinated rather than traditional yards.

In this scenario the figure of the master designer has become obsolete. The design of a yacht now requires a team of professionals and an engineering studio. I began working in this manner early in the 1970s and my studio, Giorgetti & Magrini, was perhaps ahead of its time. Today the designer is Wally Yachts, or a name such as Farr, for example, heading a team of twenty technical experts.

We are therefore unlikely to see another "Herreshoff era" or "Stephens era", but this certainly does not mean yachts and yachting will lose any of their appeal.

218 top The Moro di Venezia was the challenger in the 1992 edition of the America's Cup, the first disputed by yachts of the new America's Cup Class, a type of boat that that drew on all the design and production technology experience gained with racing class yachts. The Moro was built in advanced composites with widespread use of exotic fibers and vacuum-bagging and thermal treating of the laminates.

218 bottom and 219 bottom During the design phase, Moro di Venezia benefitted from computer aided methods: the role of the designer was by no means less important, but he was provided with crucial support by a group of specialists. The 1983 America's Cup, the historic turning point marked by Ben Lexcen's inventiveness and, apparently, the technical support of the Dutchman Peter Van Oossanen, was probably the last to see the figure of the individual designer in such an influential position.

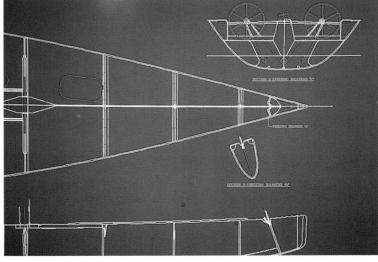

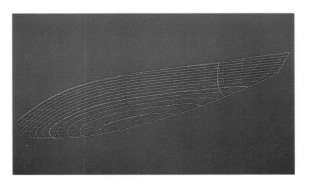

218-219 Soldini's *Fila* shows just how much a designer, the Finot Group, and the technological capacity of a yard, the Italian CNB establishment at Fano, can achieve when working on a boat that, free of all ratings considerations, has the sole aim of being as fast as possible. The boat is extremely light, has a canting ballast keel allowing the ballast to be shifted to windward, an innovative system of shrouds, and two rudders to ensure one is always under water.

219 top and right Computer Aided Design or CAD systems allow numerous different design solutions to be examined very quickly and, consequently, cheaply. Entire tank testing cycles were once necessary; that is to say, a scale model had to be built and towed across a testing tank at various speeds and various angles of heel. Each time the configuration of the design was altered a new model had to be built and the cycle repeated. Today it is sufficient to vary elements of the design and verify the results, by means of programs simulating the pressures

determined by the speed at various points of the hull. Clearly, in the design phase the system allows individual details to be modified and implemented before returning to the global configuration to evaluate the impact of the features adopted. These images, above all the composition of transverse sections (right), allow the extremes forms of this yacht, that in a victorious circumnavigation of the globe encountered wind and sea conditions that few even ocean-going yacht hulls would have resisted, to be seen at a glance.

220 top A sailmaker in a modern loft, suspended in mid-air on a kind of sling, lays fabrics and carbon fibers according to a pattern that the sail designer produced on a computer. All the America's Cup sails and those of the yachts expected to provide competitive performance are created in this way.
The sail loft with its sewing machines and sailcloth panels cut by hand and tacked to make up the composition on the vast wooden floors survives for the sails of classic boats and those of cruising boats. This photo shows the sails of Luna Rossa, the Italian yacht that won the 2000 edition of the Vuitton Cup and challenged Black Magic in the America's Cup.

The true engine of a sailing yacht is the complex system composed of the sails themselves and the mast with the shrouds supporting it, linking it to the hull and transferring the propulsive thrust. In the history of yachting, this apparatus was not subjected to modification until the late nineteenth century: from the "yachts" of Cleopatra through to the schooner *America*, sails, like clothes, were made from fabrics woven from natural fibers, and had no three-dimensional form other than the one they assumed naturally under the pressure of the wind. Masts were wooden poles and the shrouds were also made of plaited natural fibers, perhaps coated in tar to increase their longevity. It was only at the end of the nineteenth century that some one tried to "lighten" a mast by boring holes in it, transversally at first and then in the direction of the fibres. The practice only became established in the twentieth century when hollow wooden masts were used by the British America's Cup challengers. In the meantime, the

Americans had begun to build, as ever for the America's Cup, masts in curved and riveted steel or aluminium plates.

The first modern mast appeared on an American yacht in 1939; the International Rule 12-meter *Vim* designed by Olin Stephens: a hollow profile in extruded aluminium (the smelted material being forced through a matrix with the section of the finished article). Masts are still today made in the same way from the same material. Metal masts behave in a very different way to their wooden counterparts which, as wood is composed of longitudinal fibers, can and indeed must flex otherwise they would break under the combined bending and compressive stress imposed by the shrouds supporting them. The opposite is true of a profile

220-221 The mast-rigging-sail system of Moro V, a modern racing yacht: the mast is an aerodynamic profile in composite materials, epoxy resin and carbonfiber matting. The shrouds, along with the spreaders, constitute a system of stays in mono-directional wire with the dual purpose of keeping the mast upright and straight in relation to the transverse plane. The system as a whole has the function of supporting the sail area and transmitting the thrust of the wind to the hull, especially in the case of the mainsail.

220 bottom Carbonfiber is increasingly used in the manufacture of sails: only the high cost and the fragility of a fiber, as strong in traction as it is delicate in flexure, prevents an even more widespread use. Carbonfiber, for a given strength, is much lighter than the common Dacron fiber and the advantage of a lightweight sail is obvious. The carbon fabric is cut to shape and then bonded as it cannot be sewn.

221 left Today's sails are a flexible surface formed from a composition of strong and variously oriented fibers of Kevlar, carbon and other synthetic materials, compressed and kept in position between two bonded films. At one time, up to and beyond the Second World War for most boats, sails were made of panels of cloth in natural fibers. From the Thirties, however, the most advanced yachts already featured synthetic Dacron jibs and mainsails and nylon spinnakers.

221 right This photo shows the large Kevlar Genoa of EF Education. Kevlar is another synthetic fiber stronger than Dacron and less fragile than carbon. The traditional panels that allowed the type of cut to be identified immediately: the first sails had parallel panels while in the Thirties America's Cup sails had radial cuts. Subsequently triradial and even more complex geometry was introduced. Today seams with sail twine have disappeared as they add unnecessary weight with the doubling of the cloth and represent a break in the mechanical continuity of the sail.

222 top *Saving weight in the rig has a positive effect not only on the performance of the yacht, but also on the amount of physical work required of the crew. While on a J Class from the Thirties twenty men were needed on a halyard to hoist a mainsail, on one of the modern Maxis such as Longobarda 92 seen here, three are enough. The weight of the sails has dropped thanks both to materials used and the smaller sail areas carried by the smaller hulls. The efficiency of the rig has also improved thanks to low-friction blocks and more powerful winches.*

in light alloy as it may be subjected to combined bending and compressive stress but it must not flex otherwise it will fail. For this reason the shrouds on a wooden mast must not be too stiff, especially in the case of a solid rather than hollow mast: hemp, manila or cotton shrouds were ideal, much better than the overly rigid steel wires.

With the introduction of metal masts, metal shrouds were also adopted: the 1934 edition of the America's Cup seeing the simultaneous introduction of the material by the engineer Murdock on *Endeavour* and the designer Starling Burgess on *Rainbow*. What is true of the aluminium mast is also true of steel wire shrouds as they are still used today.

In truth, from the early twentieth century through to the present day notable advances

have been made in terms of both masts and shrouds: today's masts are tapering and therefore lighter and more flexible at the top, a feature made possible by the development of aluminium alloy welding techniques. Shrouds are now being made in stainless steel wire, with just a few stronger threads, or even mono-filament wires with aerodynamic sections. The basic concept, however, remains unchanged.

As we have already seen, progress in the field of sails was also very limited up to the end of the nineteenth century.

Sails made of various fabrics were used, the best being hand-woven linen: sails were very porous and were continually dampened to make them more compact and less subject to distortion (every bucket of water, however,

was a few extra pounds aloft!). One significant improvement was introduced in the second half of the nineteenth century, following America's triumphant voyage to England: the American yacht hoisted machine-woven cotton sails. However it was not until the twentieth century that a truly revolutionary development was introduced.

In 1937, *Ranger*, the America's Cup defender, was provided with sails made of Rayon, a synthetic fiber derived from hydrocarbons in place of cotton. Rayon was followed by Terylene, Tergal and lastly in the post-war period Dacron, still the most commonly used material for making sails. Currently therefore we are using materials developed in the middle of the twentieth century. Further advances have tended to

come in the way the sails are made. Today a sail is a preformed composite with panels bonded rather than sewn together. In general they are composed of two layers of transparent synthetic material that have the sole function of keeping the threads of super-resistant materials such as Kevlar or carbonfiber in place along the points of stress.

The sails are designed with aid of computers that hypothesize the concentration and direction of the forces induced by the pressure of the wind so that the majority of the weight of the fabric is composed of correctly distributed and aligned resistant material.

Today a sail is no longer a canvas sheet that assumes a form determined by the wind, but a panel that already has an efficient aerodynamic shape.

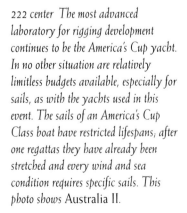

222 center The most advanced laboratory for rigging development continues to be the America's Cup yacht. In no other situation are relatively limitless budgets available, especially for sails, as with the yachts used in this event. The sails of an America's Cup Class boat have restricted lifespans; after one regattas they have already been stretched and every wind and sea condition requires specific sails. This photo shows Australia II.

222 bottom A racing yacht, like Infinity seen here, requires a budget devoted to the deck gear that accounts for over a third of the total cost. At one time, as late as the post-war period, the mast, rig, sails and gear accounted for less than 20%, the hull being far and away the most demanding element. The deck accessories have increased in number rather than cost, while the rigging is ever more sophisticated as are the materials from which it is made.

223 left Carbonfiber was widely used in the construction of America One, an America's Cup boat: the mast was no longer an aluminium extrusion as it had been up to the 1987 edition, but a laminate of carbonfiber matting and epoxy resin made in an autoclave. The large mainsail shows the carbon fibers sandwiched between the sheets of transparent mylar film, positioned according to a geometric pattern corresponding to the predicted forces. The attention paid to the mast-rigging-sails system is justified as this is in effect the yacht's engine.

223 right The deck of a Maxi, the American yacht Boomerang from 1995. Everything is designed to save weight, from the wheels to the coffee grinder columns, both in carbonfiber. The introduction of new materials has allowed weight savings that were unthinkable just a few years ago. A carbonfiber component may, for a given mechanical strength, weigh up to ten times less than the steel equivalent.

CLASSIC BOAT REGATTAS

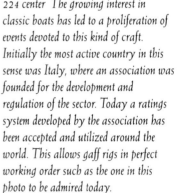

Antique furniture only attains such status after the passing of a certain period of time and when the prevailing economic conditions allow the wealthy few to pay a high price for an old wardrobe simply because it is aesthetically attractive.

The same phenomenon has now spread to the world of yachting. Up until twenty or so years ago there were only new yachts and old yachts, the latter either being abandoned or (fortunately in that they were preserved, less so in that their originality was often compromised) gradually transformed by successive owners in a slow descent from yacht to hulk, a process similar to that which produces tramp steamers.

In recent years, however, there has been increased interest, firstly amongst a select band of enthusiasts and then more widely, in classic

promotion and organization of the first classic boat rallies and formulated a "rating" system to permit competitive regattas to be staged.

The AIVE formula has been adopted throughout the Mediterranean, where nations such as France and Spain have enthusiastically embraced the classic boat theme, while links with the United States have been suggested.

In the meantime, regattas and events reserved for this type of yacht, this being a particularly appropriate use of the term given that movement looks back to the origins of the species, have multiplied and grown into important fixtures in the yachting calendar. Today, around two hundred classic boats are sailing in the Mediterranean, some of which, such as the Fife-designed *Latifa* from 1936, Herreshoff's *Mariette* from 1915 or Camper &

224 top Certain boatyards that have managed to retain the skills and technologies of the past have enjoyed a boom in recent years. The working of wood, bronze and brass has been revived by the regattas organized for classic yachts. For this reason great yachts, built by famous yards to the designs of naval architects who have contributed entire chapters to the history of sailing, have found owners willing to restore them to their original splendours. Te Vega, for example, was designed by Cox & Stevens and built in Germany by Krupp in the 1930s.

224 center The growing interest in classic boats has led to a proliferation of events devoted to this kind of craft. Initially the most active country in this sense was Italy, where an association was founded for the development and regulation of the sector. Today a ratings system developed by the association has been accepted and utilized around the world. This allows gaff rigs in perfect working order such as the one in this photo to be admired today.

boats and regattas staged specifically for this kind of craft. A classic yacht is one built in traditional materials, preferably prior to the 1950s.

For once the origins of a significant trend in the world of yachting were not Anglo-Saxon, but rather Mediterranean, and more precisely Italian. Certainly, there were individual owners who in earlier times maintained or restored wooden yachts launched many years previously, but it was in Italy that the phenomenon found fertile terrain, or rather waters, achieved official status and was regulated.

In the early Eighties a number of members of the Yacht Club Italiano, led by the President himself, created the Associazione Italiana Vele d'Epoca, which was responsible for the

224 bottom Tuiga to windward and Moonbeam, two early-twentieth-century yachts that have found new admirers. The first flies the pennant of the Yacht Club de Monaco, one of the clubs most active in the recovery of classic yachts, while the second is the property of an association which charters her. Both are magnificent examples of the work of William Fife, the famous Scottish designer and boatbuilder who, together with Charles Nicholson, was responsible for much of the history of British yachting.

224-225 A representative of the J Class era returns from the past: Astra, designed and built by Nicholson in the 1930s as an International Rule 23-meter yacht, was re-rated according to Herreshoff's Universal Rule following an agreement reached with the Americans regarding the subdivision of the classes. Still today, after a high quality restoration that has brought her back to peak fitness, she sails with the speed and performance that were the hallmark of this category of yacht.

225 bottom Another Fife yacht, Cintra, one of the first International Rule 12-meter boats. This was in 1909 and the formula had been introduced 2 years earlier. She was in fact one of the progenitors of the America's Cup 12-meter, even though today the sail pattern with a peak and a gaff topsail appears incongruous on a racing yacht. The performance provided by Cintra is nonetheless impressive and still today sailing aboard her in a regatta is an unforgettable experience.

yacht

226 left The interiors of a classic
yacht that has been subjected to a
restoration sympathetic to its original
forms and features will contain
accessories and equipment that are
compatible with the period of its
launch if not authentic. Today these
kinds of furnishings and their use may
appear to be in contrast with the
demands of modern sailing but, after
having had the pleasure of sailing
aboard Tirrenia II, I can assure you
that they offer an unmatched level of
comfort.

226-227 One of the most attractive
boats and most assiduous competitors
on the class yacht circuit: Tirrenia II,
a British yacht designed by Shepherd
in 1914. She was certainly not built as
a racing yacht but reflects that British
concept whereby the best cruising yacht
is also the best racing yachts—after
all, neither was the multiple winner of
the Fastnet, Jolie Brise, built for
racing. Tirrenia has no winches,
reflecting the conditions in which she
was launched.

Nicholson's *Creole* from 1927 to name but three, have no hesitation in passing the Pillars of Hercules and venturing out into the ocean.

Boatyards have been established, such as Fairlie Restoration in Scotland, specializing in the restoration of Fife yachts, while others such as Southampton Yacht Service, the heir to the original Nicholson, have revived their own traditions. Mention is made of these two in particular, otherwise Great Britain would for the first time in the history of yachting appear to have been excluded from something.

In Italy yards with deep-rooted traditions such as Sangermani, and other such as Beconcini or those of the Argentario region have emerged from a slow decline by specializing in

restoration work, while there are numerous other craft-based enterprises that are enjoying a second wind thanks to this new sector.

After being superseded in the America's Cup, the International Rule 12-meter class was itself falling into a terminal decline before a number of historic yachts, *Vim* and *Tomahawk* above all, were restored and relaunched.

This new interest in the yachts of the past has also resulted in the reconstruction of boats that have been lost. With design contribution from Olin Stephens, a replica of the schooner *America* had been built as early as 1967, preceded in 1963 by *Bluenose*, a replica of the winner of the Fisherman Race forty years earlier, but these were single episodes and the fruit of individual initiatives. Today there is talk of reconstructing *Britannia* and it would seem that a replica of *Westward*, the famous 1910 schooner designed by Herreshoff, is already on the slips.

In the United States, the Padanaram Yacht Company is building a wooden yacht with crossed planking belonging to the newly created W Class, a freely interpreted replica of the New York 50 designed by Herreshoff at the beginning of the twentieth century.

It really does appear that wood and brass, thrown overboard with the arrival of fiberglass, are staging something of a comeback!

227 left Creole was one of Charles Nicholson's great designs from the Twenties, one of those large schooner for which his yard was rightly famous. A yacht with an overall length of 183'6", big then and big today: for years she was considered to be the world's largest sailing yacht and has continued to sail with brief interruptions during the war and the early Eighties throughout her long career. Today she is in perfect condition.

227 right This photo shows the main deck of Creole with her helmsman and one of the two tenders. In contrast with many classic boats, Creole is still today used by her owner as a cruising and social yacht as she was originally. Her rig perhaps requires more attention that those of similar but more recent boats, but then there is no lack of sailors eager to embark on Creole.

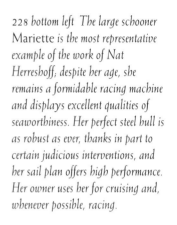

228 top left *Personally, I have nothing against replicas, although I believe little point in reviving what has been lost unless it is as an object of study. However, whenever replicas are commissioned I believe that they should remain absolutely faithful to the original design. This is not the case with America whose circular cockpit had a tiller rather than a wheel and had no deckhouse in front.*

228 center *The deck gear of a classic yacht is (the photo shows that of Mariette) if correctly reconstructed, evocative of the difficulties and physical labor involved in maneuvers a hundred years ago. The weights were vast compared with modern rigs while the block and tackle was less efficient and, above all, rigorously manual and extremely complicated. At least at first sight. Over time a generation of sailors capable of handling these rigs has been created, or rather recreated, and today the handling of many of these boats in races is impeccable.*

228 bottom left *The large schooner Mariette is the most representative example of the work of Nat Herreshoff; despite her age, she remains a formidable racing machine and displays excellent qualities of seaworthiness. Her perfect steel hull is as robust as ever, thanks in part to certain judicious interventions, and her sail plan offers high performance. Her owner uses her for cruising and, whenever possible, racing.*

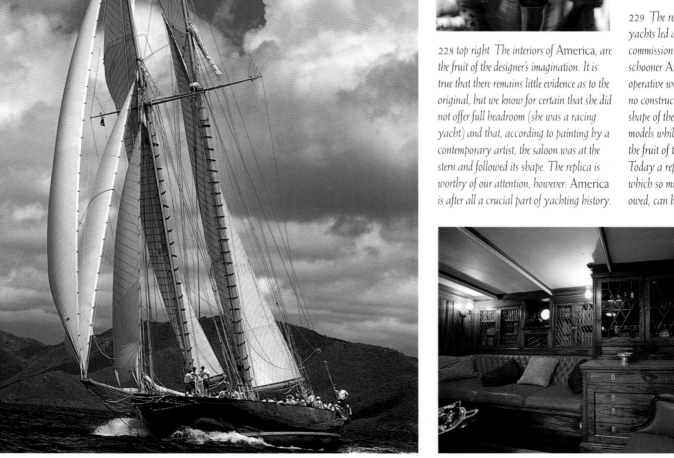

228 top right *The interiors of America, are the fruit of the designer's imagination. It is true that there remains little evidence as to the original, but we know for certain that she did not offer full headroom (she was a racing yacht) and that, according to painting by a contemporary artist, the saloon was at the stern and followed its shape. The replica is worthy of our attention, however: America is after all a crucial part of yachting history.*

228 bottom right *The interiors of Mariette have been reconstructed. During her 80 year career too much has happened to the yacht for the original furnishings to have survived. However, the design, disposition and materials faithfully replicate the original model and provide the owner with a degree of comfort worthy of more modern creations. She is still a racing yacht aboard which it is a pleasure to go cruising.*

229 *The rediscovered enthusiasm for classic yachts led a group of enthusiasts to commission Stephens to redesign the schooner America. Redesign is the operative word as in the nineteenth century, no construction drawings were produced, the shape of the hull being derived from half models while the frame and the fittings were the fruit of the experience of the boatyard. Today a replica of America, the yacht to which so much of the history of the sport is owed, can be seen sailing.*

FROM THE IOR TO THE IMS

The spread of the sport of sailing in both geographic and quantitative terms led in the 1990s to an extremely varied panorama of events and classes of boat and, consequently, places, facts and people. Regattas staged on the basis of the IOR formula introduced 20 years earlier in an optimistic attempt to standardize the sport and, in particular, to optimize the old attempts at racing different boats together, continued to survive. However, out of the IOR were born the Level Classes and, early in the Nineties, it was here that a certain staleness began to be apparent.

The 1993 edition of the most prestigious of the Level Class events, the One Ton Cup, whose origins date as far back as the nineteenth century when it was put up, albeit to a very different formula, by the Cercle de la Voile in Paris, saw just 13 participants at

Marten Marine of Auckland that launched her a year earlier in 1992.

The limitations of the One Ton Cup were actually demonstrated in that edition. The boats were by now extremely sophisticated and, in an attempt to curb the concept of planned obsolescence whereby a yacht's competitive life was restricted to the year following its launch, an age allowance was introduced that in effect signalled the surrender of the Level Class in favor of handicap racing.

This confusion was increased by the objective difficulty yacht owners faced when trying to manage a racing season that in trying to satisfy all parties saw regattas being staged throughout the world. It should also be noted that the formula privileged consistency rather than outright victories:

unquestioned and to this should be added the immeasurable appeal of sheer size: big truly is beautiful, at least in the world of sailing.

With regards to the technical aspects of the Maxi yachts, of particular significance was the 1992 edition of the Merit Cup reserved for the class and held in the Italian waters of Porto Cervo, Sardinia. This regatta was organized by the Yacht Club Costa Smeralda, which in those years had joined the yachting elite following two America's Cup campaigns, which had seen it represented in the Vuitton Cup challenger series with *Azzurra* in 1983 and *Azzurra II* in 1987. Only four Maxi yachts were in the water, but represented two contrasting philosophies. Two were sloops, that at least as far as

Cagliari in Italy. It was supposed to be a form of World Championship for yachts with an IOR rating of 30 feet 6 inches, but the interest generated hardly merited the title, despite the presence of a Japanese boat, *Cha Cha II*, competing against the Europeans. Boats from America and the rising star of yachting, *Oceania*, were conspicuous in their absence. There were, however, representatives of the latter among the crews: no less than 5 New Zealanders were found in the cockpits of the yachts, finishing first and second, both of which, for the record, were drawn by Judel and Vrolijck, German designers who had come to prominence thanks to the Level Classes. The winner, the yacht *Pinta*, thus flew a German flag, but was sailed by Russell Couts and Peter Lester, New Zealanders like the boatyard

the German champion *Pinta*, actually won only one round out of seven.

Just as these winds of crisis were blowing the IOR formula expressed its most spectacular aspect with the Class A Maxi yachts. These great boats competed in the Whitbread Round-the-World Race and a World Championship that seemed to revive the opulence of a past tied to the appeal of dimensions, that of the Big Class of the early twentieth century. The Maxi yacht races, it is true, were reserved for a limited number of participants, given the stratospheric budgets required to build and manage yachts of between seventy and eighty feet LOA, handled by crews of around thirty. However, the technical quality of yachts capable of winning an ocean race or an inshore triangle was

their rig was concerned were traditional: *Merit* owned by the Swiss financier Pierre Fehlmann and designed by Bruce Farr, and *Rothmans*, a Rob Humphreys design entrusted for the occasion to the British helmsman Lawrie Smith. Two yachts that, on paper, were at the cutting edge of hull design for inshore racing.

The adversaries of *Merit* and *Rothmans* were two Italian-owned yachts: *Longobarda '92* (formerly *Fisher & Paykel*), and *Safilo* (formerly *Steinlager*), owned by Giorgio Falk, one of the last of the gentleman drivers, an owner who willingly took the helm and had already demonstrated his ocean racing skills. Both boats were designed by Bruce Farr and were veterans, under their former names, of the Whitbread which *Steinlager* had actually won. Their ketch rigs provided extraordinary performance and apparently signalled a return to the past. In reality, the New Zealander had designed a rig with the mizzen playing a far more important role than in a classic ketch—a mizzen that allowed a staysail of significant size to be hoisted when sailing downwind. While the other boats were having to cope with vast spinnakers, *Steinlager* and *Fisher & Paykel* were thus very well balanced with no sudden and pernicious yawing, sailing under the thrust of five sails, two spankers, two jibs and the staysail, distributed along the full length of the boat; for an equivalent sail area they had a lower center of thrust and thus heeled less, were more controllable and should the wind speed increase they only had to

drop a relatively small, easy to handle sail, while the sloops were grappling with their spinnakers.

In Sardinia, the two ketches got the better of *Merit* and *Rothmans*, sparking off a heated debate: in effect the advantage they enjoyed, undeniable in strong oceanic winds, was due to the IOR formula that privileged this type of rig, rightly considering it to be less efficient. Bruce Farr had exploited this loophole in the rules to increase the sail area. At Porto Cervo, the two ketches, overtaken to windward, made up the deficit to leeward and on the reaches, aided by generally strong winds.

The previous year, instead, the class championship had been disputed by five yachts, all sloops. The three rounds were all staged in

230 Bill Koch, who was to defeat Raul Gardini in the 1992 edition of the America's Cup, participated in A Class races. His Matador II, born out of the research conducted by a group of experts at the Massachusetts Institute of Technology, won the Maxi World Championship in 1990. The costs of these boats, above all the expense of running them, with crews of 30 and containers of accessories to be shipped around the world, restricted their diffusion and their career was brief.

230-231 Seventy years on, the Maxi races revived the legendary Solent duels of the Big Class yachts. A circuit of regattas taking in the yachting capitals such as Newport and Porto Cervo carried World Championship status. These boats and races frequently served as a test bench for the America's Cup. Gardini was to launch his challenge with Moro di Venezia after his experience with Passage to Venice on the Maxi circuit.

231 bottom left Two yachts designed by Bruce Farr impressed in the 1990 Whitbread (winning the race) for the efficiency of their ketch rig with a particularly important mizzen, distanced from the mainsail as on a yawl. These were Steinlager and Fisher & Paykel, (subsequently renamed Longobarda II) and rated as a Class A for the Italian financier Gianni Varasi. In fresh winds they were capable of beating the sloop-rigged Maxis thanks to the greater sail area they could hoist and a relatively low center of thrust.

231 bottom right Vanitas belonged to the first generation of Maxi yachts: she was built in light alloy, a material that would soon be replaced by composites. Vanitas was a German Frers design from 1987. Upwind all crew members not required on the sheets would move to the windward rail, supported by the stays with their legs over the side: around fifteen men on a yacht over 16'6" wide signified a supplementary righting moment of almost 3,000 foot-pounds.

American waters, the first in the spiritual home of the America's Cup at Newport, Rhode Island, the second in Florida at Miami and the third in the Caribbean at St. Thomas. It was a championship fought out by Italians, now a significant force in the larger sailing classes, and Americans, a championship that was something of an America's Cup preview due to the presence of Raul Gardini, patron of the *Moro di Venezia* challenge, and Bill Koch who was organising the defence.

The Italian team were racing with *Vanitas*, Gardini's former *Moro di Venezia III*, an aluminium hull designed by German Frers in 1987, Gardini's *Passage to Venice*, again designed by Frers and built in composite materials by the Tencara yard which the Italian financier had established to build the America's Cup boats, and finally *Longobarda*, which had won the championship the previous year in the Mediterranean with regattas at Palma de Mallorca, St. Tropez and Porto Cervo, a Bruce Farr design in composite materials built in 1989.

The Mediterranean fleet was confronted by Bill Koch's new boat, a yacht conceived with the preparation of an America's Cup campaign in mind. The design of the yacht was entrusted to a team of technicians, Gerry Milgram from the famous Massachusetts Institute of Technology in Boston, Heiner Meldner and William Cook, with support on the structural side being provided by Hall Engineering. The yacht, named *Matador 2*, was built in composite materials with widespread use of carbonfiber by the Goetz yard in Bristol, Rhode Island. In order to define the waterlines no less than twenty-two models were tank tested. The best of these were then built as reduced scale boats for two-man crews, the winner then being scaled up to produce the actual yacht.

Bill Koch's *Matador 2* won the world championship that year, at which point it was clear that given the costs involved the formula was no longer appropriate. The Maxi yacht era came to a close at the same time as a period characterised by particular economic conditions. From then on the major economic resources would be directed towards the ever popular America's Cup.

In that period, and as a reaction to the signs of crisis on the Maxi circuit, the IOR 50-foot class was beginning to attract increasing attention. This was a class with more "reasonable" dimensions than the Class A, but greater prestige than the One Tonners which, in a period of economic euphoria, were considered to be small yachts.

As usual, the limitation on the spread of this type of yacht and events organized for it lay in the intention to involve the yachting world in its entirety. The 1991 edition of the World Championship for the class featured, for example, rounds in American waters off Miami, and in Europe at Travemunde (Germany) and Lymington (England). The result was that not all the European boats were present in America and vice-versa.

The regattas were, in any case, technically demanding and an excellent proving ground for helmsmen and crews. The 1991 victor, the Italian boat *Abracadabra*, designed by German Frers, had Enrico Chieffi and Paul Cayard in the cockpit, the pair having recently won the America's Cup Class Championship at San Diego in California. This was a newborn class invented to replace the "old" International Rule 12-meter boats in the world's most famous regatta. The 50-footers, along with the One Tonners and the Maxis effectively represented the swansong of the IOR. On the horizon was a new rating system believed to be the perfect and therefore definitive answer to the problem. Twenty years after the introduction of the International Offshore Rule, or IOR in short, a system was introduced that was new in terms of its underlying philosophy rather than its substance, the International Measurement System or IMS.

The IMS developed out of research conducted by experts at Boston's MIT and commissioned by an American owner evidently unhappy with the IOR rating attributed to his yacht. The MIT researchers were concerned above all with finding a global method of analyzing hulls rather than proceeding instead on the basis of single point measurements as had been the case with the IOR and all previous rating systems. The integrated parameters were then used to determine potential performance. The measurement is made by a laser device that analyzes the hull shape and converts the form into numerical data that can be processed by a computer.

Alongside this method, a system was developed to predict performance in relation to the wind direction and strength encountered by the yacht during a regatta, the Velocity

Prediction Program or VPP. The IOR in fact could, according to the interpretation of the designer, favor a boat in certain meteorological conditions and penalize it in contrasting weather. The IMS rendered the rating uninfluential with respects to the wind conditions encountered by a yacht during a race.

The system was completed by the proposal of the Offshore Racing Council, the international body overseeing competitive sailing, to divide the yachts into two categories, racing yachts and cruiser-racers, establishing a series of minimum demarcation standards.

The same body then determined the ratings for classes of boats racing in real time, the Level Ratings.

Considering that the earliest ratings date from the beginning of the eighteenth century, it could be said that the problem had only finally be resolved two hundred years later.

232 left Vanitas *crosses* Passage to Venice *to starboard, Gardini's older boat leading the new yacht. Both were designed by Frers but belonged to different generations: the first is still a classic yacht in terms of technology, the second has adopted the materials and construction techniques of the future. Gardini organized Tencara yard at Venice to build his yachts in composite materials.*

In the water, however, the eagerly awaited confirmation of the validity of the system instead resulted in the usual arguments.

It is not a rating system that facilitates the moving of boats and crew from one locality to another but rather economics. This is sufficient to ensure that competition will be restricted geographically and in terms of the types of boats, with the exception of the highest level events such as the immortal America's Cup, the biennial Admiral's Cup, the SORC, the Sydney-Hobart Race and so on, yachting's classics in short. And there is always the old principle whereby no matter how efficient the rating system, handicapping will always irritate those coming second.

At the IMS European Championship in 1995 (at this point the sheer number of events means that we have to be selective), fifty-three boats were in the water, but only four did not belong to the organizing nation and even these four came from countries overlooking the same sea!

Leaving aside these considerations, it was clear that the IMS tended to penalize extreme yachts and favor those with cruising capabilities. The '95 European Championship was won by *Blu Slim*, a standard IMX 38 production boat. A Farr prototype, the 39-foot *Flash*, was only third while even further back were *Osama Citizen* and *Bribon*, owned by King Juan Carlos of Spain, both also designed by Farr.

The true merit of the new rating system was that of having eliminated the excesses and distortion

induced by the hunt for loopholes, in substance those factors not foreseen or underestimated by the ratings and on which the designers tended to base the shape of their hulls. This was a strategy that became excessive above all in the hands of those designers with little new to say and who instead relied on extemporaneous invention rather than the technical validity of good design.

In the meantime, in order to increase the spectacle of the sport of sailing (it had in truth always been

spectacular, but only for those actively participating) a new type of regatta was invented, the match race between two identical, preferably production boats. This had always, or almost always, been the case in the America's Cup, the mother of all regattas, where the challenger and the defender raced against each other on the same course. However, apart from this now historic event, regattas had always been disputed by a fleet of boats.

The match race formula rewards the skill of the helmsman and, perhaps to a lesser degree, his crew. The races are short, generally on a windward-leeward course with two legs upwind and two downwind, generally of around a mile each and easy for the spectators to follow. And, most importantly, the first across the line wins. The New Zealanders emerged as protagonists in this new specialty, and it is perhaps no coincidence that, despite being later-comers to the America's Cup stage, they proved to be such effective campaigners against the weight of American experience.

A world-wide circuit, the A.C.Y. Cup, rewarded the most successful helmsman and in 1991 races were won by the Australian Peter Gilmour at Auckland, Rod Davis at Perth, Chris Dickson at Long Beach and Russell Couts at Rovigno. The last three are New Zealanders and defeated rivals from America, Great Britain, France, Denmark, Italy, Germany and possibly other nations that I have forgotten.

232-233 A single French yacht was seen on the Maxi circuit, Jacques Dewailly's Emeraude. She was consistently in the rearguard except when scoring a victory at Newport, in the first American race of the circuit, when the owner entrusted the helm to Dennis Conner. Emeraude was another German Frers design, practically a sister ship to Vanitas, the former Moro di Venezia III.

233 top left The 1990s saw the debut of a new ratings formula, the IMS replacing the IOR. The new racing prototypes had new forms and were easily recognisable with respects to boats from the previous generation. They were above all pure racing yachts: nobody would dream of going cruising with that open transom stern! Nonetheless, Flash, designed by Bruce Farr, could manage no better than third in the 1995 European Championship.

233 top right The new IMS formula favored the participation in races of cruising yachts, or at least those yachts that, designed to be built in series, had to make a number of compromises. Blu Slim is a production IMX, a 38-footer designed by the Dane Jeppesen and built in series by X Yachts, a Danish yard. She won the European IMS Championship in 1995.

Another characteristic of the new yachts designed on the basis of the IMS rule was that the stempost was almost vertical. The IMS boat was in fact a yacht without overhangs, almost vertical sides and a very flat bottom. She was not attractive and not particularly effective in races: the life of the IMS formula was even shorter than that of the IOR.

The designers had by now thoroughly analyzed and eviscerated the IOR norms, and concentrated more on the rig and materials than hull shapes: in the 1980s the Admiral's Cup was dominated by fractionated rigs even on the largest yachts while composites were the most commonly used materials. In 1981, nineteen boats were built in resin, glass or other fibers and synthetic foams, fifteen in light alloy and only four in wood. The British won again that year with *Victory*, an IOR 31-footer penned by Ed Dubois, the rising star of British yacht design. The owner Peter de Savary had launched an America's Cup campaign for 1983 and was, of course, using Admiral's Cup races to train his crew. *Dragon*, another Dubois design, and *Yeoman XXII*, designed by German Frers made up the rest of the British team.

The following edition was staged in the shadow

yacht

236 top left In 1995 the Admiral's Cup changed its rating formula once again: the IOR was abandoned in favour of one-design classes and the new IMS formula. The Mumm 36 class was one of those chosen for the event, a decision that provoked numerous protests. The Mumm 36, designed by Bruce Farr proved to be an extremely technical boat and rapidly achieved world-wide popularity.

236 top right and bottom The last edition of the millennium saw the participation of a team representing the nations of the European Union and flying the flag of Europe. In reality it was a kind of Italian second team composed of owners unhappy with the selections of the Italian Sailing Federation. It was to obtain a highly creditable second place while the official Italian team was only sixth. Merit Cup, the European team's Sydney 40, contributed to overall result with a class win.

236-237 Great Britain had two teams, evidence of the internal divisions caused by a climate of disaffection in the world of offshore racing. Alice is the Mumm 36 of the second British team representing the Commonwealth. She is rounding a buoy ahead of the French boat, Bloo, part of a team handicapped by the withdrawal in protest at the rating attributed to her of the IMS Krazy K-Yote, an advanced design featuring a wing-mast with no shrouds by Juan Kouyoumdjian. The designer was also involved in the French America's Cup challenge.

of America's Cup with Germany taking advantage to win the trophy with Italy finishing second, its best ever result in the competition. The designers were now all members of the new generation: Frers had ten boats in the race; Peterson, Holland and Dubois five each. Judel & Vrolick designed two of the three German boats, *Outsider* and *Pinta* while the third, *Sabina*, was a Jack de Ridder design. Among the Italians, *Almagores* and *Brava* were two boats that had already been seen in the Solent in 1981, the first designed by Peterson the second by Vallicelli, who also designed *Prima Donna*, the weak link that, with two no-scores in the two triangular races, was

responsible for the team missing out on what would have been a memorable victory.

The Admiral's Cup was now being disputed by smallers yachts, with the the event being dominated by the IOR 30.5 footers, the new One Tonners following the raising of the original rating limit of 27.5 feet. The 1985 edition was to see this type of boat make up sixty percent of the fleet. Germany scored follow-up victory with three designs from Judel & Vrolick: *Diva*, *Outsider* and *Rubin*. The Nineties reflected the consequences of the technical innovations and the changes to the regulations introduced during

the previous decade. Above all, as the participation of numerous One Tonners in previous years had presaged, the trophy was disputed in real time: each nation had to select a 50-footer (an IOR rating of 40.5), a Two Tonner and a One Tonner. The inshore courses were also modified, with those of the two rounds that were once staged in the Solent using the various seamarks, buoys, lighthouses and so on permanently fixed in the channel as markers, being replaced by triangular courses. These were undoubtedly more technical, but perhaps less spectacular than the ones they replaced, which had obliged the yachts to sail close in to the shore where they had to cope with shallows and currents. With the elimination of corrected time, the competition was fiercer but the number of participating nations dropped. Only eight teams competed in 1991: Australia, Germany, Denmark, Italy, France, Japan, the United States and Great Britain. France was to score a surprise victory after Italy had gone into the final round with a clear advantage—the Fastnet has

237 top Mumm 36s on a beat during one of the triangular races held in the sheltered waters of the Solent. The Italian boat Breeze 1 is leading the British Barlo Plastic, the best boat in its team and third in class, and the German Jeantex. Behind them is the red hull of the Dutch boat Mean Machine, the best of the Mumm 36s and the winner of the 1999 edition with her team, Holland's first Admiral's Cup victory.

frequently been decisive in the final Admiral's Cup standings. The same Italian team with three Bruce Farr designs, the 50-footer *Mandrake*, the Two Tonner, *Larouge* and the One Tonner *Brava* (in reality the only new yacht) was to return as one of the favorites two years later. On that occasion the Italians could manage no better than fourth behind the Germans, Australians and French after a series of unfortunate episodes, breakages, and collisions with other competitors.

The Italians were to gain revenge in 1995 by winning the first edition of a revised Admiral's Cup. The 1993 edition had, in fact, been the last

disputed on the basis of the IOR formula, while from '95 two one-design classes were adopted together with one defined by the IMS rule.

The Italians won with Pasquale Landolfi's *Brava Q8*, an IIc 40 single design by Bruce Farr built by Cookson, *Mummamia*, the Mumm 36, another one-design boat, and *Capricorn* a 46-foot IMS designed by Bruce Farr and built by the American Concordia yard.

While it retained a certain appeal, it was undeniable that the Admiral's Cup had lost a lot of its prestige: as mentioned earlier, eight

nations took part in 1993, eight in the subsequent editions and nine, but only because due to internal squabbling Italy entered two teams, in the last edition of the millennium.

The Admiral's Cup has also lost the Fastnet. The 1999 edition in fact featured a 390-mile race to Wolf Rock and back along the South coast of England in place of the legendary 600-mile ocean race that reached and rounded the Fastnet lighthouse in the Atlantic. For the record, the 1999 Admiral's Cup was won by a Dutch team for the first time in the history of the event.

MUMM 36

238 top and 238-239 The Mumm 36 is the smallest of the classes chosen for the Admiral's Cup and replaced the One Tonners. The Mumm 36 is probably the most "technical" of the contemporary yachts and has achieved considerable popularity throughout the world. The prototype was designed by the New Zealander Bruce Farr. In spite of the very exposed appearance of the cockpit, it has also demonstrated that it can handle bad weather. In fact, the boats of today with such light displacements suffer less from large waves than the heavier yachts of the past: they tend to ride over them rather than be struck by them.

The Mumm 36 is a one-design racing boat designed by Bruce Farr. The regulations governing this type of yacht are particularly restrictive and, in practice, only allow a choice of mast, boom and sails. Hull shape, dimensions and materials are instead rigidly defined as is the permitted deck gear and even the weight of the crew which must not exceed 1,466 lbs. Four yards have been awarded the concession to build the Mumm 36: the French firm Beneteau for Europe, Carrol Marine for North America, the New Zealand company Cookson for Oceania and Astillero del Estuario in Argentina for South America.

SYDNEY 40

The boat is built in glassfiber and epoxy resin sandwiched with a balsa and PVC foam core, vacuum-bagged and thermally treated.

These yachts are very light with exceptional performance, especially downwind.

Now having been built in hundreds of examples, the Mumm 36 has its own circuits with regattas in America and Europe, a World Championship and, above all, has been selected for the Admiral's Cup.
Specification:
LOA: 35' 8", LWL: 31' 8",
Displacement: 8,150 lbs, of which 3,500 lbs as ballast.
Sail area: 644 sq. ft.

The first one-design class chosen by the RORC for the new Admiral's Cup format was the Sydney 40. This is a large yacht, set between the One and Two Tonners of the past, with a large rudder and a deck layout typical of a modern racer.

Heavier foot-for-foot than the Mumm 36, compared with which it has more pronounced overhangs and, again in relation to the length, a much greater sail area, the Sydney 40 is less inclined to plane but is more powerful, in short, more of a classic yacht apart from its large cockpit with the deckhouse bulkhead virtually amidships making it instantly recognisable. The boat was designed by the Australian team of

239 top The diffusion of the Mumm 36, undoubtedly aided by its selection as an Admiral's Cup class, is demonstrated by the regattas organized in two circuits, one in America featuring events such as the SORC and others on the Great Lakes, and one in Europe with races in the Mediterranean and the northern seas from Kiel to the Solent and the Atlantic coasts of France. A highly competitive World Championship crowns this series of events.

239 bottom The Sydney 40 is a large yacht at a time when ocean racing appears to have fallen out of favor, with more technical races such as those on triangular courses taking its place. This one-design boat was penned by Murray, Burns & Dovell, and since 1995 it has been one of the classes selected for the Admiral's Cup.

Murray, Burns & Dovell with construction being entrusted to Bashford Marine, the yard building the entire range of Sydney yachts with lengths from 30 to 50 feet. The boat is of course very popular in Australian waters. The Sydney 40 design also has very severe restrictions, the owner only being allowed to specify gear and sails.
Specification:
LOA: 41', LWL: 34' 5",
Beam: 12' 4",
Draught: 8' 8",
Displacement: 12,680 lbs.
Sail area upwind: 990 sq. ft.

THE SOUTHERN OCEAN RACING CONFERENCE

Six rounds, a triangular course off St. Petersburg, a long race from there to Fort Lauderdale, almost 400 miles around the Florida peninsula, then two triangular races off Miami; the second offshore race from Miami to Nassau in the Bahamas, 200 miles traversing the Gulf Stream; lastly, a final triangle off Nassau. A series of races, all technically demanding with extremely variable wind, sea and current conditions that were, moreover, held between January and February, by no means the most comfortable season in those low latitudes. This, from the post-war period up to the 1980s was the SORC, a key event that opened the American yachting season.

Initially six clubs were involved in organizing a complex event based in three different venues: the St. Petersburg Yacht Club, the Biscayne Bay Yacht Club, the Coral Reef Yacht Club, the Miami Yacht Club and the Nassau Yacht Club. In recent years, following a downsizing of the event with the elimination of the offshore races, the St. Petersburg club has withdrawn.

Today the Southern Ocean Racing Conference is a "Not for Profit" organization with the aim of promoting significant events in the field of sailing boat regattas.

Like the Admiral's Cup in England, the SORC attained the status of an American Championship, representing in effect fifty percent of world-wide yachting, and up until the 1980s the American Admiral's Cup team was selected on the basis of results obtained in the regatta. The average number of participants was fairly high, with peaks of seventy or eighty yachts before tailing off to less than fifty in the early Eighties.

All the great designers tested their most recent boats in the SORC.

240 top Racing on the east coast of the United States has found an ideal home in the waters off Florida thanks to good winds, variable seas due to the effects of the currents and, above all, a warm sunny climate. Miami hosts the SORC, still a major event despite its decline in recent years, while at Key West an intensive week's sailing sees the most popular level classes in action. There is generally a lack of any significant foreign competition with British and Italian boats providing the rare exceptions.

240 bottom The quality of the crews is exalted when racing one-design boats in real time: tacticians take a back seat while navigation is uninfluential. The helmsman has to let the boat run while the tactician's only job is to get it into a good position on the start line. The sails and the their trimming are instead fundamental. Ever since the era of the schooner America, the United States has continued to represent the avant-garde in the cutting and assembly of sailcloth: this photo provides clear evidence.

240-241 The Mumm 30s, the smaller versions of the Admiral's Cup class, on a beat during one of the coastal SORC races. The level classes are not the only ones participating in this event although they unarguably constitute the most technically up-to-date groups. Yachts rated according to the IMS formula also compete as well as, on corrected time, others grouped in the Performance Handicap Ocean Racing Fleet, which is in effect the American equivalent.

241 top Perhaps even more so than in Europe, American waters, and in particular those of Florida where the sailing season opens, saw a proliferation of new racing classes in the early Nineties. In reality they represented nothing new other than an attempt to reduce the competing yachts to predetermined rating limits. The IOR tonnage divisions were replicated simply by changing the names of the classes. The 48-foot class was never adopted beyond these waters.

241 bottom The classes racing on corrected time were nonetheless subdivided into categories on the basis of ratings. This in effect meant that the races were actually disputed in real time, especially those with lengths of under ten miles—the majority of the events comprising the present-day SORC. Today organizers tend to prefer staging two or three short races in a single day rather than privilege longer races. The racing is undoubtedly more spectacular, which is what the sponsor wants, and there is a more even distribution of prizes, but it is no longer ocean racing.

242 left *The One Design 35 is one of the many one-design classes that flourished after the failure of the IMS, which was intended to allow everyone to race happily together. Every designer found a group of owners and a yard capable of co-ordinating themselves around a boat of a certain size, that is to say a one-design class. Some of them, such as the Mumm 36 class, have achieved widespread popularity, while others, such as the One Design 35, may be technically valid but have remained exclsuive to their home waters.*

In 1977, for example, the names that were to figure in the America's Cup in that period all featured in the SORC too, with Class A being won by Doug Peterson's *High Roller* from German Frers' *Scaramouche*, while Class B was taken by Ron Holland's *Imp* from *Gonna Gitcha* designed by Gary Mull. In Class C the young New Zealander Bruce Farr's *Sweet Okole* beat Peter Arlin's *Agnes*.

The American team for the Admiral's Cup was chosen at the end of the event: *Imp* and *Scaramouche* were joined by Britton Chance's *Bay Bea*, which had impressed despite a broken mast in the second round.

High Roller had had to decline the invitation for financial motives.

The United States were to finish second

242-243 *A large spinnaker in the water: it is difficult to say what is happening, the genoa is aloft and they are hauling on the sheet from the cockpit. The boat is still heading downwind while the following boat has already tacked. A drop immediately after gibing, a generally critical situation but the wind is gentle and there does not appear to be any threat of collision. It would be as well to recover that spinnaker in a hurry though, an unacceptable drag when racing.*

242 bottom *A fine shot of a modern genoa: cut and interconnected sailcloth panels have disappeared and the sail is constructed by laying resistant fibers in the predicted direction of the greatest stress in the area where distortion needs to be avoided. Even though the foreign contingent in the spring races off Florida is never as great as in the Admiral's Cup, the yachts at Key West and Miami are technically advanced.*

in that edition of the Admiral's Cup, hard on the heels of the British.

Doug Peterson was particularly successful in the SORC, winning in 1978 and '79 with two different boats both named *Williwaw*. Even then a racing hull aged precociously!

Class A was won by *Tenacious*, a Stephens design helmed by Ted Turner who had won the last America's Cup, with *Kialoa* coming second.

Class B went to Peterson's *Williwaw*, as mentioned, with German Frers' *Acadia* second.

Holland designs, *Midnight Sun* and *Infinity* took Classes C and D respectively.

That year the number of participants had dropped to 54. The foreign element was conspicuous by its complete absence but was to return with a vengeance in the middle of the following decade.

The Germans won in 1985 while the Italians provided the surprise of the 1986 edition.

Five Italian yachts crossed the Atlantic— aboard a cargo ship rather than under their

243 top right *The genoa hoisted, the spinnaker halyard already eased off, the crew prepares to receive the great sail on deck. The winds are light and the maneuver is routine. Key West has always attracted leading crews including some from overseas: on occasion European participants charter yachts on the spot with which they participate in the regatta. In the recent past Italians, Britons and Germans have organized the transfer of their boats, especially for the SORC.*

243 bottom *This aerial shot provides a clear view of the make-up of a modern racing yacht: The midship section is set further to the buoyant stern. At one time yachts seen from above presented an irregular rhomboid shape with the short sides to the prow, while today they are triangular. The fact is that water lines are relatively unimportant today as below the waterline, in fact, there is virtually nothing given the light displacements. For the record, the yachts seen here are Coral 45s competing in the 1997 SORC.*

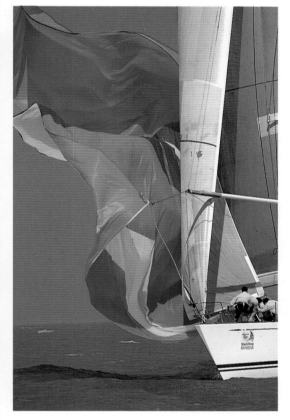

own sail as in the era of the classic British America's Cup challenges. *Almagores*, a no longer recent Doug Peterson design, was always among the first ten. *Brava*, a One Tonner designed by Vallicelli, even scored a class win in the second round. *Gemini*, an Italian Navy yacht put up a good showing, beginning with two second places behind Farr's brand-new *Snake Oil* and beating Rachel-Pugh's carbonfiber *Blade Runner*. Lastly, *Nitissima* designed by German Frers and *Templar* by Ron Holland were also consistently among the leading positions.

Strangely the participation of boats from other countries failed to lift the event, conditioned as it was by the IOR crisis.

In the last decade of the century, the prestige of the SORC continued to wane and today, now known as the Acura SORC, it is still a major event featuring many of the level classes introduced by the IMS but it no longer represents the American Admiral's Cup elimination trials, no longer features long offshore races and even the climate is more accommodating as it is now held in March.

The races are reserved for one-design classes such as the Farr 40s, the One Design 35s and the Mumm 30s which still attract foreign competitors, yachts racing with IMS handicaps, multihulls and restricted classes such as those for the Melges 24 and the Etchells.

In the last edition the Mumm 30 class was won by *Trouble*, the Farr 40 class, the most popular with 25 entries, by the Italian boat *Dawn Raid*, and the One Design 35 class by *Heartbreaker*.

WHITBREAD AROUND THE WORLD RACE

By the 1990s the great ocean races seemed to have lost the gloss and appeal that had characterized them since the first editions of the Transatlantic Race way back in 1904 through to the 1970s and the Whitbread Race.

Sailing in the Nineties took two different directions: the more technically demanding events were staged on triangular courses and in coastal waters, which is perhaps why an event such as the America's Cup has maintained its charisma. Offshore racing, on the other hand, has become an increasingly extreme sport with the single-handed events tending to attract the attention of enthusiasts and the media.

Only the Whitbread Race has continued to attract skippers and owners, although even here controversy reigned as new and more gratifying formulas were experimented. The editions staged in the Nineties saw the debut of a new class, the WOR 60s, destined to replaced the IOR Maxis that had proved to be financially too demanding and whose performance was now being matched by significantly smaller and therefore more economical hulls.

Following the 1990 edition won by the Bruce Farr-designed ketches *Steinlager* and *Fisher & Paykel*, two boats we have already encountered under different names in relation to the Maxi yacht circuit, the 1993-1994 edition was significant as it marked both the last race of the IOR Maxis and the debut of the WOR 60s.

Only four Maxis lined up for the start at Southampton, *NZ Endeavour*, sailed by the New

244 The start of the third leg of the 1993 Whitbread Around the World Race from Perth on the west coast of Australia. The yachts descended along the coast before venturing out into the Roaring Forties that would take them across the fearsome Bass Strait to Auckland. In the foreground is the huge ketch-rigged Maxi NZ Endeavour, with Grant Dalton at the helm, followed by the WOR 60 Intrum Justitia and Fehlmann's yacht Merit Cup.

245 top left The leg from Perth in Australia to the capital of New Zealand, Auckland, was by no means the longest, but it still involved 4,000 miles through the Indian Ocean at the high latitudes swept by the strong westerly winds that, encountering no land in their path, generate huge, powerful waves. La Poste, like all the Steinlager generation ketches deriving from the 1990 Whitbread winner, was at her ease in strong winds: she boasted a large sail area but a fairly low center of thrust.

245 top right Pierre Fehlmann's Merit Cup tackling strong mid-ocean winds. The Swiss owner-skipper has not missed a Whitbread since the second edition of the race in 1977 and was one of the men behind the introduction of the new WOR 60 class, designed specifically for the event. Merit Cup was to finish second overall after having won the fifth leg.

245 bottom The French boat La Poste was sailed by the great navigator Eric Tabarly after he replaced Daniel Mallé at the helm for the last legs. At the Fort Lauderdale start, this ketch designed as usual by Bruce Farr, is setting sail on the last leg that took the yachts to the finishing line at Southampton. They had started out from the English port in the September of 1993 and returned in the June of the following year.

246 top *The 1997 edition saw the usual WOR 60 yachts in the water: following their fine showing in the previous edition where they competed on a virtually even footing against the Maxis, it was decided to stage the race for this type of boat. A yacht born to race with class regulations that allowed two and half tons of supplementary water ballast to be pumped aboard to increase stability. Those who claimed these boats were unsafe had to eat their words after two editions of the Whitbread with no significant accidents.*

Zealander Grant Dalton on his third Whitbread, the Pierre Fehlman of Switzerland's *Merit Cup* that had participated in all the previous editions, the French boat *La Poste* helmed for the last legs by Eric Tabarly, and the Uruguayan *Uruguay Natural*. The first three were all ketch-rigged and designed by Bruce Farr along the lines of the earlier 1990 winners.

The WOR 60 fleet was more numerous and the boats demonstrated a new underlying concept. They were particularly light, built in composite materials with supplementary water ballast of around 550 gallons to be pumped as and when necessary into internal tanks. Despite a few

246 bottom right *Silk Cut with Lawrie Smith at the helm, leaves the start line at Freemantle. The British yacht's hopes were to be dashed as despite a victory in the sixth leg from Sao Sebastiao in Brazil to Fort Lauderdale, and a second in the eighth from Annapolis to La Rochelle, she was only to finish fifth overall. As usual, the color purple proved to be unlucky.*

246-247 *Ten WOR 60 yachts started out from Southampton. They were reduced to nine following the withdrawal of America's Challenge which despite starting out with certain ambitions and the winner of the previous edition Ross Field at the helm, had to retire due to financial difficulties at the end of the first leg. An incredible number of boats follow the yachts along the Solent as they leave British waters for nine months of ocean racing: the remarkable sight testifies to the popularity of this type of event.*

problems with delamination and consequent structural failure, the WOR 60s were to provide a convincing demonstration of their worth.

The New Zealanders dominated the event, testimony to the growth that was to take them to the top in all fields of yachting by the end of the decade, the America's Cup included.

NZ Endeavour was the best of the Maxi's, winning the class from Fehlman, while among the WOR 60s it was *Yamaha* that came home first with another Kiwi, Ross Field, at the helm. The performance of third New Zealander, Chris Dickson, at the helm of *Tokyo*, was remarkable in that he won three legs, was second in another two and eventually finished fifth overall only because of a disappointing tenth place in the fifth and final leg.

It is interesting to note that after over one hundred and twenty days of racing, the WOR 60s would have taken second place in a combined table with the Maxis, with *Yamaha* only nine hours behind *NZ Endeavour* and the second-placed WOR 60 tying with *Merit* and another two WOR 60s

finishing in front of third Maxi home.

Even the large waves and the deep depressions of the high southern latitudes had failed to get the better of these boats and they were to make the 1997-98 edition theirs. Ten boats crews started, all aboard the new WOR 60s.

The era of starts with thirty yachts lining up seemed to be a thing of the past, but this was the case with offshore racing in general.

This edition featured nine legs as if the organizers were trying to involve as many countries as possible—above all in order to find new markets for the sponsors.

As usual the race started from Southampton with the first leg finishing at Cape Town, a voyage of 7,350 miles. From here the fleet headed to Freemantle in Australia, another 4,600 miles, and then completed a 2,200-mile third leg to Sydney. From Sydney there was a relatively short 1,300 mile leg to Auckland in New Zealand before the most demanding stage of all, 6,650 miles to Sao Sebastiao in Brazil, by way of Cape Horn. Climbing 4,700 miles up through the Atlantic, the boats reached Fort Lauderdale in Florida and then it was just a short 900-mile hop to Baltimore. An Atlantic crossing to La Rochelle in France was followed by the final 450-

mile last leg to Southampton. Among the starters were three American yachts, *America's Challenge*, which was to retire with financial problems after the first leg helmed by the New Zealander Ross Field (the winner in 1993 with *Yamaha*), *Toshiba* and *Chessie Racing* instead finished sixth and seventh. There was only one British yacht, the highly fancied *Silk Cut*, designed by Bruce Farr and helmed by Lawrie Smith. She was to finish only fifth.

A sizeable Swedish presence included the female crew of *EF Education*, which despite finishing last was always very competitive, *Swedish Match* and *EF Language* helmed by Paul Cayard. The field was

248 and 249 *These photos were taken aboard* EF Language, *the winning yacht, as she sailed across the Southern Ocean. At these latitudes the waves are both very fast and very tall but a high performance yacht tends to suffer less than a traditional craft designed to meet the threat of severe conditions by being robust and consequently heavy, with a small sail area given that it was thought that abundant canvas was superfluous and that the rigging would be unable to cope with the stress. The yacht of the past was subjected to the impact of the wave whereas the modern yacht instead planes over it and tends to remain on the crest given that it is capable of a speed* similar to that of the wave itself when sailing downwind. When beating it tends leap over the crest rather than plow through. This was seen with the WOR 60 boats. The Maxis were too large and therefore it could be said that they did not count. In neither the '93 nor the '97 editions of the Whitbread did any yacht capsize or suffer serious structural damage. Previously, traditional yachts considered to be safe had capsized, many had been seriously damaged and some had lost men overboard. In the 1999 edition, Innovation Kvaerner did break her steering gear but still managed to finish (in fourth place), while Silk Cut established the world speed record by covering 450 miles in 24 hours during the second leg.

completed with a Dutch boat, *Brunel Sunergy*, a Norwegian, *Innovation Kvaerner* and *Merit Cup* racing in the colors of the Principality of Monaco and helmed by Grant Dalton, another New Zealander and the overall winner of the 1993 edition. The race was dominated by Paul Cayard aboard *EF Language* who won the first, third and fifth legs and was always holding an overall lead. In second place was Grant Dalton's *Merit*, the first boat home to Southampton. Third was another Swedish boat, *Swedish Match*. The next edition of the race will feature a new sponsor, Whitbread bowing out and its place being taken by Volvo, the first Volvo Ocean race being scheduled for 2001.

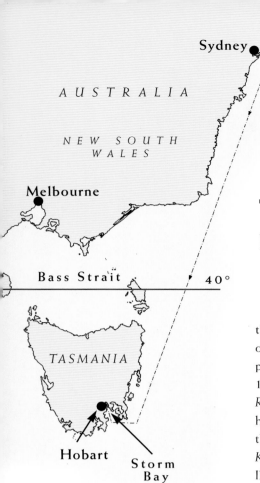

THE SYDNEY TO HOBART RACE

In the immediate post-war period, it was the Englishman John Illingworth, Commodore of the RORC, who promoted this event. He personally competed in the first edition held in 1945, winning the race at the helm of his yacht *Rani*, covering the 630 miles in six days, 14 hours and 22 minutes. The current record for the race belongs to an American Maxi yacht, *Kialoa* which in 1975, thirty years after Illingworth, crossed the finishing line after just 2 days, 14 hours and 37 minutes at sea. The difference is enormous and indicative of the difference in speed between a present day racing boat and a 1940s yacht like *Rani*.

The honor roll of this event contains international ocean racing's most famous names. *Stormvogel*, the yacht born out of the collaboration between Giles, Illingworth and Van de Stadt, won in 1965, the French boat *Pen Duick III* with Eric Tabarly at the helm in 1967, while in 1969 it was the turn of the British boats *Crusade* and *Morning Cloud* in real and

corrected time respectively.

In the 1970s, the large IOR Class A boats dominated the event: *Ondine, Kialoa, Bumblebee, Condoro, Apollo, Ragamuffin* and *Drumbeat*.

The 1999 edition saw the victory in real time of the French super-yacht *Mari Cha III*, a 145-foot long ketch designed by Philippe Briand. *Mari Cha III* is a cruising yacht and was racing as an unclassified entry as a demonstration in view of the inauguration of a superyacht-cruising category for the 2000 edition. Behind *Mari Cha III* was *Nokia*, a Bruce

Farr 60' yacht that had taken part in the 1997-98 edition of the Whitbread Race under the Swedish flag, where she finished third. Third in this race instead was the famous *Brindabella*, a Maxi yacht designed by the Australian Scott Juston which had won the race in real time in 1997.

The winner on corrected time was *Yendis*, a Farr 49 launched just a month before the start, from *Brindabella* and *Ausmaid*, a Farr 47 from 1994 which had finished second the previous year after winning in 1996.

The history of the Sydney to Hobart Race is rich in dramatic episodes: it is a demanding race, especially once the Australian coast has been left behind and the fleet encounters the Roaring Forties, that band of sea open to the westerly winds that race unobstructed around the globe. One of the most traumatic editions was undoubtedly that of 1998 when six men were lost at sea. At least another fifty-five were saved, following the sinking of their yachts, by air-sea rescue helicopters operating beyond their safety limits.

The race had started, in the best traditions of the event, on December 26, a warm Australian summer's day. 115 yachts with a total of 1,135 crew members. A fresh wind from the northeast allowed rapid progress to made as far as the Bass Strait where the fleet encountered one of the most violent storms in the history of the race.

Winds blew from the southeast at up to eighty knots generating waves of 60 to 65 feet in height, conditions determined by a deep depression—barometers registered a minimum of 928 millibars in the area of the race for no

250-251 The start of the Sydney to Hobart Race is traditionally scheduled for December 26. At least a hundred yachts set out on this ocean racing classic. This photo shows the yachts at the start in 1993: the winds are light as they were to be throughout the 630-mile race which took over four days to complete, the worst time since 1978.

less than thirty-six hours!

The consequences were tragic: six men lost, seven yachts abandoned, five sunk, seventy-one retired, fifty-five men saved from the water by the prompt and dramatic intervention of the Australian navy. Of the 115 boats that started, only 44 managed to reach Hobart, and many of these only after having sought refuge from the storm in the various bays along the coast of Tasmania.

Sayonara, an American Maxi that had already won in 1995, won in real time from *Brindabella*. Victory on corrected time instead went to a small Australian yacht, headroom (she was a racing yacht) *Midnight Rambler*, a 35-footer designed by Robert Hick, well handled in the storm by a crew from the Cruising Yacht Club of Australia.

251 top Competitive yachts and cruisers alike enter the Sydney to Hobart Race. The skyscrapers of Sydney here act as the backdrop to the start of one of the most dramatic editions of this or any other race. After setting out with a useful following wind, the fleet encountered a storm in the Bass Strait that led to the loss of six men at sea.

251 bottom Brindabella is one of the most reliable participants in the Australian race: she was second in '99 after having won in 1991 and 1997. The yacht, a Maxi racing in the IMS category, was designed by the Australian Scott Jutson for George Snow. The spinnaker has been hoisted and the genoa is almost down. The yacht is making good progress while the Australian Christmas weather is typically warm. It looks like being a good race.

252 top The yachts prepared for the BOC Challenge or other single-handed races have on-board electronics allowing perfect navigational tactics based on the developing weather patterns. The helmsmen in fact pay more attention to the movements of the depressions than those of their rivals. Communication link-ups are guaranteed in real time and respective positions are constantly monitored. The single-handed sailor is no longer a romantic adventurer, but a sportsman with a thorough technical preparation.

252-253 Competitive single-handed sailing was an established sport by the 1990s and the races had found regular sponsors. The yachtsmen involved were all well known sportsmen. The yachts sailing the oceans had the same technical specifications as other racing boats. What remained was the commitment of an individual obliged to cope with something bigger than himself, such as the spinnaker that Jean Luc Van Den Heede, a two-time competitor in the Vendée Globe and a BOC veteran, is preparing to hoist.

252 bottom Sceta Calberson is the 60-footer that the Frenchman Christophe Auguin sailed to victory in the 1995 BOC Challenge, repeating his win in the preceding edition with Groupe Sceta when he also set the record time for race. The Frenchman was perhaps favored by the enforced retirement of Isabelle Autissier as a result of a dramatic demasting in the middle of the Indian Ocean.

253 top The start of a single-handed race is an event that attracts the same audience as the other great ocean races: the second leg of the BOC Challenge starts from Cape Town and sees a fleet of spectator boats similar to the one that follows the start of the Whitbread or the Sydney to Hobart. It was Isabelle Autissier who got off to a flying start with her Charantes in the 1994 edition, the great genoa furled, the staysail full and two hands on the mainsail.

SINGLE-HANDED YACHTSMEN

Single-handed sailing has its roots in the romantic voyages of the eighteenth century, developed thanks to the spirit of adventure shared by many sailors in the nineteenth century and found existentialist motivations in the first half of the twentieth. Since then this way of going to sea, probably sailing in its purest state, has been embraced by the world of image building and promotion.

Today the great ocean races criss-cross the seven seas, from one continent to the next, under the aegis of sponsors that, while having little of that eighteenth century romance, at least have the resources to underwrite remarkably sophisticated craft and extraordinary exploits. The number of these events has increased rapidly over the last decade.

Among the many, it seems only right to

hundred days with the constant anxiety that something may have broken or that they may have had an all-too-close encounter with another vessel sailing the same route blind on auto-pilot.

Above all, it was the great French navigators who specialized in this kind of race. Bernard Moitessier and Erik Tabarly were the sport's prophets, especially the latter who was always able to attract the attention of the media and thus help to generate widespread interest.

The 1993 edition of the Vendée Globe was naturally a French triumph with Alain Gautier winning the race aboard the 60-foot *Bagages Superior*. The name of the boat unequivocally referred to her commercial sponsors. Second was another Frenchman, Yves Parlier with *Cacolac d'Aquitaine*.

253 bottom Two categories of boats are admitted to the BOC Challenge: those with hulls of up to 60 feet and up to 50 feet, the two groups racing in real time. True Blue, seen here, is the 50-footer of the Australian David Adams, 1995 class winner from the Italian Soldini aboard Kodak. After more than hundred days' sailing, less than 24 hours divided them in the final results. 29 yachts took part in that edition, 6 finishing in the larger category and 8 of the 50-footers.

mention those that have gripped the collective imagination, leaving aside the technical or sporting merits of what are always extreme events.

One of the classic races of the Nineties was the Vendée Globe, a single-handed, non-stop, round-the-world voyage departing from and arriving at Les Sables d'Olonne on the Atlantic coast of France.

The route descended the Atlantic and entered the high southern latitudes with their freezing temperatures, icebergs and giant waves generated and driven by winds that between the latitudes 40 and 55° South encountered no land to slow their race around the globe. Then it was on to Cape Horn, the scene of innumerable shipwrecks, before climbing up the Atlantic once again with its fearsome storms and even more tiring calms.

The yachtsmen faced all this for over one

The yachts prepared for a race of this kind are generally very different to those sailed by the pioneer single-handers who placed their faith in a robust boat in which they could ride out a storm. Today planing yachts place the emphasis on speed and the ability to stay above and in front of the wave rather than resist its impact. Lightweight yachts are therefore the order of the day, built in composite materials and fitted with sophisticated rigs and equipment.

This is true of the participants in the BOC Challenge, the single-handed round-the-world race in stages promoted by the British Oxygen Company. The origins of the race date back to 1968 and the Golden Globe Race, sponsored by the British newspaper the *Sunday Times*, which ended in disaster. Of the nine yachtsmen who started, only Robin Knox-Johnston actually finished the race. Ten years later, the idea of a race departing from and finishing

254 top The Australian David Adams won the 50' class in the 1994 edition of the BOC. Behind him was the Italian Soldini and, in third place, the Australian, Alan Nebauer aboard Newcastle Australia. The larger category victory went to the Frenchman Auguin from the American Pettengill aboard Hunter's Child and Jean Luc Van den Heede with Vendée Enterprises.

254 center left Isabelle Autissier competed in the 60' class of the 1994 BOC. A demasting during the Indian Ocean leg was to prevent her from scoring the victory her career and talent merited. The departure from Cape Town, with a favorable wind and good weather gave no hint of the forthcoming drama. This photo shows the roller-furling system for the foresail allowing safe sail handling from the safety of the cockpit.

254 center right The Ecureuil Poitou Charentes 2 of the Frenchwoman Isabelle Autissier seen at the start of the 1994 BOC Challenge: the new boats for this type of race boasted specifications not dissimilar to those of other racing yachts. A very broad stern requiring dual steering gear, advanced composite construction, a sophisticated with masts in carbonfiber and sails in Kevlar and mylar.

254 bottom No less than three roller-furling systems at the prow of the American Chris Beirne's Gartmore at the start of the 1994 BOC, along with a short retractable bowsprit to rig the gennaker. Even more eye-catching than the rigging is the amount of commercial logos on the sides of these boats: advertising has even invaded the world of sailing. This is not to carp as today nobody would compete in the BOC or other such financially demanding races without this economic support.

255 The American David Scully in calm winds in mid-ocean: in reality these are hours of frenetic activity as it is more difficult to keep the boat moving in these conditions than in a fresh breeze. The search for a little air is frustrating, all the more so when rivals are perhaps enjoying better conditions. Scully's Coyote was to be fourth after the four legs of the 1994-95 BOC.

at Newport, Rhode Island, well known thanks to the America's Cup of course, was taken up by the British company. The organization and launching of the event required three years and so it was not until August 28, 1982, that seventeen yachts left the small town on the Atlantic seaboard of the United States, heading for Cape Town. From here a second leg took them to Sydney from where the boats rounded Cape Horn to arrive at Rio de Janeiro. From Brazil they headed home to Newport, completing a total of 25,750 miles of single-handed sailing. Of the seventeen who started, ten finished, a reasonable percentage I would say. The race was won, it almost goes without saying, by a Frenchman, Philippe Jeantot aboard *Crédit Agricole* in 159 days. The second edition was held four years later over the same route. The result was also the same with Jeantot winning with the new *Crédit Agricole III*.

256-257 *Giovanni Soldini at the prow of his* Kodak *has just hoisted the huge gennaker rigged on the bowsprit and has consequently dropped the genoa. Soldini's yacht had a simpler and more traditional sail plan than his adversaries with jibs reeved to the stay via slides. This makes the Italian navigator's overall second place all the more admirable.*

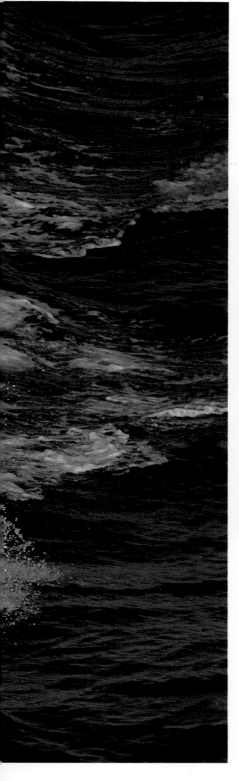

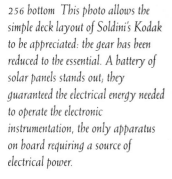

256 bottom *This photo allows the simple deck layout of Soldini's Kodak to be appreciated: the gear has been reduced to the essential. A battery of solar panels stands out; they guaranteed the electrical energy needed to operate the electronic instrumentation, the only apparatus on board requiring a source of electrical power.*

257 top *The construction of Soldini's yacht was also relatively traditional, entrusted to the by no means expert hands of the Saman community, a drug addiction clinic for young people, under the guidance of the Italian skipper himself. A good design, careful direction of the work and plenty of enthusiasm and application produced a boat that from a technical point of view gave little away to more sophisticated creations.*

257 bottom *Single-handed sailing in the Nineties had little in common with the activity in the nineteenth century or even a decade earlier. Today the navigator is in constant contact via satellite telephone both with the organizers and the rest of the world. It is all very different to when, at the end of his second Transatlantic, Tabarly was surprised to be greeted by the Newport lighthouse keeper with the words "you are the first!"*

Regattas at the end of the millennium

A record twenty-six boats lined up for the start of the 1991 edition. They were divided into two classes, yachts of up to 50 feet and yachts of up to 60 feet. The first class was won by Yves Dupasquier with *Servant IV*, while the second was taken by Christophe Auguin in one hundred and twenty days, thirty-nine less than Jeantot in 1982. As we have already seen, the boats had changed.

The edition that started in the September of 1994 retained the two-class division, but the route was slightly modified: the race starting and finishing at Charleston, again on the Atlantic coast of the United States, with a South American leg calling at Punta del Este in Uruguay. The race marked the end of the French hegemony as in the 50-foot class an Italian, Giovanni Soldini, made a name for himself by finishing second aboard *Kodak* to the winner Australian David Adams with *True Blue*. However, it was again Christophe Auguin with the 60-foot *Sceta Calberson* who won the larger class.

258-259 *Under the stern pulpit of Isabelle Autissier's Ecureuil Poitou Charantes 2 can be seen the satellite dish for telecommunications. The development of these systems today allows lightweight, compact antenna to be fitted that consume very little energy. Moreover, these systems which allow the navigator to receive meteorological information and to be constantly localizable, also allow the organizers and sponsors to transmit commentary on the race.*

259 top Seven yachtsmen entered the 60' class in the 1998 BOC, and 9 in the class for yachts of under 50': the numbers dropped considerably from the previous edition. Single-handed racing was also feeling the effects of the increase in the number of events and the difficulty in finding sponsorship. Among those who started were Isabelle Autissier and Giovanni Soldini in the 60' class, together with new names such as the Russian navigator, Fedor Konioukhov, another Russian, Victor Yazykov and a Japanese, Minoru Saito in the 50' class.

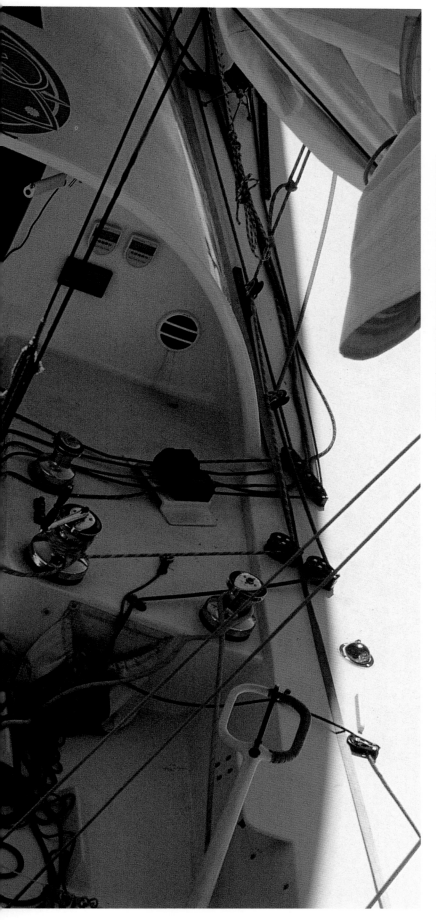

The last BOC Challenge of the Millennium was to see Giovanni Soldini triumph with his new 60-footer *Fila*. The dramatic race was so see the number of competitors reduced to three during the third leg: Soldini, the Frenchman Thiercelin and the Frenchwoman Isabelle Autissier, who was to be shipwrecked in the high latitudes far from the reach of rescue planes and boats. She was eventually found in her capsized yacht by Soldini aboard *Fila* after he changed course to go her aid when leading the race.

The last leg was a head-to-head race between Soldini and Thiercelin and for once it was not to be a Frenchman who took overall honors in a single-handed race.

Soldini's yacht was a concentrate of high technology: the ballast was a lead bulb like those fitted to the most modern America's Cup boats, linked to the hull by means of a canting keel to counter the heeling of the boat to leeward. The mast had no spreaders but rather a jockey pole tensioning the shrouds to windward. The hull was built in composite materials, vacuum-bagged and thermally treated. It gave nothing away to the most advanced racing boats.

259 bottom The Englishman Josh Hall leaning to windward in the cockpit helms his new 60-footer Gartmore out of the waters of Cape Town at the start of the second leg. Fourth in the first and second legs, he was forced to retire after his yacht was demasted during the third leg from Auckland to Punta de l'Este. The first leg had seen the retirement of the Canadian Sebastian Reidl while the other Englishman Mike Golding had abandoned when leading during the second leg. The Russian, Konioukhov finished after the maximum time limit.

258 bottom left The Frenchman, Marc Thiercelin, with Somewhere was to be the only 60' competitor other than Giovanni Soldini to complete the race. During the third leg he set the record for distance covered in 24 hours with 396.5 miles. In the 50' class, four boats retired while five reached the finish. Thiercelin was at the center of controversy, immediately resolved, following the rescue of the Frenchwoman Isabelle Autissier by the Italian Soldini.

258 bottom right Somewhere had a system of jockey poles to tension the windward shrouds, with a middle body large enough to allow a rotating mast with just a pair of spreaders. The leeward shrouds did not clutter the deck allowing the jib to be hauled taut to a narrow angle. The system was developed by the designers of the Groupe Finot. This photo of Somewhere highlights the features of the yacht's mast-sail system. The mainsail is fully battened; the mast with a diamond-pattern spreader and shroud system rotates to leeward and is kept vertical by the shrouds running to the masthead via the two jockey poles that direct the stress to the foot of the mast.

260 center This photo shows the interior of Soldini's Fila. It was designed and equipped specifically for single-handed sailing: the yachtsman sits in the nerve center from where, practically without moving, he can work at the chart table or prepare his meals. The small deck house has fixed ports that allow in the meantime the sail trim to be kept under control. Here too the sponsors' logos are in evidence: the on-board communications systems allowed images captured with a video camera to be transmitted during the voyage.

260 bottom A smiling Giovanni Soldini arrives at Punta de l'Este in Uruguay at the end of the third leg. Only fifth after the first leg, Soldini won the next three on his way to overall victory in the 1998 BOC. The route followed by the fleet had been modified: departure from Charleston, South Carolina in the United States, first leg to Cape Town as usual, then on to Auckland in New Zealand. From here the yachts headed to Punta de l'Este and then back to Charleston. 27,000 miles of single-handed sailing.

260-261 Giovanni Soldini's new yacht, the 60-footer Fila, built this time by CNB, Italian specialists in advanced composite construction. The sky light on the transom stern was installed for safety reasons as, in the case of a capsizing, it allows the yachtsman trapped inside to get out and reach the self-inflating life-raft seen in its housing on the starboard side of the transom. The working of the two rudders is clear: the windward one is out of the water and thus ineffective, the leeward rudder is instead perfectly perpendicular to the water.

260 top The seven survivors of the fleet, Giovanni Soldini and Marc Thiercelin in the 60' class and the five yachts of the 50' category, start the last leg of the 1998 BOC. The Italian's Fila moved took a convincing lead and was to win the fourth leg by a day and a half from the Frenchman. In the 50' class the Briton Garside aboard Magellan Alpha crossed the line first at Charleston while overall victory went to the Frenchman Erre Mouligne with Cray Valley.

261 top *The eye painted on the prow of Fila had a propitiatory function, as it did on the ships of the Ancient Greeks and still does on many eastern Mediterranean fishing boats. An apparent contrast with a high technology yacht capable of remarkable performance, as testified by the average speed achieved in the race of 9.43 knots and the maximum distance covered in 24 hours of 395.7 miles during the third leg.*

AMERICA'S CUP 1992:
AMERICAN WATERS ONCE AGAIN

The 1980s drew to a close, at least as far as the America's Cup was concerned, amidst contradictory signals: while on the one hand world-wide interest in the event was undeniably constant if not increasing, on the other there was a clear need for change to re-establish the natural order of things, something which the New York Yacht Club, for better or worse, had always managed to do.

There was no question, for example, that the 12-meter boats with their rating formula dating back at least seventy years, ought to be considered technologically obsolete.

The very fact that the Australians recorded the first non-American victory in 130 years had to lead to something. They had, after all, broken the Americans' plaything and following the victory of Dennis Conner's 12-meter *Stars & Stripes* that had brought the trophy back to the United States in 1987, albeit to San Diego rather than New York, a state of confusion reigned. The following year Michael Fay, a New Zealand banker, issued a challenge with a gigantic sloop-rigged yacht featuring a bowsprit and lateral platforms for the crew similar to the Australian 18-foot and highly acrobatic dinghies. This forty-meter yacht was designed to win thanks to its very dimensions. In the event, it was actually beaten by a catamaran that was much smaller but bristling with high-tech features: an aerodynamic section mast with a rigid main sail composed of a series of flaps like the wing of an airplane. She was helmed by the inevitable Dennis Conner and strolled to what was a comfortable victory such was her technological superiority.

262 The revival of America's Cup hostilities in the '90s was marked by a series of novelties: following Conner's victories, the regatta was once again staged in American waters, but those of the Pacific Ocean. Cowes was ever more distant and the same could be said of the historic holder of the cup, the New York Yacht Club. The yachts themselves were also new, the International America's Cup Class replacing the glorious Twelves. There was also to be a new challenger nation, the Moro di Venezia being an Italian yacht.

263 top The races at San Diego were staged in open waters. With the adoption of the new America's Cup Class boats, the type of course was changed: the Olympic triangle was abandoned in favor of a windward-leeward course with the first buoy upwind. This eliminated the two reaches which generally had little effect on the race, in favor of the more tactical downwind legs.

263 bottom This was the new America's Cup boat: a pure racing yacht making even fewer concessions than the 12-meters to any type of sailing other than windward-leeward racing in restricted wind and sea conditions. Compared with her predecessor she provided much more outright performance, exploited new materials and new technologies and was created more by technicians in laboratories than traditional skilled boatbuilders. A new generation of specialists in fact came into being with the America's Cup Class.

263 center left The Moro di Venezia represented the fruit of considerable efforts by Raul Gardini. The Italian businessman assembled a first rate team, "Italianizing" the leading designer of the moment, German Frers, and the world Star Class champion, Paul Cayard. Close to Venice he established a boatyard for the construction of the hulls in composite materials: this yard gave birth, one after the other, to five America's Cup Class hull, one of them being the yacht chosen for the San Diego regatta.

263 center right The class of yacht for the America's Cup resembled other contemporary racing hulls: a broad, open stern, an almost vertical, slightly more tapering prow, a broad, set-back midships section. The cockpit also had the same layout as other modern racing yachts, reaching the midships section, with all the sheets directed there and the dual wheels forward of the horse. There were no deck house or rails—anyone falling overboard had to be picked up.

CALIFORNIA

SAN DIEGO BAY

San Diego

START   FINISH

264 bottom New Zealand could count on a very well trained crew and helmsmen with great match race experience such as Rod Davies. The Kiwis were always difficult to beat when manoeuvring and never conceded errors to their adversaries. The construction of the hull, entrusted to Cookson, benefited from a decades' experience with the methodologies and above all, the five "Kiwi plastics" built for the 1986 Vuitton Cup. From a financial point of view too, the New Zealanders' challenge was very solid, being supported by Michael Fay, who had never digested the defeat inflicted upon him by Dennis Conner's catamaran five years earlier. This photo shows New Zealand 20 racing against Ville de Paris.

265 The New Zealand yacht was representing the Royal New Zealand Yacht Squadron of Auckland. It was perhaps the most extreme boat in San Diego in terms of its design philosophy: while most designers had taken a conservative route by selecting a medium-light displacement within the range offered by the ratings formula, Bruce Farr, keeping faith with the school in his country that had introduced light displacements to the IOR, designed a smaller boat weighing considerably less while the configuration of the appendages featured a rudder very similar to the ballast fin. She was a yacht with clear decks, a symptom of the attention paid to saving weight.

264 top The great adversary of the Moro di Venezia in the Louis Vuitton Cup, the event that selects the official challenger for the America's Cup, was the Bruce Farr-designed New Zealand 20. The New Zealanders were by now regular protagonists of the event. In 1987 they had come to the forefront when disputing the right to challenge the Australians with Dennis Conner. The following year it was the New Zealander banker Michael Fay who challenged Dennis Conner with a gigantic 131-foot monohull after the Americans had reclaimed the trophy.

264 center The men aboard New Zealand 20 are wearing the characteristic black strip made famous by the country's All Blacks rugby team. New Zealand was perhaps the country with the most advanced composite materials technology: not having great boatbuilding traditions they had had complete freedom in choosing the material to develop and had chosen the one of the future. Bruce Farr and Ron Holland before him had used composites in their earliest racing yacht designs and in 1987 the first New Zealander 12-meter in the America's Cup was also the world's first 12-meter built in composite materials.

That edition of the cup actually saw more intense competition in the courtrooms than on the water. Both the defender and the challenger turned to the Supreme Court, as provided for in the America's Cup Deed of Gift, either to reject the challenge or question the defence with a catamaran. The court threw out both motions, the defenders being obliged to accept Fay's challenge while the latter had to agree to race against a catamaran.

Fortunately, those with the sport of sailing, and therefore the America's Cup, at heart sat down around a table and nominated a technical commission charged with defining a new type of boat for yachting's blue riband event: the result was the new America's Cup Class.

The new boat made its debut in 1992 at San Diego, California. The cup was in the possession of the San Diego Yacht Club which received challenges issued by the Italians, French, Japanese, Australians, Spanish, Swedes and New Zealanders. The Italians got off to a great start. The campaign was led by Raul Gardini with financial backing from the chemicals colossus Montedison which, apart from cash, was to provide sound technological support. Gardini entrusted the design of the boat to German Frers, the Argentinian designer then considered to be the world's best. Naturally, he had to obtain an Italian passport, as did Paul Cayard, a Star Class champion and leading helmsman in IOR regattas.

A yard was purpose-built at Tencara, near Venice, for the construction of the five yachts, all of course built in advanced composites and all carrying the same name, Moro di Venezia.

Moro di Venezia won the challenger series, the Louis Vuitton Cup, beating New Zealand, a highly competitive Bruce Farr design, in the final. The New Zealanders had led the series 3-0, demonstrating superior speed, especially when maneuvering, thanks in part to a short bowsprit that appeared to be a throwback to the past but was actually of great help when tacking downwind. The outcome of the regatta was eventually decided in the courtroom: the Italians protested against the use of the bowsprit and the judges, without actually disqualifying the New Zealanders from the races that had already been disputed, banned the feature from the remaining races. Moro di Venezia racked up four consecutive victories against a seemingly disoriented opponent.

america's cup 1992

266 bottom and 267 top *266 bottom and 267 top New Zealand maneuvered rapidly, especially downwind and on a reach, thanks in part to the short bowsprit on which the gennaker was rigged. This feature was to be all-important in the New Zealanders' three consecutive victories. However, after they had been banned from gibing with the bowsprit in the next four races, following an official protest by the Italians, they seemed to lose their way and the Moro won the series 4-3. The top photo shows a passage during the final of the Louis Vuitton Cup.*

266 top After a long series of races disputed in three round robins by yachts from France, Spain, Japan, Sweden and Australia, it was New Zealand and Moro di Venezia that met in the final of the Louis Vuitton Cup: the winner was to challenge for the 1992 America's Cup. The final was organized on a best of seven basis, the first to win four races taking the prize. The New Zealanders' yacht was recognized as being very fast and maneuverable downwind while the Italian appeared to have the edge when beating. The races would be very close with no repetition of the disappointing 4-0 of Freemantle.

There is little to be said about the other challengers: the Japanese, the Swedes and the Spanish were making their debuts and lacked experience, the Australians were short of cash, while the French started out badly with *Ville de Paris*, designed by Philippe Briand and helmed by Marc Pajot, but then soted themselves out. They proved to be extremely competitive in the second phase of the Vuitton Cup, as they had been in 1987 with the 12-meter *French Kiss*, but by then it was too late. The San Diego Yacht Club entrusted the American defence of the cup to the syndicate led by Bill Koch and boasting more than adequate financial resources, four boats in the water and blind faith in the technology supplied by the MIT in Boston rather than the genius of a big name designer. With hindsight, however, it has to be said that the presence of an "old" wizard such as Doug Peterson was probably crucial. Bill Koch himself resembled one of the old school gentleman drivers of the Thirties. He had no interest in the commercial aspects of the enterprise but took a hands-on role in the organization and wanted to be on board even if he never took the helm. It was, after all, his money.

266-267 Moro di Venezia *on a
starboard tack to windward passes
across the bow of* New Zealand *which
still has her gennaker aloft. The Italians
were veterans of two America's Cup
campaigns disputed as mid-table
challengers: in 1983* Azzurra *had been
fourth out of seven, while* Italia *was
seventh out of thirteen in '87. Out of this
experience came a compact group of
yachtsmen with a wealth of technical
knowledge that was to prove invaluable
in the waters of San Diego.*

267 right *Raul Gardini, in the center
of the photo, with his team on the day
of the Louis Vuitton cup victory in
1992. The helmsman Paul Cayard,
first on the left, had proved, above and
beyond his undeniable sailing skills,
capable of amalgamating the crew
around him. He is seen here lifting the
cup sponsored by the famous French
marque. The event-within-an-event was
created simply to thin down the number
of potential challengers but had grown
in importance, and since 1987 had
demonstrated its value as a regatta in its
own right and as a support to the image
of the America's Cup.*

The defender boat was named *America3* and was helmed by the sixty-one year old Buddy Melges, twice world Star Class champion, Olympic gold medalist in the Soling Class and an America's Cup competitor in 1987 with *Heart of America*. Dennis Conner had a hard time raising funds but still managed to launch the latest in the *Stars & Stripes* line. He was unable to match the decisively faster *America3* however. For the first time in its history, then, the cup was to be disputed by an American yacht and a non-Anglo-Saxon challenger, a Latin boat no less. *Moro di Venezia* was by any standards an excellent yacht, but perhaps slightly inferior to

the American, especially downwind, while Paul Cayard was a first rate skipper, a worthy rival to Buddy Melges, and needed only a little more direct experience in this kind of event. However, the difference between the two teams was apparently made by the presence in *America3*'s cockpit of the timid Dave Dellenbaugh. He only took the helm for the starts but he won them all, a factor that was almost always decisive as *America3* beat *Moro di Venezia* 4-1. The cup remained in San Diego, but the New Zealanders were already planning their next challenge which came about in 1995.

268 top and bottom The 1992 America's Cup was disputed in the Pacific Ocean waters off San Diego. The regatta was contested on the basis of the new regulations whereby the first yacht to win five races took the cup. America3 was defending the colors of the San Diego Yacht Club against the Moro di Venezia representing the Compagnia della Vela di Venezia. This was the first time the America's Cup was disputed by a yacht from a non-Anglo-Saxon country. The Americans made sure not to let victory escape them, the Moro scoring only one win in the six races staged.

269 top America3 defended the
America's Cup in 1992. It is hard to say
to what extent the performance of her hull
determined the American victory. What is
certain is that the San Diego Yacht
Club's boat had no obvious weaknesses:
she was particularly effective upwind in
all conditions and held her own
downwind. Much of the merit for the win
is, however, to be attributed to the crew
and the afterguard in particular. Finally,
the logistics imposed by Bill Koch, and
the undoubted advantage of sailing in
home waters, also made vital
contributions to the yacht's success.

269 bottom right Bill Koch raises the
Hundred Guinea Cup: this is the very
cup that the Royal Yacht Squadron had
put up in 1851 for the race around
Cowes. The schooner America won
that race of course, and thus gave birth
to the legend for which Koch and many
others have been prepared to invest
fortunes. Buddy Melges, helmsman
aboard America3, also raises the cup
while behind him to the left is Dave
Dellenbaugh, the tactician and starting
helm who won each and every start,
laying a solid basis for the American
triumph.

AMERICA'S CUP: BACK TO SAN DIEGO

The challenger field was reduced compared with the previous edition: the French were back with *France 2* and *France 3*, designed by Philippe Briand, the Australians, led by John Bertrand launched the Reichel & Pugh-designed *OneAustralia* while the Japanese made their second appearance with *Nippon Challenge*, a yacht designed by Ichiro Yokoyama that relied heavily on the technology of the Land of the Rising Sun, but was entrusted to the ace New Zealand helmsman John Cutler. Lastly, there were the two New Zealand syndicates, one led by Peter Blake and blessed with very deep pockets that entered *Black Magic* designed by Laurie Davidson, Tom Schnackenberg and Doug Peterson, with Roussel Coutts and Brad Butterworth in the cockpit, and *New Zealand*, designed by Bruce Farr and helmed by Chris Dickson.

The Vuitton Cup saw a number of structural

failures, something that had perhaps never been seen before in the America's Cup. *France 2* broke her ballast fin, *France 3* broke her mast, *OneAustralia* sank after her hull failed. What had happened was simply that following the dress rehearsal with the new formula in 1992, the designers had taken systems and structures to the extremes in a process of research and development. This apart, mention has to be made of the domination displayed by the New Zealanders with *Black Magic*. In the finals they scored a 5-1 victory against the Australians of *OneAustralia* who fortunately had a spare boat.

270 left John Bertrand's Australian crew competing against Nippon Challenge, *the Japanese yacht entrusted to the New Zealander John Cutler during the World Championships that are traditionally staged a year before the Louis Vuitton Cup regatta. In truth, the World Championship has never really been considered as such by the participants who tend to see it as good training for crews. The true worth of the yachts involved is never revealed. Despite advanced technology, a sound design and the leadership of the Kiwi ace, the 1995 challenge was again to be unsuccessful for the Japanese.*

270 right Following the defeat in the final of the Vuitton Cup in 1992 against the Moro di Venezia, the New Zealanders returned to the waters of San Diego determined to exact revenge. The syndicate led by Peter Blake was flanked by another impoverished group headed by Chris Dickson. The two New Zealander teams were joined by the Japanese of Nippon Challenge, *the Australians with* OneAustralia, *the French with* France *and the Spaniards with* Rioja de Espana.

271 During the Vuitton Cup and the America's Cup itself, Peter Blake's Black Magic showed that she could count on an excellent crew: around thirty World Championship medals, two Olympic golds and 24 participations in previous editions of the America's Cup. The afterguard was composed of the skipper Roussel Coutts, the tacticians Brad Butterworth and Richard Dodson and the designer Tom Schnackenberg as navigator. The organizational qualities of Peter Blake, with two Whitbreads to his name and a lifetime dedicate to sailing, proved decisive.

272-273 Bill Koch, the 1992 winner, again put himself forward as a candidate for the defence of the cup. As usual his campaign had at least one highly original feature: he entrusted his boat to an all-female crew which included J.J. Isler, Courtney Becker, the Dey sisters and Leslie Egnot, who alternated at the helm, assisted by the navigator Annie Nelson, wife of Bruce Nelson, the designer of Young America. Responsible for the halyards was Dawn Riley who was to become the first woman to head an America's Cup challenger, America True, in the subsequent edition.

272 bottom Structural design did not always take into account the greater stresses the stiffness of the new rigs in carbon fibers and matting imposed on the hull, itself absolutely rigid. During the selection races France 2 had already suffered the loss of her ballast due to a breakage. In the Vuitton Cup OneAustralia's hull failed under the compression generated by the mast. Fortunately, John Bertrand's syndicate had sufficient financial resources to be able to bring a second boat to San Diego.

There was fierce competition among the defenders that year with three teams battling it out. Dennis Conner, with Tom Whidden and Paul Cayard, appeared to be the favourite with his Dave Pedrick-designed *Stars & Stripes*. Bill Koch, the winner in 1992, took the unusual step of hiring an all-female crew for his *America3*, the yacht being replaced a few days before the elimination trials by *Mighty Mary*. Lastly, the Pact 95 syndicate, led by John Marshall, had what proved to be the fastest boat in *Young America*, designed by Bruce Nelson.

The America's Cup proper was therefore disputed by *Young America* and *Black Magic*. The American boat was actually manned by the afterguard and crew of *Stars & Stripes* in a somewhat flexible interpretation of the rules permitted to those in possession of the trophy.

The regatta was uneventful. Never before in the 140-year history of the event had the American defender been so soundly beaten, the Kiwis scoring five wins by margins that for this

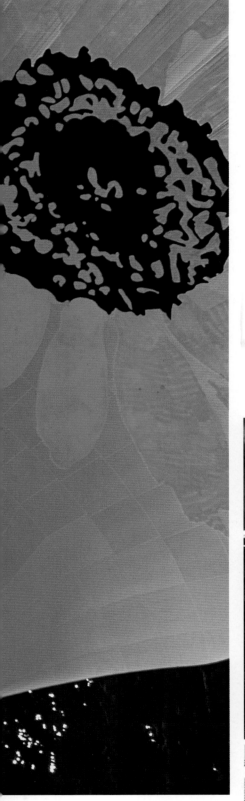

273 top An aerial view of OneAustralia, a design by the Californians Reichel & Pugh (the old rule imposing national designs, boatyards, materials and crews was by now obsolete) and the yacht with which John Bertrand was attempting to bring the cup back to his homeland. This photo shows how the evolution of the America's Cup Class hulls had led to a narrower midships section. The designers were beginning to put the experience gained with the IOR and IMS yachts behind them and to turn to earlier concepts developed with the meter-class boats.

273 bottom left Pact '95 was the name of the syndicate organized by John Marshall that had launched Young America with its mermaid-decorated prow. She was to win the Citizen Cup, the event organized to select the boat that was to defend the America's Cup won by the San Diego Yacht Club in 1992. In second place was Bill Koch's yacht, Mighty Mary with her all-woman crew while Dennis Conner's boat was only third. The crew of Stars & Stripes was nonetheless considered to be the strongest and thus, with a decision that was to spark considerable controversy, they embarked aboard Young America for the America's Cup.

273 bottom right The omnipresent Dennis Conner launched the latest Stars & Stripes, this time designed by Dave Pedrick. In the cockpit were Paul Cayard, the helmsman aboard Moro di Venezia in the previous edition, and Tom Whidden, one of the most experienced America's Cup men. Young America, designed by Bruce Nelson, was nonetheless faster than Stars & Stripes and is seen in this photo hounding Conner's boat during one of the third round robin races. The yachts are close to the marker, the spinnaker pole is already rigged and on the deck in view of the tack, the spinnaker is being hoisted.

type of racing were abyssal: 2 minutes 45 seconds in the first race, 4 minutes 14 seconds in the second, 1 minute 51 seconds in the third, 3 minutes 37 seconds in the fourth and 1 minute 50 seconds in the fifth. An indisputable and undisputed superiority.

The Americans had divided their forces with too many individuals involved. The decision to race the defender boat with a crew that had never set foot aboard her was to say the least surprising and undoubtedly risky. As was, without wanting to appear prejudiced, Koch's decision to entrust an America's Cup boat to an all-female crew without that specific experience which, as we have already seen, is fundamental in this event.

The Hundred Guineas Cup thus emigrated to the halls of the Royal New Zealand Yacht Squadron in Auckland.

274 top Tag Heuer, *seen in this photo circling at the start with Nippon Challenge, was the second boat from New Zealand. She was designed by Bruce Farr and considered to be very fast. The syndicate led by Dickson suffered, however, from a lack of funds. Almost all the teams, with the exception of the one led and financed directly by Bill Koch, took the form of a syndicate with sponsors to raise the financial resources necessary for an America's Cup campaign. On average the figure required runs into the tens of millions of dollars.*

274 bottom Approaching the upwind buoy, the spinnaker of Black Magic is "shot" to allow it to be dropped: the snap-hook of the boom is opened suddenly spilling the air from the sail which flaps as the crew struggles to recover it rapidly to prevent it ending up in the water as the yacht starts the upwind leg. Behind them approaches Young America, her spinnaker still aloft. This was in the second race of the 1995 America's Cup; Black Magic was to maintain her lead to the finish.*

275 top No mention has so far been made of the second Spanish participation in the Vuitton Cup. In 1992 the team actually reached the threshold of the semi-finals with a boat whose design was said to be the work of Bruce Farr. In 1995 the Spaniards barely managed to launch their boat, Rioja de Espana, designed by Pedro Campos on the basis of the experience gained in the previous edition. The results were disappointing with just a single victory in the four round robins.

275 bottom This photo of Tag Heuer's genoa clearly shows the unusual construction of a modern America's Cup sail. As it is no longer made of a fabric it is not strictly correct to speak of a weave. The filaments of extremely strong materials are laid according to a pattern that takes into account the direction of the forces acting on the sail. A man on the mast is now a regular feature of these races: the adjustment of the rigging is extremely sophisticated and frequently requires direct intervention while the top of the mast is at an excellent vantage point for spotting windshifts.

yacht

276 *San Diego, America's Cup Regattas 1995:* Black Magic *and* Young America, *the latter with the crew of* Stars & Stripes *aboard, square up to each other in the pre-start maneuvers. The races were to demonstrate the clear superiority of the New Zealanders who took five races in succession. With the benefit of hindsight, the decision to entrust* Young America *to a new crew that was felt to be technically superior, appears ill-judged. In this photo, the fifth and final race at San Diego:* Young America *tacks on the stern of* Black Magic *which had taken up a position of advantage in the pre-start circling. Roussel Coutts, the New Zealanders' helmsman, was to win this start too and, above all, the race, presenting to his country an unexpected but thoroughly deserved victory after a series of gradually improving performances from the debut appearance in 1987 at Freemantle to the challenger series final in 1992.*

277 *top left The selection trials for the defender had revealed glimpses of the great potential of the American boats.* America3, *however, had been replaced at the last minute by* Mighty Mary, *which was probably faster but still needed fine tuning; Dennis Conner appeared to have lost some of his charisma after the 1983 defeat and* Stars & Stripes *was short of funds.* Young America, *on the other hand, was competitive but was to be penalized by the change of crew for the final. A co-ordinated effort would perhaps have produced a different result.*

277 *top right The team led by Peter Blake celebrates its conquest of the America's Cup in San Diego. On their return home the event was to be celebrated as national triumph: in New Zealand the sport of sailing arouses passions similar to those stimulated by football in Italy or baseball in the United States. The country had begun* to make its presence felt in the world of yachting with the success of Ron Holland's boats in the IOR classes in the 1970s, and the designs of Bruce Farr: a new design philosophy of fractionated rigs and light displacements, backed up by a widespread interest in the sport among all ages and social classes.

277 *bottom right In 1992 the fleet of spectator boats that had witnessed the America's Cup races in the waters off the Californian city of San Diego from close quarters had escorted the triumphant* America3 *back to port. In* 1995 it was a New Zealander boat that had this honor. For the second time the cup was taken out of the United States, again in the hands of an Oceanic country, one of the latest arrivals on the world yachting stage, but one which clearly had the sport in its Anglo-Saxon blood.
What was surprising was the ease with which Peter Blake's yacht Black Magic beat Young America. It seemed that the 1983 defeat had ruined the United States' ability to concentrate on the event.

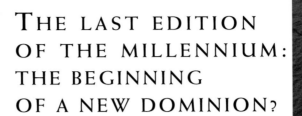

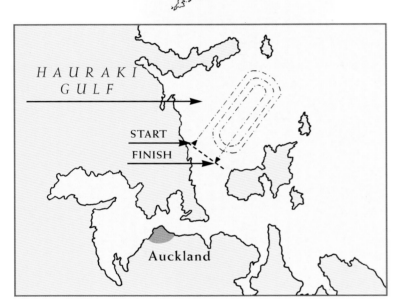

THE LAST EDITION OF THE MILLENNIUM: THE BEGINNING OF A NEW DOMINION?

The first edition of the America's Cup staged in the new millennium was to see an exceptional line up. The Americans were present in force with five syndicates. The St. Francis Yacht Club's *America One* was designed by Bruce Nelson, his fifth America's Cup boat, and helmed by Paul Cayard. The enduring Dennis Conner was present this time in the role of team leader, his new *Stars & Stripes* being designed by Reichel & Pugh and handled by the highly experienced afterguard of Tom Whidden, Ken Read and Peter Holmberg. The San Francisco Yacht Club's *America True* was designed by a technical team including Phil Kaiko and Heiner Meldner with the assistance of NASA and skippered by a woman, Dawn Riley, who had been a crew member aboard *America3* in '92 and at the helm of *Mighty Mary* in '95. The historic "owner" of the America's Cup, the New York Yacht Club, was very determined to put up a competitive challenge and its boat *Young America* was designed by Bruce Farr, along with John Marshall, one of the men with the greatest America's Cup experience, and Duncan MacLane. Her crew was led by Ed Baird, who had trained the winning New Zealand team in 1995. The fifth and final American syndicate was

278-279 An image emblematic of sailing in New Zealand: the two America's Cup Class yachts moored at Auckland and surrounded by swarms of dinghies the kids use for practice after school. The success of the sport in this country is also due to this widespread enthusiasm and dedication. In the fifth and decisive race of the America's Cup series, Roussel Coutts, the helmsman and skipper of Black Magic, had no hesitation in handing over the helm to his protégé, the very young Dean Barker.

279 bottom Black Magic demonstrated all-round superiority, perhaps a little less so in terms of hull speed: her afterguard won every start and finely judged every tack. The crew was always impeccable, the sails were perfect and the boat tacked and accelerated faster. Above all, the team appeared to possess a package of minor technical innovations, many of which were perhaps never used because the need never arose, such as that of the foresail hoisted for just a few seconds to give a little extra thrust at the start.

280 top left *America True*, the yellow boat in this photo, was to go down in history as the first challenger entered by a syndicate led by a woman. The woman in question was Dawn Riley who was already a veteran of two Whitbreads and two editions of the America's Cup: in 1992 she was aboard *America3* for a number of races, while in 1995 she helmed *Mighty Mary*. *America True* benefited from a reasonable budget and an excellent helmsman in the New Zealander John Cutler, who had steered the two Japanese challengers in the preceding editions and was a three-time world match race champion. The boat itself was valid and was designed by Phil Kaiko with support from NASA engineers.

280 bottom left *Abracadabra* following *America True* in the pre-start circling before one of the Vuitton Cup races. *Abracadabra* was flying the colors of the Waikiki Yacht Club of Honolulu in Hawaii and was thus backed by an American syndicate. At the helm was John Kolius, one of the great names in America's Cup racing afer having already challenged Dennis Conner in the defender trials in 1983, helmed the New York Yacht Club's challenger in 1987 and then trained the Moro di Venezia crew. He was blessed with a large budget, a good design team and two boats in the water: all this was not enough, however, to avoid a very poor showing in the Louis Vuitton Cup.

280-281 *Switzerland participated in the 1999 edition of the Vuitton Cup. The organization was entrusted to Marc Pajot, a veteran of 3 previous editions, who enrolled for the project a group of foreigners: the Frenchman Philippe Briand, the Dutchman Peter van Oossanen, the Wageningen testing tank expert who had already worked with Bob Miller of Australia, and the German Sebastien Schmidt. Another German, Jochen Schumann, the Olympic Finn and Soling champion, was at the helm while the Italian Enrico Chieffi was the tactician.*

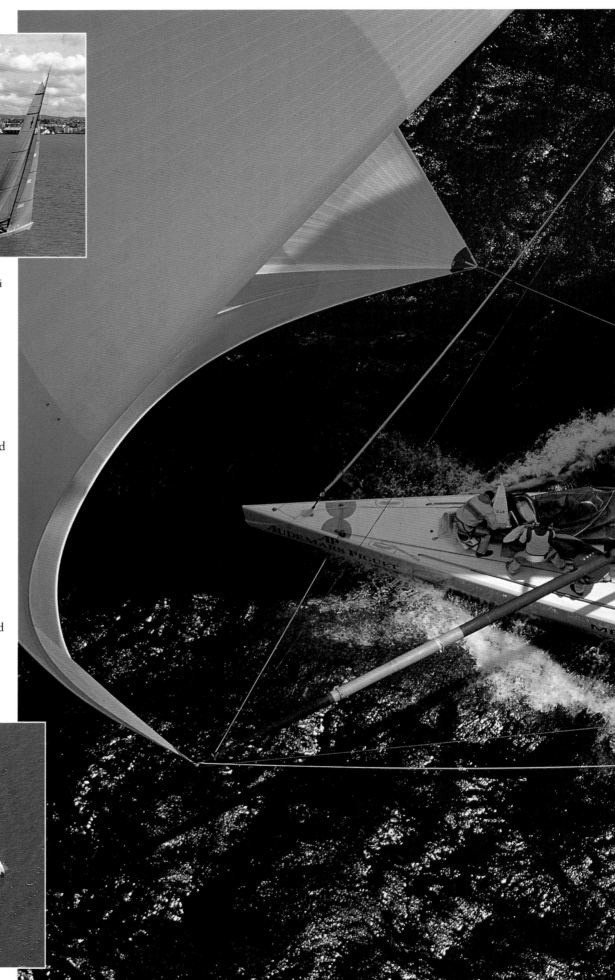

representing the Waikiki Yacht Club from Hawaii with *Abradadabra*, designed by Andy Dovell and Ian Burns and helmed by another of American sailing's greats, John Kolius. Six boats from six different nations joined the Americans in the Louis Vuitton Cup to compete for the right to challenge the Kiwis. The Italian team, promoted and sponsored by Prada and led by the fashion group's owner Patrizio Bertelli, had a boat designed by German Frers and Doug Peterson and helmed by Francesco De Angelis, with the Brazilian World and Olympic Star Class champion Torben Grael acting as tactician. The French brought *Le Defi* designed by a team whose experience had been gained in different kinds of yachts, Bernard Nivelt, Daniel Andrieu, Hervè Deavaux, Juan Kouyoumdjian and Pallu de la Barriere. An excellent match race helmsman, Bernard Pacé, was in the cockpit. The Japanese team representing the Nippon Yacht Club was led by the Australian Peter Gilmour, one of the world's best match racers, while the boat, *Idaten*, was designed by Hideaki Miyata.

281 top The Swiss boat, baptized Be Happy, was the most innovative in the fleet: Briand and the rest of the design team had come up with a hull featuring two identical fins, one at the bow and one at the stern, both ballasted and both rotating to act as rudders. The configuration was highly unusual and undoubtedly difficult to get used to. The yacht, in fact, proved to be the least efficient in the field, failing to record a single victory. Advanced features, especially for the appendages, had already been introduced for the America's Cup but always, with the exception of the famous winglets fitted to Australia II, with little success.

The Spanish boat, *Spanish Challenge*, was designed by the German Rudolf Vrolijck and skippered by the America's Cup debutante, Pedro Campos. The Swiss Fast 2000 team representing the Club Nautique de Morges with Marc Pajot at the helm of a boat with twin ballasted rudders designed by Philippe Briand and Peter van Oossanen, the technical expert at the Dutch testing tank in Wageningen where the famous winglets fitted to *Australia II* were developed. The Australians, lastly, representing the Cruising Yacht Club of Australia, were present with Syd Fisher's *Young Australia* and an extremely young crew all between eighteen and twenty-two years of age, including the skipper, James Spithill.

These eleven contenders were all aiming to challenge the new kings of the cup, the New Zealanders led by Peter Blake.

The Louis Vuitton Cup was to last for over three months and was eventually won, and almost dominated, by the Italian boat *Luna Rossa*.

Leading up to the final, the inexperienced Spanish had fallen by the wayside, as had the hard up Americans from Hawaii, the young Australians of *Young Australia*, the Swiss of the excessively radical *Be Happy* which was difficult to interpret and handle and, to the great surprise of many and the great disappointment of the ever restrained members of the New York Yacht Club, the Americans of *Young America*, rich in resources both human and financial, but psychologically undermined by the near loss of their first boat which split in two just behind the mast during a race.

282 top At the end of the three round robins (in which each boat met all the others twice) staged to select the participants in the semi-finals of the Vuitton Cup, Abracadabra, seen here dropping her spinnaker, was only ninth out of eleven participants, despite the presence of John Kolius at the helm. She was the last of the American teams and bettered only the impoverished team of Australians, all of them under twenty-two years of age, aboard the approriately named Young Australia and the Swiss boat Be Happy.

282 bottom The Japanese Nippon Challenge team came to Auckland boosted by the experience of having taken part in the previous two edition. They also had one of the highest budgets, and an invaluable asset in the form of the Australian helmsman, Peter Gilmour. They soon proved their worth in the water: Idaten demonstrated that she was one of the strongest of the challenger boats, finishing the three round robins in second place behind Prada Challenge, but ahead of all the American boats. She was unable to maintain this form in the semi-finals, however, with Luna Rossa, America One, America True and Dennis Conner all overtaking the Japanese.

282-283 The dark carbonfiber sails of Abracadabra, considered to be at the forefront of technological progress, are in striking contrast with the dolphins just visible on the flanks of the yacht. The boat helmed by John Kolius was the only one in the fleet not to have sails made by North in America. The syndicate from Hawaii had instead turned to Quantum Sail, while all the others had their own sail designs manufactured by the US sailmaker who managed to guarantee the secrecy of the individual projects.

2G35A

283 bottom As had happened in 1995 at San Diego, in New Zealand too one of the hulls split in two. A sign of the fragility of this type of boat according to some, but for myself and others, a simple and obvious consequence of structures taken to extremes in order to achieve results in an event that is by its very nature extreme. The yacht that dramatically folded in the middle of a race after falling into the trough of a modest wave was Young America, the boat upon which American hopes were concentrated and which flew the demanding pennant of none other than the New York Yacht Club. Fortunately, the budget available to the team was such that a second boat was available, but it was not sufficient to guarantee access to the semi-finals!

the Australian Iain Murray, the American Britton Chance and Dave Pedrick. They were all designers of IOR and IMS yachts as well as various one design boats. Only Briand and Chance had any America's Cup experience.

It was clear that the new hulls would have to be built in the advanced composites that had already been tested at Freemantle by *Kiwi Magic* (the first 12-meter not to be built in wood or light alloy) and that by the early Nineties were the most commonly used materials for racing hulls. It was equally clear that there was a need to open the way for carbonfiber masts and gear: the old rule preventing the use of "exotic" materials, those in other words not

284 top Luna Rossa *in one of the Vuitton Cup round robin races: "Silver Bullet" as the local press had nick-named the Italian boat, finished that phase of the competition in first place having won almost all her races. Her great rival appeared to be Dennis Conner with Stars & Stripes while all the other American teams, including America True, seen here racing against Luna Rossa, were disposed of comfortably.*

The 1987 edition of the America's Cup held at Perth had provided somewhat controversial evidence that it was time to select a new type of boat with which to dispute the trophy. The International Rule 12-meter yachts, built to a rating formula dating from early in the century, appeared to be technically and technologically obsolete.

The arguments were resolved with the appointment of a commission charged with defining a new racing class. The commission was composed of Bruce Farr, the designer from New Zealand, the French designer Philippe Briand,

commercially available, was long out of date. All these materials were widely available and easily sourced from all countries.

It was more difficult to define a formula free of the complications and thus the loopholes of the IOR while still being sufficiently flexible to allow the designers' imaginations room for maneuver, otherwise a one-design formula would have been the better option.

The America's Cup Class came into being in 1990. The formula is not dissimilar to the International Rule that had determined the form of so many yachts from 1906 up to the 1990s.

The differences compared with a 12-meter are substantially a matter of dimensions. While the first ACC boats were fairly broad and shallow, this was due above all to the experience the designers had already gained with the IOR and IMS: they were in substance Maxi class yachts. As time passed and new boats were designed, however, it was realized that certain dimensional ratios and certain forms typical of the meter classes were appropriate to match races staged in restricted wind and sea conditions. The ACC boats of the latest generation, those used in the 2000 edition of the America's Cup, resemble the old 12-meters with their narrow forms and slab sides. They provide, however, significantly greater performance.

284 center Bravo Espana, *here seen racing against* Sixième Sens, *represented Spain in the country's third America's Cup challenge following San Diego in '92 and '95. For this edition the Spanish team had revised the '95 team's Rioja de Espana, entrusting her modification to Rudolf Vrolijk, while in the meantime they also launched a new boat designed by the German. From the outset, however, the two boats were plagued by problems, above all with the rig, and a series of broken masts characterized the early phase of the expedition.*

284 bottom The French Sixième Sens team produced a great race against Luna Rossa in the third round of the Vuitton Cup. A race with numerous protests and the umpires following the two boats playing leading roles: two consecutive penalties were inflicted on Luna Rossa, who was overhauled by the French, then it was the turn of the French boat Sixième Sens to be penalized with Luna Rossa regaining the leads. The Italian yacht then managed to dispose of the second penalty without being caught but Sixième Sens, helmed by Bernard Pacé, made up ground on the last downwind leg, exploiting the boat's speed in those conditions. First across the line, however, was Luna Rossa.

284-285 Stars & Stripes, beating in a fresh wind, is sailing to windward of America One, the boat helmed by Paul Cayard. On his third America's Cup quest, Cayard was searching for the success that had escaped him on the two previous occasions. In 1992 he had been beaten by America3 when at the helm of the Italian challenger Moro di Venezia while in 1995 it had been Peter Blake's New Zealanders who had defeated him. In the meantime he had participated in the Whitbread, sailing EF Language to victory.

THE RATINGS FORMULA OF THE I.A.C.C. YACHTS:

$$[L + 1{,}25 \sqrt[2]{SV} - 9{,}8 \sqrt[3]{DSP}] : 0{,}388 = 42{,}00 \text{ meters}$$

THE 12-METER BOATS COMPARED WITH THE IACC YACHTS AS FOLLOWS:

	12 m S.I.	I.A.C.C.
LOA:	from 21/22	to 22/25 meters
LWL:	from around 14	to 17.25/18.50 meters
Beam:	from around 3.75	to 5.5 (initially)
		4 (subsequently) meters
Draught:	from 2.75	to 4 meters
Displacement:	from 26.5	to 16/20 tons
Sail area	from 300	to 600 square meters

Among the remaining teams, there was a fierce struggle between Dennis Conner with *Stars & Stripes*, Paul Cayard with *America One* and De Angelis with *Luna Rossa*. Aboard *Idaten*, Peter Gilmour was not always in tune with his crew while *Le Defi* was fast only in certain wind conditions and *America True* lacked the experience to make inroads.

In the end *Luna Rossa* and *America One* made it through to the final round of nine races which finished 5-4 in favor of the Italians who thus won the Louis Vuitton Cup and the right to compete for the America's Cup.

The Prada team's boat, perhaps faster than *America One*, won the first race, lost the second and then won two in a row. At 3-1 Cayard staged a great comeback, finely judging the starts and tactics in three races one after the other to take the score to 4-3 in favor of the Americans. The last two races, however, were won by against the odds by *Luna Rossa*.

For the first time in a century and a half of America's Cup history the trophy was to be disputed by two non-American yachts.

286 and 287 The St. Francis Yacht Club's campaign was highly regarded by the observers and was taken very seriously by all the other teams. The presence, above all, of Paul Cayard guaranteed that it would be led by a yachtsman of immense experience: the Californian helmsman, top, at the helm of America One, *had all the credentials to be considered the man to beat on this occasion. He had already reached two finals as helmsman and in 1992 he had been very close to Raul Gardini in every*

phase of the organization and management of the Moro challenge. This undoubtedly helped him during the fund raising campaign, as did his timely victory in the last edition of the Whitbread, achieved thanks to an impeccable performance throughout the race, both technically and tactically, as well as faultless organization. However, it was actually the economic aspects that were to represent the only real weakness in Cayard's team. Fund raising was, in fact, to occupy the helmsman of America One

up to the last minute, diverting his energies from the technical preparation and training of the team. The sail program, one of the fundamental aspects of an America's Cup campaign, was, above all, behind schedule and the American yacht was penalized, especially during the early phases of the Vuitton Cup, by problems with her sails. On the other hand, Cayard had been able to concentrate on the construction of the two boats designed by Bruce Nelson, considered to be one of the most reliable American designers having already penned four boats

for as many earlier challenges, and enjoying significant partnerships with the likes of Ford, Hewlett Packard and Telecordia Technologies. The first boat, USA 49, *was used in the three round robins, improved round by round and at the end of the third was lying fourth, on the same points as* America True *and Nippon Challenge's* Idaten *ahead of her. In the meantime, development work on the second boat,* USA 61, *was progressing and in the semi-finals she was to allow Cayard to move into the lead.*

288 and 289 Luna Rossa *was the third Italian challenger: following* Azzurra *in 1983 it was the turn of* Italia *and* Azzurra *again in 1987 and then* Moro di Venezia *in 1992. The campaign got underway in 1997 on deadline day for the presentation of challengers, thanks to the decisiveness and managerial talents of*

Patrizio Bertelli, the head of one of the fashion world's greatest labels, Prada. A campaign that immediately set its sights high. A challenge that, rather than being entrusted to consortia or syndicates of sponsors, was associated with an individual businessman and dedicated yachtsman, as had been the case with Bill

Koch, Gardini and many others before them. Significant technical decisions were made early on: German Frers, designer of the Moro, *and Doug Peterson, responsible for the last two America's Cup winners,* America3 *in '92 and* Black Magic *in '95, were commissioned to design the boat. At their side was a host of technical*

specialists including David Egan, responsible for mathematical models for the simulation of the hull design, Frers' son German Jr. and others. Much importance was attached to the sails with the hiring of the world number one in the field, the Italian Guido Cavallazzi, twenty years at North Sails Italia and, above all, the sail designer

on all the Italian challengers as well as John Marshall's Young America, the American defender boat in 1995. Two foreign names with enormous experience in the event were called upon for the organisation of the challenge: Laurent Esquier, involved in the America's Cup since 1974, was General Manager of the operation while Rod Davis, seven editions of the cup, three as a skipper and the World Match Race Championship in 1994, was responsible for the preparation of the crew. The helmsman and tactician pairing of Francesco De Angelis and the Brazilian Torben Grael was a proven team after numerous regattas and wins in the Admiral's Cup and the One Ton Cup. Lastly, Bill Koch's entire "package" of three sparring partner boats, America3, Mighty Mary and Kanza, was acquired for testing and working up the race boat after Koch had lost interest in the event. Out of this organization were to be born two yachts, ITA 45 and ITA 48, both named Luna Rossa.

UNA ROSSA

290 and 291 *The final of the Louis Vuitton Cup 2000 was disputed by the two strongest teams, Luna Rossa and America One, on a best of nine basis. In the first race Luna Rossa opted to use ITA 45, the boat which was considered to be the most reliable and already used in the first round robins. Racing in medium winds, the two yachts were close throughout the course until Luna Rossa was penalized. She managed to pay the penalty, however, without losing the lead and at the end just 24 seconds separated the two contenders. 1-0 to Luna Rossa. The wind was the protagonist in the second race: after a good start in soft winds Luna Rossa had a 1 minute lead at the first marker before continual variations in the breeze obliged the race committee to move the buoy. In the end America One crossed the line 1' 27" ahead to square the series at 1-1. The*

third race was characterized by strong wind blowing at 25-30 knots, critical conditions for these boats. Cayard broke halyards, spinnaker, mainsail battens, the vang and the mast showed signs of failure: he was forced to slow. The undamaged Luna Rossa was able to pull away to make it 2-1. In the fourth race Luna Rossa started poorly but managed to catch America One. During the course of a hard-fought duel De Angelis managed to oblige Cayard to concede a penalty: during the American boat's 270° turn, Luna Rossa moved into the lead and went on to win: 3-1 to the Italian boat whose stock was rapidly rising. The fifth race saw Cayard get the America One revival rolling. The Americans started ahead but were caught on the downwind leg by Luna Rossa, broaching by the latter with the

wind blowing at around 20 knots then led to the decisive passage. Cayard won after completing the race with no damage. Prada were still leading, but only by one race. In the sixth De Angelis got the better of Cayard at the start, the American being forced to chase the race. The wind kept up, never blowing less than 16 knots. America One's spinnaker held out and she managed to catch Luna Rossa on the downwind leg. The Italians manoeuvred poorly and as their spinnaker ended up in the water Cayard took advantage to win by 8″, 3-3. The wind was again strong for the seventh race and De Angelis got off to a good start. After the first pass the two boats selected different routes, always hazardous for the lead boat: when the boats crossed again it was America One in the lead by almost twenty lengths! 4-3 to Cayard. The Italians, however, against all the odds, reacted

well. America One was penalized at the start of the eighth race, partly due to the bravura of De Angelis, partly the ingenuity of Cayard. Luna Rossa started ahead and was able to cover the American boat. A lead of two lengths at the finish was sufficient to win and square the series. The ninth and final race was

to be decisive. De Angelis started well and maintained his advantage, covering his adversary throughout the race. Only on the last downwind leg did Cayard make a tentative attack, but by then it was too late. After almost 150 years a non-Anglo-Saxon Italian boat was to challenge the holder of the America's Cup.

292 top During the course of the dramatic final races in the Vuitton Cup, Roussel Coutts declared that in the America's Cup match races the New Zealanders would be much more aggressive and the duels between the boats much closer. In effect, those who had the opportunity of watching the training sessions of the

two New Zealander boats, one helmed by Coutts and the other by his young protégé Dean Barker, reported actual collisions between the two. The cup races between Black Magic and Luna Rossa did not reach these levels, but only because of the manifest superiority of the New Zealanders.

292 bottom left Whilst 11 yachts from six nations, fought to enter the year 2000 edition of the America's Cup, the defenders, as was their right, were observing them and continuing with their training and fine tuning. The Kiwis' skipper, Roussel Coutts, a world match race champion and seen here at the helm, went to sea each day putting his boats through their paces in a series of match races and simulated starts.

In the meantime the New Zealanders had developed with a technical and sporting program that was impressive in its integrity and continuity their two yachts named *Black Magic*, designed by the team of Tom Schnackenberg, the designer together with Doug Peterson of the 1995 winner and an ever-present in the cockpit of his boats even during races.

The boats were different to all the others in a myriad details that are, a few months from the conclusion of the event, still difficult to interpret. Undoubtedly much attention was paid to the aerodynamics of the rig, with that mast with a more rigid section featuring three spreaders against the four of all the others, and shrouds that undoubtedly provided less wind resistance (that stay taken to the foot of the mast whenever it was not needed, so as to avoid even the minimal turbulence generated by the slim cable was unforgettable). Then there was also a keel appendage, fin and bulb, that was probably behind *Black Magic's* greater tacking speed and acceleration.

The hull was the same, with a very swollen and power entrance and a short waterline but a significant dynamic length (she immediately reminded me of *Ranger*, the 1937 J Class, but was also a close relation of the New Zealander school developed in the 1970s with Holland and Farr).

While the challengers were exhausting themselves in their seemingly endless battle, the black-hulled yachts went to sea each day to test sails and gear, and above all maneuvers and starts: Roussel Coutts, the world match racing champion and his young disciple Dean Barker raced each other hundreds of times in hundreds of mock America's Cup situations. These were more than mere simulations, as testified by the numerous collisions between the two at the starts and during the races.

292 bottom right The two New Zealander boats were the fruit of a design concept born in the early Nineties with the creation of the America's Cup Class and honed by the design team year by year. Only Doug Peterson was missing after he decided to join the Luna Rossa team but there was no lack of talent for the fine tuning of the design, from Laurie Davidson to Tom Schnackenberg. The contribution of the latter, the co-ordinator ashore, a great sailing expert and ever present aboard as navigator, was fundamental.

293 Black Magic, the yacht of the Royal New Zealand Yacht Squadron, the holder of the cup, had no means of comparing her speed and performance against those of the challenger Luna Rossa, only modern telemetry allowing certain information regarding the challenger boats to be acquired. Peter Blake's men nonetheless had faith in their experience and match racing ability. Black Magic was to apply exemplary

match racing tactics throughout the regatta: close control of the adversary, both upwind, with a total coverage of the other boat's tacking, and downwind. When the spectators saw Luna Rossa closing on the New Zealander boat on the downwind legs what they were actually witnessing was the deliberate slowing of the latter whose only fear was that of finding less favorable wind conditions.

america's cup 2000

294 and 295 The America's Cup 2000, the thirty-first edition of the historic event, followed a well known script with only minor variations. The defender won comfortably, 5-0. In contrast with previous situations, however, there really was not such a great difference between the two teams and the final result was the sum of a series of factors all favourable to Black Magic. Roussel Coutts won every single start, whether he entered the course from the advantageous right-hand side or from the left. And when in the fifth race the New Zealanders entrusted the helm to Coutts' protégé nothing changed: Barker

too won the start. They had simply practised far more match race starts than De Angelis and it was disarming to see how, in any maneuver, departing from any situation, they always managed to cross the line ahead. Moreover, during the races, their covering tactics were always perfect: De Angelis, continually chasing his rival, was always having to invent something different and therefore to hope for a bit of good luck. He had already realized, from the very first race, who was the strongest in a head-to-head match race situation. When, in the fourth race, he found himself not in the lead but at least well placed for once (Coutts had borne up only because he did not have right of way), he felt, rightly in my opinion, that he still had to explore a different option: had he gone behind, or rather over Black Magic we would have seen the same situation as in the first race with two counter tacks by Coutts and as the yachts crossed for the third time the New Zealander slipping by. Black Magic tacked faster and Peter Blake's team, moreover, had a stiffer, lighter mast and sails that were, thanks to the work of Tom Schnackenberg, absolutely perfect. They could also count on organization just as efficient as that of the Prada team. The America's Cup remained in New Zealand.

The America's Cup 2000 was something of an anti-climax: 5-0 to the Royal New Zealand Yacht Squadron of Auckland's *Black Magic*. The New Zealanders' yacht was without doubt stronger and more efficient in an America's Cup setting; that is to say, it was not necessarily the faster boat: when the two yachts were beating side-by-side it was clear that in terms of pure speed they were evenly matched. *Black Magic* would then cross *Luna Rossa* two or three times and gain a twenty-second lead. From that point it was simply a case of controlling the race. *Luna Rossa* would gain slightly on the downwind leg but it was more a case of *Black Magic* sailing conservatively so as to keep her adversary within sight.

The New Zealanders were undoubtedly the stronger crew: the afterguard had exceptional match racing expertise while the prow demonstrated remarkable maneuvering skills. I never saw a moment's panic on board, not even when they had to repair a winch during a race, not even when a gennaker split. The crew of *Luna Rossa* were also beyond reproach—it was no coincidence that they had beaten the likes of Paul Cayard. They were simply a hair's breadth adrift of the Kiwis. That hair's breadth deriving from the historical roots of sailing, from the custom of going to sea every day after work, of practising what has become a national sport. Perhaps even deriving from descending, for better or worse, from subjects of the first man to recognize that sailing was indeed a sport, Charles II.

The America's Cup 2000 was only an episode: new challenges await and in the meantime yachtsmen continue to compete in the Fastnet, the Bermuda Race, the Admiral's Cup and the BOC Challenge. They continue, in short, to do what men have done since the days of Charles II.

america's cup 2000

america's cup 2000

296 and 297 On March 2, 2000, the crew of Black Magic celebrate the victorious defence of the America's Cup. They has just won the fifth and decisive race against Luna Rossa, an uneventful 5th race with the start won by Dean Barker, the tactics dictated by the navigator Tom Schnackenberg with the usual infallible series of maneuvers and blanket coverage. This date perhaps marks the opening of a new cycle. Never before had a non-American defender managed to retain the trophy and the right to make a second defence. The fact that this feat was performed by Peter Blake's New Zealanders was by no means casual. For some time now the country has been one of the great powers in world yachting, demonstrated by the fact that almost all of the teams present in Auckland had at least one New Zealander sailing champion among their number. From a technical point of view, for 20 years New Zealand has been at the forefront in the design and construction of above all racing yachts. Bruce Farr is the world number one and a citizen of the U.S. for professional motives only, his roots lying in New Zealand, while the constructor Cookson builds yachts for owner throughout the world. Furthermore, the group which today represents Team New Zealand is far from splitting up, having become something of a national institution and having raised new generations within its ranks: there is no doubt that the next helmsman could be Dean Barker. Lastly, the role of America's Cup defender has always brought with it a series of privileges that place the holder in a position of privilege with respects to the challenger: the logistical aspects, those associated with the regulations and the possibility of keeping one's boats under wraps until the last minute or deciding on the regatta venue only when the challenger series has been completed. The Prada team was defeated but has already signalled its intent to issue a new challenge. Luna Rossa's crew will be the challenger of record; that is to say, the co-ordinators of the challengers for the next edition scheduled for 2003. The boost to the image of the America's Cup was enormous. The ritual of the private yachts accompanying the victorious yacht as she returns to port will be repeated, testimony to the appeal a regatta born in 1851 out of the ambitious dream of a small group of American yachtsmen continues to exercise on the yachting world. As this book concludes with the regatta that represents the highest expression of the sport, the Royal Yacht Squadron in Cowes is organising a major event to celebrate in the August of 2001, the 150th anniversary of the victory of the schooner America.

GLOSSARY

ALOFT: Said of sails hoisted on the mast. Also for any object or person hoisted on or climbing the mast.

BALLAST: Heavy material used to increase the stability of the yacht.

BEAR AWAY: Turn the bow away from the direction of the wind.

BEAT: Sail against the direction of the wind.

BEND: Attach a sail to the mast system.

BOOM: Spar at the base of the sail aft of the mast, the spanker.

BOWSPRIT: Spar at the bow of the yacht on which the foresails are bent.

BULKHEAD: Athwartships dividing wall inside the yacht.

CABIN PLANKING: Flooring inside the yacht.

CATAMARAN: Twin-hulled yacht.

CENTERBOARD: Blade passing through the keel of the yacht to restrict sideways movement.

CHART TABLE: Table designed to allow the navigator to read the charts.

COCKPIT: Lowered part of the deck.

CUTTER: Twin headsail.

DECKHOUSE: The superstructure of a yacht.

DISPLACEMENT: The volume of water moved by hull when afloat and therefore the weight of the yacht.

DRAFT: The depth of that part of the hull below the waterline.

FITTINGS: Deck gear, usually in metal.

FLYING JIB: Jib hoisted unattached to forestay.

FOREMAST: The first mast from the bow of a schooner.

FREEBOARD: The height of the hull above the water.

FURL: Roll or fold up a sail.

GAFF: The spar on which a gaff sail is bent.

GAFF RIG: Type of rig with sails astern of the mast composed of a four-sided sail.

GAFF TOPSAIL: Triangular sail hoisted above the spanker.

GARBOARDS: The first layers of planking along the keel.

GENOA: Large jib, extending aft of the mast.

GUNWALE: Uppermost hull planking.

HALYARD: The rope used to hoist a sail.

HATCH: Aperture giving access to the below decks areas.

HAUL IN: Tauten a sail.

JIB: Sail hoisted before the mast.

KETCH: Two-masted rig with a taller mainmast and a shorter mizzen with the latter forward of the rudderpost.

LATEEN SAIL: Triangular sail with a yard on the longest side, used on galleys and Arab vessels in general.

LEE-WAY: Sideways movement of the yacht produced by the wind.

LEEBOARD: Mobile lateral blade acting to restrict lee-way.

LEEWARD: The side to which wind is blowing with respects to the hull.

LIE TO: Face up to the wind in the case of bad weather.

LIFELINES: Guardwires.

LINE: A rope on a yacht or a ship. A metal version is instead generally known as wire rope or cable.

LOCKER: Storage area.

LUFF UP: Turn the bow of the yacht into the wind.

MAIN DECK BEAMS: Transverse elements of the structure supporting the deck.

MAINSAIL: The sail hoisted on the mainmast.

MARCONI: Type of modern rig with a triangular mainsail.

MAST AND TOPMAST: The structures supporting the sails. The topmast of a gaff rig is, as the name suggests, the upper part of the mast.

MIZZEN: The aft sail and mast of a yawl or ketch.

OUTER JIB: Outermost foresail of a cutter rigged with three jibs.

OVERHANG: The part of the hull at the bow and stern above the water line.

PANEL: Strips of cloth composing a sail.

PLANKING: Watertight skin over the frame of a yacht.

POST: Stempost or sternpost, the hull structure element extending the keel forward or aft.

REEFS: Portions of a sail that are taken in to reduce its surface area.

RIBS: Transverse elements of the hull structure.

RIGGING: The system of ropes and wires supporting the mast.

SAMSON POST OR BITT: Part of the deck gear, used to fix mooring ropes or towing lines.

SCHOONER: Fore-and-aft rig with two or more masts.

SHEERLINE: Longitudinal line marking the upper edge of the hull.

SHEET: The rope used to adjust a sail.

SIDES: The flanks of the hull.

SKYLIGHT: Aperture on the maindeck providing light and ventilation.

SLOOP: Single-masted rig.

STANCHION: Vertical bars placed around the edges of the deck of a yacht to carry a rail or lifelines.

STAY: Part of the rigging supporting the mast towards the stern or the bow.

STROP: Piece of rope or cable used to fasten objects.

TACK1: The method by which a yacht sails against the direction of the wind.

TACK2: The lower corner of a sail bent to the deck, the boom or a spar.

TILLER: Rod used to turn the rudder.

TOERAIL: Protective border along the sides of the deck.

TOPSIDES: The yacht's sides above the waterline.

TRANSOM: Aft part of stern.

TURNBUCKLE: Coupling with dual threads used to adjust rigging.

UPWIND: Point of sailing against the direction of the wind.

WATERLINE: Longitudinal line corresponding to the level of the water when the hull is afloat.

WETTED AREA: The area of the hull below the waterline.

WINCH: Mechanism for raising the anchor or adjusting the sheets.

WINDWARD: The side from which the wind is coming with respects to the hull.

YARD: The spar on which a square sail is bent.

YARDARM: The tip of a yacht's yard or mast.

YAWL: Two-masted rig with a mainmast and mizzen, the latter aft of the rudderpost.

INDEX

BIBLIOGRAPHY

"Lo yacht origine ed evoluzione del veliero da diporto", Carlo Sciarelli, Milan, 1970

"American Yachts Their Clubs and Races", J. D. Jerrold Kelly, New York, 1884

"Gli yacht da regata", A. B. C. Whipple, USA, 1980

"Architectura Navalis Mercatoria", Chapman, 1768

"Ronde en platbodem jachten", Mr. Dr. T. Huitema, 1970

"Royal Yacht of Europe", Reginald Crabtree, 1975

"Yachting a History", Peter Heaton, London, 1955

"Enterprise to Endeavour the J class", Ian Dear, 1985

"L'arte navale", Tre Tryckare, Milan, 1963

"Histoire du yachting", Daniel Charles, Paris, 1997

"The Cumberland Fleet: Two Hundred Years of Yachting 1775-1975", Philips-Birt Douglas, London, 1978

"Yacht Club Italiano", Franco Belloni

"I velieri mercantili", Oliver E. Allen, USA, 1978

"Gli yacht", John Rousmaniere, USA, 1981

"I Clipper", A. B. C. Whipple, USA, 1980

"Yacht Racing the Aerodynamics of Sails and Racing Tactics", Manfred Curry, New York, 1927

"Vele e velieri", Franco Giorgetti, Milan, 1998

"Yacht Design", Franco Giorgetti, Milan, 1999

"Yachts on Canvas Artist Images of the Yachts from the Seventeenth Century to the Present Day", James Taylor, London, 1998

"Genoa Jib", Carlo Tagliafico & Tino Delfino, 1988

"A Century Under Sail", Stanley Rosenfeld, Boston, 1988

"The Paintings of the America's Cup", Ranulf Rayner, London, 1986

"Admiral's Cup", Daniel Gilles, 1985

"Yachting et progrès technologiques à Monaco", Monaco, 1994

"Visti in barca", Vincenzo Zaccagnino, Milan, 1990

"Mediterranean Yacht"

"A Century of Tall Ships", Beken di Cowes, Great Britain, 1985

"Un vagabond des mers du Sud", Bernard Moitessier, 1969

"Solo, intorno al mondo e Viaggio della Liberdade", Joshua Slocum, Milan, 1969

"Yachtsmann's Guide to the Rating Rule", Peter Johnson, 1971

"Victorie en solitaire", Eric Tabarly, 1964

"Twenty Challenges for the America's Cup", John H. Illingworth, 1968

"The History of Yachting", Arthur H. Clark, 1904

"Yacht Capital", Magazine

"Yacht Digest", Magazine

"Vele e motori", Magazine

"William Fife capolavori d'epoca", Franco Pace, Trieste, 1996

"C'était au temps des Yachtsmen: Histoire Mondiale du Yachting dès Origines à 1939", Grout Jack, Gallimard, 1978

"An Universal Dictionary of the Marine", Falconer William, T. Called, 1789

"The Common Sense of Yacht Design", Herreshoff L. Francis, Caravan-Marittime Bool, 1973

"Dizionario Marinaro", Castagna L., Rome, 1955

"Dizionario tecnico e nautico di marina, italiano, tedesco, francese ed inglese", Dabovich P.E. - Heinz G., Pola, 1883-1900

"Two Years before the Mast", Dana R.H., London, 1875

"Dizionario di marina", Fincati L., Genoa and Turin, 1870

"Arte navale", Imperato F., Milan, 1921

"International Maritime dictionary", Kerchove Renè de, New York, 1948

"Dizionario di marina medievale e moderno", R. Accademia d'Italia, Rome, 1937

"Yacht Designing and Planning", H.I. Chapelle, New York, 1936

"The history of American Sailing Ships", H.I. Chapelle, New York, 1949

"American Yachts and Yachting", R.F. Coffin, London, 1887

"Heavy Weather Sailing", K. Adlard Coles, London, 1967

"Racing, Cruising and Design", Uffa Fox, London, 1937

"British Ocean Racing", Douglas Phillips-Birt, London, 1960

"Corso di storia", Pietro Silva, Milano, 1942

"Yacht and Yachting", Vanderdeken, London, 1873

"La nave nel tempo", A. Vicino, Milan, 1942

PHOTOGRAPHIC CREDITS

MERPOOL/PLISSON/MARTIN-RAGET: 268-269.
MERPOOL/SEA AND SEE: 267 left.
MFA, BOSTON: 29 top.
MYSTIC SEAPORT MUSEUM: 92 left, 92 right.
MYSTIC SEAPORT, MYSTIC, CONNECTICUT:
69, 195 center, 198 top, 200 bottom, 204
bottom left.
MYSTIC SEAPORT, ROSENFELD COLLECTION,
MYSTIC, CONNECTICUT: 8-9, 33, 46 bottom
(James Burton photographer), 47 top (Image
acquired in Honor of Franz Schneider), 50
top (Courtesy New York Yacht Club), 50-51
(James Burton photogrtapher), 51 top
(Courtesy of New York Yacht Club), 51
bottom (Image acquired in Honor of Franz
Schneider),
74-75 (Charles Edwin Bolles, photographer),
75 bottom (Charles Edwin Bolles,
photographer), 80 top, 80 center, 80 bottom,
81 (James Burton photographer), 82 top, 82
bottom left, 82 bottom right, 83 top, 83
bottom, 87 top,
88 top (Charles Edwin Bolles, photographer)
89 bottom, 90 top, 90 center, 97 center
(James Burton photographer), 104 top, 108
top, 108 center, 108 bottom, 109 bottom,
110 top left, 112 top, 112 bottom, 115 top,
115 bottom, 116 bottom, 117 center left, 117
center right,
117 bottom, 118-119, 119 top, 122 top,
122 bottom (Image acquired in Honor of
Franz Schneider), 122-123 (Image acquired in
Honor of Franz Schneider), 124 top (Image
acquired in Honor of Franz Schneider), 124
bottom left, 124 bottom right, 134 top, 134
bottom, 135 (Image acquired in Honor of

Franz Schneider), 136 (Image acquired in Honor
of Franz Schneider), 136-137 (Image acquired in
Honor of Franz Schneider), 138-139, 138
bottom
left, 140 bottom, 140-141, 141 bottom,
142 top left, 142 top right, 142 bottom,
143, 144 top (Image acquired in Honor of Franz
Schneider), 144 bottom (Image acquired in
Honor of Franz Schneider), 144-145, 145, 146,
147 top left, 147 top right, 147 bottom, 151
right, 152 top right, 152-153, 153,
157 top, 157 bottom, 158, 162 top, 162
bottom, 175 bottom, 192 center, 193 top, 193
bottom, 194-195, 194 bottom, 195 top, 195
bottom, 196-197, 196 bottom, 197 top, 197
center, 197 bottom, 198 center, 198 bottom,
199 top, 200 top, 201 top, 201 bottom.
NATIONAL MARITIME MUSEUM, GREENWICH: 14
bottom, 14-15, 19 top left, 22-23, 23 top, 23
center, 23 bottom, 26-27, 36-37.
FRANCO PACE: 190-191, 199 bottom, 203 left,
205, 206, 207 center, 210 center, 212, 225
bottom, 226 left, 226 right, 227 left, 227 right,
228 top left, 228 top right, 228 center left, 228
bottom right, 229, 282 bottom, 284 top, 284
bottom, 296-297, 297 bottom right.
PEABODY MUSEUM, SALEM: 30 top, 30 bottom,
31 left, 31 right, 68-69.
THE PEPYS LIBRARY, MAGDALENE COLLEGE,
CAMBRIDGE: 24 top.
BARRY PICKTHAL/PPL/SEA AND SEE:
179 top, 179 bottom, 180 bottom.
PLISSON: 166, 264 bottom, 267 top.
PLISSON GUILLAME: 252 bottom
PLISSON LA TRINITE: 234-235
PPL/SEA AND SEE: 93 top right, 93 bottom, 168
left, 168 right, 176 top, 177 top, 177 bottom

left, 177 bottom right, 275 bottom.
G.M. RAGET/SEA AND SEE: 104-105, 167 top
right, 217 top, 224 center, 224 bottom, 280-
281.
SEA AND SEE: 64 top, 91 top, 92 top left,
92 center left, 92 bottom, 118 top, 118
bottom, 132 top, 132 bottom, 154 top,
155 top left, 155 top right, 159 center left,
163 top, 164 bottom, 204 left top, 204 right
top, 270 left.
DAVID J. SHULER/PPL MEDIALINK/SEA AND
SEE: 272 bottom.
SOTHEBY'S PICTURE LIBRARY: 1 left, 9, 36 top,
37 top, 52-53, 53 top, 54 left, 56 top, 56
bottom, 56-57, 57 top, 68, 71 top, 73
center, 85.
KAORO SOEHATA/PPL MEDIALINK/SEA AND
SEE: 215 left, 273 bottom left, 273 bottom
right, 274 bottom, 276, 277 left.
K. SOEHATA/SEA AND SEE: 264 center, 273 top.
SPARKMAN AND STEPHENS: 120 top, 121 top,
121 bottom.
STR/AP PHOTO: 259 bottom right.
HENRI THIBAULT/DPPI: 214 bottom, 215 right.
DAN THRIFT/AP PHOTO: 220 top.
RICK TOMLINSON: 10-11, 221 right, 248 top,
248 bottom, 248-249, 249 bottom right.
RICK TOMLINSON/TEAM EF: 10-11, 249
bottom left.
RICK TOMLINSON/SEA AND SEE: 235 top right.
ULLSTEIN BILDARCHIV: 60-61, 60 bottom, 61
top, 61 center, 61 bottom, 62-63, 62 bottom,
63 bottom.
ONNE VAN DER WAL/STOCK NEWPORT: 12-13,
232-233, 234 bottom, 236 top left, 240 top,
243 top, 252 center, 254 center left, 254
center right, 254 bottom, 255, 278 bottom,

296 top, 296 bottom.
J. VAPILLON/SEA AND SEE: 258 top.
WILLIAM WEST, POOL/AP PHOTO: 292
bottom right.

PRIVATE COLLECTIONS: 7, 20-21, 27, 28 top,
32-33, 34, 35, 38, 38-39, 39 bottom, 48 top,
52, 55, 70 bottom, 84 top, 84 bottom, 87
bottom, 120 bottom, 120-121.
PRIVATE COLLECTION, PHOTOGRAPH
COURTESY OF BONHAMS, LONDON: 49.
PRIVATE COLLECTION, COURTESY OF CARLO
CROCE: 16.
PRIVATE COLLECTION, ENGLAND;
PHOTOGRAPH COURTESY OF RICHARD
GREEN GALLERY, LONDON: 24-25.
LOANED BY KIND PERMISSION OF THE
PARKER GALLERY, LONDON: 91 bottom.
LOANED BY KIND PERMISSION OF THE
ROYAL CORK YACHT CLUB: 40, 41 top,
41 bottom.
LOANED BY KIND PERMISSION OF THE
ROYAL THAMES YACHT CLUB: 40-41.
PRIVATE COLLECTION, PHOTOGRAPHS
PRIVATE COLLECTION,, COURTESY OF
MADAME JACQUELINE TABARLY: 167 top left.
COURTESY OF THE YACHT CLUB ITALIANO:
64-65, 65 top, 65 center, 65 bottom, 66 top,
66 bottom, 67 top, 67 bottom, 126 top, 127
top left, 127 top right, 127 center, 127
bottom, 129 top, 133 top, 133 bottom.
PRIVATE COLLECTION, PHOTOGRAPH
COURTESY OF THE ROYAL THAMES YACTH
CLUB: 89 top.
COURTESY OF REVUE BATEAUX:
183 center right.

ACKNOWLEDGEMENTS

The Author and the Publisher would like to
thank for the precious collaboration:

Bent Aarre, Isabelle Andrieux and Chloé De
Smet of the Yacht Club de Monaco, Milt Baker
of the Bluewater Books & Charts, Lydia Barrett
of the Royal Ocean Racing Club, George
Bauer of the Newport Bermuda Race Press
Officer, Steve Benjamin of the Yale Sailing
Associates, Kristin Bierfelt and Leah Ross of
the Museum of Fine Arts Boston, Dermot Burns
of the Royal Cork of Yacht Club, Deborah
Cliffe of Bonhams, Carlo Croce and Giorgio

Oliviero of the Yacht Club Italiano, Danmarks
Museum for Lystseijlads, Captain D. Dolson of
the Royal Thames Yacht Club, Daniel
Finamore of the Maritime Art and History
Peabody Essex Museum, Ben Fuller, Daniel
Gilles, Ted Graeslund and Sören Nörby of the
Orlogsmuseet - Royal Danish Yacht Club, Jon
Humphries of Boston Yacht Club, Teri of the
Herreshoff Marine Museum America's Cup
Hall of Fame, Diana Harding of the Royal
Yacht Squadron, Irene Jacobs of the Maritiem
Museum Rotterdam, Gary Lock of Cookson
Boats, The Mariners' Museum Newport, Jeffrey

Mellefont of the Australian National Maritime
Museum, The Mercury Hobart, Susan Morris
of the Richard Green Gallery, the staff at the
Mystic Seaport Museum, Brian J. Newbury of
The Parker Gallery, Gérard Petipas of Sté du
Pen-Duick, Normann Plummer of the
Chesapeake Bay Maritime Museum, Revue
Bateaux, Daniel Roschnotti of the New York
Yacht Club, George Robinson of the Royal
Bermuda Yacht Club, San Diego Yacht Club,
Paolo Saviolo, Seawanhaka Corinthian Yacht
Club, David Taylor of the National Maritime
Museum, Chris Webster of the Tate Gallery.